The
SPIRIT
in the
GOSPELS
and
ACTS

The SPIRIT in the GOSPELS and ACTS

Divine Purity and Power

CRAIG S. KEENER

HENDRICKSON PUBLISHERS

© 1997 by Hendrickson Publishers, Inc.
P. O. Box 3473
Peabody, Massachusetts 01961–3473
All rights reserved
Printed in the United States of America

ISBN 1–56563–169–2

First Printing — May 1997

BS
2548
1 H62
K44
1997

Library of Congress Cataloging-in-Publication Data

Keener, Craig S., 1960–
   The Spirit in the Gospels and Acts: divine purity and power /
Craig S. Keener.
   Based on the author's thesis—Duke University.
   Includes bibliographic references and index.
   ISBN 1–56563–169–2 (cloth)
   1. Holy Spirit—Biblical teaching.   2. Prophecy—Christianity—
Biblical teaching.   3. Purity, Ritual—Christianity—Biblical teaching.
4. Bible   N.T.   Gospels—Criticism, interpretation, etc.   5. Bible.
N.T.   Acts—Criticism, interpretation, etc.   6. Holy Spirit
(Judaism)—History of doctrines.   I. Title.
BS2548.H62K44   1997
231′.3–dc21

          97–6228
          CIP

To Gordon Fee, Ben Aker, and the memory of George Eldon
Ladd, three scholars who through their teaching or writing on
the Spirit or the kingdom persuaded a young minister that it
was possible for a person of the Spirit to become a Bible scholar
as well. George Ladd, through his teaching on the kingdom in
his books; Gordon Fee, through his passionate New Testament
lectures on cassette tape in our library; and Ben Aker, through
his personal passion for God's word in the classroom.

TABLE OF CONTENTS

ACKNOWLEDGMENTS

This book includes research I did while a graduate student at Duke University; the Johannine portions are abbreviated and edited from part of my dissertation on Johannine pneumatology there. I am thus grateful to my dissertation committee for their insights, especially to my supervisor Moody Smith for his guidance and to E. P. Sanders for his incisive—and largely correct—criticisms, which I have taken into account in revising my thesis. I am also grateful to former Livingstone College student Brian Harvey for retyping the sections of the manuscript on Mark and Acts that I had previously written in those tight days of graduate school before I had a computer. Much of the material in the Matthew section also appears under the appropriate passages in my Matthew commentaries for IVP and Eerdmans, in progress simultaneously with this work. I also express appreciation to other Livingstone College students for helping me catch up on filing, thereby allowing me the time to get this manuscript to Hendrickson Publishers: Cal, Genese, Tonya, Crystal, Christy, and Sherry. Finally I want to thank my friends at Hendrickson Publishers for their work on this manuscript and for their friendship.

ABBREVIATIONS

Old Testament

Gen	Genesis
Exod	Exodus
Lev	Leviticus
Num	Numbers
Deut	Deuteronomy
Josh	Joshua
Judg	Judges
1 Sam	1 Samuel
2 Sam	2 Samuel
1 Kgs	1 Kings
2 Kgs	2 Kings
1 Chron	1 Chronicles
2 Chron	2 Chronicles
Neh	Nehemiah
Ps	Psalms
Prov	Proverbs
Isa	Isaiah
Jer	Jeremiah
Lam	Lamentations
Ezek	Ezekiel
Dan	Daniel
Hos	Hosea
Mic	Micah
Hab	Habakkuk
Hag	Haggai
Zech	Zechariah
Mal	Malachi

Apocrypha

Bar	Baruch
1 Esd	1 Esdras
Jdt	Judith
1 Macc	1 Maccabees
2 Macc	2 Maccabees
3 Macc	3 Maccabees
4 Macc	4 Maccabees
Sir	Sirach
Sus	Susanna
Tob	Tobit
Wis	Wisdom

New Testament

Matt	Matthew
Rom	Romans
1 Cor	1 Corinthians
2 Cor	2 Corinthians
Gal	Galatians
Eph	Ephesians
Col	Colossians
1 Thess	1 Thessalonians
2 Thess	2 Thessalonians
1 Tim	1 Timothy
2 Tim	2 Timothy
Heb	Hebrews
Jas	James
1 Pet	1 Peter
2 Pet	2 Peter
Rev	Revelation

Josephus

Ag. Ap.	*Against Apion*
Ant.	*Antiquities of the Jews*
Jos.	Josephus
J.W.	*Jewish War*

Philo

Abr.	*De Abrahamo*
Aet.	*De aeternitate mundi*
Cher.	*De Cherubim*
Conf.	*De confusione linguarum*
Congr.	*De congressu eruditionis gratia*
Contempl.	*De vita contemplativa*
Decal.	*De Decalogo*

Det.	*Quod deterius potiori insidiari soleat*
Ebr.	*De ebrietate*
Fug.	*De fuga et inventione*
Her.	*Quis rerum divinarum heres sit*
Hypoth.	*Hypothetica*
Legat.	*De legatione ad Gaium*
Leg.	*Legum allegoriae*
Migr.	*De migratione Abrahami*
Mut.	*De mutatione nominum*
Opif.	*De opificio mundi*
Plant.	*De plantatione*
Post.	*De posteritate Caini*
Praem.	*De praemiis et poenis*
Prob.	*Quod omnis probus liber sit*
Q.G.	*Quaestiones et solutiones in Genesim*
Sacr.	*De sacrificiis Abelis et Caini*
Sobr.	*De sobrietate*
Somn.	*De somniis*
Spec.	*De specialibus legibus*
Virt.	*De virtutibus*

Rabbinic Literature

ᶜAbod. Zar.	*ᶜAboda Zara*
ᵓAbot R. Nat. A	*ᵓAbot de Rabbi Nathan, Recension A*
ᵓAbot R. Nat. B	*ᵓAbot de Rabbi Nathan, Recension B*
A.M.	*Aharé Mot*
B.	*Babylonian Talmud*
Bah.	*Bahodesh*
B.Bat.	*Baba Batra*
Behuq.	*Behuqotai*
Bek.	*Bekorot*
Ber.	*Berakot*
Beṣa	*Beṣa*
B. Meṣiᶜa	*Baba Meṣiᶜa*
B. Qam.	*Baba Qamma*
Deut. Rab.	*Deuteronomy Rabbah*
Ed.	*Eduyyot*
ᶜErub.	*ᶜErubin*
Esth. Rab.	*Esther Rabbah*
Exod. Rab.	*Exodus Rabbah*
Gen. Rab.	*Genesis Rabbah*
Giṭ.	*Gittin*
Ḥag.	*Ḥagiga*
Hor.	*Horayot*
Ker.	*Keritot*
Ketub.	*Ketubot*
Lam. Rab.	*Lamentations Rabbah*
Lev. Rab.	*Leviticus Rabbah*

M.	*Mishnah*
Maʿaś.	*Maʿaśrot*
Mak.	*Makkot*
Makš.	*Makširin*
Meg.	*Megillah*
Mek.	*Mekilta*
Menaḥ.	*Menaḥot*
Mid.	*Middot*
Midr. Pss.	*Midrash Psalms (Midrash Tehillim)*
Miqw.	*Miqwaot*
Moʾed Qat.	*Moʾed Qatan*
Naz.	*Nazir*
Ned.	*Nedarim*
Neg.	*Negaʿim*
Nez.	*Nezikin*
Nid.	*Niddot*
Num. Rab.	*Numbers Rabbah*
Pesaḥ.	*Pesaḥim*
Pesiq. Rab.	*Pesiqta Rabbati*
Pesiq. Rab Kah.	*Pesiqta de Rab Kahana*
Pesiq. Rab Kah. Sup.	*Pesiqta de Rab Kahana Supplement*
Qed.	*Qedošim*
Qidd.	*Qiddušin*
Qoh. Rab.	*Qohelet Rabbah*
Roš Haš.	*Roš Haššana*
Ruth Rab.	*Ruth Rabbah*
Šabb.	*Šabbat*
Sanh.	*Sanhedrin*
Šeb.	*Šebiʿit*
Šebu.	*Šebuʿot*
Šeqal.	*Šeqalim*
Sifre Deut.	*Sifre Deuteronomy*
Sifre Num.	*Sifre Numbers*
Song Sol. Rab.	*Song of Solomon Rabbah*
Taʿan.	*Taʿanit*
Ter.	*Terumot*
Ṭohar.	*Ṭoharot*
Tos.	*Tosephta*
ʿUq.	*ʿUqšin*
VDDen.	*Vayyiqra Dibura Denedabah*
Yad.	*Yadaim*
Yeb.	*Yebamot*
Zebaḥ.	*Zebaḥim*

Other Early Jewish and Christian Literature

Apoc. Mos.	*Apocalypse of Moses*
Apoc. Pet.	*Apocalypse of Peter*
Apoc. Sedrach	*Apocalypse of Sedrach*

Apoc. Zeph.	*Apocalypse of Zephaniah*
Apost. Const.	*Apostolic Constitutions*
Apol.	*Apology*
Aristob.	Aristobulus
Asc. Isa.	*Ascension of Isaiah*
2 Bar.	*2 (Syriac Apocalypse of) Baruch*
3 Bar.	*3 Baruch*
4 Bar.	*4 Baruch*
CD	Damascus Document
CIJ	*Corpus inscriptionum iudaicarum,* ed. J. B. Frey
1 Clem.	*1 Clement*
CPJ	*Corpus papyrorum judaicarum,* ed. V.A. Tcherikover
Did.	*Didache*
Ep. Arist.	*Epistle of Aristeas*
Ep. to Eph.	*Epistle to the Ephesians*
Epiph.	Epiphanius
Gr. Ezra	*Greek Apocalypse of Ezra*
Haer.	*Adversus haereses*
Herm.	Shepherd of Hermas
Hom.	*Homily*
Jos. and Asen.	*Joseph and Asenath*
Jub.	*Jubilees*
Man.	*Mandates*
Mart. Pol.	*Martyrdom of Polycarp*
Min. Felix	Minucius Felix
Odes Sol.	*Odes of Solomon*
Oct.	*Octavius*
Phil.	*To the Philippians*
Poly.	Polycarp
Pr. Jos.	*Prayer of Joseph*
Ps.-Philo	Pseudo-Philo's *Biblical Antiquities*
Ps.-Phoc.	*Pseudo-Phocylides*
Pss. Sol.	*Psalms of Solomon*
1QapGen	Genesis Apocryphon
1QH	Qumran Hymns Scroll
1QM	Qumran War Scroll
1QpHab	Qumran Pesher Habakkuk Commentary
1QS	Qumran Manual of Discipline
4QFlor	4QFlorilegium
4QpNah	Qumran Pesher Nahum Commentary
11QTemple	Qumran Temple Scroll
Sib. Or.	*Sibylline Oracles*
Sim.	*Similitudes*
Syr. Men. Sent.	*Sentences of the Syriac Menander*
T. Ab., A and B	*Testament of Abraham,* Recensions A and B
T. Asher	*Testament of Asher*
T. Ben.	*Testament of Benjamin*
Tert.	Tertullian
T. Job	*Testament of Job*

T. Jos.	*Testament of Joseph*
T. Judah	*Testament of Judah*
T. Levi	*Testament of Levi*
T. Mos.	*Testament of Moses*
T. Naph.	*Testament of Naphtali*
T. Reub.	*Testament of Reuben*
T. Sim.	*Testament of Simeon*
T. Sol.	*Testament of Solomon*
T. Zeb.	*Testament of Zebulon*
Vis.	*Visions*

Other Ancient Literature

Ach. Tat.	Achilles Tatius
Ael.	Aelian
Alex.	*Alexander*
Apocol.	*Apocolocyntosis*
Apul.	Apuleius
Arist.	Aristotle
Artem.	Artemidorus
Chaer.	*Chaereas and Callirhoe*
Char.	Chariton
Cic.	Cicero
CIG	*Corpus inscriptionum graecarum*
CIL	*Corpus inscriptionum latinarum*
Clit.	*Clitophon and Leucippe*
De Benef.	*De beneficiis*
De Divin.	*De divinatione*
Demon.	*Demonicus*
De Nat. Deor.	*De natura deorum*
De Offic.	*De officiis*
Dial.	*Dialogue* or *Dialogues*
Dio Chrys.	Dio Chrysostom
Diog. Laert.	Diogenes Laertius
Dion. Hal.	Dionysius of Halicarnassus
Disc.	*Discourse* or *Discourses*
Educ.	*The Education of Children*
El.	*Electra*
Ench.	*Encheiridion*
Ep.	*Epistle*
Ep. Lucil.	*Epistles to Lucilius*
Epict.	Epictetus
Epig.	*Epigrams*
Eurip.	Euripides
Fr.	*Fragment*
G.A.	*On the Generation of Animals*
Geog.	*Geography*
Greek Anth.	*Greek Anthology*

Hdt.	Herodotus
Hes.	*Conversation with Hesiod*
Hist.	*Histories*
IG	*Inscriptiones graecae*
Isis	*Isis and Osiris*
Isoc.	Iscocrates
J. Conf.	*Zeus Catechized*
Juv.	Juvenal
Lat. Lang.	*On the Latin Language*
Luc.	Lucian
Lucret.	Lucretius
Lyc.	*Lycurgus*
Marc. Aur.	Marcus Aurelius
Mart.	Martial
Med.	*Meditations*
Metam.	*Metamorphoses*
Mor.	*Moralia*
N.A.	*The Nature of Animals*
Nat.	*De rerum natura*
N.H.	*Natural History*
Oed. Rex	*Oedipus rex*
Oneir.	*Oneirocriticon*
Or. (with Eurip.)	*Orestes*
Or. (with others)	*Oration*
Orph. H.	*Orphic Hymns*
Paneg.	*Panegyricus*
Petr.	Petronius
PGM	*Papyri graecae magicae*
Phaedr.	*Phaedrus*
Philostr.	Philostratus
Plat. Questions	*Platonic Questions*
Plut.	Plutarch
Progymn.	*Progymnasmata*
Rhet. ad Herenn.	*Rhetorica ad Herennium*
Rom.	*Romulus*
R.Q.	*Roman Questions*
Sat. (with Petr.)	*Satyricon*
Sat. (with others)	*Satires*
Sen.	Seneca
Sol.	*Solon*
Soph.	Sophocles
Suet.	Suetonius
Superst.	*Superstition*
Syr. D.	*Syrian Goddess*
Tac., *Hist.*	Tacitus, *History*
Thes.	*Theseus*
Tusc. Disp.	*Tusculan Disputations*
V.A.	*Life of Apollonius*
V.P.	*Life of Pythagoras*

Modern Abbreviations

AB	Anchor Bible
AGSU	Arbeiten zur Geschichte des Spätjudentums und Urchristentums
AJBI	*Annual of the Japanese Biblical Institute*
ALUOS	*The Annual of Leeds University Oriental Society*
AnBib	Analecta Biblica
ANET	*Ancient Near Eastern Texts Relating to the Old Testament*, ed. J. B. Pritchard
ANF	Ante-Nicene Fathers, ed. A. Roberts and J. Donaldson
ANQ	*Andover Newton Quarterly*
ANRW	*Aufstieg und Niedergang der römischen Welt*
ATR	*Anglican Theological Review*
ATRSup	Anglican Theological Review Supplement
ANZSTR	Australian and New Zealand Studies in Theology and Religion
ASSR	*Archives de sciences sociales des religions*
AUSS	*Andrews University Seminary Studies*
AustBR	*Australian Biblical Review*
AZLUGHJ	Arbeiten zur Literatur und Geschichte des hellenistischen Judentums
BA	*Biblical Archaeologist*
BARev	*Biblical Archaeology Review*
BASOR	*Bulletin of the American Schools of Oriental Research*
BBMS	Baker Biblical Monograph Series
BH	*Buried History*
Bib	*Biblica*
BSac	*Bibliotheca Sacra*
BibTrans	*Bible Translator*
BiT	*Bible Today*
BJRL	*Bulletin of the John Rylands Library*
BLE	*Bulletin de littérature ecclésiastique*
BNTC	Black's New Testament Commentary
BTB	*Biblical Theology Bulletin*
BZ	*Biblische Zeitschrift*
CBQ	*Catholic Biblical Quarterly*
CHL	*Commentationes humanarum litterarum (Societas scientiarum fennica)*
CHSHMC	Center for Hermeneutical Studies in Hellenistic and Modern Culture
CJ	*Conservative Judaism*
CTQ	*Concordia Theological Quarterly*
CurrThM	*Currents in Theology and Mission*
DBM	*Deltion Biblikon Meleton*
DSS	Dead Sea Scrolls
EHPR	Études d'histoire et de philosophie religieuses
EJ	*Encyclopaedia Judaica*

ÉPROER	Études préliminaires aux religions orientales dans l'empire romain
EvQ	*Evangelical Quarterly*
ExpT	*Expository Times*
FTS	Frankfurter theologische Studien
FoiVie	*Foi et vie*
GCAJS	*Gratz College Annual of Jewish Studies*
GNS	Good News Studies (Michael Glazier)
HeyJ	*Heythrop Journal*
HNTC	Harper's New Testament Commentaries
HSS	Harvard Semitic Series
HTR	*Harvard Theological Review*
HUCA	*Hebrew Union College Annual*
IBS	*Irish Biblical Studies*
ICC	International Critical Commentaries
IEJ	*Israel Exploration Journal*
Int	*Interpretation*
ITQ	*Irish Theological Quarterly*
JAC	*Jahrbuch für Antike und Christentum*
JANES	*Journal of the Ancient Near Eastern Society of Columbia University*
JBL	*Journal of Biblical Literature*
JBLM	Journal of Biblical Literature Monograph
JETS	*Journal of the Evangelical Theological Society*
JHS	*Journal of Hellenic Studies*
JJS	*Journal of Jewish Studies*
JNES	*Journal of Near Eastern Studies*
JPFC	*The Jewish People in the First Century*, ed. S. Safrai and M. Stern
JQR	*Jewish Quarterly Review*
JRH	*Journal of Religion and Health*
JSJ	*Journal for the Study of Judaism*
JSJT	*Jerusalem Studies in Jewish Thought*
JSNT	*Journal for the Study of the New Testament*
JSNTSup	Journal for the Study of the New Testament Supplement Series
JSOT	*Journal for the Study of the Old Testament*
JSS	*Journal of Semitic Studies*
JTS	*Journal of Theological Studies*
LCL	Loeb Classical Library
LEC	Library of Early Christianity, ed. W. Meeks
LumV	*Lumière et vie*
LUOSM	Leeds University Oriental Society Monograph
LXX	Septuagint
MNTC	Moffatt New Testament Commentary
MSS	Manuscripts
MT	Masoretic Text
NCBC	New Century Bible Commentary
Neot	*Neotestamentica*

NICNT	New International Commentary on the New Testament, ed. G. D. Fee
NIDNTT	*The New International Dictionary of New Testament Theology*, ed. C. Brown
NIGNT	New International Greek Testament Commentary
NovT	*Novum Testamentum*
NovTSup	Novum Testamentum Supplements
NT	New Testament
NTA	*New Testament Abstracts*
NTS	*New Testament Studies*
NedTT	*Nederlands theologisch tijdschrift*
NTTid	*Norsk teologisk tidsskrift*
OT	Old Testament
OTP	*The Old Testament Pseudepigrapha*, ed. J. H. Charlesworth
PEQ	*Palestine Exploration Quarterly*
PNTC	Pelican New Testament Commentaries
POTTS	Pittsburgh Original Texts and Translations Series
PRS	*Perspectives in Religious Studies*
PTMS	Pittsburgh Theological Monograph Series
RB	*Revue biblique*
Rel	*Religion*
ResQ	*Restoration Quarterly*
RevEtJuiv	*Revue études juives*
RevExp	*Review and Expositor*
RevQ	*Revue de Qumran*
RevRel	*The Review of Religion*
RHPR	*Revue d'histoire et de philosophie religieuses*
RivB	*Rivista Biblica*
RSPT	*Revue des sciences philosophiques et théologiques*
RTR	*The Reformed Theological Review*
SBEC	Studies in the Bible and Early Christianity
SBFLA	*Studii biblici Franciscani liber annuus*
SBL	Society of Biblical Literature
SBLDS	Society of Biblical Literature Dissertation Series
SBLMS	Society of Biblical Literature Monograph Series
SBLSCS	Society of Biblical Literature Septuagint and Cognate Studies
SBLSP	*Society of Biblical Literature Seminar Papers*
SBLSS	Society of Biblical Literature Semeia Supplements
SBS	Sources for Biblical Study
SBT	Studies in Biblical Theology
ScEsp	*Science et Esprit*
SEÅ	*Svensk Exegetisk Årsbok*
SecCent	*Second Century*
SJLA	Studies in Judaism in Late Antiquity
SJT	*Scottish Journal of Theology*
SJTOP	Scottish Journal of Theology Occasional Papers
SLJT	*Saint Luke's Journal of Theology*

SNTSMS	Society for New Testament Studies Monograph Series
SNTU	*Studien zum Neuen Testament und seiner Umwelt*
SR	*Studies in Religion/Sciences religieuses*
ST	*Scripta theologica*
StEv	*Studia evangelica*
SVTQ	*St. Vladimir's Theological Quarterly*
SzANT	Studien zum Alten und Neuen Testament
TDNT	*Theological Dictionary of the New Testament*, ed. G. Kittel and G. Friedrich
Th	*Theology*
TJ	*Trinity Journal*
TNTC	Tyndale New Testament Commentaries
TNTL	Tyndale New Testament Lecture
TZ	*Theologische Zeitschrift*
VC	*Vigiliae christianae*
VT	*Vetus Testamentum*
VTSup	Vetus Testamentum Supplements
ZDMG	*Zeitschrift der deutschen morgenländischen Gesellschaft*
ZNW	*Zeitschrift für die neutestamentliche Wissenschaft*
ZTK	*Zeitschrift für Theologie und Kirche*

INTRODUCTION

THE ARGUMENT OF THIS BOOK

This book traces samples of two streams of Jewish understandings of the Spirit in early Christian narrative literature. It is not a survey of all (or even most) relevant texts, which would unnecessarily belabor my point; I prefer working exegetically with some samples in detail rather than merely surveying broad themes by tracing every example. To say that this book is not a survey of NT pneumatology in general is not to reject the importance of such a survey, but to define the limits of this project.

I begin with a survey of early Jewish pneumatology, recognizing two primary streams of thought in the first few centuries before and after the Gospels and Acts: purification and prophecy. One could very easily divide each of these streams into subcategories: for instance, what we have labeled the "spirit of prophecy" actually includes traditional prophecy, supernatural knowledge, and (especially in the Dead Sea Scrolls) divine insights into the hidden meaning of Scripture. But the overlap among these subcategories in the ancient texts is substantial, whereas the two major streams of thought I have identified in this work remain largely distinct. I have therefore chosen, after much consideration, to retain two broad but distinguishable categories rather than imposing narrower but more ambiguous ones on the texts.

The rest of the book shows how early Christians adapted these two streams of thought. This adaptation suggests the ready availability of the categories in contemporary Judaism, not that the early Christians would have regarded contemporary Judaism as their primary source. Both functions of the Spirit also appear in the Bible that early Christians shared with other Jewish movements. Nor is this comparison exhaustive; only after one examines the elements of continuity between early Jewish and early Christian categories of pneumatology is one struck with a compelling contrast. Although the Qumran literature associates the Spirit of purity with ethics, that was contemporary Judaism's nearest parallel to the early Christian conception that the indwelling Spirit mediates God's (and Christ's) presence and moral character in the individual believer (e.g., Gal 5:16–23). That aspect of the Spirit's ministry appears most forcefully in Paul, but is evident in the Farewell Discourses of the Fourth Gospel and some examples could be adduced elsewhere in the NT. Although an examination of this contrast is beyond the scope of this book, the book points toward it as an inadvertently negative conclusion: early Christian pneumatological experience exceeded the traditional Jewish categories in which the first Christians presented it.

In my dissertation I traced the two main streams of Jewish pneumatology in the Fourth Gospel, which I believe for the most part stresses the Spirit of purification but focuses on the Spirit of prophecy (or, more specifically, the Spirit of divinely revealed insight into the Jesus tradition) in the Paraclete passages. I argued that the Fourth Gospel's pneumatology functioned as a major component of John's polemic against a cessationist stream of Judaism which could lay no claim to the spiritual experiences of John's audience and which, in the uncomfortable decades for Diaspora Judaism after 70 C.E., may have been troubled by Christian prophetism as well as by Christian messianism. To make this book of broader applicability I have retained some of the material on the Spirit of purification in the Fourth Gospel (where it is most prominent in the NT) and turned to Luke–Acts for some more obvious examples of the early Christian interpretation of the Spirit of prophecy. I believe that both streams of thought interplay freely in much early Christian thought (including the Fourth Gospel) and were inseparably connected in the early preaching of John the Baptist.

The sample Christian texts I have chosen are thus as follows: Mark 1, on John the Baptist's announcement of Spirit baptism, which proves central to Mark's Gospel; Matthew 3–4 and 12, showing how Matthew develops the Q parallel to (or source of) Mark in greater detail and in keeping with Matthean Christology; the texts supporting an explicit or implicit water/Spirit contrast in the Fourth Gospel, with special emphasis on John 3; and finally, the oft-noted Spirit of prophecy in Acts 2. Because I wish to mine these texts fairly and not merely for what I hope to find, the analyses will produce many insights not strictly limited to early Christian pneumatology. But after examining these texts and their function within their respective documents, comparisons (and perhaps contrasts) with much of the pneumatology of early Judaism should become more evident.

Although some streams of early Judaism speak almost exclusively of the Spirit of prophecy and some early Christian writers emphasize one aspect of the Spirit more than another, those extant early Christian writers that deal with pneumatology at length suggest that the Christians incorporated both aspects from the start.

THE LIMITS OF THIS BOOK

Among the many important works on biblical pneumatology that have appeared in the past decade, the massive tome on Pauline pneumatology by Gordon Fee, *God's Empowering Presence,* deserves special acknowledgment.[1] I have designed this book to complement that larger one in some small degree. The differences between the two books reflect both our respective strengths and our different purposes, but my avoidance of overlap with his work indicates my respect for and basic agreement with it, rather than disapproval of his methodology. I cannot do better what he has already done, so I simply refer readers interested in Pauline pneumatology to that work.

The present work differs from Fee's in the following respects:

(1) Whereas Fee focuses on the epistolary genre, I have selected only texts from largely narrative books of the NT, namely the Gospels and Acts.

(2) Whereas Fee examines all explicitly and many implicitly pneumatological texts in his chosen corpus, I have focused on specific texts which I believe provide important examples for the motifs we are tracing.

(3) Whereas Fee begins with a more traditional exegesis of relevant Pauline texts, I begin with contemporary Jewish literature and focus particularly on the social context of various motifs in the sample passages selected.[2]

(4) Whereas Fee also seeks the experience of the early Christians behind the text, I have tried to keep such inquiries to a minimum (although Acts, like some Pauline passages, but in contrast to the Gospels, readily lends itself to such a quest).

The present work may, however, reinforce one of the primary theses of Fee and other writers: the experience of and dependence on the Spirit was pervasive in early Christianity, which was thoroughly charismatic in the general sense of the term. Further, although some Jewish contemporaries sought revelatory experiences, the early Christians were more consistently charismatic than most of mainstream Judaism; although NT Spirit-language may fail to strike us today due to its familiarity, it radically defined early Christians as the community of the new age.

FUNCTIONAL PNEUMATOLOGY AND THIS BOOK

Although I undertook both the dissertation and this book primarily to investigate historical questions, it may have some practical value in dialogue between charismatic and noncharismatic Christians today. At my dissertation defense one professor wanted me to justify the two basic streams into which I divided early Jewish pneumatology; I admitted that a three-part schema (distinguishing inspired insight from prophecy) was also defensible, but that the Spirit of prophecy frequently overlapped with the Spirit of knowledge, so I had preferred to divide the material into two main categories. Although I suspect he thought that I had a theological motive for dividing the material this way, the potential theological implications had not yet dawned on me.

Since that time the relevance of his question has followed me: although moral purification (in Christian language, regeneration and subsequent renewal) and prophetic empowerment come from the same Spirit, they are usually distinguishable in Jewish texts (some streams of early Judaism, in fact, deal almost exclusively with the latter). The NT generally presents them as part of the same "theological" package. For instance, John's purification and revelatory themes coalesce in the reception of the Spirit in John 20:22–23; breathing alludes to God's life-giving breath to Adam in Genesis 2:7, and the commission relates to OT prophetic models. Nevertheless, that we can distinguish them indicates that it is *possible* to distinguish them, and I believe that some texts indicate that it is also possible to experience various measures of prophetic empowerment subsequent to regeneration.

In contrast to Dunn's *Baptism in the Holy Spirit* (with whose work I agree on most other points), I find Spirit-empowerments subsequent to conversion in some of the narratives of Acts, especially Acts 8. Yet Acts also seems to suggest that fully committed believers may require not merely *one* subsequent experience with the Spirit (as in some charismatic paradigms), but a succession of continuing experiences with and sudden inspirations of the Spirit in ministry crisis situations (Acts 4:8; 13:9) and probably in worship as well (13:52). The emphasis may rest less on the initial crisis experience than on the continuing Spirit-filled life (6:5; cf. 2:42–47). In other words, believers receive the Spirit at conversion, but in *practice* all believers may experience new giftings and empowerments as they pursue their Christian vocations. This is hardly the forum in which to pursue such suggestions (which I have attempted instead in my less academic *Three Crucial Questions on the Holy Spirit,* Baker, 1996), but perhaps those interested in pursuing (or refuting) such a suggestion will find some value in this work.

I hope that this study will underline the pervasively Spirit-centered character of early Christian experience. I also hope that it will thereby contribute to current discussion on how contemporary Christians can appropriate the NT model and become more Spirit-empowered in their life and ministry.

NOTES

1. G. D. Fee, *God's Empowering Presence* (Peabody, Mass.: Hendrickson, 1994); at 967 pages plus front matter, it is the most extensive treatment of Pauline pneumatology extant (and one of the few available).

2. One will thus notice my attention to primary sources where possible. I have endeavored always to credit a secondary source when my primary source is borrowed; nearly all unattributed primary sources are from my own reading in the originals or translations. I have tried to provide references to secondary sources wherever I am dependent on them or wherever I felt they might be useful to the reader. In the case of some less relevant and less accessible journal articles I have relied on *New Testament Abstracts* to catch the general sense. References to these articles are provided for the reader's bibliographic interest.

1

● ● ● ● ● ● ● ● ● ● ● ● ●

THE SPIRIT OF PURITY
AND PROPHECY IN EARLY JUDAISM

● ● ● ● ● ● ● ● ● ● ● ● ●

Other studies have addressed the function of God's Spirit in the OT[1] and early Judaism,[2] and it is not our purpose merely to duplicate these here. Although the Septuagint and, to a lesser extent, the Hebrew Scriptures, were widely used in early Christianity and therefore may have exerted the most direct influence on the development of early Christian pneumatology and pneumatic experience, they will not be the focus of the present study. These resources are widely available for the study of early Christianity and most works on early Christian pneumatology already take them into account. We are primarily interested in how other aspects of early Judaism's doctrine and experience of the divine Spirit contributed to Christian expectation and articulation of their own doctrine and experience.

The primary divisions of early Jewish divine Spirit-language treated in this chapter will be the Spirit of purification (the ethical function of the Spirit) and the Spirit of prophecy and of wisdom or instruction (these last subcategories overlap considerably).[3] Most of the extant material to be examined is more relevant to the Spirit of prophecy than of purification, especially because the later rabbis concentrated on the prophetic dimension of the Spirit to the virtual exclusion of the purifying dimension, and rabbinic literature, late though it may be, provides the most voluminous source for discussion. The greater emphasis on prophecy in this chapter reflects the contour of our extant sources.

1. THE SPIRIT IN NON-JEWISH LITERATURE

That Greek models did indeed affect Jewish practice cannot be disputed; Palestinian Judaism was thoroughly affected and permeated by Hellenism by the first century C.E. While this is true for the forms of pneumatic experience, it is not so true for the language of the Spirit itself, which early Judaism took over from older Israelite tradition. Greco-Roman[4] expressions relating to a divine Spirit are very different from the most standard Jewish usages. The Greek use of πνεῦμα in general has been summarized by Chevallier in the following ways:[5]

(1) Breath, wind

(2) A personal power, a good or bad δαίμων

(3) Anthropologically, dualistically opposed to the body

(4) Not the divine Spirit in the sense found in Jewish literature[6]

(5) Psychological dispositions

Although there is considerable overlap with the Jewish usage of רוח on points 1–3, Chevallier finds little overlap on points 4 and 5.

There were, of course, different usages of the image of the divine Spirit in Greco-Roman literature. Quintilian, for instance, observes that some think that god (*deum*) is a spirit (*spiritum*) "permeating all things" (*omnibus partibus immixtum*), whereas others, like Epicurus, think god has a human form.[7]

Among the Greeks, it was especially the Stoics and those influenced by their language that typically associated πνεῦμα with the divine.[8] "Spirit" in Stoicism was an impersonal cosmic substance, "the finest form of matter,"[9] a mixture of fire and air[10] that interpenetrated all other matter and was like the soul of the universe.[11] It was not central to Stoicism's ethics, but to its physics and metaphysics, conceptualized in terms of Stoic monism.[12] As Nock points out, the Stoics knew πνεῦμα ἱερόν (sacred spirit) but not πνεῦμα ἅγιον;[13] the Stoic concept is thus quite different from the traditional Jewish concept, although Philo may have merged the two to some extent.[14]

There is, however, one context in which there appears to be some approximation of the Jewish use of the divine Spirit in Greek literature. Before Plutarch, divine πνεῦμα was only extremely rarely associated with poetic and prophetic inspiration, although such inspiration was commonly discussed.[15] Leisegang can cite texts associating "spirit" with the inspiration of the Pythoness,[16] but apart from Strabo, most of his sources are late enough to betray Christian influence. A stronger case could perhaps be made with Plutarch's use of πνεῦμα as a source of inspiration. Plutarch, writing on the nature of inspiration, speaks of the divine spirit that inspires prophecy. He observes that one might assert,

> not without reason, that a dryness engendered with the heat subtilizes the spirit of prophecy[17] and renders it ethereal and pure; for this is 'the dry soul,' as Heraclitus has it. . . . by a sort of chilling and compacting of the spirit of inspiration [τοῦ πνεύματος] the prophetic element in the soul, as when steel is dipped in cold water, is rendered tense and keen.[18]

But the concept of "spirit" here probably has more to do with Stoic-like conceptions of a pervasive substance, or with exhalations from the earth such as those affecting the Pythian priestess at Delphi (the standard view earlier held by Plutarch), than with a spirit associated *particularly* with inspiration.[19] As Aune observes, "while Greco-Roman writers certainly had a concept of inspiration, they did not normally associate that conception with *pneuma.*"[20]

The rare similarities between Greco-Roman and Jewish usage of the divine Spirit, aside from certain postbiblical associations of πνεῦμα in Diaspora-oriented Jewish texts, may actually sometimes reflect Jewish influence on Greco-Roman tradition, given the prevalence of Jewish influences in Greco-Roman magical practices.[21] Isaacs may be right when she observes,

> In faithfully translating the Hebrew term *ruach* as πνεῦμα when it applied not only to breath and life, but also to God, the LXX played a significant part in the development of its meaning in subsequent Greek literature.[22]

Although there were definite concepts of the divine Spirit in Greek writings, and these may have affected certain perceptions and usages of Jewish "spirit" language, they do not match the primary categories of Jewish usage we will examine below. These uses have their roots in earlier Israelite imagery for the Spirit of God.

2.   THE SPIRIT OF PURIFICATION IN EARLY JUDAISM

The Spirit of God anoints God's servants for a variety of functions in the OT, including wisdom for craftsmanship,[23] and physical prowess and strength.[24] Such usages do occur in early Jewish texts, although very rarely. In Pseudo-Philo, for instance, Kenaz was clothed by the spirit of the Lord, the spirit of power, to enable him to begin striking down Amorites with the sword.[25] In general, however, reference to this function of the Spirit of God only occurs when expounding the OT texts that speak of it.[26]

More common, however, are references to the Spirit of God or Holy Spirit as the Spirit that purifies.[27] This also has OT roots, perhaps in the image of prophetic empowerment leading to transformation of character,[28] but especially in the image of eschatological cleansing by God's Spirit portrayed as water.[29] Although the image of cleansing by water representing the Spirit is not frequent in early Jewish texts, the idea of the Spirit purifying or empowering God's people to do his will occurs more than any other Spirit-image except the Spirit of inspiration and revelation. The Spirit of purification occurs less frequently than the Spirit of prophecy in part because the former appears especially in the stream of early Judaism associated primarily with the Essenes, in contrast to the more Pharisaic stream of thought and other sources. We cannot rule out its presence in common Judaism, but this aspect of the Spirit appears primarily among the Essenes.

Jubilees, after a warning against the spirit of Beliar, who leads into sin,[30] reports a prayer of Moses the intercessor and God's reply:

> "Create a pure heart and a holy spirit[31] for them. And do not let them be ensnared by their sin henceforth and forever." And the LORD said to Moses, ... "I shall create for them a holy spirit, and I shall purify them so that they will not turn away from following me from that day and forever."[32]

The language here and in the context is strikingly similar to that of Ezekiel (36:25–27), who also associates a new heart and new spirit (as well as God's own Spirit) with restoration and the keeping of God's commandments by Israel.

In the Dead Sea Scrolls, the "Holy Spirit" can refer to the Spirit of Holiness in the most natural sense, i.e., the Spirit of God who purifies or the human spirit that has been set apart to God.[33] Thus the רוח הקודש in 1QS 3.7 and 4.21 is characterized as the Spirit that cleanses or purifies from sin, with a possible background in passages like Ezek 36:25–27;[34] 4:21 compares the Spirit of Holiness to purifying waters[35] poured out on the chosen at the time of the end, and 3:4, 8–9 speak of a ritual immersion upon initiation into the community. In these contexts, especially 4:21, it is associated with the Spirit of Truth in contrast with the Spirit of Error, along with a number of other adjectival genitive constructions.[36] God's "Holy Spirit" similarly has moral associations in 1QH 9.32, although here it is also linked with the truth-teaching function of the Spirit.[37]

In CD 5.11–12 "they defile their (own) holy spirit" by reviling with their tongue against God's laws,[38] and CD 7.3–4 admonishes, "And let no one defile his holy spirit since God separated them. . . ."[39] Although these texts in the Damascus Document are less relevant to our study, neither referring to God's Spirit nor making reference to the OT purification texts, they do illustrate that the language of "holy spirit" could be applied easily enough to moral holiness,[40] possibly related to the Qumran purification baths.[41] Other texts are not clearly connected to this concept, although a possible relationship cannot be ruled out. The *Testament of Twelve Patriarchs*, for instance, of less certainly pre-Christian date, can associate the Spirit of God with doing good, as in *T. Sim.* 4:4.[42]

That some early Jewish sources omit this motif may not be significant; some mention the Spirit only rarely anyway. The relative paucity of examples of this use of the Spirit as against the Spirit of wisdom or prophetic insight need not indicate that it was virtually unknown in early Judaism. Outside of rabbinic texts, our references to the Spirit of God acting on humans are not numerous to begin with; indeed, Pryke has suggested that of ninety-seven texts definitely referring to Spirit "in the four main documents of Qumran," there are only seven clear references to God's Spirit, seventy-two referring to the human spirit.[43] Whether or not this is correct,[44] it is clear that of the Qumran texts referring to God's "Holy Spirit," a significant proportion do refer to the purifying Spirit.

Yet *Jubilees*, which shares this perspective the most clearly with documents unique to Qumran, has many other parallels with the outlook of some of the other Scrolls, suggesting that some tendencies characterized a certain kind of Palestinian Judaism, rather than early Judaism as a whole. The virtual absence of this motif from the vast body of early Jewish literature produced by the Tannaim and Amoraim cannot be ignored. Whether the Pharisees or their rabbinic successors suppressed the idea, or more likely it predominated among the Essenes to begin with, emphasis on this aspect of the Spirit was not common to all Judaism.

3. **THE SPIRIT OF KNOWLEDGE AND PROPHECY IN EARLY JUDAISM,
    EXCEPTING RABBINIC LITERATURE**

Early Jewish sources often associate the Spirit with inspiration (usually of a prophetic nature) and divine illumination or revelation in wisdom or knowledge. The latter aspect of the Spirit's work appears particularly in the Dead Sea Scrolls (e.g., 1QH 12.11–13), but because of the ambiguity of the distinction between the Spirit of prophecy and the Spirit of wisdom (cf., e.g., Eph 1:18 for an early Christian reference to the latter), we record both aspects of the Spirit's work under this category.

Despite his careful scholarship, David Aune appears to be mistaken when he writes that "the Spirit of God was identified as the Spirit of prophecy primarily within rabbinic Judaism (second century C.E. and later), not within such other sects of early Judaism as the Qumran community."[45] This view of the activity of God's Spirit among people is at least as widespread as the purifying aspect of the Spirit's activity discussed above, and more so if the exclusion of Jewish literature in Greek above is not simply coincidence.[46]

The rabbis were not alone in associating the Spirit with prophecy. Josephus, for example, notes that when the divine spirit (τοῦ θείου πνεύματος) first came to David, he "began to prophesy," a point not found in the biblical text here.[47] Best suggests that Josephus almost always uses θεῖον πνεῦμα only for the Spirit of prophecy and oracular speech.[48] Philo similarly speaks of "the Divine Spirit of prophecy," commenting on Numbers 11:16.[49] In Sirach 48:24, Isaiah foresaw the future by means of a great Spirit.[50] In the *Testament of Job*, whose pre-Christian nature, especially in the final chapters, is not beyond doubt, but certainly possible,[51] we read that Job's daughter Hemera

> spoke ecstatically in the angelic dialect, sending up a hymn to God in accord with the hymnic style of the angels. And as she spoke ecstatically [ἀπεφθέγξατο] she allowed "The Spirit" to be inscribed on her garment.[52]

This is also the case for early Palestinian Jewish literature. When Isaac was to bless Jacob's sons in *Jubilees*, "a spirit of prophecy came down upon his mouth,"[53] and the Spirit also functions as the Spirit of prophecy in the fifth book of *1 Enoch*.[54] In a later work, Pseudo-Philo, it is said,

> And when they had sat down, a holy spirit [spiritus sanctus] came upon Kenaz and dwelled in him and put him in ecstasy [extulit sensum eius], and he began to prophesy [prophetare], saying. . .[55]

Similarly, Ezra, through the Holy Spirit, is inspired to write many books.[56]

There are also references to this phenomenon in the Dead Sea Scrolls. In 1QS 8.16, the prophets revealed their message by the Holy Spirit: גלו הנבים ברוח קודשו. Although CD 2.12 is less clear, it appears again that God's Holy Spirit is identified with the Spirit of prophecy.[57]

In other early Jewish texts, the Holy Spirit also functioned as the Spirit of revelation or prophecy. The Spirit revealed matters in dreams, for example to Isaac[58] or Miriam.[59] Similarly, the Spirit could be associated with singing a spontaneously created song,[60] which would have been associated with inspiration in antiquity. One could also "see," in the sense of prophetic perception, by the Spirit.[61]

It is further worthy of note that some early Christian texts, such as the writings of Justin Martyr, carry over this same concept and language. Although Justin's *Dialogue with Trypho*[62] could reflect a great deal of Justin's own conceptions superimposed on Trypho as well as some accurate ideas attributable to a second-century Jewish teacher, he uses the concept just as freely in his own *First Apology*.[63]

It is therefore quite inaccurate to suggest that the Spirit of God was viewed as the Spirit of prophecy only in rabbinic Judaism, even though the Spirit of God in rabbinic Judaism for the most part functions only as the Spirit of prophecy. This was indeed the predominant, though far from the only, sense in which the Spirit of God was viewed in non-rabbinic Jewish texts.

4.   THE SPIRIT OF PROPHECY IN RABBINIC LITERATURE

The rabbis also could associate the Spirit with prophetic revelation and insight. For instance, Tannaitic interpreters of Joshua 2:16 remarked:

> And so Rahab said to Joshua's agents, "Go to the mountain, lest the pursuit party find you" (Josh 2:16). This shows that the Holy Spirit rested on her, for had the Holy Spirit not rested on her, how should she ever have known that they were going to return after three days. But this teaches that the Holy Spirit came to rest on her.[64]

A similar association of the Spirit with prophetic insight is found in a Tannaitic tale about R. Gamaliel II, who

> saw a gentile. He said to him, "Mabegai, take this loaf of bread." R. Le'ii ran after him . . . He said to him, "What is your name?" He said to him, "Mabegai." He said to him, "Now, did Rabban Gamaliel ever in your whole life meet you?" He said to him, "No." On the basis of this event we learn that Rabban Gamaliel divined by the Holy Spirit.[65]

In the *Mekilta,* Israel knew Pharaoh's plans against them through the Holy Spirit that rested on them.[66]

The Babylonian Gemara follows this tradition as well. That the Holy Spirit was not with Eli was clear from the way he had misinterpreted Hannah's conduct;[67] one person had given instructions specifically motivated by the Holy Spirit;[68] and no ancient priest had been inquired of who did not speak by the Spirit.[69] In light of the OT tradition, such references are all taken most naturally with reference to prophetic ability or enablement. Likewise, in the Palestinian Gemara, R. Joshua of Sikhnin in R. Levi's name says that Moses "foresaw through the Holy Spirit" Israel's subjugation under the Gentile kingdoms.[70] The association with prophecy is clearly found also in *Pesiqta de Rab Kahana*[71] and some later compilations in the *Midrash Rabbah,*[72] and McNamara finds it as "a divine power" for prophecy, praise, etc., in the Targumim.[73] One may conclude from Schäfer's data in comparing Targumim that "Holy Spirit" and "Spirit of prophecy" are functionally interchangeable, the differences mandated by style.[74]

The emphasis on the Spirit of prophecy in early Judaism has not been missed by modern students of rabbinic texts.[75] Indeed, it may in fact be the case that, if anything, modern scholars have overemphasized the identity of the Spirit as the Spirit of prophecy in rabbinic Judaism.

In rabbinic literature, the Spirit of prophecy is particularly associated with the inspiration of books of the Bible, sometimes to ensure their authority, sometimes simply assuming it. Such a usage may be implied in passing in some non-rabbinic Jewish texts,[76] but becomes far more prominent in rabbinic literature.[77] This is true in Tannaitic texts in *Sipra*[78] and *Sipre Deuteronomy,*[79] and becomes more frequent in the Gemara[80] and very common in the *Midrash Rabbah*[81] and *Pesiqta Rabbati.*[82]

What this suggests is that rabbinic Judaism not only developed the concept of the Spirit as the prophetic Spirit, almost to the exclusion[83] of other possible models,[84] but also developed that role particularly with regard to the supremacy of the Scriptures the rabbis interpreted. This is a natural development, since the rabbis' *primary* attention as legal scholars was to the biblical texts, whether they were deriving halakah or illustrating principles through haggadah. But it may also illustrate a progressive "taming" of the pneumatic dimension of early Jewish experience from the rabbinic perspective. Strongly pneumatic movements could claim an alternative epistemological base over against traditional interpretation of the Torah, and this could pose a threat to their unification of Jewish thought and practice according to what they believed was true.[85]

5. DEPARTURE OF THE SPIRIT AND CESSATION OF PROPHECY IN NON-RABBINIC SOURCES

Although Sandmel observes that prophecy was a thing of the past for rabbinic Judaism, he insists that "outside the circle of the rabbinic Sages the view that prophecy had ended simply did not exist."[86] Although this is an exaggeration, as we shall see, it is certainly true that this view prevailed much more among the rabbis than elsewhere in early Judaism.

Some scholars have traced the belief that prophecy had ended to late in the OT period,[87] but stronger arguments have been made for this belief arising in the "intertestamental" period. Hill, for example, in arguing for the latter, points to the use of pseudonymity in apocalyptic texts,[88] and argues that no prophets appear who speak with the authority of OT prophetic messengers.[89] Aside from the activities of prophets chronicled in Josephus (below), his arguments depend ultimately on the assumption that prophetic authority would be conveyed by the same conventions of genre in all periods, which does not hold true even in the OT itself.[90]

There are, however, indications that prophecy no longer maintained the role it once had, and that some parts of Judaism did not believe that prophets continued in the OT sense. First Maccabees 9:27 speaks of the cessation of prophecy, and 4:45–46 and 14:41 speak of the coming of a prophet as a future expectation[91] (although not necessarily an eschatological one).

Aune asserts here that 4:45b–46 refers to a future *clerical* prophet, not a prophet like the OT prophets, but offers no evidence in support of his contention.[92] He suggests that 9:27 only means that the ancient kind of prophets no longer appeared, and that 14:41 speaks not of a future prophet, but was meant only to restrain an idealization of the Hasmonaean program, and again refers only to clerical prophecy related to the priesthood.[93] Aune may be right (against some scholars) that the future prophet is not eschatological, but he offers no convincing reason to assume that the intended readers of 1 Maccabees should have taken "prophet" in any other than the conventional sense.

While the type of prophet "envisaged is a person with decision-making power, a man of insight," it does not therefore follow that he was this rather than a prophet with "inspired authority";[94] both types of men of God appeared in the OT, both types of divine enablement were often combined in the same characters, and the term "prophet" in itself normally implied inspiration and whatever degree of authority inspiration connoted.

First Maccabees 14:41 need not mean, indeed, that prophets were relegated only to the eschatological future; but it does clearly indicate that none were known or acknowledged in that time, and that Simon's divinely given leadership ability was not the same thing as a prophet who could tell Israel what to do.

Josephus, a Pharisee holding to a closed canon, can argue that there has been no exact succession of prophets since the time of Artaxerxes, which was why no books had been accorded canonical authority since that time.[95] In Josephus, the continuing prophetic phenomena are not, unlike those from the biblical period, associated with πνεῦμα.[96] Prophecy may have continued, but the *title* "prophet" belongs to the past and to the future. Josephus applies the term "prophet" in his own time only to those he considered "false prophets."[97] Although this could be part of Josephus' apologetic to play down the popularity of Jewish messianism and hence to isolate the Zealotic tendencies within Israel, the conjunction of his usage with that of Philo supports a broader context for the usage.[98]

In the early second century, *2 Bar.* 85:3 also indicates a belief that the prophets are no more; indeed, some early Christian texts may suggest the same belief (e.g., John 8:53). Sirach 36:14–16 probably implies an eschatological restoration or multiplication of prophecy (v. 14, λόγια) and perhaps prophets (vv. 15–16).[99]

Of course, while there may have existed in various circles a belief that prophets no longer existed as they had in biblical times, no one, including the rabbis, denied that revelatory experiences continued to be possible.[100] But biblical prophecy was seen as different from postbiblical prophecy; thus in Josephus and Philo

> πνεῦμα is confined to prophecy in the biblical period. In this way they reflect the common view that prophecy had ceased. This does not mean that they believed that inspiration had stopped. By confining πνεῦμα to the biblical period, the apologists for Judaism were making a claim for the unique character of the revelation given by God and recorded in their scriptures. This obviously lies behind Philo's claim that Moses had more of the divine πνεῦμα than anyone else. What he is asserting is the supremacy of the Mosaic Torah.[101]

6. DEPARTURE OF THE SPIRIT AND CESSATION OF PROPHECY IN RABBINIC SOURCES

If the concept of the prophetic Spirit's departure in some sense already existed in early Judaism, it was certainly developed further by the rabbis after 70 C.E.[102]

The Holy Spirit might have departed from Israel in preceding times, for instance, after Elijah was taken up to heaven;[103] but what was more widely remarked on in rabbinic texts was the teaching that the Holy Spirit had departed with the last of the biblical prophets:

> When the latter prophets died, that is, Haggai, Zechariah, and Malachi, then the Holy Spirit came to an end in Israel. But even so, they made them hear [Heavenly messages] through an echo *[bat kol]*.[104]

This Tannaitic teaching is repeated in various Amoraic texts, often in this form in the name of "our rabbis," signifying the traditioning of a standard, established earlier teaching.[105] Some later rabbis dated the departure of the Holy Spirit to the destruction of the temple,[106] or to the time of Jeremiah, with minor exceptions,[107] but the net effect was the same: the Spirit of prophecy had ceased to be available in their own time. This departure has been widely noted by modern scholars.[108]

This does not, of course, mean that revelations were not available, for as *t. Soṭa* 13:3 (quoted above) and many of the other texts argue, the heavenly voice *(bat kol)* functioned as a surrogate for the Spirit of prophecy.[109] But this substitute was at best an inferior one, and there was thus sometimes an expectation of a future time when the prophetic Spirit would be restored.

The giving of the Spirit had been associated with the eschatological salvation of Israel in the Hebrew prophets,[110] and was similarly associated with eschatology in early Christianity.[111] Isaacs points out that an eschatological role for the Spirit was rare in extant documents of Diaspora Judaism, but concedes that "this is hardly surprising, since Hellenistic Judaism was not eschatologically oriented."[112] More critical, however, is its apparent absence from first-century Palestinian Jewish texts apart from the writings of the Qumran Covenanters,[113] which leads her to suppose that the doctrine was not widespread in early Judaism.[114] Here, however, her case is almost an argument from silence, given the scarcity of references to the Spirit in early Judaism, and the fact that there is not an abundance of Palestinian Jewish literature, apart from the Scrolls, from this period.

Although rabbinic texts do not stress eschatology to the extent that most of the documents of the Qumran Covenanters or many other pre-70 and pre-135 writings do,[115] they do suggest an eschatological return of the Spirit that corresponds to the belief that it had departed for the present time.[116] The presence of the Holy Spirit on Israel in the first exodus,[117] perhaps related to the idea of God's Shekinah among Israel at that time, may also suggest an eschatological endowment of the Spirit when the future restoration is viewed as a new exodus.

7.   THE CONTINUANCE OF PROPHECY

Particularly outside the rabbinic literature, prophecy was *generally* not believed to have ceased.[118] As E. P. Sanders observes, the aristocracy may not have liked this situation, but they could not have repressed it.[119]

Josephus says that John Hyrcanus had the gift of prophecy, in that God conversed with him, and he had knowledge of future events; he also attributes this power several times to the Essenes.[120] He was also said to possess the gift himself, in the form of prediction of the future.[121] And while Jesus son of Ananias may not have received the title "prophet," his actions and message certainly characterize him as one.[122]

Similarly, even if Philo felt that prophecy had ceased with the biblical period, he felt that inspiration continued:

> Hence, Philo can speak of divine assistance which comes to him when his own literary imagination dries up.[123] In considering the relationship between πνεῦμα and conscience, we have seen that Philo certainly believed in divine guidance. Furthermore, he not only speaks of the corybantic frenzy which inspired the prophets of the past; a similar frenzy drives the ascetics of his own day out into the wilderness.[124] For Philo, it is not only the prophets of the O.T. who were inspired; so were the translators of the LXX—καθάπερ ἐνθουσιῶντες.[125]

If this is not quite as explicit as Josephus' use of προφητ- roots for the present period, it is nonetheless typical Greek language for inspiration, as well as Philo's own language for the inspiration of OT prophets, and there is no indication that this phenomenon has been repressed in the present.[126]

Josephus often reports Essene prophecy.[127] Aune argues that the prophecy in *Jewish War* 2.159 is noneschatological and very Hellenistic, and therefore probably inauthentic;[128] but given the fact that the Essenes themselves, or more probably Josephus, could have hellenized the form, this need not follow. Either way, the Essenes seem to have been respected for prophetic abilities, at least by Josephus.

Hill argues that the office of prophet continued in the Qumran community. He admits that the documents never call the Teacher of Righteousness a "prophet"; but neither did Josephus use the term for postbiblical possessors of the prophetic gift. His argument is tenuous at points; he depends, for instance, on 1QpHab 2.1–2, a reconstructed text,[129] which even in its reconstructed form would not need to point to Hill's conclusion; further, he must depend heavily on the plausible but uncertain view that the Teacher was also the author of many of the *Hodayoth*.[130] Yet despite these reservations, Hill's case is essentially sound and it remains likely that the writing and teaching of certain figures within the Qumran community, including that of the first Teacher and his successors, were understood to be prophetically inspired. As Aune notes, prophecy and the presence of the Spirit continued in early Judaism, particularly in apocalyptically oriented sects.[131]

The evidence from Qumran is not as unambiguous as we might like; the present prophetic dimension of the Spirit is especially relegated to wisdom and insight into the Scriptures, as observed above. Neverthe-less, this is different from a wholesale identification of the Spirit with prophecy, with both being relegated to the past. If Scripture interpreta-tion was thought by some to have replaced or superseded prophecy, this is nowhere stated.

Some scholars have also argued that prophecy continued in rabbinic Judaism. Abrahams, for instance, notes that Maimonides believed that prophecy belonged to good men,[132] and argues that the prophetic office was transferred to the Sages.[133] This much is true; but when he argues that while prophets had gone, the Holy Spirit continued to work in human experience,[134] his argument rests more on a theological interpretation of rabbinic literature as a whole than on the usage of the language of "Holy Spirit" in that literature.[135] Perhaps, had the question been appropriately framed, many of the ancient rabbis would have agreed with his conclusion. But this is not their usual way of speaking of the Holy Spirit, which (as noted above) is normally the Spirit of prophecy in these texts.

Aune, who depends heavily on secondary sources for his treatment of early Jewish prophecy, notes that among the rabbis there were excep-tions to the view that prophecy had ceased;[136] he fails to emphasize, however, that these examples represent a minority opinion, and that in early Jewish texts one can sometimes predict the future without necessar-ily being a prophet (especially on one's deathbed, as in some rabbinic examples).[137] R. Eliezer ben Hyrcanus, he points out, was said to have predicted suffering just before the Messiah's coming,[138] but this was part of Judaism's eschatological tradition by Eliezer's time,[139] and could thus be viewed as appropriate to a wisdom teacher, not necessarily a prophet. He cites Johanan ben Zakkai's ability to predict Vespasian's accession and the punishment on Galilee.[140] But this may simply reflect the kind of insight and miraculous powers attributed to past rabbis, similar to R. Simeon ben Yohai's[141] ability to disintegrate disrespectful people with a harsh look. Miraculous powers could safely be attributed to past guardi-ans of the tradition without opening the field up to contemporary charis-matic challengers of that tradition (contrast Josephus' willingness to attribute such powers to himself). The downplaying of current prophecy may "reflect an apologetic attempt to undermine the prophetic claims of the early Christians"[142] and, to a lesser extent, other prophetic move-ments that could challenge the epistemological hegemony and thus authority of the rabbinic movement.[143]

But even if some of the *earlier* Pharisees had wished to repress prophecy (which is not clear), it continued in popular Judaism, and from there was taken into early Christianity.[144] The eschatological intensity and widespread character of pneumatic experiences[145] were greater in many early Christian circles than elsewhere (cf., e.g., 1 Cor 14; Revelation).

But while the tendencies in parts of early Judaism that led to the general rabbinic position may have qualified the continuance of prophecy more than others, even where its continuance was affirmed, it was rarely seen in the same terms as OT prophecy. Josephus and Philo

> do not attribute this contemporary inspiration to the possession of the spirit. This they confine to the prophets of the biblical period. In so doing, they implicitly assert that the inspiration of the authors of scripture was qualitatively different from any subsequent insight.[146]

Where the Qumran documents associate prophecy and the Spirit, it is only with reference to the past, although this may be a coincidence due to the limited data with which we are working. The Spirit itself was indeed present from the vantage point of the Qumran community, but this may be, as Aune correctly points out, because apocalyptic groups like the Qumran community believed that they lived at the threshold of the new age, and thus could experience some of the power of that age in advance.[147] Boring suggests that prophecy was likewise by definition eschatological; this was true both in groups "that affirmed the presence of the prophetic Spirit (e.g. Qumran) and those that denied it (many streams of rabbinic tradition)."[148] The early Christians seem to be noteworthy for their insistence on the continuing Spirit of prophecy and continuance even of prophets among all their first-century documents which explicitly address the issue.

8.   RECIPIENTS OF THE SPIRIT AND/OR PROPHECY

Jewish literature (especially the more abundant but post-NT rabbinic texts) often speaks of those who were worthy to receive various gifts from God, even if those gifts were sometimes withheld due to the unworthiness of their generation. For instance, in the essentially rabbinic mystical treatise *3 Enoch*, R. Ishmael, being descended from Aaron, is "worthy to behold the chariot";[149] likewise, some Amoraim felt that those who did good deeds were worthy to receive the Shekinah.[150]

R. Nehemiah argued that, as a reward for their faith, Israel had been worthy of having the Holy Spirit rest on them.[151] R. Eliezer used to say that the Holy Spirit would rest on one who cleaves to God's presence.[152] But usually the Holy Spirit or Spirit of prophecy was not easily acquired. There are a number of rabbinic stories about pious rabbis who were worthy to receive the Holy Spirit, but who could not, because their generations were unworthy of its effects.[153] This story is told, for instance, of Hillel and Samuel Hakaton:

> Elders went into the upper room in the house of Gedaya in Jericho. An echo went forth and said to them, 'There are among you two who are worthy of receiving the Holy Spirit, and Hillel the Elder is one of them.' They gazed upon Samuel the Small.[154]

Similarly, Israel acquired her prophets on account of merit.[155]

Related to this is the idea that the Holy Spirit was quenched in Israel due to Israel's sins.[156] This accords with the more common image of the removal of the Shekinah, God's Presence, due to sin.[157] In any case, current generations were less worthy than the generations of great prophetic figures of the past, and the rabbis thus found fewer examples of the possession of the Holy Spirit in their own time.[158]

The Tannaim could amplify Moses' prayer that all Israel be prophets,[159] and the Amoraim could connect this prayer with Joel and, echoing Joel, argue that all Israel would be prophets.[160] But this adds little to the picture of an eschatological prophetic community already found in Joel and perhaps implied by the reception of the Spirit in some of the other prophets, and it does not indicate an emphasis on even the eschatological availability of the Spirit in rabbinic Judaism.

Other circles in early Judaism may have been more open to the current availability of the Spirit or prophecy. In Wisdom 7:27, for instance, we read that Wisdom "enters into holy souls, making them God's friends and prophets."[161] Philo, in *Her.* 259, argues that prophecy is available to every ἀστείῳ, "worthy man."[162]

Among the Qumran Covenanters, as Flusser points out, "The Holy Spirit was bestowed upon all the Elect, but not to the same degree." But only the elect had the Holy Spirit, and this distinguished them from anyone else.[163]

The presence of the Spirit was also felt to mark off the early Christians as a unique community, as Aune points out:

> In early Christianity, the presence of the Spirit within the community was the central phenomenon which convinced Christians that the eschaton had in some decisive way arrived in the person of Jesus of Nazareth.[164]

9.   THE NATURE OF PROPHECY IN THE RABBIS

That prophecy was a heavier task than prayer could be simply assumed by a Tanna arguing his case in the second century C.E.[165] Prophets had the authority to tell Israel which site God had chosen and to tell kings what they were to do.[166] Perhaps like the rabbis who temporarily had to circumvent the letter of the Law to fulfill its purpose (cf. Hillel's prozbul), prophets might temporarily supersede the letter of the Law:

> "Him you shall heed": Even if he should instruct you to violate one of the religious duties that are listed in the Torah, as did Elijah on Mount Carmel, in a case of emergency obey him.[167]

There are, of course, serious limitations on the extent to which this was allowed to be taken.[168]

The Sages essentially took over the role once granted to the prophets. A story is told of a Tanna who applies the words of Amos 7:14 to himself:

> And it happened concerning a certain student who gave instruction in the presence of Eliezer [without permission]. He said to Imma Shalom, his wife, "He will not finish out this week." And he died [that week]. After the Sabbath, sages came to him and said to him, "My lord, are you a prophet?" He said to them, "I am not a prophet nor the disciple of a prophet, but thus have I received as a tradition from my masters: 'whoever teaches law in his master's presence is liable to death.' "[169]

Although Eliezer's authority is in the tradition, his denial of filling a prophet's role is worded in the same terms as Amos's denial of *his* role as a prophet, as if to suggest that the authority of the Sages' tradition is comparable to that of the prophets.

Although in some texts the prophets could be regarded as higher than the Sages,[170] in others Sages are comparable to but higher than prophets,[171] and in still others Sages are considerably higher than prophets.[172] Indeed, Bamberger writes:

> The scholar had replaced the prophet; as R. Abdimi of Haifa put it, "prophecy has been taken from the prophets and given to the sages." A Babylonian comment on this remark declares that the scholar is more important (ᶜadif) than the prophet.[173]

Cohen notes that prophets moved in the direction of "apocalyptic seers, mystics, healers, and holy men," but prophetic authority shifted to the scribes.[174] The rabbis could view themselves as in some sense successors of the prophets.[175]

This was, perhaps, only natural, given the fact that Torah was normative, whereas there could be both true and false prophets.[176] Torah was sometimes assumed to be a step above prophecy.[177] Most often, however, no contrast was made between prophets and interpreters of Torah.[178] Just as the heavenly court or academy could be portrayed in terms mirroring the earthly academy,[179] so the prophets could be seen in anachronistic terms as Sages. Moses was the father of all the prophets,[180] and thirty prophets were among the eighty-five elders of Israel debating whether Esther's "new" laws could already be found in the Torah.[181] In this respect, they were not different from other prominent OT figures, such as Hezekiah, whom Akiba regarded as a teacher of Torah to all Israel.[182] The rabbis tended to regard the OT prophets as creative transmitters of Torah and did not oppose the two,[183] so following a tendency in early Judaism which did not originate with them.[184]

As in non-rabbinic sources,[185] prophetic enablement could be described as having God's words put in one's mouth,[186] although the same expression came to be used for Torah study.[187] But while the general rabbinic conception of prophecy would be less ecstatic than that of Philo and Josephus (below), there are indications that prophecy was not limited to Torah study and exposition, as may be indicated by the contrast between the prophet par excellence of Israel and the prophet par excellence of the nations:

> But there is quite a difference between the prophecy of Moses and the prophecy of Balaam. Moses did not know with whom he was talking, but Balaam knew. . . . Moses did not know when [God] would speak with him, until he actually was spoken with, while Balaam knew full well . . . Moses would speak with [God] only standing up . . . But Balaam was spoken with when he had fallen . . . To what is the matter comparable? To the case of the king's butcher, who knows precisely how much the king is spending on his table.[188]

There are also indications of mystical, revelatory experiences by certain rabbis.[189] The experiences attributed to R. Ishmael in *3 Enoch*,[190] and the earlier and more likely authentically based accounts[191] of R. Akiba's ascent to paradise in Tannaitic tradition,[192] suggest that these experiences, similar to those described in apocalyptic literature,[193] were not foreign to the rabbis.[194] At the same time, the dangers of such mystical revelations were not to be underestimated;[195] esoteric teachings on the laws of creation[196] and on the throne-chariot,[197] which could border on the mystical vision of God, were to be communicated only privately;[198] some matters were, in the words of a first-century visionary, ἄρρητα (2 Cor 12:4).[199]

Was this reticence to publicly communicate these teachings due to the dangers of misappropriation by non-rabbis, or inauthentic legitimation of the mystical experiences of those outside rabbinic circles? Or could these mystical experiences have included some eschatological elements that could have posed threats to rabbinic Judaism's political security? R. Akiba's support of Bar Kochba could lend credence to this last alternative, although his mysticism and his messianism could have been unrelated. (Not all eschatology would have direct political implications, some of it being quietistic; but apparently eschatology and messianic hope in general were somewhat discredited or thought to threaten political instability, for they are for some reason toned down in the Tannaitic literature.) Whatever the particular reason, certain forms of revelation no longer could function as adequate sources for communal knowledge, and the prevailing image of prophets sanctioned in rabbinic Judaism was as interpreters of the already-given Torah in accordance with the confines of developing rabbinic tradition.

10. The Nature of Prophecy in Non-Rabbinic Jewish Literature

Perhaps following the example of Saul and David, who were both anointed with the Spirit of prophecy before they could become kings,[200] or translating the Platonic notion of a wise man/philosopher as the ideal ruler, in the eschatological time prophets would rule.[201] The prophetic anointing could thus be envisioned in terms of divine wisdom to lead, even if the initial experience (as in 1 Sam 10:5–11) might be particularly ecstatic.

Yet while prophecy was not always conceived as ecstatic,[202] most of our references in Diaspora-oriented Jewish texts do include an ecstatic element. It is therefore important at this point to survey the cultural contexts of these ecstatic elements.[203]

We find prophetic ecstasy in late-second-millennium B.C.E. Palestine in the Egyptian "Journey of Wen-Amon to Phoenicia," where an ecstatic seized with some violent motion prophesies to the king of Byblos.[204] At Mari, prophecy given in trances was institutionalized,[205] and, as sometimes in Israel,[206] prophets could be designated by a term that otherwise denoted madmen.[207] Religious ecstasy was induced by various means, including intoxication, dancing,[208] ascetic fasts,[209] and even self-inflicted pain.[210] Although music was sometimes employed in Israelite prophetism,[211] some other forms of religious arousal employed by her neighbors were prohibited to Israel; nevertheless, ecstatic Israelite prophecy also existed in this period.[212]

As in the ancient Near East in the OT period,[213] so in the Mediterranean world in the NT period[214] divination was an extremely common practice.[215] But oracular prophetism maintained an important place as well. Despite a decline of some of the great oracular centers, however,[216] and the fact that the Romans tended to be much less interested in prophetism than the

Greeks,[217] prophecy had also flourished in the Eastern Mediterranean.[218] Perhaps connected with antecedents such as Mari through neo-Assyrian and other models,[219] ecstatic prophecy was found in some[220] Greek oracles apparently from the archaic period on.

Although a rationalistic Plutarch could detect the natural faculties of the Pythoness in her prophesyings,[221] prophetic possession was often thought virtually to eliminate any human elements;[222] it could be associated with "mania" or "mainesthai,"[223] and sometimes involved self-mutilation.[224] Possession could occur in the context of various cults,[225] but Aune questions whether all such possession was prophetic in nature;[226] theories of inspiration extended to music[227] and poetry,[228] law,[229] and other forms, and by no means do they all involve possession in the form in which it is found in some peripheral prophetism. But that ecstasy was seen as an acceptable phenomenon in Greek religion, at least for certain kinds of people in certain contexts, is commonly agreed upon.[230]

The acceptance of the place of the ecstatic in the Hellenistic world no doubt provided a context in which this aspect of Israelite prophetism would be developed. A Jewish sibyl, perhaps in late-first-century B.C.E. Egypt, writes that all will pronounce her a true μάντιν, though someone might call her "a messenger with a frenzied spirit" (μεμανηότι θύμῳ ἄγγελον),[231] and complains that she must prophesy with frenzy.[232]

In Pseudo-Philo, a holy spirit *(spiritus sanctus)* came upon Kenaz and "put him in ecstasy" *(extulit sensum eius)*, so that he prophesied *(prophetare)*,[233] and when he had finished speaking, "he was awakened, and his senses came back to him."[234] Likewise, in *4 Baruch* Abimelech (= Ebedmelech) the Aethiopian fell into "a great trance" (μεγάλη ἔκστασις) and awoke only sixty-six years later.[235] The charismatic sashes that enabled Job's daughters to sing in angelic languages altered their minds to think in heavenly ways.[236] Apocalyptic visionaries could also have rapturous experiences modeled on those of OT prophets like Ezekiel, who saw the throne-chariot.[237]

In Philo the images of ecstatic inspiration are most pronounced. Following Plato,[238] as well as OT forms,[239]

> Philo interpreted corybantic frenzy as a sign of true inspiration. He therefore regards the prophet as an ecstatic, totally possessed by God and His helpless instrument.[240]

He speaks of prophets experiencing an ecstasy of heavenly love, the whole mind "snatched up in holy frenzy by a Divine possession";[241] this divine frenzy could provide prophetic dreams, and be described as possession by some philosophic principle.[242] The heir of God's good things is the ecstatic soul that leaves even itself:[243] "higher than our reasoning, and in very deed divine, arising by no human will or purpose but by a God-inspired ecstasy" (ἀλλ᾽ ἐνθέῳ μανίᾳ).[244] Philo observes that

> a prophet possessed by God will suddenly appear and give prophetic oracles. Nothing of what he says will be his own, for he that is truly under the control of divine inspiration has no power of apprehension when he speaks but serves as the channel for the insistent words of Another's prompting . . . [245]

The prophets are often seized with ecstasy (ἐνθουσιάζει), so that the person is full of God, and his understanding departs.[246]

> So while the radiance of the mind is still all around us, when it pours as it were a noonday beam into the whole soul, we are self-contained, not possessed. But when it comes to its setting, naturally ecstasy and divine possession and madness [ἔκστασις . . . ἔνθεος . . . μανία] fall upon us. For when the light of God shines. . . . This is what regularly befalls the fellowship of the prophets. The mind is evicted at the arrival of the divine Spirit, but when that departs the mind returns to its tenancy. Mortal and immortal may not share the same home. And therefore the setting of reason and the darkness which surrounds it produce ecstasy and inspired frenzy.[247]

Abraham had this ecstatic, prophetic experience in Gen 15:12;[248] Moses also began his prophetic career (προφητείας) by possession (ἐνθουσιασμὸν);[249] and Philo himself would sometimes become full (πλήρης), so influenced by corybantic frenzy (ἐνθέου κορυβαντιᾶν) that he would be unconscious of what he had written.[250] As Hill points out, such language is "almost entirely derived from non-biblical Greek."[251]

Josephus, himself also not alien to ecstatic prophetic experience,[252] tells of a certain Joshua who for seven years did nothing but cry, "Woe to Jerusalem!" ignoring pain and opposition;[253] Bamberger comments on the natural association of Joshua's actions with madness.[254] Further, Josephus "not only describes the prophetic experience in terms of possession,[255] but translates the πνεῦμα θεοῦ of 1 Kgdms 10:6 as γενόμενος ἔνθεος."[256]

This sort of picture of inspiration carried over into at least some forms of early Christianity. One may compare the second-century C.E. *Odes of Solomon:*

> As the [wind] moves through the harp and the strings speak, So the Spirit of the Lord speaks through my members, And I speak through his love.[257]

All of this may suggest that the common later rabbinic understanding of the nature of prophecy was different from the popular Jewish perspective that had prevailed outside of Pharisaic ranks before a certain brand of Pharisaism rose to prominence within Palestinian, and later in a further developed form, within much of Mediterranean and Parthian Jewry. Although ecstatic phenomena and equivalents of prophecy occurred among rabbis, this experience is viewed with caution by most of the other rabbis. If one is tempted to ask why this is, the most likely answer may be the same answer that was given to why rabbinic Judaism did not allow much room for the Spirit of prophecy in the present, and barely addressed other functions of the רוח הקודש, the Holy Spirit.

11. CONCLUSION

In this chapter we have surveyed early Jewish perspectives on the divine Spirit and seen that rabbinic Judaism emphasized the Spirit of prophecy over against other possible functions of the Spirit; some other elements in early Judaism that also emphasized the Spirit of prophecy may have moved in the same direction. At least some Jewish circles, however, including at least the Essenes, also allowed a more prominent ethical dimension to the Spirit alongside the prophetic one.

We have also seen that the rabbinic understanding of the Spirit of prophecy as having ceased builds on some tendencies already present in the rest of early Judaism, developing those tendencies almost to the exclusion of rival streams of thought. The Spirit of prophecy was essentially inactive, and to whatever extent inspiration or revelatory experiences still occurred, they were often marginalized as esoteric and segregated from the body of publicly available traditions. Further, for the rabbis prophetic figures were to function as interpreters and trans-mitters of Torah, a role that had assumed central importance in rabbinic Judaism. The ecstatic element that was prominent especially in the more Diaspora-oriented circles in early Judaism did not characterize prophetic inspiration, or, if it did among some of the rabbis, was not publicly recognized by the documents' editors, whose views ultimately prevailed in the rabbinic movement.

This may suggest a polemical context for the conflict of early Jewish pneumatologies. Early Christianity, an eschatological prophetic move-ment that practiced prophecy (e.g., 1 Cor 12–14; 1 Thess 5:19–22) and was moved by eschatological, messianic enthusiasm,[258] would have posed one of the major threats to authorities who were seeking to consolidate their authority and to demonstrate their nonthreatening nature to the Roman authorities. This would have applied to many local synagogue authorities as well as to Palestinian rabbis. Thus by the time of the writing of the Fourth Gospel, pneumatology, more in a practical than a theoretical sense, may have been an issue of contention between the Johannine community and the synagogue leadership whose authority they had challenged. Yet even from the start, early Christians' eschatological enthusiasm and emphasis on direct Spirit-empowerment for holiness and prophecy would have marked them as distinctive among most mainstream groups in Jewish Palestine. Even the closest parallel, the sectarian Essenes, do not provide an adequate parallel to the intensity of charismatic experience depicted in NT texts (compare especially Fee for Pauline pneumatology), despite Josephus' trust in their occasional prophetic abilities.

But to say that Christian experience was distinctive is not to say that it was unique to the point of being unintelligible. Early Jewish pneumatology provides a context in which early Christian pneumatic experience may be understood. The intense conviction in early Christian literature is that the Spirit distinguishes Jesus and his community as the true servants of God who have begun to experience the radically new power of the kingdom era.

NOTES

1. Such as D. Lys, *RUACH* (Paris: Universitaires de France, 1962), who traces the use of רוח through various genres and (more debatably) periods; see also Fee, *God's Empowering Presence* (Peabody, Mass.: Hendrickson, 1994) 905–10; R. Stronstad, *The Charismatic Theology of St. Luke* (Peabody, Mass.: Hendrickson, 1984) 14–27.

2. E.g., M. E. Isaacs, *The Concept of Spirit* (London: Heythrop College, 1976), with an excellent survey of the use of πνεῦμα in Hellenistic Jewish texts and its application to the NT; and less recently, D. F. Büchsel, *Der Geist Gottes im Neuen Testament* (Gütersloh: Bertelsmann, 1926), with a broad survey of various contexts for Spirit language.

3. Prophecy is defined as inspired or oracular speech when it would also come under the headings of προφητ- and μαντ- or נבי roots.

4. The Persian parallel suggested by some writers (e.g., J. Finegan, *The Archeology of World Religions* [Princeton: Princeton University Press, 1952] 90, 93; H. Ringgren, *Word and Wisdom: Studies in the Hypostatization of Divine Qualities and Functions in the Ancient Near East* [Lund: Häkan Ohlssons, 1947] 170) is more verbal than conceptual ("Holy Spirit" was the Good Spirit opposed to the Evil one in Zoroastrianism; see A. T. Olmstead, *History of the Persian Empire* [Chicago: University of Chicago, 1959] 94, 96, 104; not this but Good Thought revealed vision to prophets—ibid., 96). Further, the Persian sources are difficult to date and by this period culturally remote; see, e.g., E. F. Scott, *The Spirit in the New Testament* (London: Hodder & Stoughton, n.d., foreword 1923) 46, for relevant observations on this point.

5. So M.-A. Chevallier, *Souffle de Dieu: le Saint-Esprit dans le Nouveau Testament* (Paris: Beauchesne, 1978) 37–39; for a comparison with usage in the Dead Sea Scrolls, see n. 33 below.

6. See especially Isaacs, *Spirit*, 18–19; apart from the Stoics, the references in Greek literature to a divine Spirit are rare. Thus the view that the Spirit concept in the Gospels is hellenized (Hans Leisegang, *Pneuma Hagion: Der Ursprung des Geistbegriffs der synoptischen Evangelien aus der griechischen Mystik* [Leipzig: J. C. Hinrichs'sche, 1922], especially pp. 140–43) may be open to qualification; see Isaacs, *Spirit*, 115–16, on Bultmann's improper use of Dalman's data. Πνεῦμα in Hellenistic Judaism, except when it refers to wind, normally is of divine origin (ibid., 59–64), if Isaacs is right to understand the human spirit also in this way.

7. Quint., *Inst. or.* 7.3.5 (LCL 3.84–85).

8. Isaacs, *Spirit*, i. This is not to imply that the usage is limited to Stoic texts, of course; related imagery may appear in Platonism, as Dale Martin has pointed out to me. For Gnostic texts, undoubtedly betraying Christian influences, see R. McL. Wilson, "The Spirit in Gnostic Literature," in *Christ and Spirit in the New Testament* (ed. B. Lindars and S. Smalley; Cambridge: Cambridge, 1973) 345–55; Chevallier, *Souffle*, 74–76.

9. K. Lake, "The Holy Spirit," in *The Beginnings of Christianity* (ed. K. Lake and F. J. Foakes Jackson; Grand Rapids: Baker, 1979) 5.103; see also Scott, *Spirit*, 52–53. The Spirit could be portrayed in somewhat materialistic language in rabbinic sources also; see J. Abelson, *The Immanence of God in Rabbinical Literature* (2d ed.; New York: Hermon, 1969) 212–23.

10. A. A. Long, *Hellenistic Philosophy: Stoics, Epicureans, Sceptics* (New York: Scribner's, 1974) 155–58; cf. Chevallier, *Souffle*, 41–42.

11. Long, *Philosophy*, 171; cf. E. Schweizer, *The Holy Spirit* (Philadelphia: Fortress, 1980) 29. It permeated even what was bad (Sext. Emp., *Outlines of Pyrrh.* 3.218).

12. Büchsel, *Geist*, 45–49, especially 47.

13. A. D. Nock, *Early Gentile Christianity and Its Hellenistic Background* (New York: Harper & Row, 1964) 51; also Büchsel, *Geist*, 52–53.

14. C. H. Dodd, *The Interpretation of the Fourth Gospel* (Cambridge: Cambridge, 1965) 222. Scott, *Spirit*, 58–59, and Isaacs, *Spirit*, 19, point out some clear differences Philo maintained against the Stoa in his use of πνεῦμα, apparently due to antecedent Jewish usage. M.-A. Chevallier, "Le souffle de Dieu dans le judaïsme, aux abords de l'ère chrétienne," *FoiVie* 80 (1, Jan. 1981) 43–46, especially 45–46 (on Wisdom of Solomon), observes that Hellenistic Jewish sources retain OT perspectives, but also evince an infusion of ideas from the Hellenistic world, especially Stoicism.

15. Isaacs, *Spirit*, 15; the noteworthy exceptions are Eurip. *Fr.* 192, and Plato, *Phaedr.* 265B (against his standard usage); cf. Dion. Hal. 1.31.1. Πνεῦμα was probably not associated with ecstasy in the Mysteries; cf. Büchsel, *Geist*, 104. Chevallier, *Souffle*, 39–40, cites Euripides and the inspiration of the Delphic Pythoness, Sibyls, and Bacchants, noting that by the NT era, when πνεῦμα as a term came to be applied to inspiration, it had become current to speak of the "mantic spirit," but he does not document this last remark; on pp. 40–41 he notes Plato's use of ἐπίπνοια rather than πνεῦμα for poetic inspiration, but argues that this is equivalent to Plutarch's (much later) use of πνεῦμα.

16. *Pneuma*, 32, citing Suidas, Origen, and John Chrysostom.

17. The Greek says λεπτύνειν τό πνεῦμα; the word "prophecy" does not occur, but is implied by the context.

18. *Obsolescence of Oracles* 41/*Moralia* 432F–433A (LCL 5.470f). For comments on the spirit in Plutarch, see Büchsel, *Geist,* 49–52.

19. H. W. Parke, *A History of the Delphic Oracle* (Oxford: Basil Blackwell, 1939) 22–24; Isaacs, *Spirit,* 15, 50; Schweizer, *Spirit,* 30; D. E. Aune, *Prophecy in Early Christianity and the Ancient Mediterranean World* (Grand Rapids, Mich.: Eerdmans, 1983) 34. In Dio Chrys., *On Personal Appearance* §12 (LCL 5.186–87), she "filled herself with the breath of the god"; Cic., *De Divin.* 1.36.79 notes that the power of the earth inspired *(incitabat)* the Pythian priestess, in contrast to the Sibyl's inspiration; but in 2.57.117 it is said (against the Stoic) that the subterranean exhalations that once inspired her no longer work. M. Cary and T. J. Haarhoff, *Life and Thought in the Greek and Roman World* (4th ed.; London: Methuen, 1946) 317, observe that "mephitic vapours" did not really exist in the temple.

20. *Prophecy,* 34.

21. Nock, *Christianity,* 51: the references to the "holy spirit" in magical texts may be due to Jewish influence, although this similarity may have contributed to further development of Christian pneumatology. A large body of evidence indicates that despite official Jewish opposition to magic (e.g., *m. Sanh.* 7:11 [when genuine]; p. Ḥag. 2:2 §5; *Sanh.* 7:13 §2; cf. *Roš Haš.* 3:8 §1; cf. Ps.-Phoc. 149, φάρμακα, μαγικῶν βίβλων; *Asc. Isa.* 2:5; *2 Bar.* 60:2; 66:2; *1 Enoch* 65:6), it was believed to be efficacious (*Sipra Qed.* pq. 6.203.2.2; *b. Šabb.* 61b; 66b; *b. Hor.* 10a; *b. Sanh.* 67b; *p. Ketub.* 1:1 §2; cf. charms and amulets in E. R. Goodenough, *Jewish Symbols in the Greco-Roman Period* [New York: Pantheon, 1953–65], 2.153–295; among modern Yemenite Jews, J. Ph. Hes, "The Changing Role of the Yemenite *Mori,*" in *Magic, Faith, and Healing* [New York: Free, 1964] 370; for limitations, cf. *T. Reub.* 4:9; *Gen. Rab.* 11:5; *Pesiq. Rab.* 23:8; 43:6), and appears to have been widespread in significant elements of early Judaism, which also influenced pagan magic (cf., e.g., *PGM* 1.301–5; 3.405; 4.1200–1204, 1222, 2355–56, 3007–86; 8.96–175, 470–87; 13.343–646, 815–18; 14.1061–62; 35.1–42); a wide variety of scholars have commented on this in some detail: M. Hengel, *Judaism and Hellenism* (Philadelphia: Fortress, 1974) 1.241; J. G. Gager, *Moses in Greco-Roman Paganism* (SBLMS 16; Nashville: Abingdon, 1972) 134–61; id., *Anti-Semitism,* 107–10; C. E. Arnold, *Ephesians: Power and Magic* (SNTSMS 63; Cambridge: Cambridge, 1989) 31–32; Leonhard Rost, *Judaism outside the Hebrew Canon* (Nashville: Abingdon, 1976) 63 (on Tobit); Judah Goldin, "The Magic of Magic and Superstition," in *Aspects of Religious Propaganda in Judaism and Early Christianity* (Notre Dame: University of Notre Dame, 1976) 115–47; Goodenough, *Symbols,* 12.58–63; A. Deissmann, *Bible Studies* (1923, reprint; Peabody, Mass.: Hendrickson, 1988) 277–300, 321–36; W. L. Knox, *St. Paul and the Church of the Gentiles* (Cambridge: Cambridge, 1939) 208–11; H. Koester, *Introduction to the New Testament* (Philadelphia: Fortress, 1982) 1.380–81; A. D. Nock, *Conversion* (Oxford: Oxford, 1961) 61–62; M. Smith, *Jesus the Magician* (San Francisco: Harper & Row, 1978) 69; C. D. Isbell, "The Story of the Aramaic Magical Incantation Bowls," *BA* 41 (1978) 5–16; cf. id., *Corpus of the Aramaic Inscription Bowls* (SBLDS 17; Missoula, Mont.: Scholars Press, 1975), passim; *T. Sol.; Pr. Jos.; b. Sanh.* 65b, 67b (despite the disclaimer); Apul., *Apol.,* in M. Stern, *Greek and Latin Authors on Jews and Judaism* (Jerusalem: Israel Academy of Sciences and Humanities, 1974) 2.201–5; *CIJ* 1.485 §673; 490 §679; 517 §717; 523 §724; 2.62–65 §819; 81 §833; 90–91 §849; 92 §851; 217 §1168. Although much of this material is

from the third century or later, the reputation of Jewish magicians is reflected even in Acts: 13:8; cf. 19:13–14.

22. *Spirit*, 17.

23. Exod 31:3; cf. 1 Kgs 7:14, where the writer omits reference to the Spirit.

24. Judg 13:25; 14:6, 19; 15:14; cf. 16:20; 1 Sam 11:6; cf. 18:2 (an evil spirit acting similarly). In most of these cases, however, the power was also related to the fact that they functioned as leaders in Israel; cf. Judg 3:10; 6:34. The Pauline use of strengthening by the Spirit may be related to this, especially where it may connote doing battle with spiritual powers, as in Ephesians, but the ethical sense (below) probably contributes more to the usage in the Pauline literature.

25. Ps.-Philo 27:9–10 (*OTP* 2.339–40; Latin p. 190).

26. So the Amoraic interpretation of Judg 13:25 in *p. Soṭ* 1:8 §3, where the Spirit of God becomes "the Holy Spirit." An exception to this general rule is *Pss. Sol.* 17:37, speaking of the Messiah as δυνατόν in the Holy Spirit and wise, but this again refers to anointing to be a mighty ruler (for the specifically Messianic associations of the Spirit in some texts, see M.-A. Chevallier, *L'Esprit et le Messie dans le bas-judaïsme et le Nouveau Testament* [EHPR 49; Paris: Presses Universitaires de France, 1958] 125–43; in John, cf. G. M. Burge, *The Anointed Community* [Grand Rapids, Mich.: Eerdmans, 1987] 71–110, especially 81–87); possibly also Dead Sea Scrolls references to being sustained by the Spirit's strength, especially in several of the Hymns, and probably related to the Spirit's teaching function (see G. Johnston, " 'Spirit' and 'Holy Spirit' in the Qumran Literature," in *New Testament Sidelights* [Hartford: Hartford Seminary, 1960] 38).

27. J. Coppens, "Le don de l'Esprit d'après les textes de Qumrân et le quatrième Évangile," in *L'Évangile de Jean: Études et problèmes* (Recherches Bibliques 3; Louvain: Desclée de Brouwer, 1958) 211–12, 222, also notes that both John and Qumran speak of the Spirit in terms of purification.

28. E.g., 1 Sam 10:6–7, again in the context of anointing for leadership of God's people. Thus the good Spirit from God departs from Saul to David, and an evil spirit from God torments Saul, when David is anointed king, in 16:13–14.

29. Particularly Ezek 36:25–26; Deutero-Isaiah uses the water image for the Spirit as a symbol of fertile restoration and blessing (44:3–4) and Joel retains the connection between the outpoured Spirit of God and the Spirit of prophecy (2:28–29; MT 3:1–2).

30. 1:20.

31. Probably the pure heart and the holy spirit are meant to be identical.

32. *Jub.* 1:21, 23.

33. Chevallier, *Souffle*, 52–57, summarizes the main uses of רוח in the Scrolls: wind or breath (52), invisible powers of a personal character (Spirit of Truth or of Error, 52–53), the interior dispositions of a man (54), the "Spirit of holiness" (1QH 16.2, 3, 7, 12; p. 55), the last including the use for purification (56–57).

34. Johnston, "Qumran Literature," 40. Chevallier, "Souffle dans le judaïsme," 40, says that the purifying spirit in the Scrolls performs a double function: purifying a man and revealing the truth to him. These functions are no doubt conceptually linked. B. Lindars, *New Testament Apologetic* (London: SCM, 1961) 46, finds the background for the language of 1 Thess 4:8 in Ezek 37:14.

35. Lit., מי נדה, "waters for impurity," as in 3.4.

36. In Eduard Lohse, ed., *Die Texte aus Qumran* (Munich: Kösel, 1971) 10, 14.

37. Ibid., 148; Hymn P in A. Dupont-Sommer, *The Essene Writings from Qumran* (Gloucester, Mass.: Peter Smith, 1973) 233. Cf. similarly Wis 1:5: "For the holy spirit of παιδείας will flee deceit (δόλον)."

38. Lohse, *Texte*, 74.

39. Ibid., 78. One may compare Sus 45, in which God raised up τὸ πνεῦμα τὸ ἅγιον of Daniel to defend Susanna.

40. On the Holy Spirit as purifier from sin in the Dead Sea Scrolls, see, e.g., F. F. Bruce, "Holy Spirit in the Qumran Texts," *ALUOS* 6 (1966) 52–54.

41. Suggested in passing by Johnston, "Qumran Literature," 33.

42. *OTP* 1.786; Greek text, p. 19. Cf. *T. Ben.* 8:3 (*OTP* 1.827; Greek, p. 225, counting as 8:2), although this could well be part of a Christian interpolation, as much of *T. Ben.* could be; for filling with an evil spirit (the devil's storehouse), cf. *T. Asher* 1:9 (*OTP* 1.817; Greek, p. 173): "πονηροῦ πνεύματος πεπλήρωται." The early Christian ethical use of the Spirit (which predominates in Paul with the indwelling Spirit/Christ) may also testify to the continuance of this usage.

43. J. Pryke, " 'Spirit' and 'Flesh' in the Qumran Documents and Some New Testament Texts," *RevQ* 5 (1965) 345. On the human spirit in the Scrolls, see also Johnston, "Qumran Literature," 27–36, passim.

44. A survey of Johnston's references to the Spirit ("Qumran Literature," 38–40) would at least suggest that the matter is open to dispute.

45. *Prophecy*, 200.

46. This of course has much stronger OT antecedents than the Spirit of purification, as the Spirit of Yahweh is commonly associated with prophecy; cf., e.g., Chevallier, *Souffle*, 27–29.

47. *Ant.*, 6.166; cf. 6.222. Isaacs, *Spirit*, 47–48, provides a number of other examples that illustrate Josephus' frequent association of πνεῦμα in the LXX with prophecy, and prophecy in the LXX with πνεῦμα. For an examination of how Josephus portrayed the Spirit's inspiration of Balaam and his ass in thoroughly Hellenistic terms, see J. R. Levison, "The Debut of the Divine Spirit in Josephus' *Antiquities*," *HTR* 87 (2, 1994) 123–38.

48. E. Best, "The Use and Non-Use of Pneuma by Josephus," *NovT* 3 (1959) 222–25; the one exception he finds is *Ant.* 1.27 (= Gen 1:2, too important to change), and he finds the usage restricted to the biblical period.

49. *Fug.* 186: θεῖον ἐπενεμήθη καὶ προφητικὸν πνεῦμα. For other references, see Isaacs, *Spirit*, 47. More fully on Philo's view of inspiration, see the thorough work of J. R. Levison, "Inspiration and the Divine Spirit in the Writings of Philo Judaeus," *JSJ* 26 (3, 1995) 271–323. For an angelic portrayal of the Spirit in Philo, see id., "The Prophetic Spirit as an Angel according to Philo," *HTR* 88 (2, 1995) 189–207.

50. In Sir 39:6, the righteous person is filled with the Spirit of understanding (συνέσεως) when God wills.

51. Spittler sees Montanist redaction in the final chapters.

52. 48:3 (*OTP* 1.866).

53. 31:12 (*OTP* 2.115).

54. *1 Enoch* 91:1.

55. 28:6 (*OTP* 2.341; Latin p. 195).

56. 4 Ezra 14:22; this includes the Scripture (see below).

57. On the issue of the Spirit of prophecy in the Dead Sea Scrolls, see also Bruce, "Spirit in Qumran Texts," 51, although he cites only CD 2.12; and Johnston,

"Qumran Literature," 36–37, in more detail. One should also consider references to the Holy Spirit illumining the secrets of God, following the sort of prophetic tradition one finds in Daniel; see Johnston, "Qumran Literature," 33–35, 39–40. C. Daniel, " 'Faux prophètes,' " *RevQ* 7 (1969) 59–64, believes that the Essenes called themselves "seers" and practiced prophecy; although the thrust of his article may be mistaken, evidence in Josephus suggests that Essenes would emphasize the prophetic.

58. *T. Ab.* 4, Rec. A (Stone, 10–11).

59. Ps.-Philo 9:10 (*OTP* 2.316).

60. Ps.-Philo 32:14; cf. *Mekilta* on 14:31 (cited in M. Smith, *Tannaitic Parallels to the Gospels* [Philadelphia: SBL, 1951] 64); *p. Soṭa* 5:4 §1; and later, *Pesiq. Rab.* 9:2.

61. Ps.-Philo 28:6 (*OTP* 2.341; Latin, p. 195); cf. *T. Job* 52:9 (*OTP* 1.868); 52:4 (Kraft, 84) for the prophetic vision of Job's charismatically endowed daughters; cf. *Lev. Rab.* 9:9; *Num. Rab.* 14:5; *Qoh. Rab.* 10:8 §1 for perceiving by the Holy Spirit.

62. Chs. 32–34.

63. *First Apology* 31, 44, 47, 63; cf. Theophilus, *To Autolycus* 2.33.

64. *Sipre Deut.* 22.1.2 (Neusner, 1.60).

65. *T. Pisha* 2:15 (Neusner, 2.121). In one of those rare rabbinic texts where the Holy Spirit is associated with the people of Israel as a whole, it is conceded that "If they are not prophets, they are disciples of prophets" (*t. Pisha* 4:14 [Neusner, 2.137], attributed to Hillel, though the story is probably later).

66. *Shirata* 7, lines 17–18 (Lauterbach, 2.55). For another reference to the Spirit of prophecy, cf., e.g., *Mek. Pisha* 1, lines 150ff. (Lauterbach, 1.14).

67. *B. Ber.* 31b.

68. *B. B.Bat.* 122a.

69. *B. Yoma* 73b.

70. *P. Hor.* 3:5 §2 (Neusner, 34.124).

71. 1:8; 4:3; 11:16 (Braude, 18–19, 65–66, 217).

72. *Exod. Rab.* 5:20; *Lev. Rab.* 1:3; *Num. Rab.* 13:20; 18:8; *Ruth Rab.* 4:3. R. Meir's revelatory sight in *Lev. Rab.* 9:9 (in *Deut. Rab.* 5:15, through Elijah) was mentioned above.

73. M. McNamara, *Targum and Testament* (Grand Rapids, Mich.: Eerdmans, 1972) 113.

74. P. Schäfer, "Die Termini 'Heiliger Geist' und 'Geist der Prophetie,' " *VT* 20 (1970) 306–7: *Neofiti* and the *Fragmentary Targum* always have "Holy Spirit," *Onqelos* always has "Spirit of prophecy" (except in one instance), and *Targum Pseudo-Jonathan* uses both about equally; though Schäfer observes that "Holy Spirit" has a broader range of meaning than "Spirit of prophecy." P. Schäfer elsewhere (*Die Vorstellung vom Heiligen Geist in der Rabbinischen Literatur* [SZANT 28; Munich: Kösel, 1972] 135–39) seeks to trace the origin of the term to "Spirit of the Sanctuary" (critiqued by S. C. Reif, "Review of P. Schäfer, *Die Vorstellung vom heiligen Geist,*" *JSS* 18 [1973] 158), but the standard usage, not the etymology, is our concern here. For a collection of some of the significant Targumic texts, see Schäfer, *Vorstellung*, 23–26.

75. E.g., G. F. Moore, *Judaism in the First Centuries of the Christian Era* (New York: Schocken, 1971) 1.237, 437; Abelson, *Immanence*, 238–67; A. Marmorstein, *The Old Rabbinic Doctrine of God: The Names and Attributes of God* (New

York: KTAV,1968), 99–100; S. Sandmel, *Judaism and Christian Beginnings* (New York: Oxford, 1978), 174–75; id., *The Genius of Paul* (New York: Farrar, Straus & Cudahy, 1958), 78; W. D. Davies, "Reflections on the Spirit in the Mekilta: A Suggestion," *JANESCU* 5 (1973) 98; J. Bonsirven, *Palestinian Judaism in the Time of Jesus Christ* (New York: Holt, Rinehart & Winston, 1964), 57; J. Jeremias, *New Testament Theology* (New York: Scribner's, 1971), 78; *The Universal Jewish Encyclopedia*, 1948 ed., 9.268; R. G. Horwitz, s.v. "Ruah ha-Kodesh," 14.364–68 in *EncJud*, 365. New Testament scholars less directly acquainted with rabbinic texts have tended to follow the same line: E. E. Ellis, "Christ and Spirit in 1 Corinthians," in *Christ and Spirit in the New Testament* (ed. Barnabas Lindars and Stephen S. Smalley; Cambridge: Cambridge, 1973) 274; F. F. Bruce, "The Spirit in the Apocalypse," in *Christ and Spirit in the New Testament* (ed. Lindars and Smalley) 337; M. E. Boring, *Sayings of the Risen Jesus* (SNTSMS 46; Cambridge: Cambridge, 1982) 63; id., "How May We Identify Oracles of Christian Prophets in the Synoptic Tradition? Mark 3:28–29 as a Test Case," *JBL* 91 (1972) 518; R. Bultmann, *The Gospel of John: A Commentary* (Philadelphia: Westminster, 1971) 575.

76. E.g., 4 Ezra 14:22, where Ezra restores the Scriptures by the inspiration of the Holy Spirit; cf. 1QS 8.16: "What the prophets revealed by his Holy Spirit"; Justin, *Dialogue with Trypho* 25. For Apocrypha and Pseudepigrapha in general, see Büchsel, *Geist*, 57–58.

77. E.g., Isaacs, *Spirit*, 51. W. Foerster, "Der heilige Geist im Spätjudentum," *NTS* 8 (1962) 117, rightly notes that the view that the Holy Spirit worked in inspiring biblical books is very old, but only in time did the Spirit's work tend to be *restricted* to the writing of holy texts.

78. *Sipra VDDen.* par. 1.1.3.3 (Neusner, 1.69), 5.10.1.1 (p. 119); *Shemini Mekhilta deMiluim* 94.5.12 (Neusner, 2.137); *Behuq.* pq. 6.267.2.1 (Neusner, 3.368). Also in *'Abot R. Nat.* 4A.

79. 355.17.1–3 (Neusner, 2.448); 356.4.1 (p. 451), repeating 355.17.2.

80. *B. Ber.* 4b; *Pesah.* 117a; *Meg.* 7a (attributed to R. Eleazar and R. Akiba); *p. Soṭa* 1:9 §1; cf. *Pesiq. Rab Kah.* Supplement 5:1.

81. *Gen. Rab.* 63:14; 80:8; 91:5; 92:9; 93:7; 97 (NV); *Exod. Rab.* 8:1; 27:9; 33:5; 48:6; *Lev. Rab.* 3:6, 4:1; *Num. Rab.* 10:2; 11:1; 19:15; 20:18; *Lam. Rab.* 2:20 §23; 3:58–60 §9; *Qoh. Rab.* 1:1 §1; 3:16 §1; *Song Sol. Rab.* 1:1 §§5–6, 9–10; 2:1 §3; 7:12 §1.

82. *Pesiq. Rab.* 10:2; 11:2; 20:1; 30:1; 33:2–3; 34:1; 35:1; 50:1, 4.

83. In *'Abot R. Nat.* 34A, the Holy Spirit involves only prophecy and obscure speech.

84. Whether these other models were widely available or limited primarily to Essenes (on the likely assumption that both 1QS and *Jubilees* derive from that circle) and early Christians, is not possible to say at present.

85. This is not to suggest that the Qumran sectarians would have been any more open to dissent within their own community; there the Spirit would have been restricted to communal norms. It is merely to try to explain why the view developed in rabbinic literature as it did, even if the Qumran community found a different way to restrict pneumatic challenges subsequent to the (first?) Teacher of Righteousness.

86. *Beginnings*, 174–75.

87. Cf. D. Hill, *New Testament Prophecy* (Atlanta: John Knox, 1979) 21, citing "Zech. 13.4–6; Mal. 4.5–6 and perhaps Ps. 74.9." The problem with using such texts

to make such a case, of course, arises if one suspects that Zechariah and Malachi are claiming to *be* prophecy, even if postexilic prophetic forms often differed from pre-exilic forms (much less poetry, etc.).

88. *Prophecy,* 22.

89. Ibid., 25.

90. He explicitly excludes the Sibylline Oracles from consideration, though he does not think this changes the case at all. Despite the purely hellenized form of these oracles, however, they are spoken with full authority, and Sibylline pseudonymity was a literary convention meant to increase, not decrease, one's prophetic authority. On change in OT prophecy, see M. Haran, "From Early to Classical Prophecy," *VT* 27 (1977) 385–97; but cf. S. M. Paul. "Prophets and Prophecy," *EncJud* 13.1160–64.

91. Hill, *Prophecy,* 22.

92. Ibid., 105.

93. Ibid.

94. Against Hill, *Prophecy,* 22.

95. *Ag. Ap.* 1.41. For more on the cessation of prophets in Josephus, see B. J. Bamberger, "The Changing Image of the Prophet in Jewish Thought," in *Interpreting the Prophetic Tradition* (Cincinnati: Hebrew Union College, 1969) 305.

96. Best, "Use of Pneuma by Josephus," 222–25.

97. See D. E. Aune, "The Use of προφήτης in Josephus," *JBL* 101 (1982) 419–21; cf. also Hill, *Prophecy,* 26, 28. For the eschatological prophets in Josephus (regarded by him as false prophets), see Aune, *Prophecy,* 81. But while Josephus dismisses false eschatological prophets and their signs, he accepts authentic oracles and omens; see H. C. Kee, *Miracle in the Early Christian World* (New Haven: Yale, 1983) 178–79.

98. It is, however, noteworthy that "in early Christianity this reluctance to apply the designation to contemporary figures was completely overcome, and the term *prophētēs* was freely applied to those who were regarded as inspired spokesmen of God" (Aune, *Prophecy,* 195).

99. While prophets and prophecy were added to older scriptural examples in Sirach (46:1), I am not aware of any emphasis on current prophetism in the book.

100. See especially W. A. Grudem, *The Gift of Prophecy in 1 Corinthians* (Lanham, Md.: University Press of America, 1982) 21–23, for references to the cessation of prophecy, but pp. 24–33 on the continuation of revelatory experiences understood as different from OT prophecy.

101. Isaacs, *Spirit,* 51. For a recent survey arguing that Jewish people affirmed that prophecy had ceased, see B. D. Sommer, "Did Prophecy Cease? Evaluating a Reevaluation," *JBL* 115 (1, Spring 1996) 31–47.

102. We should, however, enter a caveat here: the statement that most rabbinic literature regards the Spirit as a prophetic agent of the past (along with some of the other literature) does not mean that the rabbis had no surrogates for prophecy. As I point out in this chapter, they stressed that the prophetic function (not necessarily the quenched Spirit) had been subsumed under their task of expounding the written Scriptures. Other groups, like the Qumran sect, seem to have stressed the current "prophetic" role of the Spirit as the Spirit of wisdom, which enlightened the community to the meaning of the Scriptures. Thus the contrasts I have suggested here must not be overdrawn, although they are helpful for categorization. And yet the emphasis on the quenched Spirit of prophecy in

rabbinic texts is so explicit that it warrants the question: Why? Controversy with pneumatic sects—particularly one of the most pneumatic, early Christianity—seems a reasonable answer.

103. *T. Soṭa* 12:5 (Neusner, 3.199–200).

104. *T. Soṭa* 13:3 (Neusner, 3.201).

105. *B. Sanh.* 11a; *Soṭa* 48b; *Yoma* 9b (with an Amoraic attribution; cf. the implication also in *Ḥullin* 137b); cf. *Gen. Rab.* 37:7 (Tannaitic attribution).

106. *Num. Rab.* 15:10; *Song Sol. Rab.* 8:9 §3, both anonymous.

107. *Pesiq. Rab Kah.* 13:14: R. Eleazar vs. R. Samuel bar Nahman.

108. See especially W. D. Davies, *Paul and Rabbinic Judaism* (4th ed.; Philadelphia: Fortress, 1980) 208–15, who provides the appropriate qualifications; Bamberger, "Prophet," 306; R. Leivestad, "Das Dogma von der prophetenlosen Zeit," *NTS* 19 (1973) 288–99; Hill, *Prophecy,* 33–35. This view is commonly held; e.g., E. Rivkin, *A Hidden Revolution* (Nashville: Abingdon, 1978) 86; D. Patte, *Early Jewish Hermeneutic in Palestine* (SBLDS 22; Missoula, Mont.: Scholars, 1975) 119; C. K. Barrett, *The Holy Spirit in the Gospel Tradition* (London: SPCK, 1966) 123.

109. *B. Sanh.* 11a; *Yoma* 9b; *Soṭa* 48b; cf. Aune, *Prophecy,* 104; on p. 105 he argues that other forms of revelation were also regarded as legitimate.

110. Cf., e.g., Chevallier, *Souffle,* 31–32. For associations with the new covenant in the OT, see id., *Esprit de Dieu, parole d'hommes: Le rôle de l'Esprit dans les ministères de la parole selon l'apôtre Paul* (Neuchatel: Delachaux and Niestlé, 1966) 84–85; in early Judaism, pp. 85–88.

111. Cf., e.g., ibid., 220–22; J. D. G. Dunn, "Spirit and Kingdom," *ExpT* 82 (Nov. 1970) 36.

112. *Spirit,* 84. She refers mainly to Philo, of whom the statement is undoubtedly true, and Josephus, who had good apologetic reasons not to stress the eschatological side of Judaism. We may observe here *Sib. Or.* 4:46, possibly from the Hellenistic period: at the end of the age, God will give (δόντος) the spirit (also 4:189–90, probably ca. 80 C.E.); but in context, this may mean life at the resurrection, rather than God's Spirit in any other sense.

113. Coppens, "L'Esprit," 209, emphasizes that the Spirit is eschatological in the Scrolls, linking it with the new creation idea.

114. *Spirit,* i, 84–86.

115. Hill, *Prophecy,* 35, following Chevallier, objects that rabbinic texts used to support an eschatological return of prophecy are few and late, but this may be due to the lack of emphasis on eschatology in most of these documents, edited as they were after 135 when the Bar Kochba revolt had exposed the dangers of unbridled messianism.

116. See, in some detail, Davies, *Paul,* 208–17; R. P. Menzies, *The Development of Early Christian Pneumatology* (JSNTSup 54; Sheffield: Sheffield Academic Press, 1991) 104–8; cf. Jeremias, *Theology,* 80–81; id., *The Parables of Jesus* (2d rev. ed.; New York: Scribner's, 1972) 117, 126; D. N. Freedman, "Pottery, Poetry, and Prophecy," *JBL* 96 (1977) 23.

117. *Mek. Shirata* 7, lines 17–18 (Lauterbach, 2.55); cf. Bonsirven, *Judaism,* 57; *Ruth Rab.* 2:1.

118. Sandmel, *Judaism,* 174, as above. Foerster, "Geist," 117–18, thinks that the view that the Holy Spirit ceased with the last prophets was mainly found in

rabbinic texts addressing certain situations, and thus that it was not a dogmatic construct.

119. See E. P. Sanders, *Jesus and Judaism* (Philadelphia: Fortress, 1985) 271. The view that prophecy did not cease is articulated by Aune in *Prophecy*, following Meyer (pp. 4–5) and Cothenet (p. 6).

120. *J.W.* 1.78–80; 2.159 (though the latter applies also to biblical interpretation, perhaps along the lines of the Qumran *pesharim*); cf. *J.W.* 1.68–69. Cf. also *Ant.* 17.346 in Isaacs, *Spirit*, 49.

121. See Isaacs, *Spirit*, 48; Hill, *Prophecy*, 26–27, on *J.W.* 3.351–54. Today prophecy is often associated with prediction of the future, but while that sense was included in ancient literature (Plut., *The E at Delphi* 6, *Moralia* 387B; "Heraclitus to Amphidamas" [in *The Cynic Epistles* (ed. A. J. Malherbe; Missoula, Mont.: Scholars Press, 1977) 194–95]; Socrates, *Ep.* 1 [ibid., 222–23, line 34; 224–25, lines 12–13]; Socrates, *Ep.* 6 [ibid., 236–39]; *Sib. Or.* 3.822 [both future and past]; rabbinic references in J. Bowman, "Prophets and Prophecy in Talmud and Midrash," *EvQ* 22 [1950] 107), it was not the standard or only sense of the term.

122. See *J.W.* 6.300–309, and especially B. Noack, *Jesus Ananiassøn og Jesus fra Nasaret* (Copenhagen: Gyldendal, 1975) (briefly summarized in *NTA* 24.211); Aune, *Prophecy*, 135–37. Cf. also Josephus' presentation of John the Baptist as a "prophet," though Josephus avoids the term (ibid., 130).

123. *Abr.* 35; cf. *Migr.* 34–35; *Cher.* 27; *Somn.* 2.252, cited by Isaacs.

124. *Mut.* 39, in Isaacs.

125. Isaacs, *Spirit*, 48. The last reference is *Mos.* 2.37.

126. Of interest here is R. A. Baer, *Philo's Use of the Categories Male and Female* (AZLUGHJ 3; Leiden: E. J. Brill, 1970) 55–64, 96–98, for an important discussion of divine inspiration as divine impregnation in Philo. He also addresses Philonic texts, fewer in number but nevertheless significant, in which divine inspiration enables one to throw off sense-perception and thus become a "virgin" or asexual; this might connect the prophetic Spirit with the purifying aspect of the Spirit, but (especially if the latter was primarily limited to the Essenes) the latter may have been unknown to Philo.

127. Aune, *Prophecy*, 145, citing *J.W.* 2.159; *Ant.* 15.374–79.

128. Aune, *Prophecy*, 145.

129. Ibid., 40.

130. Ibid., 40–41. See also Boring, *Sayings*, 24.

131. Aune, *Prophecy*, 104, and the abundance of sources he cites; cf. n. 136, below.

132. I. Abrahams, *Studies in Pharisaism and the Gospels* (2d ser.; Cambridge: Cambridge, 1924) 126; he also believed, as Abrahams points out, that prophecy would be restored in the messianic age.

133. Ibid.; addressed in more detail below.

134. Ibid., 127–28; cf. also Abelson, *Immanence*, 268.

135. Although there are several references to its presence on the community gathered for Pesach; see in E. E. Urbach, *The Sages* (2d ed.; Jerusalem: Magnes Press, 1979) 1.576.

136. *Prophecy*, 104. In p. 375 n. 12, he provides a partial list of modern scholars who have also come to this conclusion.

137. E.g., R. Eliezer ben Hyrcanus in *'Abot R. Nat.* 25A. In Greek literature, one may adduce Plato, *Apol.* 39, for such a connection.

138. *M. Soṭa* 9:15 and other references in *Prophecy*, 145.

139. 1QM 15.1; *Sib. Or.* 3.213–15 (probably second century B.C.E.); *T. Mos.* 7–8 (probably first century C.E.); 4 Ezra 6–8 passim; *2 Bar.* 26:1–30:2; probably 1QH 3; war in 1QM; *Jub.* ch. 23; perhaps *Sib. Or.* 3.635–48 (probably second century B.C.E.; the advent of a royal savior [here the Egyptian king who favors God's people] follows a period of great judgments); 4QpPs (in the view of J. M. Allegro, "Further Light on the History of the Qumran Sect," *JBL* 75 [1956] 95); cf. CD 20.14–15. In a later period, *m. Soṭa* 9:15; *b. Sanh.* 97–99; *Qoh. Rab.* 2:13 §4, 2:15 §2; *Song Sol. Rab.* 8:9 §3; *Pesiq. Rab Kah.* 5:9; *Pesiq. Rab.* 15:14/15; 34:1, 36:1. It is clear in early Christian texts, e.g., Mark 13 and par.; 2 Thess 2; Rev 13.

140. *Prophecy*, 144, citing *p. Šabb.* 16:15d. Although the tradition may depend on Josephus' account of his own insight, the focus here is to what extent the view existed in rabbinic tradition, not the antiquity or accuracy of this particular tradition.

141. *B. Šabb.* 34a; *Gen. Rab.* 79:6; *Pesiq. Rab Kah.* 11:16; etc.; later transferred to R. Johanan and others (*b. B.Bat.* 75a; *Pesiq. Rab Kah.* 18:5; cf. "the rabbis" in *b. B.Meṣiʿa* 85a). Is this more related to the evil eye idea also found in the Greco-Roman world (Plut., *Table-Talk* 5.7.1–6, *Moralia* 680C–683B; *Pleasant Life Impossible* 5, *Moralia* 1090C) or to the idea that the pious man can summon forth divine fire (besides Elijah in 1 Kgs 18:38; 2 Kgs 1:10, 12; *Lives of Prophets* 21:2 [Greek §33], cf. Rev 11:5; *Jos. and Asen.* 25:6–7; *T. Ab.* 10, 14A, 12B; and perhaps *p. Ḥag.* 2:1 §4)? Cf. other images of fire falling in judgment (Lev 10:2; Num 16:35; 1QM 17.2–3; Jos., *Ant.* 4.55–56; Luke 9:54; Rev 20:9) or fire falling on altars (Exod 40:34; Plut., *Aemilius Paulus* 24.1) or during esoteric Scripture expositions (e.g., *p. Ḥag.* 2:1 §4) to validate divine authorization.

142. Aune, *Prophecy*, 104; N. N. Glatzer, "A Study of the Talmudic Interpretation of Prophecy," *RevRel* 10 (1946) 115–17, 121–22 (an already-existing tendency greatly augmented in reaction to the charismatic/prophetic activity of early Christianity). Schäfer, *Vorstellung*, 89–114, treats the quenching of the Spirit and eschatological renewal, and on pp. 116–33 those texts in which the Spirit is still available to the pious, suggesting that Christians may have used the presence of the Spirit as a polemic; Reif, "Review," 158, reiterates Urbach's view that the rabbis were reacting against early Christianity and argues that Schäfer presents no evidence to substantiate his view as better. It is not unlikely, however, that the polemic would have been operating in both directions.

143. One may wonder if *Mekilta*'s emphatic denial of Baruch's possession of the gift of prophecy (*Mekilta Pisha* 1, lines 148–166 [Lauterbach, 1.14–15]) is not intended against the circles which produced *2 Baruch* in the early second century. Likewise, Enoch was extolled in the rabbinic mystical tractate *3 Enoch* as well as other Enoch literature, Ps-Eupolemus (*OTP* 2.881); 1QapGen 2.19; *T. Ab.* 11B; *Jub.* 4:23, 10:17 (see further J. C. VanderKam, "Enoch Traditions in Jubilees and Other Second-Century Sources" [*SBLSP* 13; Missoula, Mont.: Scholars, 1978] 1.229–51); but early Amoraim argued that Enoch died and was either wicked or ambivalent, formulating this position against *minim* (*Gen. Rab.* 25:1).

144. So W. L. Knox, *St. Paul and the Church of Jerusalem* (Cambridge: Cambridge, 1925) 36.

145. 1 Cor 14:29 suggests a plurality of prophets in the Pauline congregations as at least an ideal, and given the fact that the house churches would normally seat no more than fifty persons (see J. Murphy-O'Connor, *St. Paul's Corinth:*

Texts and Archaeology [GN 56; Wilmington, Del.: Glazier, 1983] 156), and the fact that Paul is willing to use "prophets" in the present tense, we may infer that pneumatic experience was considerably more widespread than in other Jewish sects of the period for which we have evidence.

146. Isaacs, *Spirit*, 49.

147. *Prophecy*, 81, 104; see his earlier treatment of realized eschatology in *The Cultic Setting of Realized Eschatology in Early Christianity* (NovTSup 28; Leiden: Brill, 1972), especially ch. 2, "The Present Realization of Eschatological Salvation in the Qumran Community," 29–44. Sommer, "Prophecy?" 36, believes all examples of revived prophecy derive from groups that believed the eschaton was at hand. Cf. also Chevallier, "Souffle dans le judaïsme," 38–41, who contrasts the Qumran writings with rabbinic literature and suggests that the presence of the Spirit in the former is due to its partly realized eschatology. Much of early Christianity may have shared a view similar to that of Qumran.

148. *Sayings*, 111.

149. *3 Enoch* 2:4 (*OTP* 1.257), basing the case on Ps 144:15. Cf. Manoah's doubt of his worthiness to see the angel in Ps.-Philo 42:5 (he does get to see him, however; 42:6–7).

150. *B. B.Bat.* 10a; *Num. Rab.* 12:21. *ʾAbot R. Nat.* 14A; 28 §57B, attribute this worthiness for the Shekinah to thirty of Hillel's eighty disciples (Rec. A claims that their generation was unworthy, as below).

151. *Mek. Beshallah* 7, lines 135ff. (Lauterbach, 1.252–53). *Exod. Rab.* 5:20 suggests, from Num 11, that because of the elders' merit they received the Holy Spirit and so were made prophets. *ʾAbot R. Nat.* 11 §28B probably refers to *prophets* worthy to have the Holy Spirit rest on them.

152. *Sipre Deut.* 173.1.3 (Neusner, 2.50). R. Yudan in *Song Sol. Rab.* 1:1 §9 declares that whoever teaches the Torah publicly merits the Holy Spirit resting on him. One of the Amoraim by the name of R. Aha also linked obedience to reception of the Holy Spirit (*Lev. Rab.* 35:7), though in general the Spirit was not so easily received (contrast Rom 5:5; Gal 3:2). For rabbinic references to the Holy Spirit's continued availability for the worthy, see also Glatzer, "Prophecy," 122–24.

153. Simeon ben Azzai pointed out that prophecy was acquired only for the sake of Israel, not due to personal merit, *Mek. Pisha* 1, lines 148–66 (Lauterbach, 1.14–15); all the prophets were thus intensely nationalistic in their Judaism: *Mek. Pisha* 1, lines 105–6 (p. 10). For a treatment of mainly Amoraic texts following this tendency, see Bowman, "Prophets," 213–15, and for the nationalistic context of the rabbinic view of prophecy in general, pp. 205–20; Glatzer, "Prophecy," 130–36. Glatzer, "Prophecy," 136, suggests that this is in part due to a polemic against Christian ideas of the church as a new Israel; but it may also indicate a community response to Roman oppression, a comparable alternative to the apocalyptic paradigm.

154. *P. ʿAbod. Zar.* 3:1 §2 (Neusner, 33.114); this was repeated in the upper room at Yavneh with Samuel the Small, all eyes turning to R. Eliezer as the other; also in *p. Hor.* 3:5 §3; *Sota* 9:16 §2; in simpler form (but in a later collection), *Song Sol. Rab.* 8:9 §3; with thirty of Hillel's eighty disciples, according to "Our rabbis," in *b. Sukka* 28a; with the Shekinah in place of the Holy Spirit, *b. Sota* 48b. For other references to obedience to Torah being linked with reception of the Holy Spirit, see Davies, "Reflections in Mekilta," 98; id., *Paul*, 207, 218; Urbach, *Sages*, 1.577–78.

155. *Sipre Deut.* 176.1.1 (Neusner, 2.54); R. Akiba in *Mek. Pisha* 1, lines 137–41 (Lauterbach, 1.13); 176.2.2 (ibid.); the gift of prophecy was also acquired thus: so *Mek. Pisha* 1, lines 58–113 (Lauterbach, 1.5–11); R. Isaac in *b. Sanh.* 39b.

156. *T. Soṭa* 14:3; cf. also Eph 4:30; third century *T. Sol.* 26:6.

157. E.g., *Sipra Qed.* pq. 8.205.2.1, par. 206.2.6; *Sipre Num.* 1.10.3; *Sipre Deut.* 258.2.3, 320.2.1; *b. Ber.* 5b; *Roš Haš.* 31a; *Yoma* 21b; *Šabb.* 33a, 139a; *p. Sanh.* 8:8 §1; *Deut. Rab.* 5:10, 6:14; *Ruth Rab.* 1:2. The Presence withdrew due to sin but was restored due to merit: *Gen. Rab.* 19:7; *Song Sol. Rab.* 5:1 §1; *Pesiq. Rab Kah.* 1:1. On merit and the Presence, see *Sipre Deut.* 305.3.1, 312.3.1, 355.6.1; *Gen. Rab.* 60:12; *Exod. Rab.* 45:5; *Num. Rab.* 19:20; *Song Sol. Rab.* 4:5 §2, 7:6 §1; *Pesiq. Rab.* 10:2.

158. Adding more prophets to the biblical narrative was much less problematic; e.g., *p. Meg.* 1:5 §3; *Pesiq. Rab Kah.* 16:3; cf. references in Bowman, "Prophets," 205; *Jos. and Asen.* 22:13 (Levi as προφήτην), 23:8; *Herm. Vis.* 2.3.4 (and comments by E. G. Martin in *OTP* 2.463–65). That patriarchs should be prophets (expanding upon Gen 20:7; see Philonic references in Hill, *Prophecy*, 32) should not surprise us.

159. *Sipre Num.* 96.3.1 (Neusner, 2.109); but it remains a wish, as in Num 11:26.

160. See *Num. Rab.* 15 in Davies, *Paul*, 216; cf. Aune, *Prophecy*, 193; Abrahams, *Studies* (2), 127. But this tradition is late and does not appear to have been a common topic of discussion in our texts.

161. NEB.

162. Hill, *Prophecy*, 32.

163. Flusser, *Judaism*, 54; cf. also Coppens, "L'Esprit," 209, who notes that it characterized the community. Tannaim cited Hillel for the tradition, mentioned above, that the Holy Spirit rested on the community of festal pilgrims gathered for Pesach (*t. Pesaḥ.* 6:13; *p. Pesaḥ.* 6:1; *b. Pesaḥ.* 66a, in Urbach, *Sages*, 1.576). Davies, *Paul*, 200–204, regards the OT teaching of the Spirit, most frequently observed in terms of prophecy, to be associated with the community, for the growth of the community. However, the prophetic practices mentioned in 1 Sam 10:5; 19:20, presumably suggest that much prophecy was carried on that was never published because only the community-oriented prophetic message was valued by the communities that preserved them.

164. Aune, *Realized Eschatology*, 103. He does not, however, feel that all Christians were regarded as potential prophets (*Prophecy*, 195, 206, especially on Revelation); one's view on this matter may be affected in part by the various levels of meaning given to the terms "prophets" or "prophecy" in the early Christian literature (cf. 1 Cor 14:29–32).

165. *Mek. Pisha* 1, lines 38–40 (Lauterbach, 1.4).

166. *Sipre Deut.* 62.1.1–2; 70.1.3; 157.1.1; *Gen. Rab.* 73:5. Of course, prophets functioned as messengers of the suzerain King Yahweh to his vassal kings of Israel in the OT as well, and so executed a calling of higher authority than that of kings in the eyes of the Deuteronomic historians. Cf. J. S. Holladay, "Assyrian Statecraft and the Prophets of Israel," *HTR* 63 (Jan. 1970) 31–34, and, on the court of Yahweh, F. M. Cross, *Canaanite Myth and Hebrew Epic* (Cambridge, Mass.: Harvard, 1973) 186–87.

167. *Sipre Deut.* 175.1.3, on Deut 18:15–22.

168. See *t. Sanh.* 14:13; even more so, *Sipra Behuq.* pq. 13.277.1.12.

169. *Sipra, Shemini Mekhilta deMiluim* 99.5.6 (Neusner, 2.135); again in *Pesiq. Rab Kah.* 26:6/7. A similar use of Amos 7:14 by an amora is noted in *b. Ber.* 34b, *Yeb.* 121b, by Hill, *Prophecy,* 34–35.

170. *P. Sanh.* 10:1 §9, placing sages directly below prophets, prophets directly below Moses, and Moses directly below God.

171. *P. Sanh.* 11:4 §1: their teachings are more stringent than those of the prophets, and they may be accepted without signs, unlike the prophets. This is also taught in the Jerusalem *Berakot* reference noted by J. Jeremias, *Jerusalem in the Time of Jesus* (Philadelphia: Fortress, 1978) 241–42.

172. *P. Hor.* 3:5 §1: Sages are above kings, kings above high priests, high priests above prophets, and so on.

173. Bamberger, "Prophet," 306, citing *b. B.Bat.* 12a; cf. also Urbach, *Sages,* 1.306.

174. S. J. D. Cohen, *From the Maccabees to the Mishnah* (LEC 7; Philadelphia: Westminster, 1987) 23; cf. Hengel, *Judaism and Hellenism,* 1.206. Urbach, *Sages,* 1.578: in the rabbinic period, "prophecy evolved into a mystic experience."

175. E.g., *ʾAbot R. Nat.* 1A. This is often observed: Aune, *Prophecy,* 104; Hill, *Prophecy,* 34–35; Urbach, *Sages,* 1.306, 564–65, 578 (although disagreeing with the proposed connection between fixed Law and the cessation of prophecy; p. 566).

176. A false prophet (like a bad disciple) speaks what he did not hear: *t. Sanh.* 14:14–16; cf. *Sipre Deut.* 177.1.1.

177. E.g., by the early amora R. Levi, in *Pesiq. R. Kah.* 14:4 (though cf. *Pesiq. R. Kah.* 24:7); cf. Aune, *Prophecy,* 124; Glatzer, "Prophecy," 119–20, 126–30.

178. *ʾAbot R. Nat.* 4A; 6 §19B, predicates Johanan ben Zakkai's "prophecy" to Vespasian on Scripture interpretation (Isa 10:34).

179. Besides the eighteen references cited in C. S. Keener, "Matthew 5:22 and the Heavenly Court," *ExpT* 99 (1987) 46, see *ʾAbot R. Nat.* 32A; *p. Sanh.* 1:1 §4, 11:5 §1; *Pesiq. Rab. Kah.* 24:11; cf. 11QMelch. and explanation in P. J. Kobelski, "Melchizedek and Melchiresa" (Ph.D. diss., Fordham University, 1978) 123; *T. Ab.* 12A; 10B; *3 Enoch* 2:4, 5:10–12, 16:1, 18:16 (?), ch. 28, 29:1, 30:1–2; for prophetic and apocalyptic tradition, cf. G. Couturier, "La vision du conseil divin," *ScEsp* 36 (1984) 5–43.

180. *Sipre Deut.* 306.24.2. A true prophet must do as Moses did: *Sipre Deut.* 83.1.1.

181. Third-century amora R. Samuel bar Nahman in R. Jonathan's name, in *p. Meg.* 1:5 §3. For the divergent data on whether prophets could make innovations in the Law, see Bowman, "Prophets," 263–74.

182. *Sipre Deut.* 32.5.12.

183. W. D. Davies, "Reflexions on Tradition: The Aboth Revisited," in *Christian History and Interpretation* (Cambridge: Cambridge, 1967) 129–37. Thus the words of Isa 51:16, "my words in your mouth," applying in some contexts to prophecy, could be taken to apply to the study of Torah in *p. Taʿan.* 4:2 §13; *Meg.* 3:6 §2 (in *Sipre Deut.* 176.3.1 it is used prophetically, however).

184. Cf., e.g., 2 Macc 2:1–3; Hill, *Prophecy,* 27–28, on Josephus; Aune, *Prophecy,* 124, on Maccabean texts.

185. Ps.-Philo 11:2; *Jub.* 8:20.

186. *Sipre Deut.* 176.3.1, on Deut 18. This phrase can be used in the OT simply of teaching another what to say, as in Exod 4:15.

187. *ʾAbot R. Nat.* 24A; *p. Taʿan.* 4:2 §13; *Meg.* 3:6 §2.

188. *Sipre Deut.* 357.18.2 (Neusner, 2.461), citing Num 24:16; Deut 5:28; Num 24:4. For the inability to control prophetic inspiration, see the references in *Qoh. Rab.* cited by Bowman, "Prophets," 207. On *b. B.Bat.* 15b, comparing Moses and Balaam, see the extended discussion in Bowman, "Prophets," 108–14. Jewish writers often regarded Balaam as the greatest of the Gentile prophets or philosophers (Jos., *Ant.* 4.104; *Gen. Rab.* 65:20, 93:10; *Lam. Rab.* Proem 2; *Pesiq. Rab. Kah.* 15:5; in *Num. Rab.* 20:19, the Holy Spirit spoke with him); he was the only one who could explain to the nations what was happening at Sinai (*Sipre Deut.* 343.6.1; *Pesiq. Rab.* 20:1); but God kept him from cursing Israel against his will (Jos., *Ant.* 4.104; cf. *Exod. Rab.* 4:3, 20:5, 27:3), though he found another strategy to carry out his purpose (Jos., *Ant.* 4.104; *Sipre Deut.* 252.1.4; *p. Sanh.* 10:2 §8; cf. *Ta'an.* 4:5 §10). He is repeatedly considered wicked (Philo, *Conf.* 159; *Mos.* 1.48; *b. Ber.* 7a; *'Abod. Zar.* 4a; *Sanh.* 105b–106a; *Exod. Rab.* 30:20; *Num. Rab.* 20:6; *Pesiq. Rab.* 20:1; 41:3), and is contrasted with Moses (*Sipre Deut.* 357.18.1–2, above; *Exod. Rab.* 32:3; *Num. Rab.* 14:20; *Qoh. Rab.* 2:15 §2) and Abraham (*m. 'Abot* 5:19; *Gen. Rab.* 55:8). Later rabbinic polemic uses him as a type or name for Jesus (R. T. Herford, *Christianity in Talmud and Midrash* [Clifton, N.J.: Reference Book Publishers, 1966] 65ff.).

189. Schäfer, *Vorstellung*, may not conclusively demonstrate his case that the Holy Spirit's continued activity in rabbinic texts originates from mystical sources (Reif, "Review," 158), but these sources do seem to be the center of revelatory activity in extant rabbinic texts.

190. See P.S. Alexander's comments in *OTP* 1.229–38 for broader connections.

191. Bonsirven, *Judaism*, 135, comments on *t. Ber.* 3:5, 7 (that Akiba would spend hours in fervent prayer and would be left in one part of the room and be found in another) that rapturous or ecstatic experiences may be in view here; but *b. Ber.* 31a suggests that he was moved around "on account of his many genuflexions and prostrations." The latter *could* be an attempt to play down mysticism, but is more probably the realistic explanation for his movement.

192. See especially *t. Hag.* 2:3–4; *b. Hag.* 14b; *p. Hag.* 2:1 §7–8; *Song Sol. Rab.* 1:4 §1. Visions of heaven became standard fare in the apocalypses; besides Enoch's tour, see later employment of the theme in *Life of Adam* 25:3–4; *Apoc. Zeph.* 5:6; *Gr. Ezra* 5:20; *Apoc. Sedrach* 9:1; cf. Moses in *Sipre Deut.* 357.6.6.

193. Alexander, in *OTP* 1.235, suggests the "tempting" possibility "that Merkabah mysticism did not have a separate existence outside of apocalyptic till after A.D. 70 and that it was the events of the years A.D. 70–135 in Palestine which brought about a reorientation of apocalyptic and gave rise to a more or less independent Merkabah movement." Hellenistic ascents may have provided a model, but Jewish ascent traditions were not uncommon, and were sometimes associated with Moses' ascent to receive Torah (*b. Šabb.* 88b; cf. *Exod. Rab.* 42:4; *Pesiq. Rab.* 20:4; Aristob. fr. 4 [Eusebius, *Praeparatio Evangelica* 13.13.5, in *OTP* 2.840–41]; Ps.-Philo 12:1). W. A. Meeks, *The Prophet-King* (NovTSup 14; Leiden: Brill, 1967) 122–25, 141, 205–11, 241–46, 295–98; G. C. Nicholson, *Death as Departure: The Johannine Descent-Ascent Schema* (SBLDS 63; Chico, Calif.: Scholars Press, 1983) 98; and others see a polemic against Moses' ascent in the Fourth Gospel; for an early view that this is a polemic against Jewish mystic ascent traditions, see H. Odeberg, *The Fourth Gospel* (Uppsala: Almqvist & Wiksells, 1929) 72.

194. G. G. Scholem, *Jewish Gnosticism, Merkabah Mysticism, and Talmudic Tradition* (New York: Jewish Theological Seminary of America, 1965) 11–12, argues that the early Jewish mystics lived near the center of rabbinic Judaism, not near its fringes. The date of the materials is difficult to decide; D. Halperin, "Merkabah Midrash in the Septuagint," *JBL* 101 (1982) 351–63, finds traces as early as the LXX; Goodenough, *Symbols*, 1.221 (cf. also 8.17; 12.198), thinks Jewish mysticism was common, especially in the more Hellenistic circles, until halakic Judaism became dominant, and finds evidence for this in Philo (id., *An Introduction to Philo Judaeus* [2d ed.; Oxford: Basil Blackwell, 1962] 134–60). J. Neusner, "The Development of the *Merkavah* Tradition," *JSJ* 2 (1971) 149–60 thinks the earlier Merkabah traditions were expanded and made more complex with time.

195. Cf. H. W. Basser, "The Rabbinic Attempt to Democratize Salvation and Revelation," *SR* 12 (1983) 27–33; Urbach, *Sages*, 1.193. Various Jewish mystical texts show varying degrees of emphasis on responsibility to the mystic's community; see I. Chernus, "Individual and Community in the Redaction of the Hekhalot Literature," *HUCA* 52 (1981) 253–74. Such ascents could be read in light of the myth of invading heaven in OT traditions (D. J. Halperin, "Ascension or Invasion," *Rel* 18 [1988] 47–67), and some of the motifs may have come from Gnosticism in the Amoraic period (J. P. Schultz, "Angelic Opposition to the Ascension of Moses and the Revelation of the Law," *JQR* 61 [1971] 282–307). Abelson, *Immanence*, 340–56, strikes a balance between rabbinism's use and its restraint of mystical tendencies.

196. E.g., *t. Ḥag.* 2:1, 7; *b. Ḥag.* 15a; *p. Ḥag.* 2:1 §15; *Gen. Rab.* 1:5, 10; 2:4; *Pesiq. Rab Kah.* 21:5; cf. *2 Enoch* 24:3 A (rec. J is similar); perhaps 1QH 1.11, 13 (in J. M. C. Ramirez, "Los 'Himnos' de Qumran y el 'misterio' paulino," *ST* 8 [1976] 9–56 [*NTA* 22.64]).

197. E.g., *t. Ḥag.* 2:1. After a child understood the reading of Ezekiel, and was instantly consumed by fire, some rabbis wished to suppress Ezekiel (*b. Ḥag.* 13a; cf. Jerome's report of a Jewish tradition that the beginning of Ezekiel was not to be read, in G. G. Scholem, *Major Trends in Jewish Mysticism* [3d rev. ed.; New York: Schocken, 1971] 42); R. Johanan b. Zakkai refused to teach the "work of the chariot" to R. Eleazar b. ʿArak, so R. Eleazar then expounded it himself, and all the trees caught fire, bringing R. Johanan's commendation (*b. Ḥag.* 14b); a disciple of a rabbi expounded a chapter in the work of the chariot without the rabbi's permission, and was struck with a skin disease (*p. Ḥag.* 2:1 §§3–4). Throne mysticism appears to exist in the Dead Sea Scrolls; see Dupont-Sommer, *Essene Writings*, 333–34; Vermes, *Scrolls*, 210–11; Gaster, *Scriptures*, 285–88; Patte, *Hermeneutic*, 290, on the angelic litany. *T. Job* 33:9 uses similar language, but of *Job's* throne; the allusion in *Life of Adam* 25:2–3 (cf. *Apoc. Mos.* 33:2) may conflate Ezekiel's and Elijah's chariots.

198. An opinion is cited in which Torah should only be taught privately (*b. Sukka* 49b), but this is normally reserved for certain esoteric teachings (*b. Pesaḥ.* 119a; *Ḥag.* 13a; *Pesiq. Rab.* 22:2). In *b. Šabb.* 80b, a certain Galilean (his place of origin may be significant) was going to lecture publicly on the chariot passage, and so died before he could.

199. This may reflect associations with the language of the mysteries (e.g., Luc., *Lexiphanes* 10; Apul., *Metam.* 11.23; cf. *Orph. H.* 30.3, 7; W. Burkert, *Ancient Mystery Cults* [Cambridge, Mass.: Harvard, 1987] 9; A. T. Lincoln, *Paradise Now and Not Yet* [SNTSMS 43; Cambridge: Cambridge, 1981] 82;

M. Dibelius, "The Isis Initiation in Apuleius and Related Initiatory Rites," in *Conflict at Colossae* [Missoula, Mont.: SBL, 1973] 65; Aune, *Prophecy,* 65; and commentaries on 2 Cor 12:4 such as Martin, Furnish, and Barrett, loc. cit.), though it thereby acquired a broader religious semantic range (e.g., Philostr., *V.A.* 1 §1), and the idea is already found in first-century Judaism (Philo, *Det.* 175–76; *Cher.* 48; Jos., *Ag. Ap.* 2.94 [of the Law]; cf. Alexander, *OTP* 1.246–47, for the concept among Merkabah mystics).

200. 1 Sam 10:6, 10; 16:13–14. Cf. the Spirit-moved leaders of Israel in Judges (Judg 3:10; 6:34; 9:23; 11:29; 13:25; 14:6, 19; 15:14).

201. *Sib. Or.* 3:781–82, probably from second century B.C.E. Alexandria; cf. *Gen. Rab.* 73:5.

202. Cf., e.g., the angel of the Lord with the prophetic messenger formula in Ps.-Philo 38:3. Greek literature could sometimes use προφήτης as a spokesperson for a view, e.g., Diogenes, *Ep.* 21, to Amynander (*Cynic Epistles,* 114–15), or μαντέυομαι (not used of Christian prophecy in the NT) as a metaphorical extension of predicting nonsupernaturally, e.g., Ach. Tat., *Clit.* 1.9.5, 7 (LCL 30–33). Epict., *Disc.* 1.17.29 uses the μαντείαν as a parable of the philosopher; cf. 2.7.1–3 for his distaste for the real thing, and, more qualified, *Ench.* 32.3.

203. The differences between Israelite and other ancient Near Eastern prophecy have been pointed out frequently enough; e.g., A. J. Heschel, *The Prophets* (New York: Harper & Row, 1962) 465–66; Paul, "Prophecy," 1160; on prophetic succession, R. B. Y. Scott, *The Relevance of the Prophets* (New York: Macmillan, 1954) 57–62; Heschel, *The Prophets,* 472–73; for Mari, M. J. Buss, "Mari Prophecy and Hosea," *JBL* 88 (1969) 338; J. F. Craghan, "Mari and Its Prophets," *BTB* 5 (1975) 52; Heschel, *Prophets,* 471–72; for Greek vs. Jewish prophecy, cf. Büchsel, *Geist,* 43–44.

204. In *ANET* 26, including n. 13; see W. F. Albright, *Yahweh and the Gods of Canaan* (Garden City, N.Y.: Doubleday, 1968) 212; cf. C. H. Gordon, *The Ancient Near East* (New York: Norton, 1965) 159 n. 19. Other examples of ecstatic prophecy among the Hittites and pre-Islamic nomads exist; see in Paul, "Prophets," 1156. Egyptians did not necessarily have high regard for the possessed; a "man who is in the hand of the god" is classed with the blind and lame in "The Instruction of Amen-em-opet" 25 (*ANET* 424), where it refers to someone insane.

205. Haran, "Prophecy," 181; H. B. Huffmon, "Prophecy in the Mari Letters," *BA* 31 (1968) 111; cf. the possible evidence of Ebla here in G. Pettinato, *The Archives of Ebla* (Garden City, N.Y.: Doubleday, 1981) 253. This is relevant even if the ecstasy was controlled, as some have suggested due to the forms of the prophecies (W. L. Moran, "New Evidence from Mari on the History of Prophecy," *Bib* 50 [1969] 27–28).

206. Cf. 2 Kgs 9:11; Jer 29:26; Hos 9:7.

207. Albright, *Yahweh,* 212; A. Malamat, "Prophetic Revelations in New Documents from Mari and the Bible" (VTSup 15; Leiden: Brill, 1966) 210–11; cf. Paul, "Prophets," 1159; J. Lindblom, *Prophecy in Ancient Israel* (Philadelphia: Fortress, 1962) 31. For a modern study of the psychological state suggested by the possession trance, see K. Nussbaum, "Abnormal Mental Phenomena in the Prophets," *JRH* 13 (1974) 194–200. Possession trances are documented in a variety of cultures, e.g., among Australian aborigines in C. H. Berndt, "The Role of Native Doctors in Aboriginal Australia," in *Magic, Faith, and Healing: Studies in Primitive Psychiatry Today* (ed. Ari Kiev; New York: Free Press, 1964) 269.

208. Plut., *Dial. on Love* 16, *Moralia* 759AB (LCL 9.364–65), describes the use of dance in "Bacchic orgies and Corybantic revels," and compares this to the Pythia's inspiration; cf. *Table-Talk* 1.5.2, *Moralia* 623B; *Or. H.* 52.7 (cf. 40.15); cf. Walter Burkert, *Greek Religion* (Cambridge, Mass.: Harvard, 1985) 166; L. H. Martin, *Hellenistic Religions: An Introduction* (New York: Oxford, 1987) 61; W. F. Otto, *Dionysus: Myth and Cult* (Bloomington: Indiana, 1965) 143–45; Huffmon, "Prophecy," 112. Dancing can be used to stimulate trance states in various societies; see M. Eliade, *Rites and Symbols of Initiation* (New York: Harper & Row, 1958) 69; cf. the use of music in Gelfand, "Psychiatric Disorders as Recognized by the Shona," 156–73 in *Magic, Faith, and Healing*, esp. 156, 162.

209. Fasting could prepare the way for revelations in *2 Bar.* 20:5; 43:3; *Herm. Vis.* 2.2, 3.1, 10 (but cf. *Herm. Vis.* 3.13); also part of the initiation for the Lesser Mysteries of Eleusis (G. E. Mylonas, *Eleusis and the Eleusinian Mysteries* [Princeton: Princeton, 1961] 241) and maybe also the Greater Mysteries (ibid., 258). On fasting and revelations, see the commentators on ταπεινοφροσύνη in Col 2:18, especially F. O. Francis, "Humility and Angelic Worship in Col 2:18," in *Conflict at Colossae*, 168–71; Lincoln, *Paradise*, 111. In early Judaism, fasting could be used for mourning (e.g., *2 Bar.* 5:7; *T. Zeb.* 4:1–3; cf. Apul., *Metam.* 2.24) or to intensify prayer (cf. Tob 12:8; 2 Macc 13:12; *T. Ben.* 1:4–5; cf. *Did.* 1), but the rabbis strictly regulated fasting to avoid ascetic practices harmful to the body or dishonoring to the joy of the Sabbath (*t. Kip.* 4:1–2; *Taʿan.* 2:12, 14; *p. Taʿan.* 3:11 §3, 4:3 §2; *Ned.* 8:1 §1). Tribal religions sometimes use fasting to gain requests from deities (e.g., J. R. Fox, "Witchcraft and Clanship in Cochiti Therapy," in *Magic, Faith, and Healing*, 181), and in initiatory rites (Eliade, *Initiation*, 67).

210. See Lindblom, *Prophecy,* 5, 8–9, 43, 58–60; cf. Paul, "Prophets," 1156; 2 Kgs 18:28–29; Zech 13:4–6.

211. E.g., Exod 15; 1 Sam 10:5; 2 Kgs 3:15; cf. Hab 3:19; 1 Chron 25:1–6.

212. Cf. H. H. Schmid, "Ekstatische und charismatische Geistwirkungen im Alten Testament," in *Erfahrung und Theologie des Heiligen Geistes* (Hamburg: Agentur des Rauhen, 1974) 83–99; Aune, *Prophecy,* 86–87; for connections between Israelite and Mari models, see Holladay, "Statecraft," 11–12; J. Bright, *A History of Israel* (3d ed.; Philadelphia: Westminster, 1981) 88–89; cf. Pettinato, *Ebla*, 319, n. 12. R. R. Wilson, "Prophecy and Ecstasy: A Reexamination," *JBL* 98 (1979) 323–25, finds further cases of ecstasy based on more subtle phraseology in the prophets; S. B. Parker, "Possession Trance and Prophecy in Pre-Exilic Israel," *VT* 28 (1978) 271–85, feels that the experience was only marginal in Israelite prophetism.

213. Especially the Mesopotamian *baru* diviners, but the practice was widespread; cf. Gen 44:5; Taanach 1, 15th century B.C.E. (*ANET* 490); Assyrian "Hymn to the Sun-God," ca. 668–633 B.C.E. (*ANET* 388); Hittite "Investigating the Anger of the Gods" (*ANET* 497–98); "The Telepinus Myth" (*ANET* 128); Aqhat, C.2 (*ANET* 153); "Akkadian Observations on Life and the World Order" (*ANET* 434); R. R. Wilson, "Early Israelite Prophecy," *Int* 32 (1978) 10; B. O. Long, "The Effect of Divination upon Israelite Literature," *JBL* 92 (1973) 489–97; G. Mendenhall, "Mari," *BA* 11 (1948) 1–19, esp. p. 18; O. R. Gurney, *Some Aspects of Hittite Religion* (Oxford: Oxford, 1977) 45–46; id., *The Hittites* (Baltimore: Penguin, 1972) 158–59; Lindblom, *Prophecy,* 31; cf. E. Reiner, "Fortune-Telling in Mesopotamia," *JNES* 19 (1960) 23–85. For modern divination, cf., e.g., Gelfand, "Shona," 161.

214. Among pre-Roman Arabs: Philostr., *V.A.* 1 §20; Greeks: Hdt., *Hist.* 1 §§47ff.; *PGM* 4.930–1114, 3209–54; Burkert, *Religion*, 111–14; Martin, *Religions*, 40–50; Heschel, *Prophets*, 454–56; Scythians: Hdt., *Hist.* 4 §§68–69; in early Imperial Rome: R. MacMullen, *Enemies of the Roman Order* (Cambridge, Mass.: Harvard, 1966) 128–62. It could take the form of augury (as in Plut., *R. Q.* 72, *Moralia* 281B), examination of flames (Apul., *Metam.* 2.11), dream divination (Artem., *Oneir.*; Ach. Tat., *Clit.* 1.3.2) and a variety of other forms (see Aune, *Prophecy*, 23 for one breakdown of categories, following K. Latte). Divination functioned essentially on the principle of sympathetic magic. See V.P. Stogiannos, " 'Pneuma Pthona' (Pr. 16,16)," *DBM* 9 (1980) 99–114 (*NTA* 26.261), for a review of the data (in Greek).

215. It had been approved by Pythagoras (Diog. Laert., *Lives* 8.1.20, 23) and the Stoics (7.1.149; Cicero, *De Nat. Deor.* 2.3.7–4.12). There was, however, some opposition: certain Cynics (Diog. Laert., *Lives* 6.2.24; Diogenes, *Ep.* 38 [*Cynic Epistles*, pp. 160–61]), non-Stoics (Cicero, *De Divinatione*, passim; *De Nat. Deor.* 1.20.55–56; 3.6.14), and less defined opponents (cf. Artem., *Oneir.* 1, preface). Naturally the most solid opposition would be encountered in Jewish sources: Hecataeus in Jos., *Ag. Ap.* 1.203–4 (*OTP* 2.919); *Sib. Or.* 3:224–26 (probably second century B.C.E.); *Asc. Isa.* 2:5; 11QTemple col. 60 (Maier, 52–53), following Deut 18; *Sipra Qed.* pq. 6.203.2.1; *Sipre Deut.* 171.5.1; 172.1.2–4; *Ab. R. Nathan* 36A; cf. K. A. D. Smelik, "The Witch of Endor," *VC* 33 (1979) 160–79.

216. See Plut., *The Obsolescence of Oracles;* cf. G. Theissen, *The Miracle Stories of the Early Christian Tradition* (Philadelphia: Fortress, 1983) 268; Parke, *Delphic Oracle*, 381; R. M. Grant, *Gods and the One God* (LEC 1; Philadelphia: Westminster, 1986) 63. But they were still widely consulted: J. J. Collins, *The Sibylline Oracles of Egyptian Judaism* (SBLDS 13; Missoula, Mont.: SBL, 1972) 5; M. P. Nilsson, *Greek Piety* (Oxford: Clarendon, 1948) 166; Aune, *Prophecy*, 51. And they were still respected enough that oracles could be useful in a court dispute; see Quint., *Inst. Or.* 5.11.41–42 (this depended entirely on what side one argued; see 5.7.36). Their political use had, of course, been strongest in the classical period: M. P. Nilsson, *Cults, Myths, Oracles, and Politics in Ancient Greece* (Lund: Gleerup, 1951) 123–42.

217. Hill, *Prophecy*, 11. The Romans were fascinated by the Sibylline Oracles, but their cults concentrate more on divination (such as augury) than on prophetic inspiration.

218. For Greco-Egyptian prophecy, cf. *CPJ* 3.119–21 §520 (dated to the third century C.E. on paleographic grounds), probably reflecting the Potter's Oracle (which Aune, *Prophecy*, 76–77, thinks reflects the *Sitz* of ca. 130 B.C.E.); cf. Deissmann, *Bible Studies*, 235–36; Lewis, *Life in Egypt*, 98. Strabo, *Geog.* 17.1.43 (LCL 8.112–13), says that even in Egypt, with its oracle of Ammon, oracles were in decline due to the Roman satisfaction with Sibylline oracles and the Tyrrhenian prophecies based on divination.

219. See H. W. Parke, "Ecstatic Prophecy in the Near East," in *Sibyls and Sibylline Prophecy in Classical Antiquity* (New York: Routledge, 1988), app. 3, 216–20.

220. For the variety among different cults on this point, see ibid., 219; id., *The Oracles of Zeus: Dodona, Olympia, Ammon* (Oxford: Basil Blackwell, 1967) 85, 256–57.

221. *Oracles at Delphi* 7, *Moralia* 397C; but cf. Theon in ibid., 21, *Moralia* 404E. Aune, *Prophecy*, 4, does not think the Pythia experienced mantic frenzy, but this is not the view of Plutarch (*Dial. on Love* 16, *Moralia* 759B); cf. Lucan's description of her rapturous trance, cited by Richard Reitzenstein, *Hellenistic Mystery Religions* (PTMS 15; Pittsburgh: Pickwick, 1978) 71; Plato, *Phaedr.* 47). For the reputed authority and accuracy of this oracle, see Isoc., *Paneg.* 31, *Or.* 4; Hdt., *Hist.* 1 §§47ff, 65–67, 86; Plut., *Greek Questions* 12, *Moralia* 293E; 19, *Moralia* 295DE; *On Borrowing* 3, *Moralia* 828D; Plut., *Thes.* 36.1; *Lyc.* 6.5; *Sol.* 4.2; Diog. Laert., *Lives* 8.1.21; cf. Diog. Laert., *Lives* 5.91; Strabo, *Geog.* 9.3.2, 11–12; Mart., *Epig.* 9.42.4; it also posed questions to early Christianity: Justin, *First Apology* 18; Min. Felix, *Oct.* 26:6; cf. Acts 16:16.

222. So, e.g., Iamblichus, *Myst.* 3.4–6; for the Trojan Cassandra, as late as the sixth century C.E., see *Anthologia Graeca* §2, lines 189–91 (cf. lines 42–44); for Mithraic ecstatic inspiration, see *PGM* 4.738–39; Aune, *Prophecy*, 47–48. That prophesying was not always irrational (Aune, *Prophecy*, 39) is not reason to presume that it could not have been uttered ecstatically.

223. Chevallier, *Souffle*, 40, from Plutarch; Luc., *Alex.* 12. Athena puts μανίαισι in men's souls in *Or. H.* 32, line 6, but line 9 shows that she does this only to the wicked, giving prudence to the good. The etymological relationship with μάντις proposed by Plato may be correct, but does not indicate the view of all diviners in antiquity (Aune, *Prophecy*, 35); mantic frenzy was more common for peripheral intermediaries than for those in central cults (Aune, *Prophecy*, 21).

224. Luc., *Syr. D.* 51; Apul., *Metam.* 8.27–28 (the Phrygian music in 8.30 could suggest Cybele, but a differentiation is made in 9.9–10).

225. E.g., the cult of Cybele; W. K. C. Guthrie, *Orpheus and Greek Religion* (2d ed.; New York: Norton, 1966) 118. On ecstasy in this cult, see Burkert, *Religion*, 178; cf. *Orph. H.* 27.11; Lucret., *Nat.* 2.618–20; Juv., *Sat.* 3.63. For ecstasy as divine possession in the Mysteries, see Hill, *Prophecy*, 10–11; cf. Aune, *Prophecy*, 47.

226. Aune, *Prophecy*, 21; he thinks that Livy has wrongly associated the two for several cults; p. 42. Plato had distinguished various kinds of inspiration, as Plutarch, nearer our period, also points out (*Dial. on Love* 16, *Moralia* 758EF). Although possession was common in allusions to the Bacchae (e.g., Eurip., *Bacchae*; [Ps.] Plut., *Parallel Stories* 19, *Moralia* 310B; cf. Grant, *Gods*, 65; Martin, *Religions*, 93–94; Burkert, *Religion*, 292), the only author I have found who *consistently* links Bacchic or Corybantic frenzy with prophetic inspiration is Philo: *Opif.* 71; *Leg.* 3.82; *Plant.* 148; *Contempl.* 84.

227. Music and prophecy were associated in the figure of Orpheus, according to I. M. Linforth, *The Arts of Orpheus* (Berkeley: University of California, 1941) 166; Guthrie, *Orpheus*, 21. Likewise, Apollo, the god of prophecy (a prophet himself, Cic., *Tusc. Disp.* 1.47.114; Epict., *Disc.* 3.1.18; *Orph. H.* 34.4; cf. 11.21, 18.17, 27.13, 28.4; Luc., *J. Conf.* [LCL 2.76–77]; Dionysus, in Eurip., *Bacchae* 298–99; μάντις), was also associated with music: Luc., *Amber, or the Swans* (LCL 1.77); Dio Chrys., *32d Disc.* §§56–57; Marc. Aur., *Med.* 11.11; Artem., *Oneir.* 2.35; *Anthologia Graeca* §2, lines 266–70. There was also a high degree of assimilation among Orpheus, Dionysus, and Apollo: Plut., *E at Delphi* 9, *Moralia* 388E–389A; W. Burkert, *Orphism and Bacchic Mysteries: New Evidence and Old Problems of Interpretation* (CHSHMC 28; Berkeley: Center for Hermeneutical Studies, 1977) 8; Guthrie, *Orpheus*, 42–48, 113; Linforth, *Orpheus*, 171; M. Detienne, "Un

polytheisme recrit: Entre Dionysos et Apollon," *ASSR* 30 (1985) 65–75; Otto, *Dionysus*, 202–8.

228. Plato, *Ion* 533E (he compares this with Bacchic possession in 533E–534A); for oracular singers in Plato, see Aune, *Prophecy*, 38. Although they were divinely possessed, in Plato's thought, their words still had to be judged and interpreted by non-possessed governors; see E. N. Tigerstedt, "Plato's Idea of Poetical Inspiration," *CHL* 44 (1969) 64–66, 72. Plutarch associates poetry with inspiration (*Poetry* 1, *Moralia* 15E; cf. *The Oracles at Delphi No Longer Given in Verse, Moralia* 394D–409D). Hesiod in Luc., *Hes.* 7 (LCL 6.234–35) argues that the Muses inspired him and other poets (his interlocutor dissents). Horace entreats the Muses for inspiration in *Ode* 1.26; cf., e.g., 2.12.13; 3.1.3–4, 14.13–15; 4.8.29; 9.21; Juv., *Sat.* 7.10, 36–39; *CIJ* vol. 1, p. cxxiii (a pagan sarcophagus with the Muse Urania teaching music to the spouse, reused by Roman Jews); Philo, *Plant.* 129.

229. For the inspiration of lawgivers (divine sanction for laws had been important as early as Hamurabi), see M. Hadas, *Aristeas to Philocrates* (New York: Harper & Brothers, 1951) 194, on Ep. Aristeas, 240.

230. E.g., Hadas, *Aristeas*, 34, 36; A. Wikenhauser, *Pauline Mysticism* (New York: Herder & Herder, 1960) 76–77; Boring, *Sayings*, 82–83.

231. *Sib. Or.* 11:316–18 (*OTP* 1.442; Greek text, pp. 187–88).

232. Lines 320–24. Cicero concluded from pagan Sibylline use of acrostic that the form (which is Hellenistic, not classical) indicated deliberate, rather than ecstatic, thought (Parke, *Sibyls*, 139), but while there may not have been first-person speech or the same kind of possession as with the Pythia (Parke, *Sibyls*, 219), the sibyl portrays herself in the extant Jewish and Christian oracles as irresistibly moved.

233. 28:6 (*OTP* 2.341; Latin, p. 195).

234. 28:10 (*OTP* 2.342).

235. *4 Bar.* 5:8 (Kraft, 22–23); also 5:12 (ibid.). The story of a long nap also circulated concerning Epimenides (who lived ca. 600 B.C.E.), as reported by Diog. Laert., *Lives* 1.109; and Honi the Circle-Drawer, grandson of his more famous namesake, in *p. Ta'an.* 3:9 §4. Washington Irving had some Germanic and ultimately Mediterranean roots for his "original" American tale of Rip Van Winkle.

236. *T. Job* chs. 48–50; it is difficult to say if this section reflects Christian influence, perhaps from the time of the Montanist controversy. Philo's description of the worship of the Therapeutae in *Contempl.* 84, compared with Bacchic rites of strong drink, include apparently inspired singing. For inspired singing elsewhere, see *Mekilta* on 14:31–15:1 (in Smith, *Parallels*, 64); *p. Sota* 5:4 §1; *Pesiq. Rab.* 9:2; Ps.-Philo 32:14. It is possible that in Judaism this related to the heavenly (*T. Ab.* 20, Rec A; *2 Enoch* 17:1 A and J) or eschatological (*Sib. Or.* 3:715, second century B.C.E.; *b. Ta'an.* 31a; *Sanh.* 91b; *Num. Rab.* 15:11; *Qoh. Rab.* 1:11 §1; *Pesiq. Rab.* 21:1) worship.

237. See, e.g., D. S. Russell, *The Method and Message of Jewish Apocalyptic* (Philadelphia: Westminster, 1964) 160.

238. Isaacs, *Spirit*, 49, citing Plato, *Timaeus* 71D; *Ion* 533D, 543C; and Philo, *Her.* 264; *Spec.* 4.49; *Q.G.* 3.9.

239. Isaacs, *Spirit*, 51, citing 1 Sam 10:10–12.

240. Ibid., 49–50, citing *Her.* 69, 249, 266.

241. Philo, *Plant.* 39 (LCL). Baer, *Philo's Use,* 55–64, shows that Philo often portrays divine possession as impregnation.

242. *Migr.* 190.

243. *Her.* 68–69.

244. *Fug.* 168; cf. 2 Pet 1:21.

245. *Spec.* 1.65 (LCL), using ἐνθουσιῶν.

246. *Q.G.* 9. In *Q.G.* 138 every true prophet was called "seer" or "beholder" because of the eye of the soul. Contrast Aune, *Prophecy,* 150, who makes Philo's allowance for an ecstatic to be aware of his surroundings a contrast with Ps.-Philo 28.

247. *Her.* 264–65; cf. 1 Cor 14 (the parallel between Philonic and Pauline language was pointed out to me by Professor Dale Martin at Duke University).

248. *Her.* 249, 258–59.

249. *Mos.* 2.258; cf. 1.201. This is especially effective when he is about to leave his body (2.288).

250. *Migr.* 35. On Philo's own experience, see Aune, *Prophecy,* 147.

251. *Prophecy,* 32–33. One may contrast the NT literature, for whatever reason: A. D. Nock, "The Vocabulary of the New Testament," *JBL* 52 (1933) 134. For a lengthy treatment of prophets moved by the divine spirit in Philo, see H. A. Wolfson, *Philo* (4th rev. ed.; 2 vols.; Cambridge, Mass.: Harvard, 1968) 2.11–59.

252. Cf. *J.W.* 3.353.

253. Ibid., 6.300–9.

254. Bamberger, "Prophet," 305, citing *b. B.Bat.* 12b for a similar association of prophecy with madness after the temple's destruction.

255. Citing *Ant.* 6.222–23; 4.118.

256. Isaacs, *Spirit,* 50, citing *Ant.* 6.56, 76.

257. *Odes Sol.* 6:1–2 (*OTP* 2.738). Even Hellenistic magical divination seems to have influenced some strands of early Christianity, as in *Hermas* (see Aune, *Prophecy,* 17, 211, 303, following J. Reiling, *Hermas and Christian Prophecy* [Leiden: Brill, 1973] 79–96). At the same time, one should be cautious not to read in influences arbitrarily; cf. C. Forbes, "Early Christian Inspired Speech and Hellenistic Popular Religion," *NovT* 28 (3, July 1986) 257–70; Hill, *Prophecy,* 9, 29–30 (who goes too far in denying the influences, however).

258. At this point it would be possible to investigate studies of the Jesus movement as a millennial movement, discussion of signs prophets in early Judaism, and the rabbinic condemnation of the signs offered by the *minim;* but this would take us too far afield from the current study.

2

• • • • • • • • • • • • • •

JESUS AS THE SPIRIT-BRINGER
IN MARK 1:9–11

• • • • • • • • • • • • • •

This chapter could focus on either of two issues: John the Baptist's introduction of Jesus as the Spirit-bringer or Mark's exposition of that proclamation. Because the earliest Christian recollection of the Baptist's introduction of Jesus set the stage for early Christian interpretation of Jesus as the Spirit-bringer, John's introduction provides a natural starting point for the student of early Christian pneumatology. While probing some of these historical questions in a general manner, however, this chapter focuses on Mark's interpretation of the event rather than the history behind Mark's interpretation; some additional Q material will come into consideration in our following discussion of Matthew, but there, too, we look to the complete First Gospel as a whole more than to the traditions behind it.

True, Mark neither provides our only nor even our earliest source for the Baptist's proclamation. I believe that the overlap between the Baptist's fuller proclamation in Matthew and Luke and the more compressed account in Mark's introduction suggests that Q included (or possibly opened with) the Baptist's proclamation, and that Mark drew on the same tradition attested in Q (or possibly on Q itself).

Yet two factors have prompted us to restrict ourselves merely to touch elements of the historical proclamation of John while actually focusing on Mark's text. First, although I am convinced that the Gospels provide a reliable account of the Baptist's proclamation, the degree of reliability remains a matter of much debate, and engaging that debate fully would take us too far afield from the purpose of this book. Second, the written Gospel of Mark provides us a complete literary tradition as a context for interpretation that John's original proclamation does not. Whereas we can reconstruct many details of John's ministry as a context for his proclamation, the context of an entire written Gospel provides us a more complete interpretive framework from an early Christian perspective. Mark is our earliest extant narrative interpreter of Jesus as the Spirit-bringer, and provides a natural exegetical starting point for the discussion.

The Holy Spirit appears rarely in Mark's Gospel, primarily in the introduction (1:8, 10, 12) and in references to power for exorcism (3:29) and prophetic inspiration, both in the OT (12:36) and among disciples (13:11). This suggests two important points for the interpreter: Mark views the Spirit as a source of empowerment for the church's mission, and Mark gives his primary lesson on pneumatology up front, in the introduction, one of the most critical sections of his Gospel. Because a proem typically introduced a writer's main themes, and because Mark has tightened the tradition we have from Q into a concise summary of John's announcement and Jesus' baptism and testing, the Spirit plays a far greater role in Mark's Gospel than a mere concordance survey might suggest.[1]

By examining several motifs introduced in Mark 1:9–11 (the baptism pericope), this chapter seeks to elucidate the significance of the Spirit in Jesus' baptism and the events surrounding it in the context of Mark's Gospel. This Spirit passage appears to foreshadow both the suffering associated with the cross and the glory associated with the resurrection, and this has important implications for Mark's picture of Jesus as miracle-worker and Son of God. Because 1:8–13 presents Jesus not only as paradigmatic for the Spirit-baptized life but as the Spirit-baptizer, what it declares concerning Jesus' mission it likewise implies for the mission of his followers.

After we have investigated the specific literary context of the pericope in the prologue, we will focus at greater length on the major events of 1:9–11 and their significance, the function of those events in the immediate and total context of Mark's Gospel, and finally, the centrality of pneumatology to these events. Mark's abbreviation of his tradition sharpens his focus on the Spirit's attestation of Jesus in this pericope. But while John's own contrast between Spirit and fire baptism in Q (see our following chapter) probably emphasized the Spirit of purification,[2] Mark emphasizes the Spirit of prophetic empowerment (12:36; 13:11). By the context of his whole Gospel, he adapts the Baptist's emphasis, probably to summon a suffering community to revitalize its commitment to witness in the face of martyrdom.

1. MARK'S INTRODUCTION AND THE BAPTISM

The Gospels give John a prominent role as a divine spokesman. As Amos suggested that God revealed his purposes in advance to his prophets (Amos 3:7), John the Baptist comes in this passage to prepare Israel for God's climactic revelation in history. Whether the introduction consists of Mark 1:1-15,[3] of 1:1-13,[4] or of 1:1-13 with 1:14-15 as transitional,[5] it clearly introduces the identity of the Gospel's main character (Jesus) in unambiguous terms for the reader,[6] underlining both his continuity and his contrast (by virtue of his radical superiority) with what has gone before.[7] An exegesis of any part of this introduction, therefore, must take into account the purpose of the whole introduction, as well as the development of this section's motifs through the rest of the Gospel.

The Baptist himself introduces and foreshadows Jesus' mission in the passage, as elsewhere in the Gospel (6:14-29; 9:12-13; 11:30).[8] Although the rivalry between the Baptist's followers and Jesus' disciples later reflected in the literature of the Johannine and Lukan communities[9] may stand behind John's sharply circumscribed literary function in this text, the account is probably condensed to fit the general style of the introduction rather than for polemical reasons.[10] In either case, however, the Evangelist clearly wished to emphasize the forerunner's emphatic recognition of his own subordination to Jesus (1:7)[11] and consequent superiority of Jesus' baptism. Various features of this narrative, such as a citation from Malachi[12] and John's garb,[13] cast John in the role of Elijah (2 Kgs 1:8 LXX), who, in various lines of Jewish expectation in this period, was to prepare the way for the end time (Mal 4:5-6).[14] At the baptism of Jesus, the time of the forerunner had given way to the time of Jesus, whose way John had come to prepare.

i. The Setting

The setting Mark portrays is significant, both in terms of his literary connections between Jesus and John and in terms of his view of salvation history. The wilderness (1:4) is so significant to John's mission that all four Gospels justify it from Scripture (Mark 1:3; Matt 3:3; Luke 3:4); some have proposed that John first applied the Isaiah text (40:3) to himself to explain his own sense of mission (John 1:23).[15] This is possible; after all, the Qumran community applied the same Isaiah text to their own mission in the wilderness (1QS 8.13–14),[16] especially to their knowledge of the law (1QS 8.15–16). Indeed, if John knew the Qumran community he must have felt that the text applied better to his own mission; whereas they separated themselves totally from Israel, he preached directly to the crowds that came to him in the wilderness (1:5).[17]

John undoubtedly found the wilderness more hospitable than society for his message. The wilderness provided fugitives with safety from a hostile society;[18] further, John could have safely drawn crowds (1:5) in the wilderness as he could have nowhere else (cf. Jos., *Ant.* 18.118), and this region provided him the most suitable location for public baptisms not sanctioned by establishment leaders (see Jos., *Ant.* 18.117).[19] Yet probably John and surely Mark and the Qumran community found in the wilderness more than merely a place of refuge or security. What John apparently shared with the Qumranites was the expectation of the wilderness as the site of God's eschatological activity.[20] Israel's prophets had promised a new exodus in the wilderness (Hos 2:14–15; Isa 40:3), and his contemporaries acknowledged this as the appropriate location not only for renewal movements[21] but for prophets and Messiahs.[22]

Most importantly for Mark, the Baptist discharges his ministry in the wilderness as a model for Jesus (1:12)[23] and probably in fulfillment of the voice of Isaiah 40:3, which has just been cited.[24] This "wilderness" is thus the ideal site for the anticipated new exodus, a hope probably intended in Isaiah 40 itself.[25] The connection with the Jordan further strengthens the salvation-historical significance of the passage.[26]

ii. John's Apparel and Diet

John's apparel not only recalls Elijah in a general way, but along with his diet it identifies him as a holy man devoted to God alone. Usually biographers described their subjects' appearance only if appropriate factors warranted; Mark's description of the Baptist is thus significant.[27] John's garment in general resembled the typical garb of the poor,[28] as would befit a wilderness prophet cut off from all society's amenities. Camels were common enough in Palestine (cf. 10:25; Matt 23:24). Yet as noted above, John's clothing specifically evokes that of the Israelite prophet Elijah, as many commentators recognize.[29] Malachi promised Elijah's return (4:5–6), a promise which subsequent Jewish tradition developed.[30] Although the Gospel writers did not regard John as Elijah *literally* (Mark 9:4; cf. Luke 1:17), they believed that John had fulfilled the prophecy of Elijah's mission (Mark 9:13; Matt 11:14–15; 17:11–13).

John's garb tells Mark's readers two things: first, their Lord Jesus arrived exactly on schedule, following the promised end-time prophet; and second, John had to be a wilderness prophet like Elijah. Although in better times true prophets could function within society (e.g., 2 Sam 12:1–25; 24:11–12), in evil times mainly corrupt prophets remained in royal courts (1 Kgs 22:6–28; cf. Matt 11:8), God's true messengers being forced into exile (1 Kgs 17:3; 18:13). Most Jews in the first century practiced their religion seriously; but the religious establishment could not accommodate a prophet like John whose lifestyle dramatically challenged the status quo, any more than most religious establishments would tolerate him today.

John's diet is significant not for what it contained but for its exclusivity. This prophet was not the only Palestinian Jew who ate locusts.[31] Honey was the regular sweetener in the Palestinian diet,[32] readily available to the poor (e.g., Judg 14:8; 1 Sam 14:25; Isa 7:22), and was widely used in the ancient Mediterranean world.[33] Domestic beekeepers produced honey (e.g., *m. B.Bat.* 5:3); John may have acquired wild honey by smoking bees out and breaking the honeycomb (cf. *m. ʿUq.* 3:11; *Šebu.* 10:7). But whereas some of John's contemporaries ate locusts as part of their diet, John seems to have eaten nothing else. The sort of pietists that lived in the wilderness and dressed simply normally ate only the kind of food that grew by itself.[34] In the wilderness, both refugees[35] and pietists with special kosher requirements[36] might subsist on locusts. By presenting John as a special holy man, Mark's tradition presents John's witness that Jesus is the harbinger of the Spirit as all the more credible.

2. THE EVENTS OF MARK 1:9–11

Although even the language of the baptism is conformed to the earlier Scripture citation,[37] scholars are generally agreed that it represents an historical event.[38] The question here is not the accuracy of the pre-Markan tradition, but how Mark interprets that tradition in the total context of Jesus' ministry for his community of faith.

Several features emphasize the importance of the event for salvation history: the rending of the heavens, the descent of the promised Spirit, and the voice from heaven all mark out this particular recipient of John's baptism as a uniquely chosen instrument of God. Not only Scripture (1:2–3) but a prophetic "voice," John (1:3), and a heavenly "voice" (1:11) attest the identity of Jesus as the Lord, Son of God, and Spirit-baptizer.[39]

i. Rending the Heavens

Since Mark 1:10 only notes that Jesus "saw" the heavens opened, it could imply that the event was perceived only by Jesus, thus preserving the messianic secret. The fact that Mark elsewhere allows Jesus to violate the secret (e.g., 5:30–34; 11:7–11), and that Jesus is as yet unknown to the crowds, do not appreciably weaken the case here, as εἶδεν must be explained. It is possible, however, that εἶδεν anticipates the eschatological ὄψεσθε of 13:26 and 14:62 (cf. 9:1), so that the Son of man's apocalyptic vindication and glory are prefigured at his baptism.

Some scholars, like Barrett, have drawn attention to apparent parallels to the opening of the heavens in *T. Levi* 18 and *T. Judah* 24,[40] but it is generally agreed that the Testaments contain Christian interpolations[41] and both texts contain elements that look suspiciously Christian.[42] While such emphasis on eschatological figures from Levi and Judah appear in clearly pre-Christian sources,[43] the conjunction of many Christian elements in the passages currently under discussion warrants severe skepticism as to whether these testaments provide adequate background for Mark's emphasis.

Several writers have pointed to biblical eschatological language for divine revelation or deliverance here (Isa 64:1 [LXX 63:19]; Ezek 1:1),[44] and this image is probably central. Similar cosmic language sometimes appears in reference to personal deliverance in biblical and extra-biblical psalms,[45] but given Mark's later predictions concerning the apocalyptic Son of man, it probably carries a broader significance here. (Although some have denied the authenticity of the Son of man sayings[46] or even affirm a Hellenistic source for the title,[47] the criterion of dissimilarity appears decisive in favor of authenticity.[48] The meaning is more problematic; some interpret the phrase as meaning, "I";[49] others take the phrase simply to mean one identified with humanity;[50] others derive an apocalyptic figure from *1 Enoch*[51] or, more safely, the suffering and reigning figure in Daniel.[52] Scholars continue to dispute such points but we nevertheless suspect that Mark's understanding of the "Son of man" is primarily an eschatological figure modeled on Daniel 7:13–14; see Mark 2:10; 13:26; 14:62.)[53]

It is also possible, as Rhoads and Michie observe, that the "ripping" of the heavens foreshadows the "ripping" of the temple curtain at Jesus' death, thus implicitly connecting the two events,[54] although this nuance may have been too subtle even for most of Mark's intended audience upon their first hearing of the Gospel.

ii. Attestation by the Heavenly Voice

It is unclear who heard the voice from heaven; many scholars think it unlikely that the crowds heard the voice here.[55] What is significant for Mark, apparently, is not whether or not the crowds have heard, for he does not bother to clarify the point either way; what is critical is that his *readers* have heard God's pronouncement.[56]

The manifestation of a "heavenly voice" may have been a familiar concept to Mark's readers even if they did not already know about the voice to Jesus at his baptism. The *bat kol,* or "daughter of a voice," is mentioned frequently in rabbinic literature[57] and has other ancient conceptual parallels that suggest its antiquity.[58] Some scholars have felt that a *bat kol* cannot be in view here, since the *bat kol* was a second-class substitute for the Spirit of prophecy,[59] but this objection is probably untenable. First of all, the *bat kol* was a heavenly voice even more than it was a substitute for prophecy; if those roles are placed in conflict by our passage, the former role must be given preeminence. But what is probably most significant in favor of interpreting the voice here as a *bat kol* is precisely the fact that this was one means of divine communication preceding the eschatological time of the Spirit. The new era had to be introduced by witnesses of the old era, such as John the Baptist or the heavenly voice. One could also produce supporting arguments of more disputable value, depending on the date of our sources and the question of how representative these samples are. Thus the *bat kol* was reported to have been active before the Spirit of prophecy departed from Israel, in a source that might have its roots in pre-70 C.E. tradition.[60] Further, it could have eschatological ramifications in some late rabbinic sources,[61] and the idea that God could even pray to himself, not foreign to Tannaitic Judaism,[62] shows that there is nothing demeaning about the heavenly voice (even if the rabbis, as one would expect, subordinated it to the halakah).

There may be a significant connection between the heavenly voice here and an earlier biblical occurrence of the voice in salvation history, particularly at the sacrifice of Isaac (Gen 22:11–12, with ἐκ τοῦ οὐρανοῦ in LXX; cf. ἐκ τῶν οὐρανῶν here). Although the often cited parallel to Jesus' baptism in the Aqedah of *T. Levi* 18[63] may be Christian interpolation[64] or may simply have been misread by R. H. Charles,[65] its allusion to Abraham and Isaac in the context of a heavenly voice (18:6) is significant whether the text is pre-Christian or dependent on the Gospels. The language of Genesis is particularly suggestive as background for the voice at Jesus' baptism given the similarity in content (see comments on the sacrificed son, below).

iii. The Reigning Son

The content of the heavenly voice is most significant, because it identifies Jesus for the reader. The use of Scripture, always regarded by the rabbis as higher than the *bat kol* but sometimes conjoined with it,[66] can only strengthen the authority of the pronouncement.

Although some have argued that an original ambiguous παῖς under-lies the present υἱός, and referred to the servant rather than to the "Son,"[67] a mistranslation from Greek to Greek is much less likely than a mistranslation from Aramaic to Greek, and it is unlikely that Mark would have deliberately toned down ambiguous servant language in his tradition in favor of "Son." While "Son" fits Mark's titles elsewhere in the Gospel,[68] it would seem uncharacteristic of him to mute an earlier tradition where it would fit his theme of suffering.[69]

A more difficult question involves the sources of the language; schol-ars have proposed specific OT allusions as background here, and often a composite citation consisting of at least two allusions. Some have objected to the use of Ps 2:7 here on the basis of a different word order in the LXX,[70] perhaps not an insignificant argument given the few words in the citation:

Mark 1:11: Σὺ εἶ ὁ υἱός μου ὁ ἀγαπητός
Ps 2:7: υἱός μου εἶ σύ

Given the possibility that υἱός was placed later to keep ὁ ἀγαπητός with ἐν σοὶ εὐδόκησα (also not from Ps 2:7), however, and the abundant use of the psalm in other strands of early Christian tradition known to us,[71] Ps 2:7 is probably in view here.[72] In keeping with its original use as an enthronement psalm,[73] early Christian writers typically employed it for Jesus' messianic exaltation after the resurrection (Acts 13:33; Heb 1:5; cf. Mark 9:7).[74] Thus at least a proleptic enthronement appears here, validated by no less an authority than God himself.[75] The "adoption" question suggested by a proleptic enthronement[76] is probably a question Mark would not have asked, since he writes in functional rather than ontological christological categories (see below). It is after his baptism that Jesus begins to fulfill his *mission* as Son of God, to be fulfilled par excellence at a future enthronement; his personal nature is a question of a different order (as Mark 12:35–37 may suggest).

iv. Suffering Servant or Sacrificed Son?

Many writers find a second biblical allusion in Mark 1:9–11: Isa 42:1,[77] which reads in the present, most common form of the LXX:

Ιακωβ ὁ παῖς μου, ἀντιλήμψομαι αὐτοῦ:
Ισραηλ ὁ ἐκλεκτός μου, προσεδέξατο αὐτὸν ἡ ψυχή μου:
ἔδωκα τὸ πνεῦμα μου ἐπ αὐτόν. . . .

Mark 1:11, however, reads:

Σὺ εἶ ὁ υἱός μου ὁ ἀγαπητός, ἐν σοὶ εὐδόκησα.

Despite the extremely common assertion that Isa 42 is present here, the differences of wording seem insurmountably great. As Morna Hooker has observed,

> The question therefore arises whether there lies behind these passages a tradition that Jesus was identified as the Servant at his Baptism, which has already by the time of Mark become so obscured that none of the key-words has remained unchanged.[78]

"Son," "beloved," and "pleasing" were all used of Israel in other contexts besides Isa 42:1.[79] Unless it was a common messianic testimonium in its Markan form, Mark's readers cannot have been expected to have recognized it.

Several lines of defense for Mark's use of Isa 42 here have been proposed. One is that Isaiah's παῖς can mean "son" as well as "servant,"[80] but as noted earlier, this argument is considerably weakened by the fact that Mark, followed by the other Synoptics (who had either some Q material or related material surrounding Jesus' baptism), uses υἱός. If Mark changed παῖς to υἱός merely to conflate two concepts, then he also carelessly obscured the concept of the παῖς. While it is not impossible that his community already thought of the baptismal proclamation as a paraphrase of Isa 42:1, such an appeal is simply a tacit admission that no support for this view may be found in Mark's text.

A perhaps stronger argument may be that of the Spirit's conferral in both Isa 42:1 and Mark 1:10–11.[81] This, too, however, falters on the broader base of OT evidence; several other Isaiah texts along with this one could have provided the concept, without any specific text being cited. Further, the Spirit's conferral was to be expected in enthronements, and pre-Markan tradition appears to have presented the baptism more in terms of a messianic enthronement than a prediction of messianic suffering. Of course, those elements identified as messianic in the servant passages were generally those not associated with suffering in rabbinic Judaism.[82]

Probably the strongest argument that can be offered is the similarity of the citation of Isa 42 in Matt 12:18, which could suggest that the passage circulated in this form in early Christian circles.[83] But Matthew shapes his texts in accordance with his narrative, as well as the reverse;[84]

for example, while he has changed Q's "finger" to "Spirit" in 12:28,[85] he probably has conformed the Isaiah quotation to the baptism, suggesting a link between the two in Matthew that need not be found in Mark.

This could bring into question the foreshadowing of suffering in Jesus' baptism. Moule seems to ignore these implications, asserting that Jesus combines the roles of Son and suffering Servant, regardless of whether Isa 42:1 is present.[86] But there is no concept of suffering associated with Ps 2:7, and if Isa 42:1 is not present, it is difficult to see the source of servant language in this passage.

Moreover, and no less fatal to the case, is the fact that an allusion to Isa 42 need not allude to the Messiah's suffering:

> It is not clear from the Markan account that at this point Jesus was conscious of being the Suffering Servant, for the words quoted are from Isa. xlii, and not liii, but it is reasonable to infer that His sense of a suffering destiny is lineally connected with the initial experience of baptism. Cf. Luke xii.50.[87]

True, the Servant Songs, at least Isa 53, were interpreted in terms of messianic suffering by the early Christian community,[88] if not by extant sources from contemporary Judaism. But Matt 12 applies Isa 42 to Jesus' exorcism ministry as much as to his nonretaliation, and there are no other indications that a reference to one passage in the Servant Songs necessarily led to passion imagery in the early church. Thus, even were Isa 42 in view in this passage, Jesus' death would not necessarily be prefigured by the divine pronouncement.

A third text, however, has received some (though less) attention in this connection, namely Gen 22:2, which reads in the most commonly used recension of the Septuagint:[89]

Καὶ εἶπεν Λαβὲ τὸν υἱόν σου τὸν ἀγαπητόν, ὃν ἠγάπησας . . .

Again, Mark 1:11 reads:

Σὺ εἶ ὁ υἱός μου ὁ ἀγαπητός, ἐν σοὶ εὐδόκησα.

Again there are differences in the texts, but they are considerably less pronounced.

Although ἀγαπητός could conceivably reflect a variant of ἐκλεκτός (cf. John 1:34, v.1.; a variation of this in the probable text of Luke 9:35),[90] the Septuagint translators sometimes use it to translate יהיד (an *only* son), including in Gen 22.[91] Jewish literature often describes Israel as God's only child, expressing the dearness of Israel to God's heart, its special uniqueness;[92] the expression "only son" often appears in the sense of "specially beloved," particularly in reference to Isaac when Abraham was called to sacrifice him.[93] Although the Aqedah, or binding of Isaac, may not have been as prominent in first-century Judaism as some have argued,[94] there is nonetheless sufficient evidence that ancient Jewish tradition continued to meditate on the biblical event.[95] If the heavenly voice alludes to any particular usage of "beloved," then, it could be to the pathos of God's call to a father to sacrifice His son:

Καὶ εἶπεν Λαβὲ τὸν υἱόν σου τὸν ἀγαπητόν, ὃν ἠγάπησας, τὸν Ισαακ ...
(Gen 22:2)

What is at least clear in Mark is that, outside the two divine annunciations of Jesus' sonship (1:11; 9:7), his sonship is defined in terms of the cross (15:39); that he is the "beloved Son" of his Father merely heightens the pathos, the nature of God's sacrifice, and the hardness of Israel (12:6–8), justifying his inevitable judgment against the temple (12:9–11; 13:2, 14). The sacrifice is also great for the Son (14:36), for his filial relationship with the Father is severed by the horrible alienation of death (15:34).

Rhoads and Michie are therefore correct in observing that while the reader recognizes Jesus as the "anointed one" and the "Son of God" right here, the *meaning* of these terms is only unfolded as the narrative progresses.[96] The reader gets the divine annunciation in 1:11, and the disciples in 9:7, after Peter's confession and Jesus' clarification. In both contexts (1:12–13, 21–28; 8:33; 9:14–29), the proleptic revelation of glory is framed by conflict with demonic forces and indications of his mission. In Mark 1, the revelation is preceded by John's prophecy concerning Jesus' first coming; the narrative in Mark 9 is introduced by Jesus' prophecy of his second coming, and John's execution becomes the clue to Jesus' own fate. The glory and the cross, like the signs and the opposition, are inseparably intertwined throughout the Gospel, and Mark would have his readers believe that a theology devoid of either one is wholly inadequate. Yet it is the suffering the disciples are loathe to recognize; the mystery of the kingdom resides in the significance of that which is yet insignificant, the eternal reality paradoxically revealed in the anvil of finite human mortality.

If the reference to either Isa 42:1 or, more likely, to Gen 22 is to be discerned by the reader, it is because the reader already presupposes that Jesus is the Servant and/or the Father's costly sacrifice. But what indications of his suffering occur in the immediate context of the baptism, if the Scripture texts alone are insufficient witness of themselves? The text seems to attribute this function to the baptism itself, a point to which we shall turn after surveying the descent of the Spirit.

v. The Descent of the Spirit

For those who thought that the Spirit of prophecy had departed, John's prophetic witness may have counted for more than the heavenly voice. But the personal descent of the Spirit on Jesus, marking him as the Spirit-bringer and hence the kingdom-bringer, is more significant still. The descent of the Spirit like a dove may be metaphorical,[97] but whether the dove is a figurative description of a visionary event, or more likely what appeared to be a literal dove yet conveyed metaphorical significance, one must consider the function of this particular image.

In the logic of this narrative as Mark's audience would have grasped it, what did God seek to convey by sending the Spirit as a dove? A connection with Aphrodite in this context is improbable,[98] and rabbinic use of the dove for God's Spirit[99] is both rare and late. The most common rabbinic use of the dove is to represent Israel,[100] and some commentators have indeed interpreted Mark as portraying Jesus as the ideal Israelite here.[101] But although it is not unreasonable to think of Jesus as Israel's representative in this passage, it is the Spirit, and not Jesus, who is portrayed as the dove. Occasionally the divine voice appears as a dove in rabbinic literature,[102] but this is not the regular use of the imagery and thus cannot be regarded as certain background here.

The possible OT imagery here is more promising. In Gen 8:8–12, which occurs in a section of Scripture that received much attention in this period,[103] the dove appears as the harbinger of the new world (cf. *4 Bar.* 7:8). This renewed creation of the Genesis narrative, structurally parallel to the first creation,[104] appears as a common prototype of the new world in other early Christian literature.[105]

All the elements of this narrative, from the event and content of the heavenly voice to the descent of the Spirit, attest Jesus as the one John the Baptist proclaimed, the harbinger of the Spirit and the coming kingdom.

3.   THE KINGDOM-BRINGER

John's promise of one who would baptize in the Spirit appears in fuller form in the Q tradition.[106] Some scholars have seen behind the Q form of the saying an original judgment oracle mentioning only wind (to blow the chaff) and fire (to burn it).[107] While the fire certainly speaks of purifying judgment, however, both fire and wind can represent the purifying spirit of Yahweh in the Hebrew Bible, and all extant streams of tradition in which John's saying occurs include the baptism in the Holy Spirit.[108] "Fire" might have also suited Mark's purpose had he known of its presence in the Q material, but a reference to a baptism "in fire" would have entailed the inclusion of the context which explained it, expanding his introduction beyond its requisite austere length.

Our primary concern here, however, is the function of the promise of Spirit baptism in Mark's narrative. This baptism oracle is pivotal, for it connects John's baptism with that of Jesus both by continuity and by contrast. Jesus himself receives John's baptism; but it is at his baptism that he is anointed with the Spirit, and thereby qualified to bestow the Spirit on others who partake of his messianic baptism into the new era.[109] While water and Spirit baptism are not synonymous, they are closely connected;[110] yet it is not water baptism, but Spirit baptism, which is here emphasized. As Robinson notes (emphasis ours), "Terminologically *it is the 'Spirit' (vv. 8, 10, 12) which gives unity to the three sections.*"[111] Not Jesus' baptism in water, but the descent of the Spirit, is of central interest,[112] for he is thereby declared to be the Spirit-anointed Messiah[113] (cf. Matt 12:18, 28), the one who will enter into conflict with Satan (1:12–13) and lead those he baptizes to do the same.

In contrast to John's completed baptism,[114] Jesus' baptism inaugurates a new age;[115] as in many sectors of ancient Judaism, the return of the Spirit was an eschatological phenomenon, as noted in our first chapter. This Spirit baptism hence defines the mission of the eschatological kingdom-bringer. As we have also noted, although the idea of purity fits best John's warnings of impending judgment and prophetic imagery of washing in the Spirit in Isaiah and Ezekiel, the prophetic element (e.g., Joel 2:28 [3:1 MT]) is very relevant for Mark. For Mark, the Holy Spirit is the Spirit of prophecy who inspires Scripture (12:36), provides power for inspired witness (13:11), and empowers God's agents for exorcism (3:23–29).

But while Jesus, the "Mighty One" John prophesied,[116] can bind the strong man and spoil his unwilling possessions (3:27; 5:3, 7), Jesus can expect only opposition from those who prefer to remain Satan's possessions and resist the Spirit (3:22–30; 4:11–12; 5:17).[117] If the Spirit leads Jesus into conflict with Satan as a result of his anointing (1:12–13), those baptized by Jesus must expect to share not only his power over evil forces but also his suffering at their hands (10:38–39).

The anointing itself, if detached from the suffering motif elsewhere in the Gospel, could be understood in terms of a proleptic resurrection story,[118] the following temptation narrative chiastically portraying the passion. But the fact of the baptism, particularly in light of its subordination in Matthew and Luke and its virtual suppression in John, is not a motif of glory like the annunciation and anointing that accompany it. As many scholars have noted (with or without reference to Isa 42 or Gen 22), this narrative prefigures both Jesus' suffering and final triumph. Thus it must prefigure the same for Jesus' followers who, like Mark's readers (probably facing severe persecution in Rome) are likewise recipients of the Spirit and sharers in Jesus' baptism.

i. The Purpose of John's Baptism

To understand John's baptism in Gospel texts, we must explore how the earliest Christian communities would have understood baptism. Although Jews in general had long used pools for ritual immersion,[119] some have suggested the immersions at the Qumran community as the specific background for John's baptism and/or Christian baptism.[120] The Covenanters were meticulous about ritual washings,[121] and apparent connections between the Baptist and the kind of Judaism depicted in the Dead Sea Scrolls[122] have led a number of scholars to connect his baptism (and early Christian baptism) with that practiced by the Qumran community.[123] But while Qumran's initiation did include an initial washing[124] and this washing was preceded by repentance,[125] this washing (like those in some pagan cults) was simply the first among many washings for a monastic community following a reformed priesthood.[126] The ritual lustrations at Qumran are, for members of the community,[127] like the common Jewish practice of *mikveh*.[128]

Proselyte baptism was important in early Jewish conversion practice, as a specific and extremely potent form of ritual purification.[129] That Gentiles should need to be purified before joining the Jewish community is not surprising. Many Jewish texts speak ill of Gentiles, who were typically seen as oppressors of God's people and transgressors of his laws;[130] these texts reflect the hostile environment in which the Jews often found themselves. In many texts, therefore, we read that the Gentiles would be damned in the eschatological time.[131] Sanders, after dividing the eschatological fate of the Gentiles in Jewish texts into six main categories,[132] observes,

> Despite this effort to rectify the balance, it should be noted that, just as the theme of the deserved punishment of Israel recedes in post-biblical literature, that of the punishment of the Gentiles increases.[133]

This is, he believes, especially true after the sufferings of 66–70 C.E.[134]

Conversely, other texts require that Gentiles be helped and greeted in the interests of peace and honoring of the Name; mistrust was not the same as grounds for cruelty or provocation.[135] In most traditions (at least those preserved among the later Hillelite majority), righteous Gentiles would be saved even without formal conversion to Judaism,[136] provided they kept the Noahide laws.[137] This did not mean, of course, that no one was attempting to convert Gentiles.[138] In some traditions, Gentiles would actually be converted wholesale by God in the eschatological time.[139]

Yet in either of the above positions, a clear line of demarcation existed between Jew and Gentile; hence symbols that communicated transformation were critical in the conversion ritual. Circumcision was the crucial sign of entering the covenant,[140] but some of those who were spreading Judaism apparently thought exceptions could be made where Judaism would be brought into more reproach if it were carried out.[141] Such exceptions were, however, undoubtedly rare.

Both circumcision and baptism would have normally been required for new converts to Judaism. Because some Tannaim in the Babylonian Gemara, R. Joshua and R. Eliezer, debated whether baptism or circumcision by themselves would suffice for a valid conversion,[142] some scholars have held that baptism was accepted without circumcision by certain authorities.[143] But it is hard to think that R. Joshua could have openly diminished the necessity of circumcision, a commandment of the Torah; thus some have preferred to follow the Palestinian recension of this tradition, in which case R. Eliezer is saying that circumcision is sufficient without immersion, and R. Joshua is arguing that both are necessary.[144] Then again, it is easy to see how the tradition would have been modified to its Palestinian form, to conform the tradition to the normative interpretation of the Torah. Either way, the Sages as a community concurred on that occasion that both circumcision and proselyte baptism were necessary, and other texts reinforce the conclusion that proselyte baptism was a necessary part of conversion.[145]

Proselyte baptism is also pre-Christian, hence suitable background for the Christian practice. Some scholars have denied this, wishing to argue for the temporal priority of Christian baptism;[146] but their position is difficult to maintain, despite the *relative* paucity of references to proselyte baptism in pre-70 Jewish traditions (which might be explained by the relative paucity of the Jewish literature from this period in general, and specifically of references to conversion in the same literature, as well as its secondary place to circumcision for males). Given its once-for-all character, John's baptism probably adapted some elements of proselyte baptism,[147] and not just the ceremonial washings exampled at Qumran;[148] and Christian baptism may thus have originated in the same place.[149]

Although rabbinic texts strictly speaking illustrate only one stream of early Judaism and depict a period later than the NT, the antiquity of Jewish proselyte baptism may be argued on several grounds:

> (1) The Hasmonaean *mikvaoth* and references to immersions in the Dead Sea Scrolls make the antiquity and widespread character of Jewish ritual cleansing obvious; and it is almost inconceivable that the transition from the most unclean state to a state of cleanness should not have been marked by such a washing.[150]

> (2) At the end of the first century, Epictetus speaks of converts to Judaism in the Diaspora being βεβαμμένου (pf. of βάπτω), as if this is well-known;[151] and Epictetus was undoubtedly not alone in this knowledge.[152]

> (3) *M. Pesaḥ.* 8:8 makes *tebillah* a matter of dispute between the first-century adherents of Beth Hillel and Beth Shammai;[153] this point is considerably weakened, of course, if proselyte baptism was not originally in view here,[154] but Tannaitic tradition in the Tosefta supports the antiquity of the proselyte baptism interpretation.[155]

> (4) Given that rabbinic Judaism was in a position of far greater power than the early Jewish Christians were, and usually ignored or condemned their teachings, it would be quite unlikely that they would have borrowed initiatory baptism from the Christians, and hardly more likely that they would have developed it and approved it on their own once it had become associated with the Jewish Christians.[156]

Other arguments, for instance that some definite symbol of transition was necessary for women converts, are less substantial but can supplement the case.

While it might be Christian anachronism to call proselyte baptism a "baptism of repentance," sincerity of heart was required in conversion for it to be valid.[157] False proselytes *might* derive *some* benefit from God,[158] but only conversions from pure motives were ultimately valid.[159] Some proselytes signified their changed allegiance by taking Jewish names.[160]

In John's preaching this baptism was associated with repentance (Mark 1:4). Repentance was an important teaching in early Judaism,[161] and when conjoined with baptism connoted sincerity of intention.[162] If John is here understood as offering a new proselyte baptism to which even Israel must submit, however, this is not mere repentance for a single act; it is the wholesale turning from a pagan way of life to an unconditional allegiance to the one true God. The eschatological warnings of John are thus a suitable preparation for the radical summons of the kingdom of God (1:15), even though only Matthew makes explicit John's preaching of the "kingdom."

ii. The Theological Significance of Jesus' Baptism

Because John's baptism was a baptism of repentance (1:4), Jesus' submission to it necessarily identified him with the company of the repentant elect.[163] That is, his baptism was intended to be vicarious in a very loose sense of that term;[164] his only apparent disclaimer to "goodness" (10:18) is intended to undermine the self-righteousness of a suppliant (10:20) and to emphasize that true devotion to the one God (10:18) is expressed in one way: radical allegiance to Jesus (10:21). Throughout Mark's Gospel, despite the repeated frailty and misunderstanding of finite disciples, Jesus' perfection remains a constant.

What narrative Mark gives us thus leaves little reason to suppose that Mark believed Jesus submitted to a baptism of repentance because he needed to repent. Rather, the pure one shared in the experience that rightly belonged to others; the πολλοί of 10:45 and 14:24 are the repeatedly erring πολλοί of the narrative (e.g., 10:48; 14:56), and this, taken together with the irony of 15:31 and other clues, suggests that Mark's Jesus was innocent and suffered on behalf of others.

Thus Jesus' baptism naturally prefigures his suffering in Mark 10:39-40, just as the cup, perhaps reminiscent of the cup of divine wrath in the biblical prophets, refers to his death in the same passage (cf. 14:25, 36; 15:23, 36).[165] That passage explicitly corrects a misunderstanding of the kingdom, and informs all would-be disciples that baptism with Mark's Jesus is a commitment to the death.

iii. Markan Christology and the Disciples' Mission

The Jesus of Mark enters into conflict with Satan in the Gospel's introduction, passing his tests and so demonstrating his Spirit-empowerment. The rest of Mark's Gospel recapitulates and develops this theme: a Spirit-empowered Jesus assaults the devil's kingdom by healing the sick and driving out demons (3:27-29), while the devil continues, behind the scenes, to strike at Jesus through the devil's religious and political agents.[166] Disciples are called to share Jesus' mission, hence both his sufferings (e.g., 8:34; 10:39-45; 13:9) and his power (4:40; 9:19, 29; 11:21-24). This proposal assumes, of course, that Mark presents Jesus' charismatic activity in a positive light, not that he uses Jesus' suffering to play it down.

In 1971 Theodore Weeden argued the view that Jesus' signs were a negative phenomenon, charging that Mark refutes a *theios anēr* Christology. In his 1979 paperback edition Weeden conceded that the category *theios anēr* might be in question, but maintained his view that the Second Gospel nevertheless polemicized against a triumphalist expectation of signs and charismatic experiences in the Markan community.[167] For Weeden, the voice at the baptism declaring Jesus as Son is inseparably connected with Jesus' role as a *theios anēr*, a divine man wonder-worker.[168] Yet he feels that the second half of the Gospel challenges this understanding of Jesus' mission actually promulgated by Mark's opponents.[169] Does the cross repudiate the charismatic view of Jesus as a wonder-worker, or does it merely qualify the character of a mission that must include suffering as well as miracles?

iv. A Divine Man?

The voice at Jesus' baptism identified him as God's Son, but divine sonship exhibited a wide range of potential nuances in antiquity. The pagan world used divine sonship in various ways,[170] and Hellenistic usage is not uniform.[171] Scholars have long sought to understand Jesus' sonship in Hellenistic categories, however,[172] including that of the *theios anēr*.[173] But it has more recently been argued that the *theios anēr* is actually a later, composite category, the basic elements of which had not yet been fused in the time of Mark:

> To call Moses a *theios anēr* because he is a miracle-working philosopher may only impede the exegesis of the texts. In Artapanus where Moses' capacity as a miracle worker is highlighted, the almost complete lack of philosophical criteria is notable. In Philo and Josephus, on the other hand, Moses is presented as the paradigm of the philosophical virtues, at the apparent expense of traditional stories about his teratological prowess.[174]

This objection does not lose its force from the later rabbinic traditions which combine miracle haggadah with the portrait of Moses as the great teacher;[175] regardless of possible Hellenistic influence, these conceptions pull together existing strands of OT and later Jewish thought rather than looking to paradigms such as Apollonius or Diogenes. Otto Betz has argued that a document rooted in Jewish faith (as early Christian documents ultimately were) should be understood first in that light:

> Was the Son of God in Mark, with the miracles which he performed, depicted essentially along Hellenistic lines? I doubt it. At this point, too, Bultmann has overestimated Hellenistic influence. Quite apart from this, the 'divine man' type seems to me to be an artificial construction, but even if such a

type did exist, the New Testament scholars should be more inclined to look back to the 'men of God' of the Old Testament.[176]

Martin Hengel likewise objects to this presupposed Hellenism on similar grounds:

> If they [Bultmann, Bousset, and others] were right [concerning the suffering and rising of the son-deity in the Mysteries affecting Christianity], then a few years after the death of Jesus an 'acute Hellenization,' or more precisely a *syncretistic paganization of primitive Christianity*, must have come about among the spiritual leaders of Jewish Christianity like Barnabas or the former scribe and Pharisee Paul. Moreover, this must have taken place either in Palestine itself or in neighboring Syria . . . It is clear that such an extraordinary historical development would have been in radical and irreconcilable contradiction to the preaching of Jesus.[177]

It is not, of course, impossible that Mark articulates his Christology partly by alluding to concepts which would be familiar in some form to his Hellenistic readers. But it cannot be forgotten that his readers knew Jesus to be Jewish, and they could be more tolerant of various widespread miracle motifs related to prophetic figures in the Septuagint than of some correlation of Jesus to their former pagan gods set in a Jewish narrative context.

v. God's Beloved Son in Mark

Others have sought the background of Mark's use of the term in ancient Jewish patterns of filial obedience[178] or special agency.[179] Although these motifs, like some associated with the *theios anēr*, have undoubtedly exerted direct or indirect influence, they are not specific enough of themselves to explain the special sonship of Jesus in the Markan text.

In Jewish literature Israel was often portrayed as a son or the sons of God.[180] Any righteous or wise man could be called God's υἱός,[181] perhaps even his μόνος υἱός,[182] in Hellenistic Jewish literature, but the language could be especially applicable to apocalyptic figures,[183] devout rabbis,[184] and wonder-workers.[185] Still, these Jewish parallels exhibit the same weakness most prominent in the Hellenistic theories of Bultmann and others. Mark does not present his readers with *a* son of God, but with *the* Son of God, his beloved, i.e. unique, Son.[186]

The most natural way to understand "Son of God," then, is in a messianic sense; the oracle of 2 Sam 7 was midrashically expanded and applied to an ultimate ruler both in some psalms of the temple cult (Pss 2, 89, 132) and by later prophets (Isa 9:6–7; etc.), and the postexilic Chronicler may idealize the reigns of David and Solomon to conform to expectations of a future Davidic kingdom. While it may be true that, apart from a florilegium from Qumran Cave 4,[187] "Son of God" was not used as a messianic title in extant Jewish materials,[188] it was a perfectly natural christological reading of the OT. Some of the deficiency in rabbinic material may be accounted for on the basis of anti-Christian polemic, as one Amoraic source may suggest:

> R. Abbahu illustrated thus: A human king may rule, but he has a father and brother; but God said: 'I am not thus; I am the first, for I have no father, and I am the last for I have no brother, and besides Me there is no God, for I have no son.'[189]

Rabbinic sources nevertheless often preserve the equivalence between the eschatological "Son of David" and the Messiah.[190]

As noted above, the thesis of a polemic against a *theios anēr* Christology which Mark supposedly includes in his Gospel only for the purpose of refuting it[191] must at the least be seriously modified;[192] but Mark's narrative modifies even the idea of a messianic Son. Far from Zealot or merely apocalyptic messianic categories, Jesus is identified with a suffering Son of man (e.g., 8:29–34). As James Robinson observed, Mark's Christology is functional:

> The present analysis has served to show that the loftiness of Jesus, although unquestioned by Mark, is not central in his presentation, which is rather concerned with Jesus' struggle, action and suffering.[193]

Indeed, for Mark, the royal Son of David (10:47–48) is actually the heavenly Lord who now hears the prayers of the church (12:35–37, with 12:29–30).[194] Jesus' sonship was demonstrated by miracle-working, as it would continue in the form of answers to prayer (e.g., 9:29; 10:51 vs. 10:36). It was also demonstrated in obedience unto death (14:36), expressions to be carried on through the witness of his followers (1:17; 3:14–15; 4:40; 6:7–13, 30, 37–41; 9:18–19; 11:22–25; etc.). And, as Kingsbury points out, the heavenly voice is God's, and the verdict must therefore be positive; Jesus is the Son of God for Mark and his community, and this has positive force.[195]

vi. Jesus the Miracle-Worker as a Paradigm

Although the Second Gospel qualifies Jesus' miracle-working mission as secondary to his passion, it never portrays the miracles themselves in a negative light. Two applications seem to flow from the narratives. First, Mark's audience could take courage from the stories of Jesus' power; not only did he invite his followers to share his sufferings, but he had power to still a storm and rebuke sickness and death in answer to pleas of faith or desperation (e.g., 1:40–42; 4:38–41; 5:23, 41–42). But second, Jesus expected his disciples to share his miracle-working power as well as his sufferings.

Thus Jesus rebukes his disciples for fearing in the midst of a storm, either expecting them to have trusted Jesus' presence to keep the boat secure, or expecting them to have stilled the storm themselves (Mark 4:38–40). The disciples rightly learned more about Jesus' identity from this event (4:41), but they still lacked faith to act in his name on their own (4:40). Thus shortly after this event they fail to recognize Jesus' supernatural knowledge (5:31). Yet Jesus authorized them to expel demons as he did, and the disciples successfully carried out this mission (6:6–13, 30) as a paradigm for later Christian evangelism (13:10). It is not too disheartening, that after sharing his power they nevertheless doubt his power to provide food for a multitude like Elisha of old (6:35–37), except that they make the same mistake twice after this, like faithless Israel in the wilderness (8:4, 16–21). The disciples' inability to expel a single demon while Jesus was away earns the title "unbelieving" (9:18–19) and a warning about their inadequate prayerfulness (9:28–29).

Finally, Jesus draws a twofold lesson from the cursing of the fig tree. Because judgment on the fruitless tree frames the temple-cleansing narrative, it undoubtedly functions in Mark's Gospel as a literary parable of impending judgment on the temple.[196] But Jesus also draws an explicit lesson for his disciples concerning the act of power: "removing mountains" was a metaphor for performing what seemed virtually impossible,[197] and he promises that even the smallest amount of faith is adequate to uproot such mountains.[198] Jesus plainly applies the lesson of the fig tree to the disciples' learning how to pray with faith (11:20–25). This pericope decisively refutes any argument suggesting that Mark opposes signs; a persecuted community needs faith all the more.[199]

But just as Jesus encountered opposition because of his miracles (3:5–6), the disciples could expect the same. Their commissioning as miracle-workers forms a brief frame around the detailed narrative of John the Baptist's execution (6:6–30), prefiguring that of Jesus, which in turn prefigures that of the disciples. As important as Jesus' miracles are to his suffering church, the cross is still more critical, and believers must share that as well (8:34); before Jesus faces his passion he warns the disciples about their cross (13:9–13; cf. 14:37–38). To "share" Jesus' baptism (10:38–39) is to share his mission: and that is to take up the cross to follow Jesus. The Spirit who enabled Jesus to expel demons also hurled Jesus (the term is ἐκβάλλει, the same word used for expelling demons) into the wilderness where he would be tested by the devil; that same Spirit empowers believers to engage the tester as Jesus did, both by signs and by suffering. In popular modern parlance, Mark might be called a charismatic posttribulationalist.

Thus, while Mark is not as explicit as Luke–Acts, he is certainly more charismatic than Weeden allows (unless he is so inept as to leave precisely the contrary impression from the one he intended). Yet his charismatic exegesis of Jesus is not born of Hellenistic mysticism, but of apocalyptic realism in a world of opposition: the kingdom is manifested in the Spirit of prophecy now, but its prophetic testimony increases the birth-pangs of the Messiah that must precede the ultimate and full revelation of the kingdom (13:7–13). Miracle-working and suffering because of the Gospel are both inseparable corollaries of union with Christ in Spirit baptism, because baptism declares both Christ's cross and his glory. Indeed, throughout Mark's Gospel miracles occur only in the context of a conflict with Satan and his religious and political agents.[200]

4. CONCLUSION

The focus of Mark's introduction is plainly christological, but this passage also provides our primary insight into Mark's view of the Spirit, first of all with reference to Jesus and secondly in the lives of those who follow him. The Spirit empowers God's servants for mission, an emphasis sharing some common elements with the early Jewish emphasis on the Spirit's empowerment of prophets; but Mark (and early Christian tradition) develop this emphasis in terms of their message of the cross (cf. 1 Cor 1:18). Mark's introduction builds three successive scenes around the work of the Spirit, laying the groundwork for the whole of his Gospel. John the Baptist announces the coming Spirit-baptizer in 1:8, the "mightier" one powerful enough even to free the devil's possessed captives (1:7; 3:27; cf. Luke 11:22). When the Spirit comes on Jesus in 1:10, he becomes the model for the Spirit-baptized life; those he later baptizes in the Spirit should follow his paradigm. When in the next pericope the Spirit thrusts Jesus into the wilderness for the devil's testing (1:12–13), we learn the purpose Mark wishes to emphasize for Spirit baptism: the Spirit equips believers to confront hostile powers as they proclaim and demonstrate the reign of God.

The pericope of Jesus' baptism introduces a tension that continues throughout Mark, and portrays the ideal disciple who is baptized in the Spirit by Jesus according to the model Jesus who is baptized in water by John. Jesus worked miracles and suffered opposition, and his witnesses are expected to do the same. Both facets of the kingdom occur in conflict with Satan and his demonic realm of sin in the present age, the tension generated by the eruption of the age to come into history. In modern terms, a Spirit-empowered disciple is to be a charismatic post-tribulationist, taking seriously Jesus' claims to a radical faith that both delivers people from the clutch of Satan's kingdom and suffers the apocalyptic pangs that are the cost of this battle. Mark is not opposed to signs, but signs must be understood in the context of mission; and the mission in which the Spirit leads the disciples must always stand under the shadow of the cross, until "the Son of man comes in glory."

NOTES
· ·

1. M. R. Mansfield, *"Spirit and Gospel" in Mark* (Peabody, Mass.: Hendrickson, 1987) 38–39, rightly follows E. F. Scott and M. D. Hooker in affirming that Mark introduces the Spirit so strongly in the prologue that the rest of the Gospel may take the Spirit for granted.

2. John's reference to "baptism" (employing a water image) may allude to OT passages emphasizing both themes (cf. Joel 2:28 [MT 3:1]; Ezek 36:25–27). Probably both nuances of "the Holy Spirit" were thus implicit in his words and understanding. But while John may not have distinguished the two, his emphasis in the "Spirit and fire" saying is undoubtedly the Spirit of purification.

3. See H. Anderson, *The Gospel of Mark* (London: Oliphants, 1976) 63–64; L. E. Keck, "The Introduction to Mark's Gospel," *NTS* 12 (1966) 352–70. J. Dewey, *Markan Public Debate* (SBLDS 48; Chico, Calif.: Scholars, 1980) 144–45, portrays 1:1–8 as a chiasm within a larger inclusio (εὐαγγέλιον) in 1:1, 15.

4. E.g., N. R. Petersen, *Literary Criticism for New Testament Critics* (Philadelphia: Fortress, 1978) 53–54; J. M. Robinson, *The Problem of History in Mark and Other Markan Studies* (Philadelphia: Fortress, 1982) 78–79.

5. J. D. Kingsbury, *The Christology of Mark's Gospel* (Philadelphia: Fortress, 1983) 50. Probably most who take the shorter introduction take 1:14–15 as transitional.

6. See D. Rhoads and D. Michie, *Mark as Story* (Philadelphia: Fortress, 1982) 40; M. D. Hooker, *The Message of Mark* (London: Epworth, 1983) 5.

7. For an explanation of the contrast, see Robinson, *Problem of History,* 70; the continuity is implied in the Isaiah prophecy, especially on the reading of E. J. Pryke, *Redactional Style in the Marcan Gospel* (Cambridge: Cambridge, 1978) 35–38, who takes ἐγένετο as copulative (p. 38).

8. For more details, see Anderson, *Mark,* 65; Robinson, *The Problem of History,* 74; W. Marxsen, *Mark the Evangelist* (Nashville: Abingdon, 1969) 33.

9. On which see R. Bultmann, *The History of the Synoptic Tradition* (rev. ed.; reprint, 1963; Peabody, Mass.: Hendrickson, 1993) 165; J. Painter, "Christology and the Fourth Gospel," *AusBR* 31 (1983) 51; M. Hengel, *The Charismatic Leader and His Followers* (New York: Crossroad, 1981) 36; for a later period, cf. J. Daniélou, *The Theology of Jewish Christianity* (London: Darton, Longman

& Todd, 1964; Chicago: Henry Regnery, 1964) 62. Some (e.g., R. Kysar, "The Contributions of the Prologue of the Gospel of John to New Testament Christology and Their Historical Setting," *CurTM* 5 [1978] 359) acknowledge the possibility but think Bultmann's claims exaggerated; others find the Baptist's function in the Fourth Gospel to be that of witness (e.g., M. D. Hooker, "John the Baptist and the Johannine Prologue," *NTS* 16 [1970] 354–58; M. Rissi, "Jn 1:1–18," *Int* 31 [1977] 398), although this role is filled by the Baptist for a reason. On Matthew's solution, cf., e.g., M. Dibelius, *Jesus* (Philadelphia: Westminster, 1949) 77.

10. Cf. E. Trocmé, *The Formation of the Gospel according to Mark* (Philadelphia: Westminster, 1975) 55, who argues that Mark condensed this material to reduce the Baptist's status to that of forerunner, though he observes later (p. 160) that the baptism was summarized like the temptation (1:12–13) and preaching (1:14–15) "in order to hasten on to the formation of the little group of disciples (1.16–20)."

11. On the sandals and the role of the slave, cf. Anderson, *Mark*, 72–73; *b. B.Bat.* 53b (by irony); Urbach, *Sages*, 1.386; D. Daube, *The New Testament and Rabbinic Judaism* (reprint, 1956; Peabody, Mass.: Hendrickson, 1994) 266; W. D. Davies, *The Sermon on the Mount* (Cambridge: Cambridge, 1966) 135. See in greater detail comments on Matthew's parallel to this passage in our next chapter. On the similarity of Matthew's variant, see the koine usage in J. H. Moulton and G. Milligan, *The Vocabulary of the Greek Testament* (Grand Rapids: Eerdmans, 1982) 106, or the Aramaic solution proposed by T. W. Manson, *The Sayings of Jesus* (London: SCM Press, 1957) 40. Although the "cultural humility" model (cf. B. J. Malina, *The New Testament World* [Atlanta: Knox, 1981] 78) may play a significant role, for Mark this announcement functions as a sort of christological confession.

12. E.g., Hurtado, *Mark*, 3.

13. Cf. Hooker, *Message of Mark*, 9; W. L. Lane, *The Gospel according to Mark* (NICNT; Grand Rapids, Mich.: Eerdmans, 1974) 51; G. E. Ladd, *A Theology of the New Testament* (Grand Rapids, Mich.: Eerdmans, 1974) 35; Hengel, *Charismatic Leader*, 36; Anderson, *Mark*, 72.

14. Later Babylonian Amoraim pictured Elijah as alive (e.g., b. Moed Katan 26a); sometimes eschatologically, sometimes in the present age, he was sent as God's messenger, often of deliverance to rabbis (*b. ᶜAbod. Zar.* 17b; *Šabb.* 33b; *Taᶜan.* 21a; *Yoma* 19b–20a; *Sanh.* 113b; *Gen. Rab.* 33:3; *Deut. Rab.* 5:15; cf. Mark 15:35), but usually as God's messenger to teach and settle halakic disputes (*b. Ber.* 3a; 35b; *B.Meṣiᶜa.* 3a; 30a; 59b; 85b; *B.Bat.* 94b; *Menaḥ.* 32a; 45a; *ᶜAbod. Zar.* 36a; *Ḥag.* 9b; *Ketub.* 106a; *Giṭ.* 42b; *Gen. Rab.* 71:9; *Song Sol. Rab.* 4:12 §5). He could fly and be ranked among the angels (*b. Ber.* 4b) and was a sudden avenger of God's honor (*b. Ber.* 6b; *Qidd.* 70a). Often he was disguised (*b. ᶜAbod. Zar.* 17b; *Gen. Rab.* 33:3), but contrast Mark 9:4. Rabbis referred to his eschatological coming; cf. the expression "until Elijah comes" (e.g., *b. Menaḥ.* 63a) and some passages above; many texts associate his future coming with the Messiah (*b. ᶜErub.* 43b; *Sukka* 52b; *Gen. Rab.* 71:9; 83:4; *Exod. Rab.* 3:4; 18:12; *Lev. Rab.* 34:8; *Deut. Rab.* 6:7; *Song Sol. Rab.* 2:13 §4; 8:9 §3; *Pesiq. Rab.* 15:14/15; 35:4). Although Babylonian Elijah material predominates, most of the eschatological material derives from Palestinian sages, but many purportedly Tannaitic materials in the later collections are too fanciful to derive from the period alleged. The Gospels may reflect earlier stages of such tradition than remain extant in most documents (outside

LXX sources like Malachi and Sirach). On Justin, *Dialogue with Trypho* 8:4, 49, cf. H. P. Schneider, "Some Reflections on the Dialogue of Justin Martyr with Trypho," *SJT* 15 (1962) 169. In general, cf. H. M. Teeple, *The Mosaic Eschatological Prophet* (JBLM 10; Philadelphia: SBL, 1957) 4–8, 106.

15. Robinson, *Problem of History*, 13.

16. Cf. W. H. Brownlee, "A Comparison of the Covenanters of the Dead Sea Scrolls with Pre-Christian Jewish Sects," *BA* 13 (1950) 71; R. E. Brown, "The Dead Sea Scrolls and the New Testament," in *John and Qumran* (ed. J. H. Charlesworth; London: Geoffrey Chapman, 1972) 4.

17. Cf. 1QS 8.13–14; 9.19–20; F. F. Bruce, "Qumrân and Early Christianity," *NTS* 2 (1956) 177; cf. C. H. H. Scobie, "John the Baptist," in *The Scrolls and Christianity* (ed. Matthew Black; London: SPCK, 1969) 68. Although Mark freely blends texts (Isa 40:3; Mal 3:1) in the standard Jewish manner, linking them by means of the common phrase, "prepare the way" (R. N. Longenecker, *Biblical Exegesis in the Apostolic Period* [Grand Rapids, Mich.: Eerdmans, 1975] 138), naming the more well-known prophet in his composite quotation, Matthew simplifies Mark's citation by including only the quotation actually from Isaiah (cf. J. Meier, *Matthew* [Wilmington, Del.: Michael Glazier, 1980] 23).

18. E.g., Heb 11:38; Rev 12:6; *Pss. Sol.* 17:17; *Song Sol. Rab.* 2:13 §4; cf. similarly prophets like Elijah (1 Kgs 17:2–6; 2 Kgs 6:1–2).

19. The location also shows John's prophetic devaluation of society's obsessions: prophets regularly abandoned societal comforts, status symbols, and even basic necessities (cf., e.g., 1 Kgs 13:8–9, 22; 20:37; Isa 20:2; Jer 15:15–18; 16:1–9; 1 Cor 4:8–13).

20. Although John was clearly not part of the Qumran community at this point—they did not accept those who differed from them in any respects (see J. Pryke, "John the Baptist and the Qumran Community," *RevQ* 4 [1964] 483–96)—evidence suggests that he baptized near them (see Jeremias, *Theology*, 43).

21. Cf. G. Theissen, *Sociology of Early Palestinian Christianity* (Philadelphia: Fortress, 1978) 48–50.

22. Matt 24:26; Acts 21:38; Jos., *Ant.* 20.189; *J.W.* 2.259, 261–62; cf. G. R. Beasley-Murray, *A Commentary on Mark Thirteen* (London: Macmillan, 1957) 84.

23. Cf. the parallels (and differences) in W. H. Kelber, *Mark's Story of Jesus* (Philadelphia: Fortress, 1979) 17; U. Mauser, *Christ in the Wilderness* (SBT 39; London: SCM, 1963) 90.

24. See Bultmann, *History*, 246; Robinson, *Problem of History*, 73; Anderson, *Mark*, 69; Marxsen, *Mark the Evangelist*, 37.

25. Kingsbury, *Christology of Mark's Gospel*, 59; cf. the new exodus language in Isaiah ("way" through the "wilderness" and other recurrent motifs, also found in Hosea and Jeremiah: cf. Isa 12:2 with Exod 15:2; Isa 35:10; 45:13; 49:11–12; 51:9–11; Hos 2:14–15; 11:1–5, 10–11; 12:9), and various modern treatments, such as T. F. Glasson, *Moses in the Fourth Gospel* (Naperville, Ill.: Allenson, 1963) 15–19; D. Daube, *The Exodus Pattern in the Bible* (London: Faber & Faber, 1963), particularly 11–12; R. R. De Ridder, *Discipling the Nations* (Grand Rapids, Mich.: Baker, 1971) 36ff. (briefly mentioned, e.g., D. A. Hagner, *Hebrews* [NIBC; Peabody, Mass.: Hendrickson, 1990] 65). In the Scrolls, cf. CD 5.19; 7.21; T. H. Gaster, *The Dead Sea Scriptures* (Garden City, N.Y.: Doubleday, 1976) 327–28; in rabbinic texts, cf. *b. Ber.* 12b (Ben Zoma and "the Sages"); *Exod. Rab.* 2:6; *Lev. Rab.* 27:4; *Pesiq.*

Rab. 31:10; cf. Bonsirven, *Judaism,* 202; cf. R. N. Longenecker, *The Christology of Early Jewish Christianity* (London: SCM, 1970) 39–40.

26. See Rhoads and Michie, *Mark as Story,* 65; Kingsbury, *Christology of Mark's Gospel,* 59; Robinson, *Problem of History,* 73; Larry Hurtado, *Mark* (San Francisco: Harper & Row, 1983) 9.

27. J. Drury, *Tradition and Design in Luke's Gospel* (London: Darton, Longman & Todd, 1976) 29. Some material in this section also appears in my forthcoming commentaries on Matthew.

28. G. E. Wright, *Biblical Archaeology* (Philadelphia: Westminster, 1962) 191–92.

29. The Synoptic miracle traditions and passages like Luke 9:61–62 (cf. 1 Kgs 19:20; Luke 10:4 with 2 Kgs 4:29) transferred some Elijah images to Jesus, but for Jesus these were inadequate (cf. Luke 9:8, 19–20, 33–35). The antiquity of the eschatological Elijah tradition is guaranteed, though scholars still dispute the antiquity of his messianic forerunner role: e.g., C. Milikowsky, " 'lyhw whsyh (Elijah and the Messiah)," *JSJT* 2 (1982–83) 491–96; Schneider, "Reflections," p. 169; M. M. Faierstein, "Why Do the Scribes Say That Elijah Must Come First?" *JBL* 100 (1981) 86; J. A. Fitzmyer, "More about Elijah Coming First," *JBL* 104 (2, 1985) 295–96; D. C. Allison, "Elijah Must Come First," *JBL* 103 (1984) 256–58. The Gospels' "honey" probably refers to bee-honey rather than the more obscure vegetable "honey" suggested by A. B. Bruce, "The Gospel according to Matthew," in *The Expositor's Greek Testament* (Grand Rapids, Mich.: Eerdmans, 1979) 1.80 (cf. C. H. Kraeling, *John the Baptist* [New York: Scribner's, 1951] 195 n. 11; or date honey in Jos., *J.W.* 4.468–69); the spiritual honey of *Jos. and Asen.* 16.14/7–8 is also irrelevant.

30. E.g., Sir 48:10; cf. 4 Ezra 6:26; *ṭos. ʾEd.* 3:4; *Sipre Deut.* 41.4.3; 342.5.2; see Howard M. Teeple, *The Mosaic Eschatological Prophet* (JBLMS 10; Philadelphia: Society of Biblical Literature, 1957) 4–8; W. L. Lane, *The Gospel according to Mark* (NICNT; Grand Rapids, Mich.: Eerdmans, 1974) 324.

31. See Bruce, "Matthew," 80; A. W. Argyle, *The Gospel according to Matthew* (Cambridge: Cambridge, 1963) 36.

32. E.g., Exod 3:8; 13:5; Prov 24:13; 25:16, 27; *Jub.* 1:7; Sir 11:3; 24:20; *t. B.Bat.* 1:9; *Bek.* 1:8.

33. E.g., Petr., *Sat.* 38; Cary and Haarhoff, *Life and Thought,* 112.

34. 2 Macc 5:27; Jos., *Life* 11.

35. E.g., *Qoh. Rab.* 10:8 §1.

36. E.g., CD 12.14; 11QTemple 48.1–5; cf. S. L. Davies, "John the Baptist and Essene Kashruth," *NTS* 29 (1983) 569–71.

37. Robinson, *Problem of History,* 73–74: it is "proclaimed." His attempt to elucidate Gnostic "parallels," however (pp. 29–39), seems misguided; cf. D. O. Via, *Kerygma and Comedy in the New Testament* (Philadelphia: Fortress, 1975) 86–87.

38. Jeremias, *Theology,* 45; J. R. Michaels, *Servant and Son* (Atlanta: John Knox, 1981) 25; E. Schweizer, *The Good News according to Mark* (Atlanta: John Knox, 1970) 37; cf. V. Taylor, *The Gospel according to St. Mark* (2d ed.; London: Macmillan, 1966) 158. Of course, this does not deny the presence of interpretive elements (Anderson, *Mark,* 23, 75; Bultmann, *History,* 247, cf. p. 253). Marxsen (*Mark the Evangelist,* 58) naturally points out the emphasis on Galilee in 1:9. (This emphasis appears to be significant regardless of the provenance he defends; for

a Galilean provenance, cf. Marxsen, *Mark*, 66; cf. especially L. D. Vander Broek, *The Markan Sitz im Leben* [Ph.D. diss., Drew University, 1983; Ann Arbor, Mich.: University Microfilms International, 1983]; against a Galilean provenance, cf. Anderson, *Mark*, 28–29. For a Roman provenance, see Ernest Best, *Mark: The Gospel as Story* [Edinburgh: Clark, 1983] 35–36; against Vander Broek, *Sitz im Leben*, 8–12.) Taylor, *Mark*, 159, points to "in those days" as editorial, although he does not give the phrase eschatological significance as does J. D. Kingsbury, *Matthew: Structure, Christology, Kingdom* (Philadelphia: Fortress, 1975) 30, in Matt 3:1.

39. The heavenly voice alone would have been inadequate, for Jewish tradition that commented on it allowed that it testified of others as well (e.g., *Sipre Deut.* 357.10.3; *b. B.Bat.* 58a; *Ketub.* 104a; *Soṭa* 21a; *p. ʿAbod. Zar.* 3:1 §2; *Hor.* 3:5 §3; *Soṭa* 9:16 §2; *Pesiq. Rab Kah.* 9:2) and that it remained subordinate to Scripture (*b. Ḥul.* 44a=*Pesaḥ.* 114a; *p. Moʿed Qat.* 3:1 §6), but here it confirms the witness of Scripture and a prophet. Jesus is not a mere prophet but the subject of other prophets' messages.

40. *The Holy Spirit and the Gospel Tradition*, 43–44, following Charles in thinking these are not interpolations.

41. J. H. Charlesworth, "Christian and Jewish Self-Definition in Light of the Christian Additions to the Apocryphal Writings," in *Jewish and Christian Self-Definition* (Philadelphia: Fortress, 1980–82) 2.35–41; id., *The Old Testament Pseudepigrapha and the New Testament* (SNTSMS 54; Cambridge: Cambridge, 1985) 38–39, 99; id., *The Pseudepigrapha and Modern Research with a Supplement* (SBLSCS 7–S; Missoula, Mont.: Scholars Press, 1981) 211–13; cf. Dupont-Sommer, *Essene Writings*, 303; Daniélou, *Theology*, 14 (Jewish-Christian work using several earlier Testaments); Rost, *Judaism*, 144–45; cf. very early dating in E. J. Bickerman, "The Date of the Testaments of the Twelve Patriarchs," *JBL* 69 (1950) 245–60. For relationship with the Scrolls (if any), cf. F. M. Cross, *The Ancient Library of Qumran & Modern Biblical Studies* (rev. ed.; Grand Rapids, Mich.: Eerdmans, 1980) 44; C. Rabin, "The 'Teacher of Righteousness' in the 'Testaments of the Twelve Patriarchs'?" *JJS* 3 (1952) 127–28; P. Grelot, "Notes sur le Testament araméen de Lévi," *RB* 63 (1956) 391–406; id., "Le Testament araméen de Lévi est-il traduit de l'hébreu?" *REJ* 114 (1955) 91–99; J. T. Milik, "Le Testament de Lévi en araméen," *RB* 62 (1955) 398–406, although, given the widespread nature of the testamentary genre, the Testaments as a whole could be independent from the Qumran patriarchal testaments and yet be early. Jeremias, *Theology*, 50, thinks *T. Levi* 18:6–7 and *T. Judah* 24:2–3 probably use Jewish-Christian traditions about Jesus' baptism.

42. Compare the preceding note; note particularly the conjunction of the same motifs in *T. Levi* that occur in Jesus' baptism, though the same motifs are rarely even coupled in other ancient Jewish literature, suggesting dependence in one direction or the other.

43. The blessings on Levi (31:12–17) and Judah (31:18–20) may be stressed in *Jubilees* because only those two tribes still had viable identities in the author's day. Longenecker (*Christology*, 114) regards *Jubilees* as proto-Essene and sees the Levitical emphasis as preliminary to the two messiahs of 1QS, though later Qumran literature toned it down to one figure. But cf. B. Noack, "Qumran and the Book of Jubilees," *SEÅ* 22–23 (1957–58) 201; R. H. Charles, *The Book of Jubilees* (London: Black, 1902) xiv. At any rate, even in the period when Qumran stressed

only a single messiah (if that was not throughout its history), it was the messiah "of Aaron and of Israel," suggesting a continuing eschatological role for Levi.

44. E.g., Kingsbury, *Christology of Mark's Gospel*, 64; Hooker, *Message of Mark*, 11; Schweizer, *Mark*, 37. Cf. *Jos. and Asen.* 14:2/3; John 1:51; Rev 4:1; 11:19; 15:5; 19:11.

45. See Ps 18:7–16 in context and some of the Qumran hymns. Perhaps this explains the curious figure of 1QH 3, who is sometimes portrayed in possibly or probably messianic terms (J. Baumgarten and M. Mansoor, "Studies in the New *Hodayot* [Thanksgiving Hymns]—II," *JBL* 74 [1955] 188; R. Gordis, "The 'Begotten' Messiah in the Qumran Scrolls," *VT* 7 [1957] 191–94; R. E. Brown, "The Messianism of Qumran," *CBQ* 19 [1955] 66–72), sometimes the opposite (L. H. Silberman, "Language and Structure in the Hodayot [1QH 3]," *JBL* 75 [1956] 96–106; critiqued by W. H. Brownlee, "Messianic Motifs of Qumran and the NT, II," *NTS* 3 [1956–57] 209–10). The most natural reading to me seems to be a use of eschatological messianic woes language for the sufferings of the psalmist.

46. E.g., J. R. Donahue, *Are You the Christ?* (SBLDS 10; Missoula, Mont.: SBL, 1973) 184–85; cf. A. J. B. Higgins, *Jesus and the Son of Man* (Philadelphia: Fortress, 1964), denying the earthly Son of man sayings (118) and suggesting that Jesus referred to a heavenly advocate, not himself (193).

47. The obvious Aramaism refutes a Hellenistic reading (*pace* W. O. Walker, Jr., "The Origin of the Son of Man Concept as Applied to Jesus," *JBL* 91 [1972] 482–90, and in *The Bible in Its Literary Milieu* [ed. V.L. Tollers and J. R. Maier; Grand Rapids, Mich.: Eerdmans, 1979] 156–65; Dibelius, *Jesus*, 47). Even Koester, who thinks early Christian prophets connected Jesus and the Son of man without identifying the two, recognizes the phrase's derivation from an Aramaic source (*Introduction*, 2.88–89).

48. Cf. Jeremias, *Theology*, 275–76; I. H. Marshall, "The Synoptic Son of Man Sayings in Recent Discussion," *NTS* 12 (1966) 327–51; B. Gerhardsson, *The Origins of the Gospel Traditions* (Philadelphia: Fortress, 1979) 57; R. T. France, "The Authenticity of the Sayings of Jesus," in *History, Criticism, & Faith* (ed. Colin Brown; Downers Grove, Ill.: InterVarsity, 1976) 113; H. Riesenfeld, *The Gospel Tradition* (Philadelphia: Fortress, 1970) 14; W. G. Kümmel, *The Theology of The New Testament* (Nashville: Abingdon Press, 1973) 106; H. Riesenfeld, "The Mythological Background of New Testament Christology," in *The Background of the New Testament and Its Eschatology* (Cambridge: Cambridge, 1964) 94–95. For a similar suggested Matthean usage for suffering representative/example for God's people, cf. M. Pamment, "The Son of Man in the First Gospel," *NTS* 29 (1983) 116–29.

49. E.g., Lane, *Mark*, 297, following Vermes; contrast Jeremias, *Theology*, 261, n. 1.

50. R. Leivestad, "Exit the Apocalyptic Son of Man," *NTS* 18 (1972) 243–67; contrast B. Lindars, "Re-Enter the Apocalyptic Son of Man," *NTS* 22 (1975) 52–72. For ideas of the representative man in certain contexts, O. Cullmann, *The Christology of the New Testament* (Philadelphia: Westminster, 1963) 138–41; C. G. Montefiore, *The Synoptic Gospels* (New York: KTAV,1968) 1.44; cf. 1.65).

51. Scholars dispute whether the Son of man in *Enoch*'s Similitudes (e.g., 46:3; 48:2–6, 10; 69:26–29) is pre-Christian (T. F. Glasson, "The Son of Man Imagery: Enoch XIV and Daniel VII," *NTS* 23 [1976] 82–90) or not (G. Vermes, *Jesus and the World of Judaism* [Philadelphia: Fortress, 1984] 89–99), and wheth-

er the Son of man is preexistent and heavenly (e.g., Bright, *History*, 457) or merely a messianic figure of some sort (e.g., Sandmel, *Judaism*, 88–89; Bonsirven, *Judaism*, 189); or even alludes to Enoch in some way (cf. Charlesworth, *New Testament*, 18, 88–89; R. G. Hamerton-Kelly, *Pre-Existence, Wisdom, and the Son* [Cambridge: Cambridge, 1973] 41). Such questions if unanswered may make a NT derivation from *1 Enoch* (e.g., F. C. Burkitt, *The Earliest Sources for the Life of Jesus* [Boston: Houghton Mifflin, 1910] 66ff.; Ladd, *Theology*, 145–58) problematic.

52. Daniel seems to provide some chronologically safer and no less plausible connections than the Similitudes (Hooker, *Message*, 71–72; E. Lohse, *Mark's Witness to Jesus Christ* [New York: Association, 1955] 44; T. W. Manson, *The Servant-Messiah* [Cambridge: Cambridge, 1961] 72–74; see especially Longenecker, *Christology*, 82–92).

53. At this point Justin, *Dialogue with Trypho* 31–32, might preserve a reliable tradition concerning a Jewish view (cf. L. V. Barnard, *Justin Martyr* [Cambridge: Cambridge, 1967] 48; id., "The Old Testament and Judaism in the Writings of Justin Martyr," *VT* 14 [1964] 404; W. A. Shotwell, *The Biblical Exegesis of Justin Martyr* [London: SPCK, 1965] 73; though cf. A. J. B. Higgins, "Jewish Messianic Belief in Justin Martyr's *Dialogue with Trypho*," *NovT* 9 [1967] 301–2). For other notes on rabbinic discussions, see Moore, *Judaism*, 2.335–37; W. Bousset, *Kyrios Christos* (Nashville: Abingdon, 1970) 53 (using only late sources); cf. E. Stauffer, *Jesus and His Story* (New York: Knopf, 1960) 163.

54. See Rhoads and Michie, *Mark as Story*, 46. I had previously noticed but subsequently dismissed the same connection independently; the strength of the connection rests on the thesis that the passion is central and thus proleptically prefigured repeatedly throughout the Gospel.

55. Anderson, *Mark*, 75; Kelber, *Mark's Story*, 18–19; Hooker, *Message of Mark*, 13; Robinson, *Problem of History*, 81; Kingsbury, *Matthew*, 14 (on Matthew's account!). C. E. B. Cranfield, "The Baptism of our Lord—a Study of St. Mark 1.9–11," *SJT* 8 (1955) 58, argues that it was a vision but a real communication to Jesus; Bultmann, *History*, 248, thinks it describes an objective happening as in Matthew and Luke, because it is a faith legend.

56. Cf. Q. Quesnell, *The Mind of Mark* (AnBib 38; Rome: Pontifical Biblical Institute, 1969) 132.

57. E.g., *b. B.Bat.* 58a; 73b; 85b; *Mak.* 23b (R. Eleazar); *Ḥul.* 44a (R. Joshua, but later tradition); *Ketub.* 104a (Judah ha-Nasi, but later tradition); *Soṭa* 21a (Hillel the Elder, but later tradition); *ʿErub.* 54b; *Šabb.* 33b (R. Simeon b. Yohai, but later); 88a (R. Eleazar); *Pesaḥ.* 114a (= *Ḥul.* 44a); *Lev. Rab.* 19:5–6; *Lam. Rab.* 1:16 §50; *Ruth Rab.* 6:4; *Qoh. Rab.* 7:12 §1 (R. Nehemiah, but may be later); *Song Sol. Rab.* 8:9 §3 (speaking of early times but very anachronistic); cf. Urbach, *Sages*, 1.579; Sandmel, *Judaism*, 175; Barrett, *Spirit*, 39–40; F. F. Bruce, *New Testament History* (Garden City, N.Y.: Doubleday, 1972) 168 n. 20. On this passage, cf. Trocmé, *Formation of Mark*, 57 n. 1.

58. E.g., Jos., *Ant.* 13.282–83 (cf. *Song Sol. Rab.* 8:9 §3); Artapanus in Eusebius, *Praeparatio Evangelica* 9.27.36; Plut., *Isis* 12, *Moralia* 355E; *Mart. Pol.* 9; cf. N. B. Johnson, *Prayer in the Apocrypha and Pseudepigrapha* (JBLM 2 (Philadelphia: SBL, 1948) 62–63.

59. Hooker, *Message of Mark*, 12–13.

60. The tradition in *b. Pesaḥ* 94a; *b. Ḥag.* 13a, is attributed to R. Johanan ben Zakkai (though it could be argued that Johanan assumes that the Spirit had

ceased functioning temporarily because the temple was destroyed in Nebuchad-nezzar's time, the period of which he spoke, this is unlikely: the prophets were still active); cf. similarly R. Isaac in *b. Sanh.* 39b.

61. E.g., *Lev. Rab.* 27:2 (R. Jeremiah b. R. Eleazar).

62. R. Jose b. Halafta (ca. 150 C.E.) as cited in Bonsirven, *Judaism,* 5.

63. Longenecker, *Christology,* 115 (though noting that this could be Jewish-Christian interpolation and redaction); cf. B. Gärtner, *The Temple and the Community in Qumran and the New Testament* (Cambridge: Cambridge, 1965) 117.

64. E.g., Schweizer, *Mark,* 38.

65. M. Black, "The Messiah in the Testament of Levi XVIII," *ExpT* 60 (1948–49) 321–22; cf. *OTP* 1.795 (tr. H. C. Kee), regarding only "in the water" as an interpolation.

66. E.g., *b. Yoma* 22b; conversely, cf. *b. Sanh.* 104b (late).

67. The arguments for this position are summarized in I. H. Marshall, "Son of God or Servant of Yahweh? A Reconsideration of Mark i.11," *NTS* 15 (1969) 327; Marshall argues, 327–32, that υἱός is original.

68. See especially Kingsbury, *Christology of Mark's Gospel,* passim.

69. One may note, for example, the probable use of Isa 53 in Mark 10:45 (*pace* Anderson, *Mark,* 257; Hooker, *Message of Mark,* 93; id., *Jesus and the Servant* [London: SPCK, 1959] 74–79 [she does allow general OT influence]). See W. J. Moulder, "The OT Background and the Interpretation of Mark X.45," *NTS* 24 (1977) 127 (Luke 22:27 as Jesus' most explicit reference to himself as Servant); Jeremias, *Theology,* 293–94; V.Taylor, *The Atonement in New Testament Teaching* (London: Epworth, 1945) 14; Higgins, *Son,* 43–44; note especially the Semitic formulation of the saying and its unique parallels with Isa 53. The scarcity of Jesus' teaching on such vicarious atonement is not a necessary argument against its authenticity; see M. Hengel, *The Atonement* (Philadelphia: Fortress, 1981) 34. R. Bultmann, *Jesus and the Word* (New York: Scribner's, 1958) 214, speaks of this as "a Hellenistic variation of an older saying" preserved in Luke 22:27; J. Jeremias, *The Central Message of the New Testament* (New York: Scribner's, 1965) 46, says Luke 22:27 is the hellenized version, with Matthew and Mark retaining a very Semitic form of the saying!

70. Cranfield, "Baptism," 61.

71. On Acts 13:32–33 (interpreting the psalm concerning Jesus' resurrection/enthronement), cf. N. A. Dahl, "The Story of Abraham in Luke–Acts," e.g., in *Studies in Luke–Acts* (ed. L. E. Keck and J. L. Martyn; Nashville: Abingdon, 1966) 148; M. D. Goulder, *Type and History in Acts* (London: SPCK, 1964) 53; M. Hengel, *The Son of God* (Philadelphia: Fortress, 1976) 23; cf. R. J. Bauckham, *Jude, 2 Peter* (Waco, Tex.: Word, 1983) 219 (noting messianic usage, with references, especially to Lövestam); on Heb 1:5, see Longenecker, *Exegesis,* 177. Lindars, *Apologetic,* 211, appears to me to be mistaken when he emphasizes the metaphysical as over against the resurrection interpretation of Heb 1:5. Psalms 2:7–8 and 110:1 are also linked in 1 Clem. 36, but Clement is probably dependent on Hebrews here, citing Heb 1:3–4 and then Ps 104:4 (Heb 1:7).

72. E.g., Marshall, "Son or Servant?" 332–33; but this is the view of nearly all the commentators below (Mansfield, *Spirit and Gospel,* 27, is an exception).

73. See Bright, *History of Israel,* 225–26; W. Harrelson, *From Fertility Cult to Worship* (Garden City, N.Y.: Doubleday, 1969) 86–87. However the psalm was originally applied, it was widely regarded as messianic in later Judaism (e.g.,

b. *Sukka* 52a; Longenecker, *Christology,* 113). Cf. R. de Vaux, *Ancient Israel* (New York: McGraw-Hill, 1961) 109, for comparison with ancient coronations; much of the language of the psalm can be compared with royal boasts and coronations in *ANET.*

74. See D.-J. Kim, "Mark—a Theologian of Resurrection" (Ph.D. diss., Drew University, 1978) 92.

75. Kingsbury, *Christology of Mark's Gospel,* 66.

76. Rhoads and Michie, *Mark as Story,* 105; Dunn, *Jesus and Spirit,* 65–66; contrast Cranfield, "Baptism," 61–62; Menzies, *Pneumatology,* 152–53; cf. W. Wrede, *The Messianic Secret* (Cambridge: Clarke, 1971) 224–25 (a baptism initiating Jesus' ontological messiahship but awaiting the resurrection for its accompanying dignity would be possible, but it is unlikely that Jesus is "Son" at the baptism only proleptically).

77. Marshall, "Son or Servant," 335; Jeremias, *Theology,* 53–54; Kingsbury, *Christology of Mark's Gospel,* 40, 65; Bruce, *History,* 168; Schweizer, *Mark,* 37; J. A. T. Robinson, *Twelve New Testament Studies* (London: SCM Press, 1962) 162; Taylor, *Mark,* 162 (with Isa 44:2). We do not here contest the possibility of influence by the language ("echoes": Robinson, Taylor), but only that the phrasing is intended to evoke the picture of the Servant which appears to be clearer later in Mark.

78. *Servant,* 72; cf. Anderson, *Mark,* 79–80. The Servant tradition appears to have been predominantly non-messianic in pre-Christian Judaism (L. Goppelt, *Jesus, Paul, and Judaism* [New York: Nelson, 1964] 83; Hooker, *Servant,* 47 [on Isa 53, but her argument is essentially that the prophet would not have introduced new ideas, an argument I do not find persuasive]; cf. R. Simlai in W. D. Davies, *The Gospel and the Land* [Berkeley: University of California, 1974] 60, who takes the Servant as Moses; but Simlai is third century C.E.). Others, however, have contended for a pre-Christian messianic Servant tradition: W. Zimmerli and J. Jeremias, *The Servant of God* (Naperville, Ill.: Allenson, 1957) 57ff.; H. J. Schoeps, *Paul* (Philadelphia: Westminster, 1961) 134–35, 139; J. N. D. Kelly, *A Commentary on the Epistles of Peter and Jude* (BNTC 17; reprint, 1969; Peabody, Mass.: Hendrickson, 1993) 126 (following *TWNT,* but noting that sufferings were missing for the messianic Servant). J. W. Doeve, *Jewish Hermeneutics in the Synoptic Gospels and Acts* (Assen: Van Gorcum, 1954) 147–48, demonstrates how rabbinic exegetical methods would naturally connect Isa 53 with Dan 7:13ff. (though it should be noted that the rabbis could justify anything exegetically if it accorded with tradition). Some have thought that Qumran's Teacher of Righteousness is described in terms of Isaiah's Servant Songs (Brownlee, "Motifs," 18–20; Dupont-Sommer, *Essene Writings,* 361–63). Justin Martyr, *Dialogue with Trypho* 13, 43 (on which cf. E. F. Osborn, *Justin Martyr* [Tübingen: Mohr, 1973] 103), attests Christian rather than Jewish usage. Sirach 1:6 LXX shares ῥίζα and ἀπεκαλύφθη with Isa 53:1–2 LXX, which could interpret the Servant as personified wisdom, but the source is probably Prov 8:1, etc. *Pesiq. Rab.* 31:10 and the *Kabbalah* (C. D. Ginsburg, *The Kabbalah* [London: Routledge and Kegan Paul, 1955] 141–42) are too late to be of value. Zimmerli and Jeremias, *Servant,* 70–71, are probably correct that anti-Christian polemic toned down messianic associations, but there are still severe limitations in our evidence. Also on this targum, see F. F. Bruce, *The Acts of the Apostles: The Greek Text* (Grand Rapids, Mich.: Eerdmans, 1951) 193; E. M. Yamauchi, "Concord, Conflict, and Community," in

Evangelicals and Jews in Conversation (ed. M. H. Tannenbaum, M. R. Wilson, and J. A. Rudin; Grand Rapids, Mich.: Baker, 1978) 165–66; and Zimmerli and Jeremias, *Servant*, loc. cit.

79. Hooker, *Servant*, 72–73.

80. Schweizer, *Mark*, 38.

81. Ibid.

82. See note 78 above, especially the last lines about the targum. But, given the polemic in which the rabbis were engaged by the *minim* (usually though not exclusively Jewish Christians in earlier rabbinic sources), it is difficult to say to what extent our rabbinic sources accurately reflect the pre-Christian situation.

83. Schweizer, *Mark*, 37–38.

84. Matthew's infancy narratives are one case in point; cf. George M. Soares Prabhu, *The Formula Quotations in the Infancy Narrative of Matthew: An Enquiry into the Tradition History of Mt 1–2* (Rome: Biblical Institute Press, 1976).

85. *Pace* C. S. Rodd, "Spirit or Finger," *ExpT* 72 (1961) 157–58. Matthew changes the more Semitic "finger" to fit his own context, perhaps as midrash on Isa 42 just cited; Luke includes the Spirit whenever he can, suggesting it was there missing from his source (cf. also E. Schweizer, *The Good News according to Matthew* [Atlanta: Knox, 1975] 287; R. H. Gundry, *Matthew* [Grand Rapids, Mich.: Eerdmans, 1982] 235).

86. *The Gospel according to Mark* (Cambridge: Cambridge, 1965) 12. Marshall, "Son or Servant?" 326–27, provides the history of linking of Isa 42 and Ps 2:7 in Mark 1:11.

87. Taylor, *Mark*, 618–19.

88. Jeremias, in Zimmerli and Jeremias, *Servant*, 93; E. Schweizer, "The Son of Man Again," *NTS* 9 (1963) 257; V. Taylor, "The Origin of the Markan Passion-Sayings," *NTS* 1 (1955) 159–67.

89. See Best, *Mark as Story*, 81; Marshall, "Son or Servant?" 335 (probably); Kingsbury, *Christology of Mark's Gospel*, 65 (probably); Taylor, *Mark*, 162 (echoes).

90. Cf. Marshall, "Son or Servant?" 328.

91. C. H. Dodd, *The Parables of the Kingdom* (London: Nisbet & Company, 1936) 130 n. 1; Ladd, *Theology*, 164; Schweizer, *Mark*, 41.

92. *Exod. Rab.* 52:5 (possibly Tannaitic: attributed to Simeon b. Yohai); *Lev. Rab.* 2:5 (Simeon b. Yohai); *Song Sol. Rab.* 2:1 §1; 2:14 §2; 3:11 §2; 5:16 §3 (naturally predominates in *Song Sol. Rab.*); *Jub.* 31:15, 20; cf. 19:27.

93. E.g., *Gen. Rab.* 55:7 (Freedman and Simon): " 'THY SON.' 'Which son?' he [Abraham] asked. 'THINE ONLY SON,' replied He. 'But each is the only one of his mother?'—'WHOM THOU LOVEST.' " He loved them both, so God specified Isaac. Cf. *Gen. Rab.* 59:9 (Isaac is "the beloved one of the world"); *Pes. Rab.* 40:6 (= *Gen. Rab.* 55:7); *T. Abr.* 7, 8A; thus μονογενής in Jos., *Ant.* 1.222, is the beloved Isaac. See further Th. C. De Kruijf, "The Glory of the Only Son (John i 14)," in *Studies in John* (ed. W. C. van Unnik; NovTSup 24; Leiden: Brill, 1970) 123; R. L. Roberts, "The Rendering 'Only Begotten' in John 3:16," *ResQ* 16 (1973) 7, 13; I. J. Du Plessis, "Christ as the 'Only begotten,' " *Neot* 2 (1968) 22, 29; cf. also some of the commentaries on John (e.g., J. H. Bernard, *A Critical and Exegetical Commentary on the Gospel according to St. John* [2 vols.; ICC; Edinburgh: T. & T. Clark, 1928] 1.23–24; E. C. Hoskyns, *The Fourth Gospel* [2d rev. ed.; ed. F. N. Davey; London: Faber & Faber, 1947] 149). Cf. *b. Pesaḥ.* 118a; *Gen. Rab.* 98:13;

Song Sol. Rab. 1:9 §2, where God is "The Unique One of the World" (cf. *Num. Rab.* 10:5; also C. G. Montefiore and H. Loewe, *A Rabbinic Anthology* [New York: Schocken, 1974] 150 §408).

94. See E. P. Sanders, *Paul and Palestinian Judaism* (Philadelphia: Fortress, 1977) 28–29.

95. In the literature, e.g., *Jub.* 18:13 (going beyond Genesis in connecting it with Mount Zion); later traditions in *Gen. Rab.* 56:4 (Samael tried to prevent it); 56:8 (Isaac wanted to be bound); *Exod. Rab.* 15:11 (connected with Israel's redemption); *Pes. Rab.* 40:6 (Abraham rejoiced to bind Isaac, Isaac rejoiced to have his throat cut, etc.); cf. Longenecker, *Christology*, 115; Urbach, *Sages*, 1.502–7; Goodenough, *Symbols*, 9.71–77, for Jewish art; E. Best, *The Temptation and the Passion* (SNTSMS 2; Cambridge: Cambridge, 1965) 171; J. Swetnam, *Jesus and Isaac* (AnBib 94; Rome: Biblical Institute, 1981) 23–80. For suggested relations between this and early Christian soteriology, see the (usually excessive) views in Swetnam, *Isaac*, 5–22, 80–85; Schoeps, *Paul*, 141; J. E. Wood, "Isaac Typology in the NT," *NTS* 14 (1968) 583–89; M. Wilcox, " 'Upon the Tree,' " *JBL* 96 (1977) 85–99; R. L. Rubenstein, *My Brother Paul* (New York: Harper & Row, 1972) 109–11 (though his psychoanalytic approach—e.g., God's "infanticidal tendencies" on 66ff.—proves unhelpful).

96. Rhoads and Michie, *Mark as Story*, 104–5.

97. Cf. Taylor, *Mark*, 160; Anderson, *Mark*, 78 (probably correct about the dove-like descent, although the particular associations ought still to be investigated).

98. Cf. Plut., *Isis* 379D (LCL 5.164–65).

99. I. Abrahams, *Studies in Pharisaism and the Gospels* (1st ser.; Cambridge: Cambridge, 1917) 48–49; Barrett, *Spirit*, 38 (following Abrahams). The hovering of the brooding Spirit in Gen 1, compared to a dove in *b. Ḥag.* 15a (so Taylor, *Mark*, 160–61; Hooker, *Message of Mark*, 11–12, less strong), is not prominent enough to be probable.

100. E.g., *b. Šabb.* 49a; 130a; *Exod. Rab.* 20:6; *Song Sol. Rab.* 2:14 §§1–2 (§2 purportedly from the School of R. Ishmael); cf. Goodenough, *Symbols*, 8.41–46. But many diverse symbols were adopted for Israel by the rabbis that may not have been as perspicacious to other segments of Jewish thought, and since so many symbols represented Israel it is hard to see why one should be preferred over another.

101. Lane, *Mark*, 57.

102. *B. Ber.* 3a (probably reflecting Tannaitic tradition); cf. Abrahams, *Studies* (1), 47.

103. Cf. Qumran's *Genesis Apocryphon*, as well as *Jubilees* and the Enoch literature in particular. Later rabbis focused less on the prepatriarchal era, but it was of great importance to the popular forms of Judaism behind much of the literature now called the Pseudepigrapha. Cf. 1 Pet 3:18–22; 2 Pet 2:4–5; Jude 6, 14; and perhaps 1 Cor 11:10 for similar traditions in early Christian literature.

104. The narratives of Adam, Noah, Abraham, Jacob, and to some extent Joseph are structurally parallel in blessing, curse, and fruitfulness, and the first three are separated by parallel genealogies of equally schematized length.

105. 1 Pet 3:20–21; 2 Pet 3:6–7; cf. Matt 24:38. Other possibilities, such as a dove alluding to sacrifice (Mark 11:15) or harmlessness (Matt 10:16; omitted in Luke 10:3) do not fit this context; salvation-historical language is used here.

Although it is possible that the dove is simply used as the most appropriate of flying creatures to land on Jesus, the other OT language in the context suggests that the dove probably has special significance here.

106. If Mark is not dependent on Q here (he may be), the promise's parallel occurrence in the Q tradition defends it on the criterion of multiple attestation, and if the Fourth Gospel is likewise independent the case from multiple attestation is stronger.

107. See H. J. Flowers, *"En pneumati hagiō kai puri,"* *ExpT* 64 (1953) 155–56; Manson, *Sayings,* 41 (citing Acts 19:1–6 against Spirit); cf. Bruce, "Matthew," 84; for wind in winnowing, e.g., *Lev. Rab.* 28:2; *Qoh. Rab.* 5:15 §1.

108. See Bruce, "Spirit in Qumran Texts," 50. Perhaps John's baptism was to symbolize cleansing by the spirit of judgment and burning (Isa 4:4; Mal 3:2) that would deliver from eschatological fire (so J. D. G. Dunn, "Spirit," in *NIDNTT* [Grand Rapids, Mich.: Zondervan, 1978] 3.695); cf. also the fiery stream idea of L. W. Barnard, "Matt. III.11//Luke III.16," *JTS* 8 (1957) 107.

109. Cf. Robinson, *Problem of History,* 74. For the essential identity between John's and Christian baptism, cf. R. Bultmann, *Theology of the New Testament* (New York: Scribner's, 1951) 1.39.

110. On the difference, see Meier, *Matthew,* 25; J. K. Parratt, "The Holy Spirit and Baptism," *ExpT* 82 (1971) 231–35; on the similarity of Christian water baptism and Spirit baptism (John's may function paradigmatically but this is not in view here), see G. R. Beasley-Murray, "The Holy Spirit, Baptism, and the Body of Christ," *RevExp* 63 (1966) 177–85; id., *Baptism in the New Testament* (Grand Rapids, Mich.: Eerdmans, 1962) 275–78; A. Richardson, *An Introduction to the Theology of the New Testament* (New York: Harper & Brothers, 1958) 357.

111. Robinson, *Problem of History,* 76–77.

112. See J. D. G. Dunn, *Baptism in the Holy Spirit* (SBT 15, 2d ser.; London: SCM, 1970) 33–34.

113. See Dunn, *Baptism,* 27; G. W. H. Lampe, *The Seal of the Spirit* (London: Longmans, Green, 1951) 35; Kingsbury, *Christology of Mark's Gospel,* 64; Schweizer, *Mark,* 37; cf. Bonsirven, *Judaism,* 218; Jeremias, *Theology,* 54–55. The language need not be Hellenistic here (Kingsbury, *Christology of Mark's Gospel,* 62–63), and the context suggests the OT functional anointing idea rather than any fusion of natures.

114. The aorist here may contrast with Jesus' eschatological baptism; cf. F. J. Botha, *"Ebaptisa* in Mark i. 8," *ExpT* 64 (1952) 268, who describes it as a "timeless aorist."

115. Dunn, *Baptism,* 24; cf. Beasley-Murray, *Baptism,* 290; R. E. O. White, *The Biblical Doctrine of Initiation* (Grand Rapids, Mich.: Eerdmans, 1960) 87; Robinson, *Problem of History,* 9; Hooker, *Message of Mark,* 11; Robinson, *Twelve Studies,* 169.

116. Harnack's allusion to the worshipped Morning Star here (cf. W. Ramsay, *Luke the Physician* [London: Hodder & Stoughton, 1908] 232) has almost nothing to commend it. Jesus' "might" is vindicated in the baptism and proved in the temptation, where he encounters and overcomes the tempter by resisting him.

117. On the conflict in 1:9–13 and its function in the conflict motif throughout the Gospel, see Vander Broek, *Sitz im Leben,* 161; Anderson, *Mark,* 81; Kelber, *Mark's Story,* 19; Kingsbury, *Christology of Mark's Gospel,* 69; Robinson, *Problem of History,* 76 (though cf. Anderson's remarks, p. 81); Rhoads and Michie,

Mark as Story, 42. On the wild beasts, cf. G. Bilezikian, *The Liberated Gospel* (BBMS; Grand Rapids, Mich.: Baker, 1977) 145 (citing beasts in imperial Rome). On eschatological approaches, see Kelber, *Mark's Story,* 19; Anderson, *Mark,* 82; W. F. Hambly, "Creation and Gospel," *SE* 5 (1968) 69; on allusions, see Michaels, *Son,* 45, who sees possible allusions to Dan 4; one might think of the Roman story of Romulus and Remus, to which allusion is not uncommonly made in Roman texts (cf., e.g., Mart., *Epig.* 2.75).

118. See Kim, "Theologian of Resurrection," 92; Robinson, *Twelve Studies,* 162–63 n. 7 (with Lampe) on ἀναβαίνων. There are significant literary connections between the pericopes. See, e.g., Kingsbury, *Christology of Mark's Gospel,* 60; cf. also: 1:9a/16:6 (Nazareth); baptism/burial, 1:9a/15:42–47; coming up/resurrection, 1:10a/16:6; heavens opened/veil rent (1:10b/15:38); annunciations, 1:11/15:39/16:6. But note that such connections tie the event to the cross as well as to resurrection; cf. the fewer and weaker parallels with the temptation: 1:13 clarified by 8:31–38 (cf. Matt/Luke) as temptation to avoid the cross (15:30–31; cf. Matt 27). Mark 1:13b's wild animals could allude to Ps 22:16, but Matt and John use this more clearly than Mark 15:29, 34. The angels of 1:13c appear in the passion temptation (but only in Luke 22:43; cf. Matt 26:53; Luke lacks them in the earlier temptation of ch. 4, however). The baptism and transfiguration, of course, are clearly linked (Kingsbury, *Christology of Mark's Gospel,* 48–49; Trocmé, *Formation of Mark,* 56–57), which is what really makes the case. For an attempt to place the connection between baptism and death/resurrection in Mark's *Sitz,* see E. Johns and D. Major, *Witness in a Pagan World* (Guildford: Lutterworth, 1980) 44.

119. See, e.g., Y. Yadin, *Masada* (New York: Random House, 1966) 164; M. Pearlman, *The Zealots of Masada* (New York: Scribner's, 1967) 179; N. Avigad, *Discovering Jerusalem* (Nashville: Nelson, 1980) 139–43; R. Reich, "A Miqweh at 'Isawiya near Jerusalem," *IEJ* 34 (1984) 220–23.

120. E.g., B. E. Thiering, "Inner and Outer Cleansing at Qumran as a Background to New Testament Baptism," *NTS* 26 (1980) 266–77; id., "Qumran Initiation and New Testament Baptism," *NTS* 27 (1981) 615–31; D. Smith, "Jewish Proselyte Baptism and the Baptism of John," *ResQ* 25 (1982) 13–32.

121. E.g., Jos., *J.W.* 2.129; 8.150; cf. *Ant.* 18.19. But non-Essene Jews who could afford it may have also been more meticulous than halakah demanded; see the Upper City Jerusalemites in Avigad, *Discovering Jerusalem,* 142. B. G. Wood, "To Dip or Sprinkle?" *BASOR* 256 (1984) 45–60, argues for dipping in ritual purifications. The *mikvaoth* archaeologists have uncovered argue strongly in favor of immersion as the form of washing, as in later rabbinic texts.

122. E.g., Gaster, *Scriptures,* 2 (but cf. p. xii); Jeremias, *Theology,* 43; O. Betz, *What Do We Know about Jesus?* (Philadelphia: Westminster: 1968) 34–35; M. Black, *The Scrolls and Christian Origins* (London: Nelson, 1961) 94, 97, 100–101.

123. E.g., Anderson, *Mark,* 70–71; G. Vermes, *The Dead Sea Scrolls in English* (2d ed.; New York: Penguin, 1981) 45 (with reservations).

124. See 1QS 5.8–23 and texts in Josephus cited by F. M. Cross, *The Ancient Library of Qumran and Modern Biblical Studies* (rev. ed.; Grand Rapids, Mich.: Baker, 1980) 95 n. 96a. C. T. Fritsch, *The Qumran Community* (New York: Macmillan, 1956) 7; Thiering, "Initiation and Baptism," 615–31; id., "Cleansing," 266–77; Brownlee, "Comparison," 58; Brown, "Scrolls," 4; cf. Robinson, *Twelve Studies,* 16.

125. 1QS 5.8–23; Black, *Scrolls and Origins*, 94, 100–101.

126. Cf., e.g., Jos., *J.W.* 2.150. This has been argued by many scholars, e.g., G. R. Driver, *The Judaean Scrolls: The Problem and a Solution* (Oxford: Blackwell, 1965) 496–506; H. Ringgren, *The Faith of Qumran* (Philadelphia: Fortress, 1963) 221; J. T. Milik, *Ten Years of Discovery in the Wilderness of Judaea* (London: SCM, 1959) 102–3; Pryke, "John the Baptist," 483–96; M. Simon, *Jewish Sects at the Time of Jesus* (Philadelphia: Fortress, 1967) 75. Such purifications were not thought to purify the soul from sin; see E. F. Sutcliffe, "Baptism and Baptismal Rites at Qumran?" *HeyJ* 1 (1960) 179–88.

127. Cf. Hurtado, *Mark*, 4; Pryke, "John the Baptist," 495; Lane, *Mark*, 48.

128. Cf., e.g., Jos., *Ant.* 6.235; *m. Para.* 11:6; *t. Miqw.; b. Ber.* 51a; *Šabb.* 64b.

129. Cf. *p. Qidd.* 3:12 §8.

130. E.g., 1 Macc 5; *Jub.* 1:9, 15:34, 22:16–18, 20–22, 23:24, 24:25–33; Ps.-Philo 7:3, 12:4 (*OTP* 2.302, cites also *4 Ezra* 6:56; *2 Bar.* 82:5 in this connection); 4QpNah 1.1; *m. ʿAbod. Zar.* 2:1; *Ter.* 8:12; *Sipre Deut.* 213.1.1; *Gen. Rab.* 80:7. On Gentiles' sacrifices, e.g., *p. Ter.* 1:1, 3:8; *Pesiq. Rab.* 48:1. For a broad sampling of rabbinic texts on the issue of Gentiles, see Montefiore and Loewe, *Anthology*, 556–65.

131. 1QM 11.12–13; 14.7; 15.1–2; 17.1–2; *t. Sanh.* 13:2; *b. Roš. Haš.* 17a (including the wicked of Israel in the judgment); *Lev. Rab.* 13:2; *Num. Rab.* 19:32; *Qoh. Rab.* 1:9 §1; *Pesiq. Rab.* 10:5, 11:5; cf. *1 Enoch* 99:4. Cf. texts in Bonsirven, *Judaism*, 65–68.

132. *Jesus*, 214.

133. Ibid., 215.

134. Ibid. E. E. Urbach, "Self-Isolation or Self-Affirmation in Judaism in the First Three Centuries," in *Jewish and Christian Self-Definition* (ed. E. P. Sanders; Philadelphia: Fortress, 1980–82) 2.278–84, thinks that the predominantly negative perspective toward Gentiles reflects the pre-70 period, and that it was emended at Jamnia to avoid the profanation of God's name. J. Jeremias, *Jesus' Promise to the Nations* (SBT 24; London: SCM, 1958) 40–41, perhaps overemphasizing the negative perspective, suggests that the negative view increased to a climax with such statements as that of R. Eliezer b. Hyrcanus (ca. 90 C.E.), "No Gentile will have a part in the world to come"; Moore, *Judaism*, 2.385–86, cites texts showing that R. Eliezer was believed to have changed his mind. See Sanders, *Jesus*, 215, for a critique of Jeremias on this point.

135. CD 12.6–8; *m. Giṭ.* 5:9; *Qoh. Rab.* 11:1 §1; though cf. qualifications in Bonsirven, *Judaism*, 154. The obligation to treat foreigners well for the sake of reputation occurs in Isoc., *To Nicocles* 22, *Or.* 2; the point in Ps.-Phoc. 39–40 may be directed toward just treatment of the Jews in Alexandria, rather than for witness to Gentiles.

136. *Ep. Aristeas* 279 (Ptolemy Philadelphus); *t. Sanh.* 13:2; *Sipre Deut.* 307.4.2. For righteous individuals among the nations, cf. also *Sipra A.M.* pq. 13.194.2.15; *b. Ḥul.* 92a; *Lev. Rab.* 1:3.

137. *Mek. Bah.* 6:90ff.; *Sipre Deut.* 343.4.1; *b. Yeb.* 48b; *ʿAbod. Zar.* 64b ("the Sages"); *Sanh.* 56ab (bar.); 59a (purportedly Tannaitic); 74b; *Gen. Rab.* 26:1 (Tannaitic); 34:14; *Exod. Rab.* 30:9; *Deut. Rab.* 1:21; *Pesiq. Rab Kah.* 12:1; cf. Urbach, "Self-Affirmation," 275–78; Moore, *Judaism*, 274–75. The Noahide law tradition in its finished form may be later, but there may be allusions to it in Pseudo-Phocylides (see P. W. Van der Horst in *OTP* 2.569), the idea appears as early as *Jubilees*, and there is evidence for it in Philo and Josephus (J. P. Schultz,

"Two Views of the Patriarchs," in *Texts and Responses* [ed. M. A. Fishbane and
P. R. Flohr; Leiden: Brill, 1975] 48–49). In *Jub.* 6:4–10 (with 6:15–16, providing an
inclusio around 6:11–14), Noah's covenant prefigures Israel's covenant, but the
Noahide laws are implied in 7:20–25 (although the conclusions drawn from this by
L. Finkelstein, *Pharisaism in the Making* [New York: KTAV,1972] 223–27, are
overstated; see Schultz, "Views," 44–45).

138. Cf. Jos., *Ant.* 20.34–36; *Ag. Ap.* 2.210; *m.* ʾ*Abot.* 1:12 (though only if הבריות
include Gentiles); *b. Šabb.* 31a (purportedly Tannaitic); *Sanh.* 99b; *Gen. Rab.*
39:14, 47:10, 48:8, 84:8, 98:5; *Num. Rab.* 8:4; *Qoh. Rab.* 7:8 §1; *Pesiq. Rab Kah.* Sup.
1:6; *Pes. Rab.* 14:2, 43:6. For further discussion, see B. J. Bamberger, *Proselytism in the Talmudic Period* (New York: KTAV,1968) 13–19 (OT period), 19–24
("intertestamental" period), 222–25 (early rabbis), 225–28 (the royal house of
Adiabene), 267–73 (on Matt 23:15); Urbach, *Sages,* 1.549–54, passim; D. Flusser,
"Paganism in Palestine," 1065–1100 in *JPFC,* 1097; cf. the information in
D. Georgi, *The Opponents of Paul in Second Corinthians* (Philadelphia: Fortress,
1986) 83–164, although his conclusions may go too far. Although formal "missionaries" were not employed, those who spread the message were deeply committed
to it: S. B. Hoenig, "Conversion during the Talmudic Period," in *Conversion to
Judaism* (ed. D. M. Eichhorn; New York: KTAV,1965) 49; K. Lake, "Proselytes
and God-Fearers," *Beginnings,* 5.75; J. N. Sevenster, *The Roots of Pagan Anti-
Semitism in the Ancient World* (NovTSup 41; Leiden: Brill, 1975) 203. Active
proselytizing may have been modeled after Hellenistic models (cf. E. R. Goodenough, *The Church in the Roman Empire* [New York: Cooper Square, 1970] 9;
Culpepper, *School,* 117), and may have been stifled by the wars with Rome
(S. Applebaum, *Jews and Greeks in Ancient Cyrene* [SJLA 28; Leiden: Brill,
1979] 343; J. G. Gager, *Kingdom and Community* [Englewood Cliffs, N.J.:
Prentice-Hall, 1975] 137; for other perspectives, cf. S. J. D. Cohen, "Conversion
to Judaism in Historical Perspective," *CJ* 36 [1983] 31–45).

139. 1QH 6.12–14; 1QM 12.14 (in both instances, the purpose is to emphasize
Israel's eschatological glory); *Sib. Or.* 3:710–26 (second century B.C.E.), perhaps
1:129; *T. Zeb.* 9:8 (textually uncertain); *t. Ber.* 6:2; *Num. Rab* 1:3. In some texts
Gentiles would survive, under the Messiah's yoke; *Pss. Sol.* 17:30. For surveys of
the diverse opinions on the lostness of the Gentiles in ancient Jewish texts, see
Sanders, *Paul,* 206–12; Bonsirven, *Judaism,* 66–70.

140. E.g., Jdt 14:10; Sirach 44:20; Jos., *Ant.* 20.34–48; *t.* ʿ*Abod. Zar.* 3:12; *Ber.*
6:13; cf. *T. Levi* 6:3, 6–7; *Exod. Rab.* 30:12.

141. Jos., *Ant.* 20.40–42, though contrast Eleazar of Galilee, 20.43–44.

142. *B. Yeb.* 46a.

143. N. J. McEleney, "Conversion, Circumcision, and the Law," *NTS* 20 (1974)
319–41; cf. Lake, "Proselytes," 78–79.

144. Bamberger, *Proselytism,* 49–52; cf. J. Nolland, "Uncircumcised Proselytes?" *JSJ* 12 (1981) 173–94. In support of this, cf. *b. Yeb.* 71a.

145. *T.* ʿ*Abod. Zar.* 3:11; *b. Ber.* 47b; ʿ*Abod. Zar.* 57a; *Yeb.* 46ab; *p. Qidd.* 3:12
§8; cf. *t. Zabim* 2:7.

146. T. M. Taylor, "The Beginnings of Jewish Proselyte Baptism," *NTS* 2
(1956) 193–98; Smith, "Proselyte Baptism," 13–32; Robinson, *Studies,* 16 n. 12;
S. Légasse, "Baptême juif des prosélytes et baptême chrétien," *BLE* 77 (1976)
3–40.

147. Parallels, as well as differences, are observed by many scholars, e.g., Taylor, *Mark*, 155; White, *Initiation*, 78–79; Argyle, *Matthew*, 23; Hooker, *Message of Mark*, 9.

148. For some degree of relationship with Qumran, see Brown, "Scrolls," 4; Robinson, *Twelve Studies*, 16; J. Jeremias, "The Qumran Texts and the New Testament," *ExpT* 70 (1958–59) 68–69; Anderson, *Mark*, 70–71; against Pryke, "John the Baptist," 483–96; J. Delmore, "La pratique du baptême dans le judaïsme contemporain des origines chrétiennes," *LumV* 26 (1956) 165–204.

149. Although some argue against proselyte baptism as a source (Beasley-Murray, *Baptism*, 18–31; Anderson, *Mark*, 71; cf. W. F. Albright, *From the Stone Age to Christianity* [Baltimore: Johns Hopkins, 1946] 290), the opinion is increasingly shifting in the direction of recognizing it as a source, with whatever modifications: L. H. Schiffman, "At the Crossroads," in *Jewish and Christian Self-Definition* (ed. E. P. Sanders; Philadelphia: Fortress, 1980–82) 2.128; L. Goppelt, *Theology of the New Testament* (Grand Rapids, Mich.: Eerdmans, 1981–82) 1.37; Bruce, *History*, 156; Ladd, *Theology*, 41; W. A. Meeks, *The First Urban Christians* (New Haven: Yale, 1983) 150; H. Falk, *Jesus the Pharisee* (New York: Paulist, 1985) 151; earlier in the century, Abrahams, *Studies* (1), 42; Montefiore, *Gospels*, 1.8.

150. Cf. similarly K. Pusey, "Jewish Proselyte Baptism," *ExpT* 95 (1984) 141–45.

151. *Disc.* 2.9.20, despite the interpretation of the Loeb editor that these are Christians, probably based on ignorance of the Jewish practice. Stern, *Authors on Judaism*, 541, interprets it correctly.

152. It is probably implied by Juv., *Sat.* 14.104, who would then be regarding it as a matter of common knowledge in Roman society that after Jews circumcised their converts they led them to the place of washing. *Sib. Or.* 4:165, which Collins thinks is a non-Christian work of ca. 80 C.E., very possibly refers to proselyte baptism also. Cf. Justin Martyr, *Dialogue with Trypho* 29.1, for a mid-second-century reference.

153. Schiffman, "Crossroads," 128–31; definite early attestation is not possible here, but "the transmission of this statement in the names of three separate Tannaim may indicate that it was widespread," and probably reflects an authentic early dispute. Cf. T. F. Torrance, "Proselyte Baptism," *NTS* 1 (1954) 154.

154. Taylor, "Baptism," 196.

155. See Abrahams, *Studies* (1), 37.

156. Cf. also Cohen, *Maccabees*, 53; Schiffman, "Crossroads," 128; White, *Initiation*, 320.

157. *Pesiq. Rab Kah.* 12:20 (a proselyte by repentance); note the comparison in *b. Ta⁽an.* 16a, and admonitions concerning true repentance, e.g., *Pesiq. Rab.* 44:1; cf. also the requirements for entering the Qumran community in 1QS 3.4–7; 5.13–14; Black, *Scrolls*, 94, 97.

158. *P. Sanh.* 6:7 §2 (Gibeonites, converted from impure motives, were still avenged by God); *Num. Rab.* 8:4.

159. *T. Demai* 2:5; *Sipre Deut.* 356.5.7; *b. Qidd.* 62a; *Yeb.* 47a; *p. Git.* 1:4 §2; *Qidd.* 4:1 §§2–3; *Num. Rab.* 5:3, 8:4, 9; cf. *b. Šabb.* 33b; *Yeb.* 24b (Tann.); *Pesiq. Rab.* 22:5; *T. Jos.* 4:4–6; also the discussion in Urbach, *Sages*, 1.387–88. This would be true in the messianic time, according to some rabbis, e.g., in *⁽Abod. Zar.* 3b. J. Neusner, "The Conversion of Adiabene to Judaism," *JBL* 83 (1964) 60–66

argues for political as well as authentic motives in the conversion of Helene and Izates.

160. E.g., *m. Yad.* 4:4; *Sipre Deut.* 253.2.2; *b. Ber.* 28a; *Šabb.* 33b.; *CIJ* 1.384 §523: "Veturia Pau(l)la, 'prosélyte' (portant) le nom de Sara"; also Bamberger, *Proselytism,* 234; cf. also the inscriptional references to the proselyte Salome in E. M. Meyers and J. F. Strange, *Archaeology, the Rabbis, & Early Christianity* (Nashville: Abingdon, 1981) 68; and J. Finegan, *The Archeology of the New Testament* (Princeton: Princeton, 1952) 247; and to the proselyte Judah, in ibid. B. Bagatti, *The Church from the Circumcision* (Jerusalem: Franciscan Printing Press, 1971) 237, is mistaken to suppose that these should represent Jewish converts to Christianity. Proselytes are common in the Diaspora; e.g. *CIJ* 1.20 §21; 141 §202; 159 §256; 340–41 §462; 384 §523; 424 §576.

161. E.g., *Manasses* 7; *T. Ab.* 10A; 11B; Philo, *Virt.* 175–86; *m. Yoma* 8:8–9; *b. Roš Haš.* 16b; *B.Mesiʿa* 59a; *Yoma* 86ab; *Šabb.* 153a (purportedly Tannaitic); *Midr. Pss.* 90:12; 93:2; *Gen. Rab.* 1:4; 22:13; 38:9; *Exod. Rab.* 31:1; *Lev. Rab.* 15:4; *Num. Rab.* 13:3; 14:1 (insufficient); *Deut. Rab.* 2:12, 24; *Qoh. Rab.* 7:8 §1 (purportedly Tannaitic); 7:14 §1; *Lam. Rab.* 3:43–44 §9; *Song Sol. Rab.* 5:16 §1 (Tannaitic); 8:6 §2; *Pesiq. Rab.* 33:6; 44:7; 47:1. The portrayal in R. Bultmann, *Primitive Christianity in its Contemporary Setting* (New York: Meridian, 1956) 71, is too negative here. It is clear that Jewish *shub* was more holistic than Greek *metanoia* (cf. Ladd, *Theology,* 38–39; F. V.Filson, *A New Testament History* [Philadelphia: Westminster, 1964] 100).

162. 1QS 5.13–14; *b. Taʿan.* 16a; *Pesiq. Rab.* 44:1; Bonsirven, *Judaism,* 116; in the NT, cf. Dunn, *Baptism,* 15–17. Jewish teachers warned against fake conversions, as noted above.

163. Hooker, *Message of Mark,* 10; cf. Filson, *History,* 36.

164. Taylor, *Mark,* 618; Cranfield, "Baptism," 54–55.

165. Cf. Robinson, *Twelve Studies,* 160; Lampe, *Seal,* 39. Compare especially the logia in Luke 12:49–50, which may connect our saying with the fire baptism, intensifying the connection between Jesus' suffering and baptism and that of his followers; see Robinson, *Twelve Studies,* 161; Dunn, *Baptism,* 42; cf. P. S. Minear, *The Kingdom and the Power* (Philadelphia: Westminster, 1950) 135; for the apocalyptic significance of this passage, cf. A. J. Mattill, Jr., *Luke and the Last Things* (Dillsboro, N.C.: Western North Carolina, 1979) 4.

166. Mansfield, *Spirit and Gospel,* 30–31, with others, rightly qualifies Robinson's overemphasis on this theme; nevertheless, the theme remains important. Once introduced in the prologue, the theme may thenceforth be taken for granted no less than the Spirit may be; see n. 1 above. Attributing most examples to Mark's tradition rather than his redaction does not explain why he preserves these examples so prominently (e.g., the first miracle, 1:21–28) in his narrative.

167. T. J. Weeden, *Mark—Traditions in Conflict* (Philadelphia: Fortress, 1971). He qualifies his thesis in the 1979 preface (p. vii) in response to Holladay's critique.

168. Ibid., 56–59.

169. Ibid., 60–69.

170. For Canaanite usage in the early OT period, cf. W. F. Albright, *The Biblical Period from Abraham to Ezra* (New York: Harper & Row, 1963) 45; for Emperor worship, cf. A. Deissmann, *Light from the Ancient East* (Grand Rapids, Mich.: Baker, 1978) 346–47. (Bousset, *Kyrios Christos,* 207 n. 142, argues that

Deissmann's connection with Paul in this regard is anachronistic, since Emperor worship had not yet assumed such proportions; in the East, this is questionable, but he is probably correct that such was not the understanding of "son of God" in most Hellenistic circles, since it was one example among many in paganism.) The category is not altogether illogical in polytheism, and it follows that not all usages are genetically related; cf. e.g., the use in the early Chou (Zhou) dynasty, ca. 1050–770 B.C.E., in C. Jochim, *Chinese Religions* (Englewood Cliffs, N.J.: Prentice-Hall, 1986) 29.

171. Cf., e.g., Dio Chrys., *32d Discourse* §95 for heroes (Alexander and Heracles) who claimed to be sons of Zeus; W. M. Ramsay, *The Cities of St. Paul* (London: Hodder & Stoughton, 1907) 143, for use in the Phrygian mysteries. See 146–47 for fluidity of divine conceptions.

172. E.g., Deissmann, *Bible Studies*, 166–67 (though the NT idea goes back to the OT, the Gentile Christians no doubt understood it in Hellenistic terms); Bousset, *Kyrios Christos*, 207 (with too much optimism on parallelism between Christian and pagan imagery here); for the divine man as a miracle worker, cf. Reitzenstein, *Mystery-Religions*, 26–27. See especially Bultmann, *Theology*, 1.130–32.

173. On the Hellenistic Jewish use of the motif, as well as some general considerations, see Georgi, *Opponents*, 122–64; on social aspects, see 390–94; on the man of God image in Sirach, see 394–99; see also "The 'Divine Man' in Jewish Apologetics," 399–406; "*Theios anthrōpos* in Pagan Missionary Activity and Propagandistic Ideology," 406–9 (he argues it included wonder-working as a propagandistic device).

174. D. L. Tiede, *The Charismatic Figure as Miracle Worker* (SBLDS 1; Missoula, Mont.: SBL, 1972) 240. Cf. also C. H. Holladay, *Theios Aner in Hellenistic Judaism* (Missoula. Mont.: Scholars, 1977). For similar critiques from other scholars, cf. Nock, *Gentile Christianity*, 45; Hengel, *Son of God*, 25.

175. E.g., Moses' battles with angels during his legendary ascent to the throne of glory to receive the Torah: *b. Šabb.* 88b; *Exod. Rab.* 42:4; *Pesiq. Rab.* 20:4.

176. *Jesus*, 64.

177. *Son*, 18. Cf. similarly H. N. Ridderbos, *Paul: An Outline of his Theology* (Grand Rapids, Mich.: Eerdmans, 1975) 90–91. For the current state of the question on the divine man, see the review in Kingsbury, *Christology of Mark's Gospel*, 33–37.

178. M. D. Hooker, *A Preface to Paul* (New York: Oxford, 1980) 55–65.

179. R. P. Martin, *Mark: Evangelist and Theologian* (Grand Rapids, Mich.: Zondervan, 1972) 106; cf. Cullmann, *Christology*, 275.

180. E.g., *Jub.* 2:20 (cf. 19:29); 1QH 9.35–36; *Pss. Sol.* 17:30; for other non-rabbinic references, cf. Hengel, *Son of God*, 51; *b. Šabb.* 31a; 128a (citing Tannaitic sources); *Sukka* 45b; *Exod. Rab.* 46:4–5; *Num. Rab.* 5:3; 10:2; *Deut. Rab.* 1:6; 3:15; *Lam. Rab.* Proem 23 (R. Judah ha-Nasi); see Bonsirven, *Judaism*, 48–49. This was often presented by parables: *b. Yoma* 76a (R. Simeon b. Yohai); *Exod. Rab.* 15:30; *Lev. Rab.* 10:3; *Num. Rab.* 16:7 (R. Joshua); *Deut. Rab.* 2:24; 10:4; *Lam. Rab.* Proem 2; 1:17 §52; 3:20 §7; *Song Sol. Rab.* 2:16 §1; *Pesiq. Rab.* 15:17.

181. E.g., Wis 2:18; 5:5.

182. Philo, *Sobr.* 55–56.

183. E.g., Abel, in *T. Ab.* 12 A.

184. E.g., R. Ishmael b. Elisha according to *b. Ber.* 7a.

185. Honi the Circle-Drawer, in *b. Ber.* 19a; cf. also Charlesworth, *Pseudepigrapha and New Testament*, 82, following Vermes. On Jesus in this category, cf. Cohen, *From Maccabees to Mishnah*, 122; J. Neusner, *Judaism in the Beginning of Christianity* (Philadelphia: Fortress, 1984) 25, 35–44 (in general). H. C. Kee, *Community of the New Age* (Philadelphia: Westminster, 1977) 62, derives these traditions in Judaism from the OT.

186. Cf. Hengel, *Son of God*, 24. He notes (p. 30) that the term was never used as a title except for *divi filius*, and (p. 32) that most of Wetter's sources had been influenced by Christianity.

187. See Longenecker, *Christology*, 93: Hengel, *Son of God*, 44. For Jewishness of the term in the NT, see Longenecker, *Christology*, 98; cf. Hengel, *Son of God*, 21–23.

188. Jeremias, *Parables*, 73; Montefiore, *Gospels*, 1.85 (though he allows the messianic exegesis of Ps 2); H. Conzelmann, *An Outline of the Theology of the New Testament* (New York: Harper & Row, 1969) 76 (though cf. OT usage, 76–77); G. B. Stephens, *The Johannine Theology* (New York: Scribner's, 1894) 104–5. *Fourth Ezra* 13:37, 52, may evince Christian redaction for the Latin version.

189. *Exod. Rab.* 29:5 (*Midrash Rabbah* 2.339–40).

190. *B. Sanh.* 97b–98a; *Gen. Rab.* 88:7; *Song Sol. Rab.* 2:13 §4; *Pesiq. Rab.* 15:14/15. On the Scrolls, see Gaster, *Scriptures*, 447 ("Messianic Florilegium" on 2 Sam 7:10–14); J. A. Fitzmyer, *Essays on the Semitic Background of the New Testament* (2d ed., SBS 5; Missoula, Mont.: Scholars Press, 1974) 113–26; Kee, *Community*, 126. In general, see the references in Longenecker, *Christology*, 109.

191. Weeden, *Traditions in Conflict*, 52–69, 165.

192. Cf., e.g., Vander Broek, *Sitz im Leben*, 131–89; Kingsbury, *Christology of Mark's Gospel*, 63; Bilezikian, *Liberated Gospel*, 143–44; cf. F. J. Matera, *What Are They Saying about Mark?* (New York: Paulist, 1987) 18–37, for a summary of views on Christology, and 36–37 for Matera's interpretation. With Kingsbury, *Christology of Mark's Gospel*, 56, we hold that a Christology against the "Son of God" would portray Mark as an unreliable narrator (regardless of the variant in 1:1).

193. *History*, 117.

194. See Mansfield, *Spirit and Gospel*, passim (esp. 103). That Mark's audience would hear his Gospel as referring to their risen Lord fits early Christian practice in general (even if one discounts Mansfield's hypothesis of a connection with Pauline Christianity [*Spirit and Gospel*, 153–60]). See A. J. Hultgren, *The Rise of Normative Christianity* (Minneapolis: Augsburg Fortress, 1994) 53, who finds the attesting presence of the Spirit among believers in all the earliest streams of Christianity. On early Christian spirituality, see B. Thurston, *Spiritual Life in the Early Church* (Minneapolis: Augsburg Fortress, 1993).

195. *Christology*, 40–42. Mark 10:35–45 shows a false understanding of Jesus' impending kingdom in Jerusalem; so also the πολλοί of 10:48, who wanted Jesus to get on with the *real* business of setting up the kingdom rather than stopping to heal a blind man. As Via, *Kerygma and Comedy*, 92, points out, a polemic against heresy does not necessitate a narrative format.

196. Cf., e.g., Hooker, *Message of Mark*, 82; F. F. Bruce, *The New Testament Documents* (5th ed.; Grand Rapids, Mich.: Eerdmans 1980) 73–74; Lane, *Mark*,

400; L. Gaston, *No Stone on Another* (NovTSup 23; Leiden: Brill, 1970) 83; A. De Q. Robin, "The Cursing of the Fig Tree in Mark XI," *NTS* 8 (1962) 281.

197. E.g., (often with reference to mastering difficult subjects) *'Abot R. Nat.* 6A; 12 §29B; *b. Ber.* 63b; *Sanh.* 24a; cf. also Manson, *Sayings,* 206; Jeremias, *Theology,* 161; D. E. Nineham, *Saint Mark* (PNTC; Philadelphia: Westminster, 1977) 305; cf. *T. Sol.* 23:1. Presumably these Jewish teachers, like Jesus, echo a more popular and generally applicable idiom. Jewish tradition reports teachers who commanded objects to uproot to validate their halakah, but others regarded signs as inadequate for this purpose (*p. Mo'ed Qat.* 3:1 §6).

198. Isaiah promised that Israel would become powerful enough to crush mountains (Isa 41:15); Zechariah promised that mighty mountains would become like plains before God's Spirit-empowered leaders for his people (Zech 4:6–7), and especially before the Lord himself (Zech 14:3–5).

199. See especially S. E. Dowd, *Prayer, Power, and the Problem of Suffering* (SBLDS 105; Atlanta: Scholars Press, 1988) for a thorough and excellent examination of this issue.

200. As in John, response to Jesus' signs is crucial (unbelief being a common but negative response). Far from being negative, Jesus' signs extol him (see Rhoads and Michie, *Mark as Story,* 105; cf. Kingsbury, *Christology of Mark's Gospel,* 76–77).

3

• • • • • • • • • • • • •

MATTHEW'S PERSPECTIVE
ON THE SPIRIT-BRINGER

• • • • • • • • • • • • •

We have selected three passages for brief examination in Matthew: 3:7–4:11; 12:15–45; and 9:35–10:15. The first passage provides Matthew's interpretation (following Q) of the same event that we surveyed in Mark's introduction. Like Mark, Matthew includes the three occurrences of the Spirit in consecutive paragraphs (John's announcement, the descent at Jesus' baptism, and leading Jesus into the wilderness for testing), but he also includes substantially more material in two of these paragraphs. We therefore will limit our treatment of Markan material in Matthew to comments specific to Matthean redaction of this material. At the same time, Matthew includes and edits substantially more Q material regarding John's sayings, and includes a small amount of uniquely Matthean material (from the standpoint of our extant sources; e.g., 3:14–15). Thus we will treat briefly John's proclamation, Jesus' baptism by John, and finally the testing narrative.

Matthew's redaction of material in chapter 12 betrays an interest in the Spirit that casts significant light on his baptismal narrative as well; the later passage even suggests that the heavenly voice of 3:17 refers to Isa 42 rather than to Gen 22 (in contrast to Mark). Here Matthew clarifies the relationship between the Spirit and opposition, again clarifying the difference between the divine Spirit's empowerment for miraculous works and magical enablement by other spirits.

Finally, we will briefly examine relevant points in 9:35–10:15 (especially 9:35–10:1, 7–8). Even though this discourse explicitly mentions the

Holy Spirit once (inspired speech in the face of persecution in 10:20), it is in the commissioning of his disciples in the passage that Matthew most directly implies that Jesus' charismatic ministry provides a model for the missionary teachers of his community who are making disciples for Jesus (28:19). The disciples proclaim the same kingdom message and demonstrate it in the same miraculous ways as Jesus, immediately after Matthew's first mention of the Beelzebub accusation in response to Jesus' miracles (9:34). Matthew's incorporation of material from various other sources, especially Mark's end-time discourse, also makes clear that he was applying this missionary discourse to his community's own mission.[1]

1.   JOHN'S WARNINGS OF JUDGMENT (3:1–12)
....

Josephus presents the Baptist's mission like a moralizing philosopher for his hellenized audience.[2] By contrast, the Gospel accounts preserve a greater ring of authenticity: John was a wilderness prophet proclaiming impending judgment. Repentance (3:2, 6, 8) was the only appropriate response to the coming kingdom (3:2), fiery judgment (3:7, 10–12) and the final judge who would be more than a merely political Messiah (3:11–12).

The warnings in this passage serve a twofold function for Matthew's audience, who felt oppressed by a Pharisaic establishment (presumably at Yavneh) and needed instruction for their labors in the Gentile mission: judgment against persecutors vindicates the oppressed righteous, but judgment also warns the righteous not to become wicked (cf. Ezek 18:21–24). By narrowing Q's "crowds" to "Pharisees and Sadducees" (3:7; cf. Luke 3:7), Matthew expects his readers to take special encouragement from the coming judgment: their Pharisaic opponents, for all their claims to represent the truest form of Judaism, were spiritual Gentiles (3:6, 9). Yet Matthew also expects his readers to recognize that they, too, can become like these Pharisees (24:48–51; cf. Amos 5:18–20).

i. John's Mission to Israel

Although some Jewish traditions denied that those who are righteous like Abraham needed repentance,[3] most acknowledged that all people have sinned[4] and all need repentance.[5] Yet John's call is more radical than these traditions; his "repentance" refers not to a regular turning from sin after a specific act, but to a once-for-all repentance, the kind of turning from an old way of life to a new that Judaism associated with Gentiles converting to Judaism. In various ways John warns his hearers against depending on the special privileges of their heritage.

First, John's baptism confirms that he is calling for a once-for-all turning from the old way of life to the new, as when Gentiles convert to Judaism. As noted in the previous chapter, none of the other sorts of regular ceremonial washings qualifies easily as background for John's baptism; only the baptism of Gentiles into Judaism signified the kind of radical change John was demanding. Proselyte baptism appears in early Palestinian Jewish texts (e.g., *m. Pesaḥ.* 8:8; *t. ʿAbod. Zar.* 3:11) and Gentile commentators knew of it as well (Epict., *Disc.* 2.9.20; perhaps Juv., *Sat.* 14.104; cf. *Sib. Or.* 4.162–65). Thus John treats his fellow-Jews as if they were Gentiles, calling them to turn to God on the same terms they believed God demanded of Gentiles.[6]

Second, John's hearers were not acting like good descendants of the patriarchs anyway. Scholars sometimes read "offspring of vipers" (3:7; 12:34; 23:33; cf. Luke 3:7) as "offspring of Satan,"[7] even though Matthew's source has the plural and avoids Genesis' term for "serpent." More likely, Matthew alludes to the ancient view that vipers were mother-killers. In the fifth century B.C.E., Herodotus declared that newborn Arabian vipers chewed their way out of their mothers' wombs, killing their mothers in the process. Herodotus believed that they did so to avenge their fathers who were slain by the mothers during procreation (Hdt., *Hist.* 3.109); later writers applied his words to serpents everywhere.[8] Calling his hearers vipers may have been an insult, but calling them "offspring of vipers" accused them of eating their own mothers, indicating the utmost moral depravity.[9] The image of vipers fleeing wrath may derive from serpents fleeing the stubble set on fire to ready the fields for winter sowing[10] or a tree-serpent fleeing those who will destroy the forest.[11] That Matthew applies this phrase to religious leaders is significant.

Third, by employing the image of a tree's fruit, both John and Jesus demand that one's life match one's profession (3:8; 7:16–17; 12:33; 13:22–23; 21:34, 43).[12] The prophets had already applied the image of a tree being cut down to judgment against a nation (Ezek 31:12–18; Dan 4:23). Although Jewish teachers used trees symbolically in a variety of ways, some have thus pointed out the specific Jewish symbol of trees to stand for nations, in this case, for Israel;[13] if this suggestion is correct, it might further drive home the point. In Matthew, however, the trees must also refer to the Pharisees and Sadducees, who must bear fruit in keeping with repentance (3:8) or face the ax and fire (3:10). Kraeling suggests that Palestinians would use wood from such a tree "for domestic and manufacturing purposes,"[14] but most small trees that could not bear fruit would be especially useful for firewood.

Fourth, that God could raise up children for Abraham from stones (cf. Gen 1:24; 2:9) warns John's hearers not to take their status as God's people for granted. Most Jewish people believed they were chosen in Abraham,[15] but John responds that this ethnic election is insufficient to guarantee salvation unless it is accompanied by righteousness (cf. Amos 3:2; 9:7). Although Greeks also had stories of people formed from stones (e.g., Ovid, *Metam.* 1), John's words make better sense in his own setting in Jewish Palestine: prophets were not above using witty word-plays at times (e.g., Amos 8:1–2; Mic 1:10–15; Jer 1:11–12), and "children" and "stones" probably represent a wordplay in Aramaic.[16] Because the biblical tradition had long used stones to symbolize God's people (Exod 24:4; 28:9–12; Josh 4:20–21; 1 Kgs 18:31) or covenants (Gen 31:46; Josh 4:20–24), John's hearers would understand his point quite clearly. God was so sovereign that he could choose the elect even on a basis that contradicted their view of the covenant (cf. Rom 9:6–29).

ii. John's Message of the Coming Judge and Judgment

In all four Gospels, John thought himself and his own baptism min-uscule compared with the coming one and his baptism. In three successive paragraphs Mark depicts God anointing Jesus with the Spirit at baptism (Mark 1:10), thereby qualifying Jesus to bestow the same Spirit on others (1:8) and indicating that participation in his baptism includes sharing his sufferings (1:12).[17] In contrast to this abbreviated program in Mark's introduction, however, Matthew and Luke follow a longer form of the Baptist's saying in a fuller context which speaks of a judgment-baptism in fire as well as in the Spirit (cf. also Luke 12:49–50 in light of Mark 10:38–39). Although both the Spirit and fire will provide a purifying function for Israel as a whole, the "trees cut down and cast into the fire" (3:10) are individuals (3:7–8), as are the chaff. Contrary to the interpretations of some, the righteous will be baptized in God's Spirit, whereas the wicked will be baptized in fire (3:11 in context; also Luke 3:16 with 3:9, 17).[18]

Some think that John's original proclamation addressed only the threshing floor image of wind blowing the chaff so it could be separated from the wheat and burned.[19] In this case, John would have thought not of the "Holy Spirit" but of a "purifying wind," which would be translated much the same way.[20] But four reasons militate against taking John's original words as referring merely to "wind and fire": his contemporaries usually understood "holy spirit" as a reference to God's Spirit or to a purified human spirit; wind, like fire, can represent God's purifying Spirit in the OT; and many, especially John's contemporaries in the wilderness, associated the Spirit with purification;[21] and all extant traditions apply the saying to God's Spirit.[22] Thus it is more likely that John offered another wordplay like the Aramaic one probably presupposed in 3:9; he announced the promised outpouring (a water image) of God's Spirit for the end time (e.g., Joel 2:28–29; Isa 44:3; Ezek 39:29) as an agent like wind separating the wicked from the righteous for judgment. Although Matthew and Luke retain Mark's emphasis on the Spirit, itself possibly derived from Q, they report more of John's preaching of judgment.[23]

John proclaimed first of all that the kingdom was coming. In Matthew's summary of their preaching, both John and Jesus announce the same message: "Repent, for the kingdom of heaven is at hand!" (3:2; 4:17). The "kingdom of heaven" employs a typical Jewish periphrasis for God ("heaven"),[24] and simply means the "kingdom of God."[25] Scholars today widely recognize that God's "kingdom" is his "reign,"[26] recognizing its background in contemporary Jewish usage.[27]

Because virtually every stratum of Gospel tradition testifies that Jesus regularly announced the kingdom, there should be no doubt that this was a characteristic emphasis of Jesus' teaching.[28] Scholars have often debated whether Jesus emphasized a present or future kingdom, however. While evidence seems to favor a future (impending) kingdom especially clearly,[29] many have noted an emphasis on the presence of the kingdom in the Gospels, especially in the kingdom parables (e.g., 13:32)[30] and sayings like the one about entering the kingdom as a child (18:3) and a child being great in the kingdom (18:4). If one examines the Gospels as a whole, their picture of the kingdom is both present and future.[31] It was only natural for Jesus' first followers, once they recognized that Jesus would come again to establish his kingdom fully, to conclude that the expected kingdom would come in two stages corresponding to Jesus' first and second comings.[32]

Matthew intends his missionary audience to find in the preaching of John and Jesus a model for the disciples' preaching, and hence his community's preaching as well (10:7). Those who believed in the coming day of the OT God of justice must get their lives in order; Matthew uses Jesus' kingdom announcement in 4:17 as an introduction for the more detailed exposition of the demanded ethics in chapters 5–7. John combines images of harvest with the coming of God's kingdom (3:2), impending wrath (3:8), and eternally destructive fire (3:10–12; cf., e.g., 4 Macc 12:12; *Jub.* 36:10). Most Jewish residents in Palestine expected a time of impending judgment against the wicked and deliverance for the righteous.[33] But most expected judgment on other peoples and only on the most wicked in Israel.[34]

Farmers destroyed useless products after the harvest. Earlier biblical writers had employed the natural agricultural image of harvest and threshing-floor (3:8, 10, 12) as judgment and/or end-time imagery;[35] the image also recurs elsewhere in Jesus' sayings (Matt 9:38; 13:39; 21:34) and early Judaism.[36] Fire naturally symbolized future judgment:[37] people used chaff for various purposes, one of the most prominent of which was fuel,[38] but whereas chaff did not burn eternally,[39] John depicts the wicked's fire as "unquenchable." John does not simply echo the Jewish consensus of his day, because opinions divided on the character of hell.[40] He specifically affirms the most hideous available image of his day, namely that hell involved eternal torment.

John warned that the coming judge would be incomparably powerful. Judgment is coming, but what is the identity of this coming judge whom John announces (3:11–12)? Although the Spirit would rest on the Davidic Messiah (Isa 11:1–2; cf. 42:1; 61:1), no mere mortal could pour out the Spirit; this was the gift of God alone (Isa 44:3; 59:21; Ezek 36:27; 37:14; 39:29; Joel 2:29; Zech 12:10) just as no mere mortal could baptize in fire, i.e., judge the wicked. Further, John exalts the coming one to a role reserved for God in biblical tradition. The most servile tasks performed by a household servant involved the master's feet: washing the feet,[41] carrying sandals, or unfastening thongs of sandals.[42] To be involved in such work was to be a slave. Thus although ancient teachers usually expected disciples to function as servants,[43] later rabbis entered one caveat: unlike slaves, they did not tend to the teacher's sandals.[44] Whereas the Hebrew Bible regularly called the Israelite prophets "slaves of God"[45] (ancient hearers would have received the image of being God's slave as one of great honor),[46] the prophet John here claims his unworthiness even to be Christ's slave.[47] Against prior biblical revelation, John's proclamation of a coming king (e.g., Isa 9:6–7; Jer 23:5–6) who would also function as judge (perhaps Dan 7:10, 13–14) make good historical sense; so, against his own proclamation, do his later doubts about Jesus (11:3//Luke 7:19).

Indeed, the text which introduces John in Matthew (3:3) and Mark (1:2–3) is instructive: the one whose way John prepares is none other than the "Lord" himself (Isa 40:3); Matthew's readers would not need to know Hebrew to realize that John was preparing the way for the one Matthew's narrative hailed as "God with us" (1:23). It is against this backdrop of John's proclamation of a judge whose slave he was unworthy to be that his reticence to baptize Jesus, and God's testimony to Jesus' identity, appears in 3:13–17.

2.   THE BAPTISM OF GOD'S SON

Although Jesus alone did not need John's baptism—he was the giver of the true baptism (3:11)—he submitted to it to fulfill God's plan

(3:14–15). After Jesus' public act of humility, God publicly identified Jesus as his own Son (3:16–17; cf. 2:15), i.e., as the mightier one whose coming to bestow the Spirit John had prophesied (3:11–12). Matthew hastens over the baptism itself in a participle ("having been baptized," which the NIV properly fleshes out as "as soon as Jesus was baptized") to his main point: God's vindication of Jesus, who accepted the humiliation of baptism.

i. John Recognizes Jesus as the Ultimate Baptizer

Given the embarrassment of some early Christian traditions that Jesus accepted baptism from one of lower status than himself, it is now inconceivable that early Christians made up the story of John baptizing Jesus.[48] That John himself would admit Jesus' greater status as in 3:14 is not unreasonable;[49] given John's witness to a mightier one (3:11–12), subsequent witness to the Spirit descending on Jesus (3:16–17), and subsequent witness that he had at least initially assumed that Jesus was the Christ (11:3), an objection like the one he offers in 3:14 is not unlikely. Why would the fire-baptizer seek baptism like an ordinary mortal?[50] Whereas John recognizes Jesus' superiority, however, Jesus humbly identifies himself with John's mission: "it is proper for *us* to do this to fulfill all righteousness."[51]

Despite John's undoubted knowledge of the association between the Spirit and prophecy,[52] John recognized that Jesus had come to bestow the Spirit in fuller measure than even he as a prophet had received, and he desired this baptism (3:11; cf. 11:11–13).

ii. Jesus "Fulfills All Righteousness" by Identifying with His People

Since "fulfilling righteousness" elsewhere in Matthew may pertain to obeying the principles of the law (5:17, 20; cf., e.g., *Sib. Or.* 3.246), Jesus presumably here expresses his obedience to God's plan revealed in the Scriptures.[53] Matthew's readers familiar with the Scriptures would already understand that Jesus sometimes "fulfilled" the prophetic Scriptures by identifying with Israel's history and completing her mission (2:15, 18).[54] This baptism hence represents Jesus' ultimate identification with Israel at the climactic stage in her history: confessing her sins to prepare for the kingdom (3:2, 6). Jesus' baptism, like his impending death (cf. Mark 10:38–39 with Mark 14:23–24, 36), would be vicarious, embraced on behalf of others with whom the Father had called him to identify.[55]

iii. God Acclaims Jesus as His Son

In this passage, God declares his approval of Jesus in several ways (3:16–17), which we survey very briefly here because in most cases these features of Matthew's narrative function the same way their analogues did in Mark. First, the heavens part, reflecting biblical language for God's revelation or future deliverance.[56] Second, Jesus saw the Spirit descend on him like a dove. Third, God shows his approval of Jesus by a "heavenly voice," a concept with which Matthew's Jewish readers were undoubtedly familiar, as we noted in the preceding chapter. Although many scholars doubt that the crowds hear the heavenly voice,[57] Matthew's change of Mark here suggests that he viewed the parting of the heavens as an objective experience and not merely Jesus' vision. Further, his change of Mark's "You are my son" to "This is my son" suggests a public theophany and testimony to Jesus.[58]

The fact of the voice is important, but what the voice says is more important, for this is what declares Jesus' identity to the reader. The results of our analysis here would be much the same as in Mark, except that in the context of Matthew's Gospel, an allusion to Isa 42 *is* intended here. Matthew 12:18 suggests that Matthew read Isaiah's servant into the heavenly voice, for he reads the voice's recognition oracle into his own translation of Isaiah. Because Jesus is son of Abraham (cf. Gen 22:2) as well as son of David (Matt 1:1), but especially because Jesus is the suffering servant (8:17; 12:18), Jesus' mission includes suffering as well as reigning. As in Mark, Matthew's Jesus also shares his mission with his followers (5:11–12; 10:22; 16:24–27; 19:27–29; 24:9–13).

3.   THE SPIRIT LEADS JESUS INTO TESTING

Although space precludes us from treating the temptation narrative in detail, we should note two significant features of this narrative in passing.

i. The Spirit Brings Jesus to the Test

First, the Spirit no longer merely leads Jesus into the wilderness where he will be tested (Mark 1:12–13); in Matthew he leads him into the wilderness for the express purpose of testing by the devil.[59] Although the community prays, "Lead us not into testing," probably in the sense, "Let us not succumb to the test" (6:13; 26:41), testing itself must come and the one tested must find strength from the Spirit who leads one into that conflict.[60] This is true whether the prayer envisions the final test, as many scholars think,[61] or whether it includes all tests in this age,[62] which better fits the broad early Jewish usage of such prayers.[63] While Satan remains the agent of testing as in Mark, Matthew's Gospel places Jesus' conflict with Satan more clearly in the broader context of the latter's role in God's sovereign purposes, an idea not foreign to Judaism. The Hebrew Bible usually makes God the author of "testing" (Gen 22:1; Deut 13:3), but in the sense that he proves the depth of a person's commitment, not in the sense of seeking to make a person fall.[64]

Just as 3:13–17 announces Jesus' sonship and 4:1–11 defines it, 3:13–17 reports that the Spirit empowers Jesus for his mission as God's Son and 4:1 reports that the Spirit guides him to where his sonship must be defined (4:1, 3, 6). Matthew expressly informs his community that the purpose of the Spirit's first leading of God's Son was that he might be tested. This narrative would have functioned in two critical ways for Matthew's community as they faced opposition from the leadership at Yavneh and on other fronts. First, this narrative again presents Jesus as the vicarious advocate of his people, repeatedly relinquishing his own power and position for his mission to save his people from their sins (1:21).

But second, no less than Matthew's discourse sections (28:19), this narrative provides a *model* for his followers in testing (6:13), for Jewish teachers instructed by example as well as by word.[65] Jesus' followers are destined for testing (6:13; 26:41), but Jesus their forerunner has gone before them and shown them how to overcome. Jesus had to be tested and overcome the tester before he could do anything else.[66] Jesus here also resembles earlier biblical characters who learned the depth of God's grace that sustained them; they could boast not in their success in the test, but in God's empowerment without which they could not have overcome. Jesus went into the testing only after the Father had empowered him in the Spirit.

ii. The Test Defines Jesus' Mission

The second point is that this testing narrative, like the narrative that preceded, unfolds Matthew's Christology. As many scholars have noted,[67] the narrative compares Jesus with figures in Israel's history, first of all with Israel itself.[68] Matthew makes this biblical background clear even in simple ways like saying the Spirit "led" Jesus into the wilderness (following Q; Mark employs a much stronger "impelled," Mark 1:12), reflecting a common biblical motif of God guiding his people in the wilderness (e.g., Ps 107:7; Isa 63:14).[69] In this narrative Matthew presents Jesus as Israel's—and Matthew's community's—champion, the one who succeeded where Israel had failed in the wilderness.

The narrative also connects Jesus with one of the primary figures of Israel's history, Moses. If John had been a model of sacrificial obedience for living in the wilderness and subsisting on locusts (see preceding chapter), Jesus who *fasts* in the wilderness is even more so. Jesus' fast especially recalls that of Moses in Exod 24:18; 34:28; as does that of Elijah in 1 Kgs 19:8.[70] The synoptic writers and their tradition recognized that Jesus, like most of his heroic predecessors in biblical history (Abraham, Joseph, Moses, David, Job), had to pass the period of testing before beginning his public ministry. But whereas some of his predecessors almost succumbed to their test, restrained only by God's favor (e.g., 1 Sam 25:13–34), Jesus provides the perfect model for triumphing in testing.

More specifically, however, this narrative defines Jesus' mission as Son of God (3:17) vis-à-vis some contemporary models of divine sonship (which the narrative attributes to Satan). Granted that Jesus is God's Son (the Greek construction of Satan's suggestions allows one to read "*since you are God's Son*," challenging not his call in 3:17 but seeking to redefine and co-opt it), what kind of divine son is he?[71] Although this defining of Jesus' sonship probably appears at least as early as Q, it remains important for Matthew, who in chapter 12 must explicitly distinguish the Spirit's miraculous work from that of the devil. Matthew may also respond to an internal threat within the community, if the false charismatics against whom he polemicizes (sometimes in terms reminiscent of his denunciation of the Pharisees, cf. 3:7–10; 12:24, 33–37; 23:33) have penetrated that far (7:15–23; 24:24).[72]

iii. The Three Tests and Jesus' Mission

The devil tests Jesus with three roles into which other Palestinian charismatic leaders had fallen, from the crassly demonic sorcerer's role to those which some Jews justified as pious. Jesus' refusal in each case allows Matthew to define Jesus' call over against the charges of his opponents (12:24; 26:55; 27:11, 40–43). First, Jesus was not a magician (4:3). Magicians typically sought to transform one substance into another to demonstrate their power over nature.[73] Jesus' opponents cannot deny his power but wish to attribute it to Satan, as if he were a magician (12:24);[74] many Jews associated demons with the worst kind of sorcery.[75] Unlike most of Jesus' religious contemporaries, however, the reader knows the true story and just how false the charge of Jesus' association with magic was. Even after a forty-day fast, Jesus resisted the temptation to turn stones into bread. Even to a person much less hungry (cf. Gen 3:6; Exod 16:2–3; Ps 78:18), the temptation could seem a natural one: like OT prophets, Jesus fed multitudes[76] and certainly could have used his God-given power to feed himself; but Jesus instead waits on God to act for him (4:11).

In customary portrayals, magicians were those who manipulated spiritual power and formulas, but Jesus acted from an intimate, obedient personal relationship with his father (6:7–9). Like a father disciplining his children, God humbled Israel in the wilderness, teaching his people that he would provide their bread while they were unemployed if they would just look to him (Deut 8:1–5).[77] Jesus accepts his father's call in the wilderness and waits for his father to act.

Second, this narrative's Jesus was not a deluded visionary (4:5–6) like Josephus' "false prophets" who wrongly expected God to back up their miraculous claims.[78] By wanting Jesus to jump over an abyss known to invite certain death without God's intervention (cf. Jos., *Ant.* 15.412), the devil perhaps wants Jesus to presume upon his relationship with God, to act as if God were there to serve his Son, rather than the reverse. Leading religious teachers echo Satan's theology at the cross: if Jesus is God's Son, let God rescue him from the cross (27:40–43). They probably think they echo a wisdom saying undoubtedly widely known in many recensions of the Greek Bible: "For if the righteous man is a son of God, God will help him, and deliver him from the hand of those who resist him" (Wis 2:18); instead they merely echo the devil. The context of the wisdom saying depicted the situation more accurately: the wicked want to condemn the righteous to death unjustly because he claims to be a child of God and to have a good future (Wis 2:16–20).

In this passage Jesus understands Scripture accurately and alludes not only to the passage he cites but also to its context. When he warns against "putting God to the test" (Deut 6:16) he alludes to Israel's dissatisfaction in the wilderness (e.g., Exod 17:2–3). Although God was supplying their needs, they demanded more than their needs, forgetting the greatness of God's deliverance. Matthew reminds his readers that the God of Israel is not a pagan god to be manipulated with words or sacrifices (6:7–9); his servants must be prepared to do his will whether or not it accords with their own (26:42; cf. 6:10).

Finally, Jesus was not a political revolutionary, contrary to the assumptions and charges of the Jewish aristocracy (26:55, 61; 27:11–12).[79] The devil took Jesus on a "high mountain," whether a visionary, mythical mountain[80] or transporting him to a literal one (which could provide at best a representative sampling of the nearer kingdoms).[81] Many citizens of the Roman Empire felt that Rome ruled the earth's kingdoms;[82] to rule the earth would include the subjection of the Roman emperor. Although most Jewish people agreed that evil angels ruled the nations,[83] they also recognized that the devil's authority was delegated;[84] hence they might be suspicious of the devil's certainty that he could give kingdoms.[85] Nevertheless, the devil claimed delegated authority, and by offering Jesus the sort of political kingdom revolutionary leaders sought, the devil offered Jesus the kingdom without the cross (although the cross was precisely where many revolutionaries ended up). The religious leaders later echo Satan's temptation here (27:42–43).

Yet in this instance not only Jesus' opponents but his own disciple Peter echoes Satan's theology exactly: the messianic kingdom without the cross (16:22). Jesus likewise pushes away Peter in disgust[86] as he had Satan, even to the point of calling Peter "Satan" (16:23; cf. 4:10). Correcting a teacher was rare;[87] further, disciples "followed" their teachers (8:22; 9:9–10; 10:38; 19:21), walking behind them out of respect when they walked. Thus, though Jesus "turned" to confront Peter literally behind him (16:23), he now ordered him to "get behind" him figuratively (16:23), returning to a position of discipleship.[88] But Peter was not only out of order; he was the devil's agent. Satan offered Jesus the kingdom without the cross at Jesus' temptation (4:8–9); Peter now offers the same temptation and encounters the same title.[89] By valuing the things humans value (like lack of suffering), Peter shows himself in league with the devil (16:23; cf. Jas 3:15; 4:7). That Peter is a "stumblingblock" (16:23; not in Mark) plays on his name ("rock") negatively just as 16:18 does positively.[90]

Later a disciple seeking to defend Jesus strikes with the sword (26:51), but Jesus informs him that God does not need his servants' violence to defend his purposes; retaliation only breeds more violence (26:52), and God is able to defend his purposes by himself when he wishes to do so (26:53).[91] Jesus' mission involved the cross (26:54), and whether his disciples liked it or not, so did their mission (16:23–26). Thus Matthew's temptation narrative fulfills, among other functions, the same function as its analogue in Mark, developing the idea of 3:13–17 more sharply.

4. THE SPIRIT-ANOINTED HUMBLE SERVANT

Although Jesus' empowerment by the Spirit in 3:16 is critical to Matthew's Gospel, 12:28 becomes a central crux for the interface of his pneumatology and Christology. Yet 12:28 is central in large measure because Matthew defines Jesus' Spirit-empowerment contextually in terms of the Isaiah quotation in 12:18. In the context of 12:18, 12:28 announces Jesus' eschatological identity in terms of his being the Messiah and first embodiment of Israel's mission empowered by the Spirit in the new era. If the Spirit is active, the kingdom is surely at hand.

In 12:1–14 Matthew employs two of Mark's Sabbath controversy stories to illustrate the conflict between Jesus' rest and the Pharisees' rest (11:28). The conflict over the nature of the Sabbath further illustrates two entirely different approaches to the law (5:20).[92] These Pharisees illustrate the principle that Jesus was hidden "from the wise and learned" (11:25).

Rather than contending with the Pharisees further, after these conflicts Jesus withdraws (12:15) and warns those who are beginning to realize his power not to tell others about it (12:16; in the same context in Mark 3:12 it was the demons who recognized his identity and on whom he enjoined silence). So far would Jesus go in not breaking a reed (12:20) that he would offer his cheek to those smiting him with one (27:30; cf. Mic 5:1–2). Thus Jesus demonstrates that he prefers not to fight others when it is not necessary (12:19–20; cf. 10:23; Gen 26:14–22). Although his opponents may think him a youthful upstart,[93] the Scriptures mandate Jesus' identity and his destiny (12:21).

The quotation from Isaiah 42:1–4 in this passage especially looks forward to the conflict in the following narrative: whereas his opponents misinterpret his identity, his empowerment by the Spirit demonstrates that he is the chosen one of Isaiah's prophecy (12:18, 28). Matthew quotes more of the passage than the "Spirit-endowed" or "chosen servant" part, however, to emphasize the meek character of Jesus' first coming (21:5) and especially the final line, which reinforces Matthew's theme of the Gentile mission (2:1–12; 24:14; 28:19): Gentiles will hope in Jesus.

In this passage Matthew reads Jesus as Isaiah's "servant of Yahweh." Although *Targum Pseudo-Jonathan* (fifth century C.E., including earlier material) calls the servant "Messiah" in Isa 42:1; 43:10; and 52:13,[94] Judaism in Jesus' day rarely applied the servant passages to the Messiah. In its immediate context, Isaiah 42:1–4 refers to Israel, not to a more specific figure within Israel (44:1, 21; 49:3). But Matthew's reading also makes sense of the context, developing it in a different direction: God's servant Israel failed in its mission (42:18–19), so God chose one person within Israel to restore the rest of his people (49:5–7); this one would bear the punishment (cf. 40:2) rightly due his people (52:13–53:12).[95]

Translating freely from the Hebrew, Matthew conforms the language of Isa 42 to God's praise of his Son in Matt 3:17 ("my beloved . . . in whom I am well pleased").[96] As Matthew repeatedly pointed out earlier in his Gospel (1:1; 2:15, 18; 3:15; 4:1–2), Jesus' mission is not a wholly new event, but one rooted in the history of his people. For Matthew the Servant Songs help to define Jesus' identity (3:17; 8:17; 20:28). From this text Matthew reminds his readers that at his first coming Jesus was not a political or warrior messiah; he humbled himself as a suffering servant until the time when he would lead "justice to victory" (12:20).

5.   GOD'S SPIRIT VERSUS BEELZEBUB
. . . .

Convinced that Jesus is not God's agent and annoyed by the popular response to Jesus (12:23; cf. 7:28; 8:27; 9:8), the Pharisees resort to the only other possible explanation for his supernatural power over demons (12:22; cf. 9:32–34): it comes from the devil (12:24). In a lengthy response, Jesus not only refutes their charge, but turns it back on them (12:25–45).[97]

People often thought magicians performed their acts through the help of spirit agents,[98] hence the charge here is that Jesus was a sorcerer.[99] This is no small charge: even if Jesus' contemporaries could not enforce the sentence, magic was a capital offense.[100] Jesus' acts of power exceed those normally performed by magicians; thus his opponents attribute his power to the most powerful of malevolent spirits, Satan himself.[101]

This narrative describing Jesus' triumphant response to their charge provides ammunition for Matthew's audience, who undoubtedly confronted the same accusations about their ministry and that of their Lord.[102] Rather than deny testimony concerning Jesus' miracles, later Jewish sources continued to charge Jesus with sorcery;[103] because many associated magic with Egypt,[104] Jesus' youthful stay in Egypt (2:13–19) was also used against him.[105] Perhaps equally relevant to Matthew's readers, later Jewish sources also complained that Christians, who were still working miracles well into the second century, were working them by Satan's power.[106]

i. God's Enemies Challenge God's Attestation

That Jesus can "know their thoughts" (12:25) further attests his power; but while Jewish teachers normally characterized as a prophet or pious man one who could know others' thoughts,[107] they can attribute Jesus' knowledge to the same source as they attributed his exorcisms. Jesus' early followers affirmed him as the bearer par excellence of the spirit of prophecy; some of his opponents viewed him as a false prophet (Deut 13:1–5; 18:9–20).

ii. True Exorcists Are God's Servants

Jesus presents a world sharply divided into God's kingdom and the devil's kingdom, and indicates through various arguments that one cannot be working for both kingdoms at the same time. Jesus first asks why the devil would work at cross-purposes with himself (12:25–26). Perhaps the devil might permit a few exorcisms to bring fame to a sorcerer and gain ground in the long run; Jesus' widespread expulsion of demons, however, constitutes no minor strategic retreat, but a whole-sale assault on Satan's kingdom on earth. The necessity of concord or harmony for survival[108] and warnings about divided kingdoms[109] represent common wisdom in ancient society.

Jesus next questions why his opponents single out his ministry of exorcism while approving exorcisms performed by their own disciples (12:27).[110] Jewish exorcists were common, and employed a variety of magical techniques (incantations, pain compliance techniques like smelly roots, or invocation of higher spirits to get rid of lower ones),[111] quite in contrast to Jesus, who merely commanded authoritatively and the demons obeyed in fear (cf. also 8:16–17).[112] Although the miracles of Elijah and Elisha provide the role model for many of Jesus' miracles, the closest OT model for exorcisms would be David in 1 Sam 16:14–23;[113] early Judaism viewed David's son Solomon as exorcist par excellence.[114] Jesus claimed to act by God's Spirit (12:28), quite in contrast to his opponents who probably would not have thought that the Spirit was available in their time (cf. chapter one above).[115]

Third, if Jesus was driving out demons by God's Spirit, this action constituted proof that the time of the kingdom was upon them (12:28). Most Pharisees apparently believed that the prophetic Spirit had been quenched when the last biblical prophets had died, and that the Spirit would be restored only in the time of the kingdom (see chapter one, above). Although many Pharisees apparently rejected miracles as proof of truth,[116] Jesus summons them to consider an alternative explanation for his miracles, namely that the promised Spirit and kingdom have come on the scene. Indeed, the Greek construction here can sometimes be rendered, "*since* I drive out demons by the Spirit, the kingdom has come on the scene." If the kingdom has not already "come" in some sense in this verse,[117] it is at least quite imminent.[118]

Matthew strategically interprets "finger of God" in his source (cf. Luke 11:20) as "God's Spirit,"[119] showing that Jesus is the promised harbinger of the Spirit (12:18), the first agent of God's kingdom. This means that the earlier Gospel tradition saw Jesus' exorcisms (not just the

Spirit's coming) as a sign of God's impending reign.[120] This end-time interpretation of Jesus' exorcisms lacks parallels in magical exorcism texts;[121] that it also lacks substantial parallels in Jewish messianic and end-time expectation[122] may support the authenticity of the saying; early Christians had available no other prominent source for the idea than Jesus himself. Yet this eschatological interpretation makes good sense: as the climax of history approaches, the forces of God's kingdom and the devil's are arrayed in battle against one another.

Fourth, Jesus had defeated the strong man, "binding" him (tying him up) so that he could plunder the possessions in the strong man's house. That is to say, Jesus invaded Satan's domain and defeated him in order to recapture the human lives that Satan had enslaved through demon-possession or other means (12:29).[123] Far from being authorized by the demons' ruler, Jesus had authority over the devil—one spirit that no mere magical incantation could thwart (cf. *T. Sol.* 6:8). Jesus does not speak here as a magician. That "no one plunders a strong man" was common wisdom;[124] if Jesus' parable about binding alludes to specific earlier language, it is not to magical terminology but to God as the divine warrior delivering his people in Isa 49:24–25.[125]

Since Jesus claims a specific act of binding prior to his ministry of exorcism, he probably refers back to his defeat of Satan at the temptation.[126] Although ancient magical texts regularly speak of "binding" or tying up spirits magically so one can rule them, Jesus' parable does not refer to magical binding;[127] rather, he claims that his integrity before God in defeating temptation has given him power over Satan (Acts 19:13–20). In establishing the first stage of his kingdom Jesus *already* defeated the devil and has delegated his authority over evil spirits to those who are truly his followers, those who submit to his reign (10:8). The final "binding" of Satan awaits his future defeat.[128]

Finally, this list of arguments concludes with Jesus' warning that whoever is not on his side is on the other side (12:30). This saying (already located in the comparable section in Q; Luke 11:23; cf. Mark 9:40) also reflects common wisdom in both Greek[129] and Jewish[130] life. Jesus allows no would-be disciples to straddle the fence: one either follows him or opposes him, just as one does with the devil.

iii. Blasphemy against the Spirit[131]

Although Q may have originally declared that Jesus expelled demons by God's "finger" (Luke 11:20), and Mark omits this statement, most of the same material in Q (Matt 12:22–27, 29; Luke 11:14–19, 21–22; Matt

12:30, 43–45, and Luke 11:23–26 also agree against Mark here) appears in the blasphemy against the Spirit pericope in Mark (3:22–27). This may suggest that Matthew simply follows Mark in joining the accusation of Spirit-blasphemy to the charge against Jesus, but more likely it suggests that Luke has deferred his treatment of Spirit-blasphemy to apply it more directly to unfaithful Christians (Luke 12:8–10), as he also imports Markan Spirit material from elsewhere to complete the section (Luke 12:11–12; Mark 13:11). Thus it is likely that Matthew 12:28 correctly interprets Q here: Jesus acts by God's "finger," and those who revile his activity therefore revile God's *Spirit* (Matt 12:31–32).

Jewish teachers acknowledged that deliberate sin against God's law ("sin with a high hand"; cf. Num 15:30–31; Deut 29:18–20; CD 8.8), such as deliberate blasphemy against God, was unforgivable;[132] some recognized that atonement could purify even these sins, but only for the genuinely repentant.[133] Even such a sin as Peter's denial of Jesus (26:69–75) clearly does not count in the unforgivable category (28:10–20); the context of "blaspheming against the Spirit" here refers specifically to the sin of the Pharisees, who are on the verge of becoming incapable of repentance. The sign of their hardness of heart is their determination to reject *any* proof for Jesus' divine mission, to the extent that they even attribute God's attestation of Jesus to the devil.[134]

The Spirit's empowerment attests Jesus' identity, and those who reject that attestation reject not Jesus but the one who sent him (10:40); Matthew's community could expect the same treatment (10:24–25) despite their own charismatic empowerment (9:35–10:1, 7–8, 20).

iv. Jesus Returns the Charge

Matthew rearranges the material in Q and climaxes with 12:43–45, probably to emphasize that while Jesus is a genuine exorcist, "this generation" led by his opponents would invite the demons back in yet stronger force, and so would become more demonized than before his coming. In other words, not Jesus and his followers, but their opponents, are the devil's vassals.

Reusing some Q material from the sermon on the mount/plain (7:16–20; Luke 6:43–45), Matthew reminds his readers also of John's denunciation of the fruitless leaders (3:7–10). That one's speech reveals one's heart may represent conventional wisdom;[135] Jewish wisdom, like Mediterranean wisdom in general, regularly exhorted appropriate use of one's tongue.[136] On the day of judgment (cf. 10:15; 11:22)[137] each person would give account to God (cf. Rom 14:12), one's words often revealing the character of one's heart (Matt 15:11).[138] Their speech, Jesus says, is what gives them away; by criticizing the Spirit's work of miraculous empowerment, they show themselves to be servants of the devil. This is the sort of corrupt fruit one expects from corrupt trees like these interlocutors, he charges.

v. Sufficient Evidence

The request for a sign (cf. 16:1–4; John 6:30) revealed the evil character of that "generation's" hearts (cf. 11:16; 16:4; Deut 32:5);[139] Jesus had already been providing signs and his opponents were disputing their validity (12:22–24). One may compare the similar situation in 16:1–4, where, ignoring the signs of a prophet in 15:21–39, his opponents, "testing" him,[140] want a sign "from heaven."[141] In that text the very sinfulness of the generation becomes part of the sign (16:2–4).[142]

The whole of 12:39–45 constitutes Jesus' response to his opponents' charges ("generation" in 12:39, 45, frames the section). Jesus explains that his generation needs no greater sign that he is from God than his own message. He first insists that the only sign the sign-seekers would be given was the sign that God supplied the Ninevites: Jonah's restoration after three days on the edge of death (12:39–40).[143] One should keep in mind, however, that the Ninevites did not witness Jonah's resuscitation for themselves; indeed, there is no evidence he even recounted it to them.[144] The Ninevites experienced the effects of a divine sign they never recognized, and this may be Matthew's point (not clear in Luke 11:29, 32): the Ninevites repented without recognizing a sign, whereas Jesus' opponents were too hard-hearted to repent despite the many signs he had been giving them (cf. 11:20–24; Jonah 1:16; 4:2). All the Ninevites needed was Jonah's preaching of the truth, yet Jesus was greater than Jonah (12:41; cf. 12:6).[145]

Jesus' second example is that Solomon's wisdom was enough to prove his divine appointment, and that a distant queen heard and came to him (as some Gentile seekers had done with Jesus: 2:1–12; 1 Kgs 10:1–13).[146] Yet one greater than Solomon is here. The images of the Ninevites and the Queen of Sheba condemning Jesus' generation in Israel at the judgment would have horrified Jesus' hearers, many of whom expected Israel's final vindication against the nations at that judgment day. Indeed, if God accepted Nineveh's repentance, surely he would accept Israel's (*Pesiq. Rab Kah.* 24:11). At the same time, however, Jewish readers could respond to the book of Jonah as if it threatened Israel's judgment by Nineveh's comparatively quick repentance (*Mek. Pisha* 1.81–82).[147]

vi. A Demonized Generation (12:43–45)

Although this paragraph occurs in the same general context in Luke, Matthew specifically places it within the discussion of "this evil generation" (12:39, 45) and uses it to *conclude* Jesus' response to his opponents. Whatever else the parable might say about exorcism, Jesus' point is what it says to that generation: although Jesus was exorcising the generation, its evil leaders were setting it up to be demonized all the worse by rejecting Jesus' reign.[148]

The story includes many clearly Palestinian elements[149] and the story line is quite basic. When an unclean spirit leaves a person and enters the desert seeking a place to dwell[150] it finally returns with seven times the original force and the man ends up worse than before his exorcism. ("Sevenfold" represents the rhetoric of amplified punishments.)[151] If one translates the passage literally, the sentence is conditional: the demons will return *if* the house is left empty.[152] Were Jesus' opponents accusing him of being in league with Satan through his exorcisms (12:24)? Jesus here returns the charge: it is they, not he, who are redemonizing their generation, for they leave the house empty in which God, the only true alternative to the devil, should reign (cf. 23:38–39).

6. MORE LABORERS FOR THE HARVEST

Although most of Matthew's pneumatology so far examined has exhibited a christological focus, Matthew's Christology (hence also his pneumatology) also provides an example for his community (ancient biographies typically provided positive or negative examples).[153] Matthew 9:35 constitutes a summary statement similar to 4:23–25 (which also precedes a kingdom discourse), making clear that the incidents he has reported are merely some prominent examples of Jesus' many works and teachings. At this strategic point, however, Matthew indicates that Jesus' mission prefigures that of his followers. As Jesus perpetuated John's message concerning the kingdom (3:2; 4:17), his followers will do the same (10:7). As Jesus demonstrated the kingdom by compassionately healing (9:35), his disciples must do the same (10:8). In short, this is the point in the Gospel at which Matthew clarifies the suggestion of 3:11 and 16 that much of Jesus' mission is likewise the mission of Jesus' disciples: those whom Jesus baptizes in the Spirit find their model in the Spirit-filled ministry of Jesus.

Matthew rearranges material from various sections of his sources in chapter 10 to emphasize not merely a past, historical mission with little current significance, but one that provides a model for his community.[154]

i. Sheep without a Shepherd

In keeping with his thoroughgoing distinction between true prophets and false, between Jesus' miracles and works of magicians, Matthew emphasizes that Jesus' motivation was compassion[155] and that this attitude reflected the character of the God of the OT. When lacking God-appointed leaders, God's people in the Hebrew Bible often appear as "sheep without a shepherd" (Num 27:17; 1 Kgs 22:17; 2 Chron 18:16), inviting the compassionate Lord to shepherd his people himself (Ezek 34:11–16), including feeding them (Ezek 34:2–3; Matt 14:19–20), healing them (Ezek 34:4; Matt 9:35), and bringing the lost sheep back (Ezek 34:4–6; Matt 18:12–14). This implies that the religious leaders of Israel who purported to be their shepherds had failed to obey God's commission (Ezek 34:2–10; Matt 23).

ii. Jesus Seeks More Workers

Given the magnitude of the needs, Matthew's Jesus seeks to extend his ministry of compassion, expressed in preaching and healing (9:35–36). Jewish teachers understood that each of them could handle only so many students by themselves, even if the students were yet minors.[156] Miracle-working teachers sometimes expected their disciples to work miracles, although the disciples were not always successful;[157] Jesus' disciples sometimes fell short of their teacher, too (17:16).[158] The term Jesus uses for "workers" here recurs in 10:10, indicating that the workers Jesus wished to send forth into the harvest were his own disciples. Those exhorted to pray for laborers in 9:38 become the laborers in the next chapter.

The mission was no less urgent than the harvest, which sometimes required unusual or extravagant measures to bring in all the grain (e.g., 20:1–16). Gathering the wheat in the harvest has eschatological ramifications in view of the approaching kingdom (3:12; 13:30), and the urgency of harvest was a potent image that provided other Jewish teachers with similar analogies.[159]

7. JESUS' AGENTS

Jesus' instructions here show that the disciples would carry on most aspects of his mission (9:35–38). Historical data clearly limits Matthew's freedom to adjust the account; although Matthew stresses the Gentile mission (28:19), his Jewish readers are well aware that before the cross

Jesus sent his disciples only to Israel (10:5–6). Yet Matthew provides these instructions not merely as a matter of historical interest but as a living message to his own readers; had Matthew's interest been *merely* historical he would not have rearranged this section so thoroughly to be relevant to his readers.

Thus he includes some material not relevant to the first mission but which his community would recognize as particularly relevant in their own day, including prosecution before synagogue and pagan courts (10:17–18).[160] Likewise Matt 11:1 does not actually report the disciples' mission (contrast Mark 6:12–13) because for Matthew the mission must continue in his own generation. Summoning his community to greater commitment to the Gentile mission, he provides instructions for those who would go forth to evangelize, and, in more general ways, for the churches that send them.

i. Jesus Authorizes Others to Expel Demons and Heal[161]

Jesus' authorization means that they were to carry on his own mission of healing (9:35), because the laborers were so few (9:37). In OT narratives God's servants frequently trained others, delegating authority to them; thus Elijah trained Elisha and also apparently led a revival of wilderness prophets (cf. 2 Kgs 2:3–18); Samuel also was training a prophetic movement that had not existed when God first began calling him (1 Sam 3:1; 19:20–24).[162]

ii. Jesus "Apostles" his Agents

Jesus "sends," or "apostles" these disciples (10:5).[163] The language used here for "sending" probably connotes commissioning agents with delegated authority. Surrounding cultures had long used heralds and ambassadors, the latter acting on the sender's authority and responsible to carry out his wishes;[164] philosophers could likewise send disciples to teach in their stead and act as their representatives.[165] Ancient Israelite circles also used formal agents or messengers (e.g., Prov 10:26; 13:17; 22:21; 25:13; 26:6), and agency eventually became a legal custom so pervasive that both Roman and Jewish law recognized the use of agents, or intermediary marriage-brokers, in betrothals.[166]

Sources suggest that an agent did not necessarily have high legal status;[167] even slaves were permitted to fill the position.[168] Yet agents carried delegated authority, because they acted on the authority of the one who sent them. Thus later teachers commonly remarked that a person's agent *(shaliach)* is "equivalent to the person himself."[169] How one treats Jesus' messengers or heralds therefore represents how one treats Jesus himself (10:40–42). Because the agent had to be trustworthy to carry out his mission, teachers sometimes debated the character the pious should require of such agents.[170] This also implies, of course, that a *shaliach*'s authority was entirely limited to the extent of his commission and the fidelity with which he carried it out. Jesus may authorize his disciples to perform charismatic acts of compassion (9:36) in his name, but this does not authorize them to use his power to get whatever they want (4:3).

While some scholars reject the "agent" background for early Christian apostles,[171] the early and broad Mediterranean parallels for the general concept supports the idea,[172] and it was accepted as NT background as early as Jerome *(Comm. in Ep. ad Gal.* 1.1) and advocated by Lightfoot in the last century.[173] The concept of agency informs the early Christian idea of apostleship in a general way,[174] but differences also exist.[175] These differences point us to a specific *kind* of "agent" in this passage: in biblical history, *God's* agents were the prophets. The connections in this text between Jesus' commissioned messengers and prophets should not be overlooked (10:41).[176]

iii. Initial Mission to Israel Alone

Readers could interpret Jesus' limitation of his disciples' initial mission to Israel as an indication that the mission discourse reports history only, rather than being prescriptive for Matthew's own community. More likely, it indicates that just as Jesus successfully authorized his first disciples to proclaim the kingdom in the region where Matthew's audience knew that the disciples first ministered, he could successfully authorize disciples to proclaim the kingdom to the nations (28:18–20).

Matthew's Jewish-Christian community is already well aware that Jesus commissioned disciples to minister to the people of Israel during his own earthly ministry; he makes no attempt to conceal this commission.[177] The very number of central disciples (10:1) signifies a mission to Israel. Twelve naturally could symbolize the twelve tribes of Israel, and many contemporary interpreters understood other references to "twelve" in this manner.[178] The Qumran community included a leadership of twelve special officers, a number which comported well with their vision of themselves as the true remnant of Israel.[179] Although Jesus had many disciples, he apparently selected a core group of twelve (e.g., Mark 3:16; 1 Cor 15:5) to make a statement similar to that of the Qumran community:[180] Jesus' disciples were the leaders of the true remnant of God's people (19:28). The tradition of the Twelve, which is older than any given list of the names themselves, is a nearly certain bedrock tradition going back to the historical Jesus.[181]

This limitation fits the historic priority of Israel in salvation history (cf. Rom 1:16; 2:9–10; 15:8–9), was practical (these disciples were not yet equipped to cross cultural boundaries), and undoubtedly would not have been at all objectionable to the disciples themselves (cf. Acts 10:28). Jesus' concern for the "lost sheep" of Israel (10:6; 15:24) echoes his complaint that his people were "helpless" like "sheep without a shepherd" (9:36; cf. 10:16). The biblical prophets complained that the irresponsibility of Israel's shepherds allowed the sheep to go astray (Jer 50:6; Ezek 34:5); the text may also recall Isa 53:6. Jewish people often thought that ten of the twelve tribes were lost and would be restored only in the end time;[182] Jesus' choice of "twelve" apostles signified the imminence of the end-time regathering of God's scattered people (10:1).[183]

Nevertheless, Jesus' orders address geography *more* than ethnicity; the NIV mistranslates "way of Gentiles" as "among the Gentiles." Jesus merely prohibited taking any of the roads leading to Hellenistic cities in Palestine.[184] Since Samaria and Gentile territories surrounded Galilee, Jesus' orders de facto limited his disciples' mission geographically, restricting their activity to Galilee.[185] Because Jesus' earliest followers extended this prohibition beyond its minimal sense, it undoubtedly remained in the background of early Christian opposition to the Gentile mission.[186]

In contrast to other commandments in this chapter, however, Matthew indicates that Jesus later revokes this one, specifically clarifying that this one command was a temporary measure during his earthly ministry. The critical prerequisite of the end which the church can fulfill is world evangelization (24:14), and the Gospel's climactic conclusion is the commission to disciple *all* nations until the end of the age (28:19–20). Indeed, the contextual literary function of 10:5 may best explain why Matthew both retains and emphasizes it: by highlighting that the gospel's recipients are Jewish, hence that *Jewish* people may reject the kingdom and be treated as Gentiles (10:14–15), this verse implies a supraethnic view of the covenant that ultimately necessitates the Gentile mission.[187]

iv. The Disciples' Message is the Kingdom

Their message precisely echoes that of Jesus' opening proclamation in 4:17. That Matthew intends the kingdom to remain his community's message is clear not only from the fact that Matthew nowhere revokes it but from the exactly parallel formulation in his Gospel's conclusion: "as you go" is a participle in both instances (10:7; 28:19). That Jesus has all authority in the universe (28:18) and appears alongside the Father and the Spirit (28:19) indicates his rule or kingdom, especially in view of the allusion to Dan 7:13–14 in Matt 28:18. To make disciples for this king is to proclaim the good news that God's future kingdom is already active in this age (cf. 28:20). Acts concurs that the kingdom message is the gospel of Christ (Acts 8:12; 20:24–25; 28:31).

v. Signs Authenticate the Kingdom Message

As Jesus demonstrated God's rule with signs (9:35), so must the disciples (10:1, 7–8). Harrington observes that "the disciples' mission (vv. 7–8) replicates and extends the mission of Jesus in preaching the coming of God's kingdom and in healing the sick (see 4:23)."[188] Jesus' commands in 10:8 are all sharp, parallel statements that would communicate emphasis in both Aramaic and Greek.[189] Various early Christian circles doubted that hardhearted people would be satisfied with signs (15:37–16:1; cf. John 11:47–48; 12:10–11; Acts 4:16–17), but believed that signs could draw other people's attention to the kingdom message (11:3–6, 21, 23; cf. John 2:11; Acts 4:29–30; 9:35, 42).

vi. Jesus' Agents Disdain Profit

In contrast to some maligned classes of moral teachers,[190] Jesus' disciples were to disdain profit, their simplicity testifying to the sincerity of their conviction as in the case of their master (8:20).[191] Peasants, at least in the poorest parts of the empire like Egypt, often owned only one cloak (cf. 5:40);[192] Cynics also voluntarily limited themselves to a single cloak; since some Cynics were known in Hellenistic cities of Syria,[193] a Cynic connection is not impossible. Yet more to the point, Essenes showed their devotion to God by a simple lifestyle, those who lived in the wilderness devoting all their goods to the community.[194] Josephus also indicates that Essenes did not take provisions when they traveled, expecting hospitality from fellow Essenes in every city.[195] Perhaps most relevant is the model of Israel's ancient prophets in times of national apostasy.[196] Manson remarks that the disciples here depend on the people of the land, "like an invading army."[197]

In a traditional Jewish proverb, God commissioned Torah teachers to offer Torah freely as he did;[198] some early Jewish teachers prohibited accepting pay for teaching.[199] The prophetic model may again be most relevant; one may compare Elisha's unwillingness to accept Naaman's gifts, preferring to allow the Aramean God-fearer to remain wholly indebted to Israel's God; his servant Gehazi, however, determined to profit from Naaman and suffered for it (2 Kgs 5:20–27). Elisha reminded Gehazi that the current time of spiritual crisis rendered the acquisition of material possessions a vain pursuit (2 Kgs 5:26).

On long trips, one typically brought both a change of clothes and money in a bag tied to one's belt or fastened around one's neck;[200] Jesus forbids the normal basic apparatus for travel. Jesus' prohibition of the "bag" (10:10; Mark 6:8; cf. Prov 7:20) prohibits begging,[201] the survival method of the otherwise equally simple Cynics.[202] Mark allows at least staff and sandals,[203] but Matthew's demand for simplicity is still more radical, prohibiting even these.[204] In contrast to Mark, Matthew not only prohibits taking money on one's journey, but acquiring any money while there.[205]

The "staff" was an instrument for self-protection (sometimes against robbers, perhaps against wild beasts) and perhaps as an aid in walking on uneven paths. Some Jewish teaching forbade the staff, but usually only on the Sabbath (m. Roš Haš. 1:9), holy days (2:9), or in the temple.[206] Thus these prohibitions might underline the sacredness of the mission.[207] The point of the prohibitions can hardly be limited to this explanation, however, for this explanation fails to account for details such as "the additional prohibition of two tunics,"[208] which at least some early Christians applied to discipleship in general (Luke 3:11). The obedience of Jesus' disciples to their calling in this text challenges missionaries from the Matthean community likewise to count the cost (cf. 1 Cor 4:11–12; 2 Cor 4:8–9; 6:4–5; 11:23–27). The best Cynics also recognized that the significance of their lifestyle lay in the values it reflected rather than merely the simplicity itself.[209]

Churches provided hospitality for traveling apostles, prophets, and evangelists in the late first century, but Christians had to become wise about hucksters and charlatans. One early church document warns that if a prophet wants to stay more than three days or asks for money, he is a false prophet (Did. 11:5; cf. 2 Cor 11:7–15); Matthew may have had such false teachers in mind as he dictated this warning.[210]

vii. Trusting God for Provision

The missionaries could travel light, not depending on normal means of support (cf. 6:19–24), because they trusted God's provision (6:25–34).

Ancient Mediterranean peoples emphasized hospitality,[211] and Jewish travelers, who avoided inns when possible due to inns' unsavory moral reputations, particularly stressed this virtue.[212] Because strangers could abuse this system, however, Jewish people outside Palestine depended heavily on letters of recommendation showing that the traveler was of good reputation.[213] Like the early Christians (2 John 10–11; *Did.* 11–12), most Jews would not embrace one they believed to be a messenger of false teaching.[214] But like Paul in 2 Cor 3:1–6, this passage emphasizes that Jesus' messengers had better backing than a letter of recommendation; the authority of Jesus himself stood behind them (10:40–42).

Hospitality implied a potential reciprocal obligation, to be fulfilled when the host himself might be in need; but because the disciples brought a spiritual gift of far greater worth than the hospitality they sought, they fulfilled their reciprocal obligation immediately.[215] Indeed, the initial burden of obligation lay primarily on the host (1 Cor 9:14; 1 Tim 5:18).

viii. Responding to Christ's Messengers

The hearers would be judged by whether they embraced Jesus' messengers, just as they would be judged by how they responded to Jesus himself (10:40–42). The missionaries were to use one home as their base of operation for evangelizing the community (10:11–12; cf. Mark 6:10; Luke 10:7). They would find the home first by inquiring from those they encountered who might prove receptive to their message (10:11), then by finding if the household welcomed them to stay there (10:12–13). Greetings constituted an essential aspect of social etiquette in Mediterranean antiquity[216] and social convention dictated particular rules for how to greet persons of varying rank (23:7),[217] as they still do today in most Middle Eastern society.[218] But Jews also viewed their greetings as "wish-prayers":[219] *shalom,* "peace," meant, "May it be well with you" (e.g., 1 Chron 12:18). Just as a curse undeserved will not take effect (Prov 26:2), Jesus declares that the blessings will be efficacious only if they prove appropriate.

Those who received the agents of Christ received Christ himself (10:40–41; 25:35–40), even if the only hospitality they had available to offer was a cup of water (10:42). But those who rejected Christ's agents were to be treated like pagans (10:14). Just as Jewish travelers returning to the holy land might shake the dust of Gentile lands from their feet,[220] or those entering the holy temple might shake the relatively profane dust of the land of Israel from their feet,[221] so Jesus' disciples were to treat those who rejected their message as unholy (Acts 13:51; cf. 18:6; 22:23).[222] God would treat these nations not merely like Gentiles in general, but worse than Sodom and Gomorrah (10:15), for they were rejecting a greater revelation, a greater opportunity for repentance, than Sodom and Gomorrah had (11:23–24).[223] The prophets had employed Sodom as the epitome of evil that merited judgment (Isa 13:19; Jer 50:40; Zeph 2:9) and regularly applied the image to Israel (Deut 32:32; Isa 1:10; 3:9; Jer 23:14; Lam 4:6; Ezek 16:46–49). Later Jewish texts also employed Sodom as the epitome of immorality.[224] Sodom's rejection of angelic messengers (Gen 19) merited less damnation than Jesus' contemporaries' rejection of him (cf. Matt 12:6, 41–42; 23:35–36).

Jesus' messengers are to carry on his mission, proclaiming the same message of the kingdom he proclaimed, authenticating the message through the same signs he performed, countering false accusations by following the simple itinerant lifestyle he followed while preaching, and recognizing that hearers would be judged according to their response to Jesus' agents as they were judged according to their response to Jesus. The only difference Matthew's Gospel makes explicit between the first disciples' mission in their narrative world and his contemporaries' mission is that the mission is no longer limited to Israel, but for all peoples (28:19).

8. CONCLUSION

For Matthew, the empowering Spirit is essential in defining Jesus' mission as God's servant rather than the devil's. He empowers Jesus for his call and through his time of testing. Jesus as the true Son of God depends not on magic, on signs that would exalt him, or on political power (4:1–11); rather, he depends on the Spirit, as the meek one who waits for God's vindication and the spread of justice to the Gentiles (12:18–21). The miracles he does are by God's Spirit, not by Beelzebub, and indicate the coming kingdom of God (12:28). The Spirit equipped the forerunner of Matthew's community, and so would equip Matthew's community itself, not for miraculous (12:38; 16:1) or political (22:17; 26:52) triumphalism (both of which had failed Judea in the recent revolt against Rome), but for miracles motivated by compassion (9:35–10:1) and empowerment to endure the test (4:1; 10:17–20). For Matthew's community, which knew both true and false charismatics (7:15–23), this distinction was essential. Because the Matthean believers also had to defend themselves as well as their Lord against charges of sorcery by successors of the Pharisees (perhaps partly on the basis of the view that prophets in the OT mold had ceased), Matthew emphasizes that Jesus and his true followers pass the tests for true prophets, reversing the charge of Satanic allegiance toward their accusers.

NOTES

· ·

1. Much of the material in this chapter has been borrowed from two commentaries I am currently writing on Matthew, the more popular for InterVarsity Press and the more academic for Eerdmans. See more detailed documentation in the latter.

2. See J. P. Meier, "John the Baptist in Josephus: Philology and Exegesis," *JBL* 111 (1992) 234.

3. E.g., *Manasses* 3:8; cf. *T. Ab.* 10A; *ʾAbot R. Nat.* 14A.

4. 1 Kgs 8:46; 1 Esd 4:37–38; Sir 8:5; *T. Ab.* 9A; 4 Ezra 8:35; Moore, *Judaism,* 467–69; Bonsirven, *Judaism,* 114.

5. Sanders, *Paul,* 174–80; Montefiore and Loewe, *Anthology,* 315–33.

6. F. F. Bruce, *The Time Is Fulfilled* (Grand Rapids, Mich.: Eerdmans, 1978) 61.

7. Manson, *Sayings,* 40.

8. Ael., *N.A.* 1.24; Pliny, *N.H.* 10.170; Plut., *Divine Vengeance* 32, *Moralia* 567F.

9. In the fourth century B.C.E., Aristotle declared that vipers produce eggs internally but bring forth their young alive. However, he made no comments on the nature of their delivery (Arist., *G.A.* 1.10, 718b–30). Likewise Strabo altogether omits discussions of Indian vipers' birth (Strabo, *Geog.* 15.1.45). Not all writers in subsequent centuries agreed with Herodotus; in the second or third century C.E. Aelian, following a no longer extant work of Aristotle's successor Theophrastus, at one point agrees that the mother's womb bursts, but argues that it is through no malice of the offspring (Ael., *N.A.* 15.16); but he elsewhere concurs with and elaborates on Herodotus' account, as noted above. Ancient Mediterranean peoples considered parent-murder one of the most hideous crimes conceivable (e.g., Sen., *De Clementia* 1.23.1; Epict., *Disc.* 1.7.31–33; Plut., *Rom.* 22.4; Marc. Aur., *Med.* 6.34; Apul., *Metam.* 10.8; Diog. Laert., *Lives* 1.59; 1 Tim 1:9), continuing to recall Nero's matricide (Mart., *Epig.* 4.63.3–4; *Sib. Or.* 4:121, 5:30, 8:71). Most people believed that even children who justly avenged their fathers erred in personally carrying it out against their mothers, and thus the Furies would torment them (e.g., Eurip., *El.* 1238–91; *Or.* 531–32, 549–63).

10. Bruce, *Matthew,* 82.

11. Jer 46:21–23; R. T. France, *Matthew* (TNTC; Grand Rapids, Mich.: Eerdmans, 1985) 92.

12. Q follows the literal Semitic and LXX idiom "make fruit" (common in the Greek of the NT) here (M. Black, *An Aramaic Approach to the Gospels and Acts* [3d ed.; Oxford: Clarendon, 1967] 138–39). Judaism also insisted that repentance be demonstrated practically (*m. Yoma* 8:8–9; Montefiore, *Synoptic Gospels,* 2.15).

13. Rom 11:16–17; cf. F. Mussner, "1QHodajoth und das Gleichnis von Senfkorn," *BZ* 4 (1960) 128–30; more narrowly Kraeling, *John the Baptist,* 43–44.

14. Kraeling, *John the Baptist,* 44.

15. Cf., e.g., Neh 9:7; Mic 7:20; Sanders, *Paul*, 87–101; M. J. Borg, *Conflict, Holiness, & Politics in the Teachings of Jesus* (SBEC 5; New York: Mellen, 1984) 207.

16. Often noted; e.g., Manson, *Sayings*, 40; Argyle, *Matthew*, 36; J. C. Fenton, *Saint Matthew* (Philadelphia: Westminster, 1977) 56; Gundry, *Matthew*, 47.

17. Cf. Robinson, *Problem of History*, 76–77, and our preceding chapter.

18. This proclamation represents eschatological judgment on Israel, not mere purification of the individual; in detail, see Menzies, *Pneumatology*, 137–44.

19. As depicted in various texts in the OT and as late as, e.g., *Lev. Rab.* 28:2; *Qoh. Rab.* 5:15 §1.

20. Bruce, *Matthew*, 84; Flowers, "Pneumati"; cf. Dunn, "Spirit," 695; Isa 4:4; Mal 3:2. Barnard, "Matt. III," 107, suggests the image of a fiery stream.

21. See ch. 1, above.

22. Cf. Bruce, "Spirit in Qumran Texts," 50; Aune, *Prophecy*, 132.

23. Although Menzies is correct that Luke's pneumatology is almost entirely prophetic, I would argue that Luke's dependence on tradition qualifies that emphasis in Luke 3:16; *Pneumatology*, 145. That prophecy can involve *proclamation* of judgment is not, as he hopes, sufficient to explain the context of being *baptized in* fire here.

24. E.g., Dan 4:26; Luke 15:18; 3 Macc 4:21; 1QM 12.5; *1 Enoch* 6:2; 13:8; *m. ʾAbot.* 1:3; *t. B. Qam.* 7:5; *Sipra Behuq.* pq. 6.267.2.1; *Sipre Deut.* 79.1.1; 96.2.2; *b. ʿAbod. Zar.* 18a, bar.; *B. Qam.* 76a; *Moʾed Qat.* 17a; *Ned.* 45a, bar.; *Pesaḥ.* 66b; *Taʿan.* 14b; *Num. Rab.* 7:5; 8:4; *Ruth Rab.* 7:1; *Qoh. Rab.* 7:8 §1; 7:27 §1; 9:12 §1.

25. Some Jewish texts use "kingdom of heaven" as a periphrasis for "kingdom of God" (e.g., *Sipra Qed.* pq. 9.207.2.13; *p. Qidd.* 1:2 §24), as many scholars note (e.g., Goppelt, *Theology*, 1.44; Bonsirven, *Judaism*, 7; Marmorstein, *Names and Attributes*, 93; Moore, *Judaism*, 1.119, 2.309). Matthew naturally preferred this synonymous expression common in the Pharisaic-type circles he was engaging; M. D. Goulder, *Midrash and Lection in Matthew* (London: SPCK, 1974) 63; Jeremias, *Theology*, 97; contrast R. A. Guelich, *The Sermon on the Mount* (Waco: Word, 1982) 77. The contrast between "kingdom of heaven" and "kingdom of God" that characterized some earlier dispensational interpreters has been widely abandoned; R. L. Saucy, *The Case for Progressive Dispensationalism* (Grand Rapids, Mich.: Zondervan, 1993) 19.

26. Scholars widely concur that the Hebrew, Aramaic, and Greek terms signify the concept "reign," "authority," or "rule" (e.g., Dodd, *Parables*, 34; N. Perrin, *The Kingdom of God*, 24; Betz, *Jesus*, 33; contrast Aalen, "Reign").

27. E.g., Ps 22:28; 103:19; 145:11, 13; Dan 7:18, 22, 27. Like the OT (e.g., Isa 6:5), Jewish teachers could speak of God's present rule, especially among people who obeyed his law (e.g., *m. Ber.* 2:2; *Sipra A.M.* pq. 13.194.2.1; *Sipre Deut.* 313.1.3; 323.1.2; see Bonsirven, *Judaism*, 176). But Jewish people also looked for the kingdom as God's future rule, when he would reign unchallenged (e.g., Isa 24:23; Wis 5:16; *Jub.* 1:28; *Mek. Shirata* 10.42–45; cf. Moore, *Judaism*, 1.423; 2.309; Bonsirven, *Judaism*, 176–77; R. B. Laurin, "The Question of Immortality in the Qumran Hodayot," *JSS* 3 [1958] 344–55), as attested in regular Jewish prayers; see, e.g., W. O. E. Oesterley, *The Jewish Background of the Christian Liturgy* (Oxford: Clarendon, 1925) 65, 70. When Burton Mack thinks the Cynic concept of philosophic rulership comes closer to Jesus' proclamation of the reign of Israel's God than the Jewish notion (which is, as we have noted, already found

in the Hebrew Bible), his interpretation probably reveals more about Mack's prejudices than about Jesus; cf. Mack, *A Myth of Innocence* (Philadelphia: Fortress, 1988) 70–74.

28. See especially Sanders, *Jesus and Judaism*, 139–40.

29. Sanders, *Jesus and Judaism*, 151–54, 231–32; cf. Burkitt, *Sources*, 69; A. Schweitzer, *The Quest of the Historical Jesus* (New York: Macmillan, 1968) 223–397.

30. See Dodd, *Parables*; Jeremias, *Parables*, passim.

31. E.g., J. D. G. Dunn, *Jesus and the Spirit* (London: SCM, 1975) 89; R. H. Stein, *The Method and Message of Jesus' Teachings* (Philadelphia: Westminster, 1978) 60–79; Ladd, *Theology*, 70–80; Aune, *Cultic Setting*, 3–4; A. E. Harvey, *Jesus and the Constraints of History* (Philadelphia: Westminster, 1982) 91.

32. One should also compare present and future aspects of God's rule in Jewish texts, above, even if this may not provide the whole explanation. Some scholars, who maintain that Jesus' future kingdom is an unrealistic hope for modern people, label the kingdom a myth and translate it into existential language more appropriate for their own academic circles of thought, e.g., Bultmann, *Theology*, 1.24; N. Perrin, *Jesus and the Language of the Kingdom* (Philadelphia: Fortress, 1976) 30–32; R. C. Tannehill, *The Sword of His Mouth* (SBLSS 1; Missoula, Mont.: Scholars Press, 1975) 56; Borg, *Conflict*, 248–63; cf. R. Bultmann, *New Testament Mythology and Other Basic Writings* (Philadelphia: Fortress, 1984) 137–38. But their position appears to presuppose modern contempt for apocalyptic thought rather than a detailed historical argument; see Sanders, *Jesus and Judaism*, 7, 27, 125–27. Further, the future kingdom is hardly irrelevant to the persecuted and oppressed, who nurture hope that God's justice will ultimately triumph and vindicate them.

33. Some hellenized Jews like Philo stressed judgment far more rarely; cf., e.g., *Congr.* 171–72: God, being good, would not literally send famine or death.

34. Cf. Sanders, *Jesus and Judaism*, 96.

35. E.g., Ps 1:4; Isa 17:13; Hos 13:3; cf. Jer 4:11–13; 13:24.

36. See 4 Ezra 4:30–32; cf. *Sipre Deut.* 312.1.1; 343.5.2; *Num. Rab.* 4:1; cf. also early Christian references, perhaps derived from the Jesus tradition (Jas 5:7–8; Rev 14:15).

37. E.g., Isa 26:11; 66:15–16, 24; cf. 2 Thess 1:6–7.

38. E.g., *CPJ* 1.199.

39. Kraeling, *John the Baptist*, 42; Ladd, *Theology*, 37.

40. E.g., *'Abot R. Nat.* 41A; cf. also 36A. Many believed that it was eternal for at least the worst sinners: 4 Macc 9:9; 12:12; *t. Sanh.* 13:5; probably *1 Enoch* 108:5–6; Ps.-Philo 38:4; *Asc. Isa.* 1:2; *3 Enoch* 44:3; *p. Ḥag.* 2:2 §5; *Sanh.* 6:6 §2; cf. Plut., *Divine Vengeance* 31, *Moralia* 567DE. In the most common Jewish view, most sinners endure hell only temporarily and are then destroyed (cf. 1QS 4.13–14; *Gen. Rab.* 6:6; most sinners in *t. Sanh.* 13:4; *Pesiq. Rab Kah.* 10:4; *Pesiq. Rab.* 11:5) or released (*Num. Rab.* 18:20; other texts are unclear, e.g., Sir 7:16; *Sipre Num.* 40.1.9; *Sipre Deut.* 311.3.1; 357.6.7; *'Abot R. Nat.* 16A; 32 §69B; 37 §95B). Many Jewish storytellers conflated Gehenna with the Greek Tartarus, e.g., *Sib. Or.* 1:10, 101–3, 119; 4.186; 5.178; 11.138; cf. *Gr. Ezra* 4:22; *b. Giṭ.* 56b–57a; *p. Ḥag.* 2:2 §5; *Sanh.* 6:6 §2; *Apoc. Pet.* 5–12. Although Luke does not reject future eschatology in his effort to contextualize for Greek readers (Acts 17:31–32; 23:6; 24:15; contrast, e.g., Jos. *Ant.* 18.14, 18; *J.W.* 2.163; Philo, *Sacr.* 5, 8), Matthew's

emphases retain more of their original Jewish flavor; cf. C. Milikowsky, "Which Gehenna?" *NTS* 34 (1988) 238–49; Goulder, *Midrash in Matthew,* 63.

41. Cf. *Jos. and Asen.* 7:1; 13:15/12; 20:4 (with *OTP* 2.210 note); *Gen. Rab.* 60:8; J. Carcopino, *Daily Life in Ancient Rome* (New Haven: Yale, 1940) 274. Although Jerusalem's streets were reportedly cleaned (*b. Pesah̨.* 7a; for other cities, M. Avi–Yonah, *Hellenism and the East* [Jerusalem: Hebrew University, 1978] 124), less tidy Eastern towns' streets might have included "refuse" and the droppings of "scavenging dogs, pigs, birds, and other animals" (R. L. Rohrbaugh, "The Pre-Industrial City in Luke–Acts," in *Social World of Luke–Acts* [ed. J. H. Neyrey; Peabody: Hendrickson, 1991] 135). But one could also assume this servile posture for hospitality (e.g., Gen 18:4; *T. Ab.* 3A; 3B); those of humble status or without servants would necessarily do so; wives and children could adopt this servile posture toward the *pater familias;* see, e.g., Hierocles, *On Duties: How to Conduct Oneself toward One's Parents* 4.25.53 (in Malherbe, *Exhortation,* 92–93); 1 Sam 25:41; cf. C. K. Barrett, *The Gospel according to St. John* (2d ed.; Philadelphia: Westminster, 1978) 440.

42. E.g., Diog. Laert., *Lives* 6.2.44; *b. B.Bat.* 53b, though both sources ridicule treating slaves in such a demeaning manner; see Daube's and Urbach's citations below. "Loosening" (Mark 1:7; Luke 3:16) and "carrying" (Matt 3:11) the sandals convey the same sense of servility, hence communicate the same point despite the variation in wording; cf. data in Daube, *New Testament and Judaism,* 266. They may also reflect the same Aramaic verb; cf. Manson, *Sayings,* 40.

43. E.g., Exod 33:11; 1 Kgs 19:21; 2 Kgs 5:20; 6:15; Zeno in Diog. Laert., *Lives* 7.1.12; Cleanthes in Diog. Laert., *Lives* 7.5.170; *t. B. Meṣiᶜa.* 2:30; cf. *p. Soṭa* 5:5 §4; Daube, *New Testament and Judaism,* 266, cites also *b. Ketub.* 96a.

44. *B. Ketub.* 96a, cited by various commentators (many following Billerbeck); cf. Davies, *Sermon,* 135; L. Morris, *The Gospel according to John* (NICNT; Grand Rapids, Mich.: Eerdmans, 1971) 141.

45. E.g., 2 Kgs 9:7, 36; 10:10; 14:25; 17:13, 23; 21:10; 24:2; Ezra 9:11; Isa 20:3; Jer 7:25; 25:4; 26:5; 29:19; 35:15; 44:4; Dan 3:28; 6:20; 9:6, 10; Amos 3:7; Zech 1:6; cf. *ᵓAbot R. Nat.* 37 §95B; D. B. Martin, *Slavery as Salvation* (New Haven: Yale, 1990) 55–56; W. Sanday and A. Headlam, *A Critical and Exegetical Commentary on the Epistle to the Romans* (5th ed.; ICC; Edinburgh: Clark, 1902) 3; E. Käsemann, *Commentary on Romans* (Grand Rapids, Mich.: Eerdmans, 1980) 5. Cf. especially David (e.g., 2 Sam 3:18; 7:5, 8, 19–21, 25–29; 1 Kgs 3:6; 8:24–26, 66; 11:13, 32, 34, 36, 38; 14:8; 2 Kgs 8:19; 19:34; 20:6; 1 Chron 17:4, 7, 17–19, 23–27; 2 Chron 6:15–21, 42; Ps 78:70; 89:3, 20; 132:10; 144:10; Isa 37:35; Jer 33:21–22, 26; Ezek 34:23–24; 37:24–25; cf. *ᵓAbot R. Nat.* 43 §121 B) and Moses (e.g., Exod 14:31; Num 12:7–8; Deut 34:5; Josh 1:1–2, 7, 13, 15; 8:31, 33; 9:24; 11:12, 15; 12:6; 13:8; 14:7; 18:7; 22:2, 4–5; 1 Kgs 8:53, 56; 2 Kgs 18:12; 21:8; 1 Chron 6:49; 2 Chron 1:3; 24:6, 9; Neh 1:7–8; 9:14; 10:29; Ps 105:26; Dan 9:11; Mal 4:4; cf. Ps.-Philo 30:2, *famulum; ᵓAbot R. Nat.* 43 §121B). Cf. also the patriarchs (Gen 26:24; Exod 32:13; Deut 9:27; Ps 105:6; 2 Macc 1:2; *Jub.* 31:25; 45:3; *T. Ab.* 9 A; *2 Bar.* 4:4; *ᵓAbot R. Nat.* 43 §121B) and Israel as a whole (Lev 25:42, 55; Deut 32:43; Isa 41:8–9; 42:1, 19; 43:10; 44:1–2, 21; 45:4; 48:20; 49:3; Jer 30:10; 46:27–28; Ezek 28:25; 37:25; *2 Bar.* 44:4; *t. B. Qam.* 7:5; *ᵓAbot R. Nat.* 43 §121B; *Gen. Rab.* 96 NV; *p. Qidd.* 1:2 §24; cf. Tob. 4:14 v.l.).

46. Inscription in F. C. Grant, ed. *Hellenistic Religions* (Indianapolis: Bobbs-Merrill, 1953) 122; Martin, *Slavery,* xiv–xvi (citing Soph., *Oed. Rex* 410; Plato,

Phaedo 85B; Apul., *Metam.* 11.15; inscriptions), 46, 49 (against, e.g., F. W. Beare, *A Commentary on the Epistle to the Philippians* [2d ed.; London: Black, 1969] 50); cf. Rom 1:1 (cf. P. S. Minear, *Images of the Church in the New Testament* [Philadelphia: Westminster, 1960] 156). Slaves of rulers exercised high status: e.g., Epict., *Disc.* 1.19.19; 4.7.23; inscriptions in *The Roman Empire* (ed. R. K. Sherk; TDGR 6; New York: Cambridge, 1988) 89–90 §47; Suet., *Gramm.* 21, in S. Dixon, *The Roman Mother* (Norman: Oklahoma University, 1988) 19; cf. Char., *Chaer.* 5.2.2.

47. E.g., Anderson, *Mark*, 72–73; Taylor, *Mark*, 157.

48. Sanders, *Jesus and Judaism*, 11; Mansfield, *Spirit and Gospel*, 25–26; against Bultmann, *History*, 251.

49. *Pace* Dibelius, *Jesus*, 77.

50. Meier, *Matthew*, 26.

51. Ibid., 26–27.

52. See ch. 1, above.

53. For the obedience interpretation, see also B. Przybylski, *Righteousness in Matthew and His World of Thought* (SNTSM 41; Cambridge: Cambridge, 1980) 94; for the view that Jesus here "fulfills" prophecy, see Meier, *Matthew*, 27; id., *The Vision of Matthew* (New York: Paulist, 1979) 57–58.

54. Cf., e.g., Davies, *Sermon*, 15; Longenecker, *Exegesis*, 144–45; Meier, *Vision*, 55; Bruce, *Documents*, 41; D. Patte, *The Gospel according to Matthew* (Philadelphia: Fortress, 1987) 37; Gundry, *Matthew*, 34.

55. Lampe, *Seal*, 39; cf. G. Barth, "Matthew's Understanding of the Law," in *Tradition and Interpretation in Matthew* (by G. Bornkamm, G. Barth, and H. J. Held; Philadelphia: Westminster, 1963) 138; R. E. H. Uprichard, "The Baptism of Jesus," *IBS* 3 (1981) 187–202.

56. See our chapter on Mark 1. Although narrative connections within the Gospel are important, reading Jesus' "going up" from the water (3:16) as a type of his ascension (Robinson, *Twelve Studies*, 162–63 n. 7) would probably read too much into the phrase, since Matthew never so much as narrates the ascension.

57. E.g., Kingsbury, *Matthew*, 14; Hill, *Prophecy*, 59; Kelber, *Mark's Story*, 18–19; Cranfield, "Baptism," 58; M. Borg, *Jesus: A New Vision* (San Francisco: Harper & Row, 1987) 41, 53 n. 19.

58. Meier, *Vision*, 58.

59. Some also believed the wilderness to be a special haunt of demons (12:43; cf. 4 Macc 18:8; W. M. Alexander, *Demonic Possession in the New Testament* [Edinburgh: Clark, 1902] 29; Jeremias, *Theology*, 69).

60. The primary test early Christians would face and which the heroes Jesus' hearers revered had faced was persecution, the temptation to apostasy (Manson, *Sayings*, 170; cf. 1 Pet 5:8–9). Jewish teachers came to regard martyrdom or perseverance in dangerous tests as the ultimate way to "hallow God's name" (6:9; Moore, *Judaism*, 2.105–7).

61. Cf. Schweitzer, *Quest*, 364; J. Jeremias, *The Prayers of Jesus* (Philadelphia: Fortress, 1964) 105–6; R. V.G. Tasker, *The Gospel according to St. Matthew* (TNTC; Grand Rapids, Mich.: Eerdmans, 1961) 74; A. George, "Ne nous soumets pas à la tentation," *BVC* 71 (1966) 74–79; Brown, "Scrolls," 4; Meier, *Matthew*, 62. The eschatological interpretation makes good sense of the whole context of the sermon: one must get right in view of the coming kingdom (4:17). Most Jewish pietists also expected a period of suffering before the time of the kingdom (1QH

3), and they prayed for protection for that time (*b. Pesaḥ.* 118a). Scholars rightly note the prominence of the final tribulation in the Gospels (W. F. Albright and C. S. Mann, *Matthew* [AB; Garden City, N.Y.: Doubleday, 1971] 76–77) and that one cannot distinguish between the present and future time of testing in the Dead Sea Scrolls (Perrin, *Kingdom,* 197–98).

62. The very lack of distinction between present and future testing means that an eschatological community would regard the present as the time of tribulation (cf. perhaps CD 20.14–15). While the omission of the Greek definite article may not constitute a decisive argument against the future interpretation (cf. D. A. Carson, "Matthew," in *The Expositor's Bible Commentary* [Grand Rapids, Mich.: Zondervan, 1984] 8.83; *pace* Schweizer, *Matthew,* 156; Moule, *Mark,* 66–67; I. H. Marshall, *Commentary on Luke* [NIGTC; Grand Rapids, Mich.: Eerdmans, 1978] 461; id., *Kept by the Power of God* [Minneapolis: Bethany, 1974] 68), the conjunction of "lead us not into testing" with "deliver us from the evil one" suggests that present trials are in view (cf. 13:19; Gundry, *Matthew,* 109). Further, the future cast of the first petitions need not support the future cast for this "test"; the first petitions refer to the coming kingdom, not to the tribulation that precedes it. "Watching" to be ready for testing (26:41) might even prefigure watching for the ultimate test: not the tribulation, but the judgment at the Son of man's coming (24:42–25:13). In the whole context of Matthew, "testing" here probably includes the final tribulation but is not limited to it; this petition is not strictly eschatological. If a specific allusion is intended in this context, it may be to the time of the exodus. God released his people from slavery (cf. perhaps 6:12), fed them with manna (6:11), and they, like Jesus, were tested in the wilderness (6:13; cf. 4:1–2). C. B. Houk, "Peirasmos, the Lord's Prayer, and the Massah Tradition," *SJT* 19 (1966) 216–25, and J. J. Lewis, "The Wilderness Controversy and Peirasmos," *Colloquium* 7 (1974) 42–44, may be correct in finding an allusion to the exodus narrative, but they find more than Matthew's language warrants in reading, "lest we test *God*" (Exod 17:1–7; Houk, "Peirasmos," 223; more tentatively Lewis, "Controversy," 43; cf. M. B. Walker, "Lead Us Not into Temptation," *ExpT* 73 [1962] 287).

63. Most other Jewish prayers that requested protection from temptation meant testing in the present time (Montefiore, *Synoptic Gospels,* 2.103; cf. Abrahams, *Studies* (2), 101; Jeremias, *Prayers,* 105; *b. Sanh.* 64a).

64. Cf. Best, *Temptation,* 49–50. Contemporary and later Jewish literature also recognized that God sent testing (e.g., *Jub.* 17:17; Sir 2:1; 36:1; Wis 3:5–6; 10:10; 11:9; Jdt 8:25; *Pss. Sol.* 16:12–15; *Gen. Rab.* 55:2; *Num. Rab.* 17:2; cf. *Jub.* 19:3), but viewed as evil testing whose goal was stumbling (4 Macc 9:7).

65. Biographies often recounted the protagonist's refusal to turn from a heroic vocation for other temptations; see P. L. Schuler, *A Genre for the Gospels* (Philadelphia: Fortress, 1982) 96. Jewish teachers sometimes told stories of their predecessors' invulnerability to sexual or other temptations (*'Abot R. Nat.* 16A), although other stories illustrated their predecessors' vulnerability to temptation (e.g., *b. Qidd.* 81a in Urbach, *Sages,* 1.480).

66. Cf. H. Schlier, *Principalities and Powers in the New Testament* (New York: Herder & Herder, 1961) 40.

67. Those who propose a Buddhist (R. Thapar, *A History of India* [Baltimore: Penguin, 1966] 119; cf. Montefiore, *Synoptic Gospels,* 2.19, 21; Manson, *Sayings,* 45) or even general Greco-Roman (e.g., Barrett, *Spirit,* 52; M. Dibelius, *From*

Tradition to Gospel [Cambridge: Clarke, 1971] 245) background for the account miss the clearer background in Israel's testing in the wilderness.

68. Widely noted, e.g., Teeple, *Prophet*, 75–76; Dunn, *Baptism*, 30; Riesenfeld, *Gospel Tradition*, 76; Albright and Mann, *Matthew*, 36; R. F. Collins, "The Temptation of Jesus," *Melita Theologica* 26 (1974) 32–45; Meier, *Vision*, 59–61; Gundry, *Matthew*, 53; France, *Matthew*, 98.

69. God led his people (e.g., Ps 80:1; 143:10), especially in the exodus: Exod 13:18, 21; 15:13, 22; Deut 8:2; Neh 9:12; Ps 77:20; 78:14, 52; 106:9; 136:16; Isa 48:21; Jer 2:6, 17; 23:8; Hos 11:2–4; Amos 2:10; Acts 13:17; Bar 2:11; *1 Enoch* 89:22; 4 Ezra 14:4; *Sib. Or.* 3.255; *Pesiq. Rab.* 12:8; for his leading in the new exodus, cf., e.g., Rom 8:14; *Pss. Sol.* 17:40–41; *Pesiq. Rab.* 30:2. The Bible also connected the Spirit's presence with the exodus (Isa 63:10–11, 14; Hag 2:5).

70. Many recognize the Moses allusion (e.g., Gundry, *Matthew*, 55; France, *Matthew*, 98; cf. 2:16, 20), although the Scripture *citations* allude to Israel as a whole. Later Jewish literature had others repeat Moses' forty-day fast, e.g., Adam in the *Life of Adam and Eve* 6:1. Cf. Zosimus's fast from wine and bread for forty years in the desert in *History of Rechabites* 1:1 (possibly dependent on Christian desert monasticism); contrast Abaris' continual magical fast (B. L. Blackburn, " 'Miracle Working ΘΕΙΟΙ ΑΝΔΡΕΣ' in Hellenism," in *Gospel Perspectives* [ed. Wenham and Blomberg] 6.191) and Baruch's seven-day fast which did not make him hungry (*2 Bar* 21:1; contrast Matt 4:2). Ancients also recognized that forty days without food could precipitate death by starvation (Diog. Laert., *Lives* 8.1.40).

71. Cf. Gundry, *Matthew*, 55; F. W. Danker, *Jesus and the New Age* (St. Louis: Clayton, 1972) 55; *T. Job* 37:8 v.1.

72. Although one could find in 7:15–23 Jewish exorcists' attempts to use God's sacred name (12:27; Jos., *Ant.* 8.47; cf. *m. Sanh.* 10:1; H. Bietenhard, "ὄνομα," in *TDNT*, 5.243), as yet unaware of their judge's identity as Jesus (cf. 25:31), it almost certainly refers instead to false Christian charismatics whose disobedience Christ finally reveals (10:26; Aune, *Prophecy*, 223). "In his name" means "as his representatives" (e.g., 10:41–42; 18:5) rather than employing the magical techniques by which ancient exorcists invoked names of higher spirits to expel lower ones (cf. Acts 19:13–16). Although some could prophesy and work signs by demonic power (e.g., 2 Thess 2:9; Rev 13:13–16; cf. Jer 2:8; 23:13), one could also manifest charismatic empowerments by the divine Spirit, yet be wicked (1 Sam 19:24). Matthew is not anticharismatic; that he must warn his community against the wrong kind of prophets, yet fails to attack prophetism in general, strongly suggests that both he and his community accept some prophets as genuine (5:12; 10:8, 40–42; 23:34; cf. J. R. Michaels, "Christian Prophecy and Matthew 23:8–12," in *SBL Seminar Papers 1976*, 305–10; Hill, *Prophecy*, 156; Aune, *Prophecy*, 215). The *Didache* similarly provides moral tests for prophets precisely because its community accepts the validity of prophets (e.g., *Did.* 11).

73. E.g., *p. Ḥag.* 2:2 §5; *Sanh.* 6:6 §2. Magicians also sometimes metamorphosed themselves or others (Apul., *Metam.* 1.9; 2.1, 5, 30; 3.21–25; 6.22; Blackburn, "ΘΕΙΟΙ ΑΝΔΡΕΣ," 190, 193; cf. J. S. Mbiti, *African Religions and Philosophies* [Garden City, N.Y.: Doubleday, 1970] 256–58). Some later teachers denied that demons could create (Alexander, *Possession*, 33, cites *b. Ḥul.* 105b, probably following Edersheim), but some rabbis believed they themselves had harnessed God's creative power (e.g., *'Abot R. Nat.* 25A); some Jews felt they

could harness demons to do their bidding (e.g., *T. Sol.* 7:8). Magic was widespread, yet not only in Palestinian Judaism (e.g., Wis 17:7; *m. Sanh.* 6:4; 7:11; Ps.-Phoc. 149), but even among Greeks and Romans, the charge of sorcery was a serious one (cf., e.g., Apuleius' defense; Kee, *Miracle,* 213; Smith, *Magician,* 75–76; Theissen, *Miracle Stories,* 239–42).

74. Cf. Bultmann, *History,* 255–57; Smith, *Magician,* 105.

75. Ps.-Philo 34.2–3; *b. Sanh.* 67b; Smith, *Magician,* 97–99; Arnold, *Ephesians,* 18.

76. Matt 14:13–21; 15:29–38; 16:9–10; cf. 1 Kgs 17:14–16; 2 Kgs 4:3–6, 42–44.

77. Cf. Robinson, *Twelve Studies,* 54; Barrett, *Spirit,* 51–52.

78. E.g., Jos., *Ant.* 20.168; *War* 2.259. Smith, *Magician,* 105, and others point out that claims to be able to fly also characterized magicians. Early Christianity's closest parallel to this claim (Acts 8:39) is not analogous (cf. C. S. Keener, *The IVP Bible Background Commentary* [Downers Grove, Ill.: InterVarsity, 1993] 346–47).

79. Cf. P. F. Ellis, *Matthew: His Mind and His Message* (Collegeville, Minn.: Liturgical, 1974) 108; cf. John 18:36.

80. Manson, *Sayings,* 44, cites *1 Enoch* 24–25; *2 Bar.* 76:3; cf. Meier, *Matthew,* 30; France, *Matthew,* 99; Luc., *Charon.*

81. Gen 13:14–15; Deut 34:1–4.

82. E.g., Rev 17:18; Jos., *J.W.* 2.361; 3.473.

83. Dan 10:13, 20–21; cf. C. S. Keener, *Paul, Women, & Wives* (Peabody, Mass.: Hendrickson, 1992) 64–65.

84. Cf. John 12:31; 16:11; 2 Cor 4:4; 1 John 5:19; *T. Sol.* 1:12.

85. Cf. Luke 4:6. Contrast Dan 4:25; cf. *m. ʾAbot* 3:15.

86. "Get away from me!" indicates disgust; cf. Isa 30:22 MT; *m. ʿAbod. Zar.* 3:6; *Šabb.* 9:1; God thus addresses Satan in *Pesiq. Rab.* 20:2.

87. *ʾAbot R. Nat.* 1A. Some sages believed that even teaching law in the presence of one's teacher merited death from God (*Sipra Shemini Mekhilta deMiluim* 99.5.6).

88. Some suggest here the mistranslation of a Semitic idiom for "Get *from* behind me," i.e., "You are no longer my disciple" (Smith, *Parallels,* 30; cf. Black, *Aramaic Approach,* 218; in *T. Job* 27:1, possibly reflecting the gospel tradition, such a construction would signal "stop hiding"); but such a final repudiation leaves no trace either in the gospel tradition or in subsequent testimony concerning Peter's role in early Christianity. Although "get behind me" was not a typical rebuke (Smith, *Parallels,* 30), "go" was a fairly typical harsh response to a foolish or hostile statement (e.g., Epict., *Disc.* 3.23.12–13; cf. Jas 4:13; 5:1; Mart., *Epig.* 1.42). Weeden, *Traditions in Conflict,* 65, and Kelber, *Mark's Story,* 47–48, even find in Jesus' rebuke of Peter Markan exorcist language. It was known that teachers and prophets gave very firm warnings to their disciples (CD 8.20–22).

89. O. Cullmann, *The State in the New Testament* (New York: Scribner's, 1956) 27. Although Jewish writers occasionally spoke of "satans" in the plural, i.e., demons (Gaster, *Scriptures,* 224, 262 n. 16; Alexander, *Possession,* 25, 30; repeatedly in the Aramaic incantation texts, e.g., 23.3–4; 58.1; 60.10; 66.5), Jesus compares Peter to Satan himself because he spoke Satan's lines (cf. Luke 22:31; John 13:27; Acts 5:3; *T. Job* 26:6/7; 27:1).

90. Meier, *Vision,* 117; id., *Matthew,* 185.

91. Cf. R. J. Sider, *Christ and Violence* (Scottdale, Penn.: Herald, 1979) 23–24.

92. Cf. similarly S. Bacchiocchi, "Matthew 11:28–30," *AUSS* 22 (1984) 289–316; Patte, *Matthew,* 167.

93. Cf. Luke 3:23; on respect for age, see, e.g., Sir 8:6; 1 Pet 5:5; *4 Bar.* 5:20; Ps.-Phoc. 220–22; *Syr. Men. Sent.* 11–14, 76–93; *t. ʿAbod. Zar.* 1:19; *Meg.* 3:24; Plut., *Lycurgus* 14, *Sayings of Spartans, Moralia* 227F; Diog. Laert., *Lives* 2.41; 8.1.22–23; cf. Plut., *Whether an Old Man Should Engage in Public Affairs, Moralia* 783B–797F. Still, the age requirements for some important offices extended to as young as twenty-five (CD 10.6–7) or thirty (*m. ʾAbot* 5:21), and exceptional youths were recognized (Sus 50; Sir 51:13; Wis 8:10; 1 Tim 4:12; *p. Taʿan.* 4:1, §14; Plut., *Pytheas, Sayings of Kings and Commanders, Moralia* 187E).

94. F. F. Bruce, *The Books and the Parchments* (Old Tappan, N.J.: Revell, 1963) 143 n. 1; Moore, *Judaism,* 2.327; cf. S. L. Edgar, "The New Testament and Rabbinic Messianic Interpretation," *NTS* 5 (1958) 50, for other late references.

95. For a similar recognition of a possible distinction among figures Isaiah intertwined through corporate personality, cf. W. S. LaSor, D. A. Hubbard, and F. W. Bush, *Old Testament Survey* 2d ed. (Grand Rapids, Mich.: Eerdmans, 1996) 310–12, and sources cited there.

96. Cf. Gundry, *Matthew,* 229; Schweizer, *Mark,* 37–38; K. Stendahl, *The School of St. Matthew and Its Use of the Old Testament* (Philadelphia: Fortress, 1968) 110.

97. Matt 12:28//Luke 11:20, Q material, demonstrates that where Mark depends on an earlier source like Q, Matthew, Luke, or both feel free to add appropriate material from the original source. This multiple attestation also favors the authenticity of the passage.

98. Cf., e.g., *1 Enoch* 65:6; *Asc. Isa.* 2:5; but especially magical papyri (e.g., *PGM* 1.88–90, 96–100, 164–66, 181–85, 252–53; 2.52–54).

99. Cf. also John 7:20; 8:48; 10:20; D. E. Aune, *The New Testament in Its Literary Environment* (LEC 8; Philadelphia: Westminster, 1987) 56.

100. Meier, *Matthew,* 134; cf. *p. Ḥag.* 2:2 §5; *Sanh.* 7:13 §2.

101. Beelzebul is probably a corruption of a pagan deity's name (2 Kgs 1:2), but appears as the prince of the demons in the third-century *T. Sol.* 3 (perhaps through Christian influence).

102. Mark had already employed the tradition in a similar way; cf. Mansfield, *Spirit and Gospel,* 62.

103. On Jewish accusations that Jesus was a magician, see also J. Klausner, *Jesus* (New York: Menorah, 1979) 27–28, 49–51, 293; G. Dalman, *Jesus Christ in the Talmud, Midrash, Zohar, and the Liturgy of the Synagogue* (New York: Arno, 1973) 45–50; Herford, *Christianity in Talmud,* 50–62; S. Gero, "Jewish Polemic in the Martyrium Pionii and a 'Jesus' Passage from the Talmud," *JJS* 29 (1978) 164–68; E. M. Yamauchi, "Magic or Miracle?" in *Gospel Perspectives* (ed. France, Wenham, and Blomberg) 6.90–91; W. Horbury, "Christ as Brigand in Ancient Anti-Christian Polemic," in *Jesus and the Politics of His Day* (Cambridge: Cambridge, 1984) 183–95. The earliest Jewish and pagan sources reflecting this view admittedly date from the second century (D. E. Aune, "Magic in Early Christianity" in *ANRW* 2.23.1, 1525; D. Flusser, *Judaism and the Origins of Christianity* [Jerusalem: Hebrew University, 1988] 635), but several reasons suggest that the later charge of sorcery reflects a first-century one: (1) no *potentially* relevant sources predate the second century anyway, hence second

century sources reflect our earliest available data; (2) charges of magic are common in societies that accept its existence (see Mbiti, *Religions*, 262); (3) Gospel texts would probably not respond to a nonexistent charge (Sanders, *Jesus and Judaism*, 166); and (4) fitting Jesus into the ancient category of "magician" would be easy enough if one ignored other features of his ministry, as his opponents did (cf. at length Smith, *Magician*; for critique on many points see, e.g., Yamauchi, "Magic," 95–96; C. L. Blomberg, "Concluding Reflections on Miracles and Gospel Perspectives" in *Gospel Perspectives* [Sheffield: JSOT, 1986] 449).

104. E.g., *ʾAbot R. Nat.* 28A; 48 §32B; *b. Qidd.* 49b; *Exod. Rab.* 9:6; 20:19.

105. See Dalman, *Jesus in Talmud*, 33; A. Plummer, *An Exegetical Commentary on the Gospel according to S. Matthew* (London: Elliot Stock, 1910) 17.

106. Dalman, *Jesus in Talmud*, 37–38; Herford, *Christianity in Talmud*, 211–15; Bagatti, *Church from Circumcision*, 95–96.

107. E.g., *t. Pisha* 2:15; *Mek. Shirata* 7.17–18; *p. Ḥag.* 2:2 §5; *Sanh.* 6:6, §2; *Pesiq. Rab Kah.* 4:3; *Jos. and Asen.* 23:8; *Lives of Prophets* 17.2.

108. Ps.-Phoc. 74–75; also a common topic of Greek speeches.

109. *T. Sol.* 5:5; 15:8 (though perhaps following the Gospels).

110. We read "sons" here as "apprentices" or "disciples" (cf. Jeremias, *Jerusalem*, 177).

111. Tob 6:7–8, 16–17; 8:2–3; Jos., *Ant.* 8.45–49; *Jub.* 10:10–13; cf. 1QapGen 20; Justin Martyr, *Dialogue with Trypho* 85; *T. Sol.* 5:13; for name invocation of spirits to counter other spirits, as in pagan magical texts, cf. Aramaic incantation text 3.8–9; 50.7–8; *T. Sol.* 2.4; 5.5; 8.5–11; 18; cf. also late rabbinic sources purporting to depict an account of Johanan ben Zakkai (*Num. Rab.* 19:8; *Pesiq. Rab.* 14:14). For more detail, see Alexander, *Possession*, 126–28; cf. here Meier, *Matthew*, 134–35; V. Taylor, *The Formation of the Gospel Tradition* (2d ed.; London: Macmillan & Company, 1935) 129.

112. Cf. G. H. Twelftree, " 'ΕΙ ΔΕ . . . ΕΓΩ ΕΚΒΑΛΛΩ ΤΑ ΔΑΙΜΟΝΙΑ . . . ,' " in *Gospel Perspectives*, 6.383; G. Vermes, *Jesus the Jew* (Philadelphia: Fortress, 1973) 23, 63–65. Curing disease with a mere word (8:3, 8) was also quite unusual, contrasting with most of the popular magicians of the day (Anderson, *Mark*, 97).

113. Cf. Betz, *Jesus*, 66; Barrett, *Spirit*, 53; Ps.-Philo 60.

114. E.g., *T. Sol.* 5.10; Aramaic incantation text 47:1–2; *p. Ketub.* 12:3 §11; *Pesiq. Rab Kah.* 5:3.

115. Although the sources are rare and late, one may note in passing that some later teachers even felt that good demons existed, and those who knew the Law well could teach rabbis (Alexander, *Possession*, 36).

116. Bonsirven, *Judaism*, 16.

117. E.g., Dodd, *Parables*, 28 n. 1.

118. Cf. Sanders, *Jesus and Judaism*, 134–36.

119. E.g., Gundry, *Matthew*, 235; Schweizer, *Matthew*, 287; *pace* Rodd, "Spirit"; Dunn, *Jesus and Spirit*, 45–46; Menzies, *Pneumatology*, 186–89. Matthew's earlier citation of Isa 42 provides contextual reason for the change in Matthew.

120. E.g., G. E. Ladd, *The Gospel of the Kingdom* (Grand Rapids, Mich.: Eerdmans, 1978) 48.

121. Theissen, *Miracle Stories*, 278–79.

122. Cf. Sanders, *Jesus and Judaism*, 134–35; *pace* Barrett, *Spirit*, 59; Betz, *Jesus*, 59–60.

123. Cf. Ladd, *Gospel of Kingdom*, 48; Fenton, *Matthew*, 198–99; Jeremias, *Theology*, 94.

124. *Pss. Sol.* 5:3; Charlesworth, *Pseudepigrapha and New Testament*, 79.

125. Also Manson, *Sayings*, 86; Robinson, *Problem of History*, 78; Hooker, *Message of Mark*, 37.

126. Jeremias, *Parables*, 122; J. Weiss, *Jesus' Proclamation of the Kingdom of God* (Philadelphia: Fortress, 1971) 81; Rhoads and Michie, *Mark as Story*, 42.

127. Incantations for warding off demons are at least as old as the Egyptian *Book of the Dead* (e.g., Spells 40, 41, 136). Although "binding" had wider figurative usages (e.g., 22:13; Plato, *Cratylus* 403C; *PGM* 12.160–78; 14.256) and, on analogy of the literal judicial usage of imprisoning or releasing (Jos., *J.W.* 1.111), sometimes referred to demons' present or future imprisonment (*1 Enoch* 10:4–6, 11–14; 13:1; 14:5; 21:3–4; *Jub.* 10:7; *T. Levi* 18:12; Rev 20:2; cf. *1 Enoch* 22:11; 90:23), it became common in magical exorcisms (e.g., Tob. 8:1–2; Smith, *Magician*, 127; Twelftree, "ΕΚΒΑΛΛΩ ΤΑ ΔΑΙΜΟΝΙΑ," 385; cf. *T. Sol.* 3:7; 18). "Binding" demons appears as part of magical texts in Aramaic incantation text 3.2, 7; 5.1–2 ("conquered . . . bound"); 5.3–4 ("I am binding you with the evil and strong spell"); 10.1 ("wholly bound and sealed and tied in knots . . . that you . . . depart from the house"); 27.2–3; 47.1–3; texts also speak of demons binding persons (e.g., Tob 3:17; Deissmann, *Light*, 304–7). One could also "bind" demons to manipulate them to do one's will in sorcery (e.g., *PGM* 3.99–100; 101.1–3; cf. also in R. S. Kraemer, *Maenads, Martyrs, Matrons, Monastics* [Philadelphia: Fortress, 1988] 108–9; cf. Alexander, *Possession*, 36–40), "loose" them to attack others (*PGM* 4.2246–48) or use such demons to "bind" people in love or other spells (e.g., *PGM* 101.8–9, 16–17, 36; 4.355–56, 376–88, 395; 7.912–13; 15.1; 32.1–19; *IG* 3.97.34–41 in M. R. Lefkowitz and M. B. Fant, *Women's Life in Greece and Rome* [Baltimore: Johns Hopkins, 1982] 258 §251).

128. Cf. 13:30; Rev 20:2; Twelftree, "ΕΚΒΑΛΛΩ ΤΑ ΔΑΙΜΟΝΙΑ," 391–92.

129. Cf. Suet., *Julius* 75; Plut., *Sayings of Kings*, Peisistratus 3, *Moralia* 189C.

130. Cf. Flusser, *Judaism and Origins of Christianity*, 510–11, though he wrongly postulates dependence, which overstates the case.

131. For a discussion of authenticity of the blasphemy against the Spirit saying, see Marshall, *Kept by Power*, 77–78. Apart from its context in the Didache (11:7), none of Boring's arguments that this must be a prophecy later than Jesus himself bear any weight (*pace* Boring, *Sayings*, 159–60; Theissen, *Sociology*, 28).

132. *Jub.* 15:34; 1QS 7.15–17, 22–23; *p. Ḥag.* 2:1 §9; *Šebu.* 1:6 §5; cf. Heb 6:6; CD 8.8; 10.3; for Pythagoreans treating apostates as if dead, see W. Burkert, "Craft versus Sect: The Problem of Orphics and Pythagoreans," in *Self-Definition*, 3.18.

133. CD 10.3; Jas 5:19–20; *p. Šebu.* 1:6 §5; *Ruth Rab.* 6:4.

134. "Will be forgiven" may reflect an Aramaic construction meaning forgiveness in the present rather than only in the future (Gundry, *Matthew*, 237).

135. Cf. Bultmann, *History*, 108 n. 1; G. Dalman, *Jesus-Jeshua* (New York: Macmillan, 1929) 227; Manson, *Sayings*, 60; one ancient story line also apparently recognized that one could ruin one's own defense in court and be convicted by one's own words (Luke 19:22; *Num. Rab.* 16:21).

136. E.g., Sir 4:29; 5:11; 20:18; Syr. Men., *Sent.* 301–13; Ps.-Phoc. 20; *m. ʾAbot.* 1:15, 17; 3:13; ʾAbot R. Nat. 1, 26A; Philo, *Conf.* 33ff.; Ahiqar 98–99, sayings 15–16;

Sen., *Dialogues* 5.10.1; Plut., *Lectures* 3, *Moralia* 39B; Dio Chrys., *32d Disc.* 2; Diog. Laert., *Lives* 1.69–70, 87, 92, 104; 5.40; 7.1.21, 23–24; 7.5.172.

137. The expression refers to the final judgment: cf. Jdt 16:17; *1 Enoch* 10:6, 12; 84:4; 94:9; 96:8; 97:3; 98:8; 99:15; 1 John 4:17; 4 Ezra 7:38; *2 Enoch* 50:4, 5A; 51:3; *T. Levi* 1:1; cf. *T. Moses* 1:18.

138. At least some groups regarded "idle" or "vain" words as profane on a day holy to the Lord (CD 10.18); Jesus here indicates that even such careless words spoken without thought will testify concerning one's character in the judgment day.

139. Dalman, *Jesus-Jeshua*, 52–53.

140. The religious leaders (there "scribes and Pharisees," here "Pharisees and Sadducees") had challenged Jesus after other miracles (15:1–20); the Gospel's first reference to testing (4:1; cf. 6:13; 19:3; 22:35) suggests that the devil is their theological source (cf. Robinson, *Problem of History*, 93).

141. A "sign from heaven" could mean "from God" ("heaven" often functioned as a circumlocution for God's name: e.g., Luke 15:18; Rom 1:18; Dan 4:26; *1 Enoch* 6:2; 13:8; 1QM 12.5; 3 Macc 4:21; *m. ʾAbot.* 1:3; *t. B.Qam.* 7:5; *Sipra Behuq.* pq. 6.267.2.1; *Sipre Deut.* 79.1.1; 96.2.2) but in this context probably means a sign in the heavens (e.g., Plummer, *Matthew*, 221), like those which many people believed presaged the fall of Jerusalem (Jos., *J.W.* 6.288–91) and the end (cf. Matt 24:29–31; 27:45, 51–53). Jewish teachers sometimes debated the interpretation of such signs, for instance, what eclipses at evening predicted versus eclipses in the morning (*t. Sukka* 2:6). Presumably they here ask Jesus to predict a sign in the sky, which essentially reduces them to the level of astrologers or diviners, something forbidden in the Hebrew Bible (Deut 18:10; cf. *Jub.* 12:16–17). Matthew thus contrasts these religious leaders starkly with pagan astrologers who came to worship King Jesus in 2:1–12. If one wishes to construe the Pharisaic request in its worst possible light, magical texts promised signs from the sky for magicians, which signs would become their divine "messengers" or spirit-guides (*PGM* 1.74–76, 154). By contrast, some Greek rationalists sought nontheistic explanations for celestial phenomena (Epicurus in Diog. Laert., *Lives* 10.99).

142. The generation's sinfulness could constitute a sign, because many Jews expected such a generation immediately preceding God's eschatological kingdom (CD 20.14–15; *2 Bar.* 26:12; *m. Soṭa* 9:15; *b. Sanh.* 97a; *Pesiq. Rab.* 15:14/15). The description of that generation resembles Moses' complaint against Israel (Deut 32:5), a generation that had repeatedly tested God in the wilderness and rejected his prophet Moses (Ps 78:18–20).

143. "Three days and three nights" (Jonah 2:1; cf. Hos 6:2) was standard Jewish language covering a period including any parts of three days (references in Gundry, *Matthew*, 244–45). Jewish teachers apparently only accepted the witness of one's death after three days had passed (Dalman, *Jesus-Jeshua*, 188). Some Jewish sources apply the "heart of the earth" to the realm of the dead (Gundry, *Matthew*, 244, who also compares Jonah 2:3; but cf. Ezek 28:2). The resurrection was an end-time event (Dan 12:2); Jesus' resurrection was a clear indication that the kingdom time was at hand (12:39–40).

144. Jonah 3:1–4; cf. 3 Macc 6:8; Justin, *Dial.* 107.

145. Matthew might also expect his community to recall that Jesus prophesied Jerusalem's destruction (23:38–24:2) as Jonah prophesied Nineveh's, but the

specific tradition that Jonah also prophesied Jerusalem's demise (cited by G. Schmitt, "Das Zeichen des Jona," *ZNW* 69 [1978] 123–29) is later and too narrow.

146. That some later Jewish traditions amplify her paganism (*T. Sol.* 19:3) is probably irrelevant; that Jesus' and Matthew's audience would have viewed her as a Gentile was sufficient. Origen and Jerome viewed her as a black African (C. H. Felder, *Troubling Biblical Waters* [Maryknoll: Orbis, 1989] 12–13; F. M. Snowden, *Blacks in Antiquity* [Cambridge, Mass.: Harvard, 1970] 202–3); both Ethiopian and Arabic (Manson, *Sayings*, 91) traditions about her claim her for themselves; for further discussion, see Felder, *Troubling*, 22–36; W. L. Hansberry, *Pillars in Ethiopian History* (Washington, D.C.: Howard University, 1981] 33–58.

147. Jewish traditions attested in some rabbinic sources indicate that Gentile converts to Judaism would testify against the nations in the judgment (*Pesiq. Rab.* 35:3); the repentant poor would testify against those who used poverty as an excuse against repentance; the repentant rich and so forth would do likewise (e.g., ʾ*Abot R. Nat.* 6A; 12 §30B; *b. Yoma* 35b; *3 Enoch* 4:3).

148. Cf. Jeremias, *Parables*, 106; Argyle, *Matthew*, 99.

149. Jeremias, *Parables*, 197–98; cf. Bultmann, *History*, 164.

150. For desert haunts for some demons, cf. 4:1, above; cf. Isa 13:21; *2 Bar.* 10:8; *T. Sol.* 5.11–12; Kraeling, *John the Baptist*, 28.

151. Gen 4:15, 24; Lev 26:18; Ps 79:12; for other "sevenfold" amplifications, cf. *1 Enoch* 72:37; 91:16; cf. *T. Sol.* 8:1.

152. Jeremias, *Theology*, 154.

153. On the moralistic function of biographies, see, e.g., Aune, *Environment*, 36; cf., e.g., S. Mason, *Josephus and the New Testament* (Peabody, Mass.: Hendrickson, 1992) 63.

154. Cf. S. Brown, "The Mission to Israel in Matthew's Central Section," *ZNW* 69 (1978) 73–90. J. A. Grassi, "The Last Testament-Succession Literary Background of Matthew 9:35–11:1 and Its Significance," *BTB* 7 (1977) 172–76, is probably correct that 9:35–11:1 reflects "succession" language, but the specifically testamentary background he suggests, and especially his attempt to root it in Gen 49:1–33, is too narrow; better, though still too narrow, is the suggestion of R. E. Morosco, "Matthew's Formation of a Commissioning Type-Scene out of the Story of Jesus' Commissioning of the Twelve," *JBL* 103 (1984) 539–56, that roots it in Moses' commission in Exod 3–4. Some Jewish teachers stressed that disciples must do some of the master's works during his lifetime lest they face undue hostility later (*Sipre Deut.* 305.1.1).

155. *Pace* some commentators, the literal sense behind the metaphor translated "had compassion" had long before lost significance (A. C. Thiselton, "Semantics and New Testament Interpretation," in *New Testament Interpretation* [ed. I. H. Marshall; Grand Rapids, Mich.: Eerdmans, 1977] 81).

156. S. Safrai, "Education and the Study of the Torah," in *JPFC* 957.

157. *P. Taʿan.* 3:8 §2; cf. 2 Kgs 2:14; 4:31.

158. See comments by B. J. Malina, *Windows on the World of Jesus* (Louisville, Ky.: Westminster/Knox, 1993) 131.

159. A late-first-century teacher made nearly the same statement in *m.* ʾ*Abot* 2:15, probably concerning study and teaching of Torah (see *m.* ʾ*Abot* 2:16).

160. See F. F. Bruce, *The Message of the New Testament* (Grand Rapids, Mich.: Eerdmans, 1972) 68; R. E. Morosco, "Redaction Criticism and the Evangelical: Matthew 10 a Test Case," *JETS* 22 (1979) 323–31; G. Theissen, *The*

Gospels in Context (Minneapolis: Fortress, 1991) 56–57; F. W. Beare, *The Gospel according to Matthew* (San Francisco: Harper & Row, 1981) 252; A. Edersheim, *The Life and Times of Jesus the Messiah* (Peabody, Mass.: Hendrickson, 1993) 295; Meier, *Matthew,* 102–3; *pace* Schweitzer, *Quest,* 361; J. Wilkinson, "The Mission Charge to the Twelve and Modern Medical Missions," *SJT* 27 (1974) 313–28.

161. Some documents emphasize "authority" over demons in contexts referring to commanding them or manipulating them for magical purposes (e.g., *T. Sol.* 1:5), but Jesus and his disciples simply silenced them and cast them out (e.g., Mark 1:22–27).

162. In an early second-century tradition, the disciples of the prophets (תלמידי הנביאים) succeeded them: Joshua and Moses, and Elisha and Elijah, though Baruch proved an exception (*Mek. Pisha* 1.150–53; cf. *'Abot R. Nat.* 1A; *'Abot R. Nat.* 1 §2B; the baraita in *Pesiq. Rab.* 51:2). Joshua appears as Moses' successor also in Sir 46:1; *T. Moses* 1:7, 10:15, and Elisha as Elijah's, apparently, in Sir 48:12.

163. Cf. A. M. Hunter, *The Message of the New Testament* (Philadelphia: Westminster, 1944) 63.

164. E.g., Jos., *Ant.* 18.1, 265; Pliny, *Ep.* 10.18.190–91.

165. E.g., Diog. Laert., *Lives* 7.1.9.

166. B. Cohen, *Jewish and Roman Law* (New York: Jewish Theological Seminary of America, 1966) 295–96.

167. *B. Ketub.* 99b–100a.

168. *B. Giṭ.* 23a.

169. E.g., *t. Taʿan.* 3:2; *m. Ber.* 5:5.

170. E.g., *m. Demai* 4:5; *t. Demai* 2:20.

171. E.g., F. S. Malan, "The Relationship between Apostolate and Office in the Theology of Paul," *Neot* 10 (1976) 57; A. Ehrhardt, *The Apostolic Ministry* (SJTOP 7; Edinburgh: Oliver Boyd, 1958) 5.

172. Cf., e.g., K. H. Rengstorf, *Apostolate and Ministry* (St. Louis: Concordia, 1969) 27; G. Dix, *The Apostolic Ministry* (ed. K. E. Kirk; London: Hodder & Stoughton, 1947) 228–30.

173. J. B. Lightfoot, *St. Paul's Epistle to the Galatians* (3d ed.; London: Macmillan, 1869) 93–94, citing Epiph., *Haer.* 30.

174. See K. Lake, "The Twelve and the Apostles," in *Beginnings,* 5.37–59.

175. Käsemann, *Romans,* 5–6; J. A. Kirk, "Apostleship since Rengstorf," *NTS* 21 (1975) 252. W. Schmithals, *The Office of Apostle in the Early Church* (Nashville: Abingdon, 1969) 108, objects that the evidence for sending agents by twos (Mark 6:7; Luke 10:1; Acts 13) is late and rare; but while most rabbinic evidence is by its nature late, it is abundant (cf. *p. Roš Haš.* 2:8 §4; more fully, W. L. Liefeld, "The Wandering Preacher as a Social Figure in the Roman Empire" [Ph.D. diss., Columbia University, 1967] 225–26; cf. Jeremias, *Theology,* 235). He further neglects the historic model of paired heralds traversing a distance (e.g., Homer, *Iliad* 1.320; see C. H. Gordon, *The Ancient Near East* [New York: Norton, 1965] 110) as well as the frequent custom of disciples (J. E. Stambaugh and D. L. Balch, *The New Testament in Its Social Environment* [LEC 2; Philadelphia: Westminster, 1986] 144; Safrai, "Education," 968).

176. Cf. Boring, *Sayings,* 89. Some figures viewed by Jewish teachers as agents included Moses (*Sipra Behuq.* pq. 13.277.1.13–14; *'Abot R. Nat.* 1A, v.1.),

Aaron (*Sipra Sav Mekhilta DeMiluim* 98.9.6), the biblical prophets (*Mek. Pisha* 1.87; *'Abot R. Nat.* 37 §95 B), or, most generally, anyone who carried out God's will (*Sipra Sav Mekhilta DeMiluim* 98.9.5). Jewish teachers who saw the prophets as God's commissioned messengers were consistent with the portrait of prophets in their scriptures; Israel's prophetic messenger formulas echo ancient Near Eastern royal messenger formulas such as, "Thus says the great king," often addressing Israel's vassal kings for the suzerain king Yahweh (Holladay, "Statecraft," 31–34; V.W. Rabe, "Origins of Prophecy," *BASOR* 221 [1976] 127). Old Testament perspectives on prophets inform the early Christian view of apostleship (Grudem, *Prophecy,* 43–54), although they do not exhaust its meaning (cf. Hill, *Prophecy,* 116–17); early Christianity clearly maintained the continuance of the prophetic office (Acts 11:27; 21:10; 1 Cor 12:28), while seeming to apply to apostles the special sort of position accorded only certain prophets in the OT (such as prophet-judges like Deborah and Samuel, and other leaders of prophetic schools like Elijah and Elisha).

177. Most scholars concur that historically, Jesus limited his mission primarily or exclusively to Israel (Sanders, *Jesus and Judaism,* 11; Ellis, *Matthew,* 49).

178. Perhaps even the twelve signs of the zodiac (e.g., *Pesiq. Rab Kah.* 16:5; *Pesiq. Rab.* 4:1; 29/30A:6; cf. Jos., *J.W.* 5.217).

179. F. F. Bruce, "Jesus and the Gospels in the Light of the Scrolls," in *Scrolls and Christianity,* 76.

180. Bruce, "Jesus and Scrolls," 75; Sanders, *Jesus and Judaism,* 104.

181. Sanders, *Jesus and Judaism,* 98–101. In contrast to the slight variations in the canonical lists, one may compare the forms in the *Apostolic Church Orders* and the *Epistola Apostolorum* (Lake, "Apostles," 41).

182. Jeremias, *Theology,* 235; Sanders, *Jesus and Judaism,* 96–97; though contrast some in *m. Sanh.* 10:5; *t. Sanh.* 13:12.

183. Cf. Jeremias, *Theology,* 235; Sanders, *Jesus and Judaism,* 98–106.

184. Manson, *Sayings,* 179; cf. Jeremias, *Promise,* 19 n. 3, who renders the phrase "toward" Gentile populations.

185. See Gundry, *Matthew,* 185.

186. Cf. Acts 11:3; Meier, *Matthew,* 106–7.

187. In the context of his whole Gospel, Mark's account of the sending of the Twelve (Mark 6:7–13) may also imply a universal commission; cf. S. J. Anthonysamy, "The Gospel of Mark and the Universal Mission," *Biblebhashyam* 6 (1980) 81–96.

188. D. J. Harrington, *The Gospel according to Matthew* (Collegeville: Liturgical, 1982) 45; in Mark, cf. J. Delorme, "La mission de Douze en Galilée," *Assemblées du Seigneur* 46 (1974) 43–50.

189. Jeremias, *Theology,* 21–22; they need not represent prophetic speech, *pace* Boring, *Sayings,* 145–46.

190. Cf., e.g., A. J. Malherbe, " 'Gentle as a Nurse,' " *NovT* 12 (1970) 203–17; Liefeld, "Wandering Preacher," 260.

191. Although Jesus still had a home of some sort in Capernaum (4:13), his traveling ministry left him and his disciples at the mercy of others' hospitality. In practice, then, Jesus was essentially homeless, even more dependent on others than were the Levites in biblical law. Radical philosophers also demanded readiness to abandon possessions (Epict., *Disc.* 2.2.15; 4.8.31), and the founder of the

Qumran community mourned that enemies had banished him into the wilderness "like a bird out of the nest" (Betz, *Jesus*, 72).

192. Theissen, *Sociology*, 34–35; cf. *CPJ* 1.239–40 §129.5.

193. S. Freyne, *Galilee, Jesus, and the Gospels* (Philadelphia: Fortress, 1988) 241.

194. 1QS 1.11–13; 6.22–23; Jos., *Ant.* 18.20; *J.W.* 2.122; Philo, *Prob.* 76; *Hypoth.* 11.4–5; J. A. Fitzmyer, "Jewish Christianity in Acts in Light of the Qumran Scrolls," in *Studies in Luke–Acts*, 243; D. L. Mealand, "Community of Goods at Qumran," *TZ* 31 (1975) 129–39; cf. H.-J. Fabry, "Umkehr und Metanoia als monastisches Ideal in der 'Mönchsgemeinde' von Qumran," *Erbe und Auftrag* 53 (1977) 163–80.

195. Jos., *J.W.* 2.124–25.

196. E.g., 1 Kgs 18:13; 2 Kgs 4:38; 6:1; cf. W. A. Meeks, *The Moral World of the First Christians* (LEC 6; Philadelphia: Westminster, 1986) 106.

197. Manson, *Sayings*, 181.

198. Dalman, *Jesus-Jeshua*, 226; cf. *Sipre Deut.* 48.2.7.

199. Jeremias, *Jerusalem*, 112; Gundry, *Matthew*, 187.

200. Stambaugh and Balch, *Social Environment*, 38.

201. See Deissmann, *Light*, 108–9.

202. Meeks, *Moral World*, 107. Cynics typically wore rough robes (e.g., Epict., *Disc.* 4.8.12) and carried only a bag and a staff (Epict., *Disc.* 3.22.10; Crates, *Ep.* 16, 23, 33; Diogenes, *Ep.* 7, 26, 30; Diog. Laert., *Lives* 6.1.13; 6.2.22–23, 76; cf. Anacharsis, *Ep.* 5). Many of these references also emphasize that Cynics let their beards grow long, but coins indicate that Palestinian Jews in this period generally already had beards, so this feature of Cynic lifestyle would not be relevant to mention.

203. Perhaps as protection against snakes (Schweizer, *Matthew*, 239).

204. Mark probably toned down the more radical formulation in Q; see Luke 10:4; Boring, *Sayings*, 145.

205. Cf. Mark 6:8; Gundry, *Matthew*, 186.

206. *M. Ber.* 9:5; *Sipre Deut.* 258.2.2, which also require the removal of profane dust from one's feet (cf. 10:14).

207. Cf. Schweizer, *Matthew*, 239.

208. Gundry, *Matthew*, 187.

209. Julian, *Or.* 6.200C–201C in Malherbe, *Exhortation*, 35; cf. Petr., *Sat.* 14; Diogenes, *Ep.* 15.

210. Cf. Gundry, *Matthew*, 186.

211. E.g., *Rhet. ad Herenn.* 3.3.4; Cic. *De Offic.* 2.18.64; Epict., *Disc.* 1.28.23; A. J. Malherbe, *Social Aspects of Early Christianity* (2d ed.; Philadelphia: Fortress, 1983) 95.

212. Gen 19:3; Judg 19:20; Tob 5:10–15; 7:8–9; 10:6–10; Ps.-Phoc. 24; *T. Job* 10:1–4; Luke 11:6; Acts 16:15; 1 Tim 3:2; Titus 1:8; Heb 13:2; 1 Pet 4:9; see more extensively J. Koenig, *New Testament Hospitality* (OBT 17; Philadelphia: Fortress, 1985).

213. E.g., Rom 16:1–2; cf. C.-H. Kim, *Form and Structure of the Familiar Greek Letter of Recommendation* (SBLDS 4; Missoula, Mont.: SBL, 1972); other sources in Keener, *Paul, Women, & Wives*, 251.

214. Cf. Sir 11:29, 34; *t. Demai* 3:9; *Sipre Deut.* 1.10.1; *p. Giṭ.* 5:10 §5.

215. Cf. Crates, *Ep.* 2.

216. E.g., Isoc., *Demon.* 20, *Or.* 1; cf. *p. Ta'an.* 1:4 §1; 4:2 §8.

217. Cf. *t. Ber.* 2:20; *p. Hor.* 3:5 §3; *Ketub.* 12:3 §6; 2 John 10.

218. D. F. Eickelman, *The Middle East* (2d ed.; Englewood Cliffs, N.J.: Prentice Hall, 1989) 234.

219. On the concept of "wish-prayers," see G. P. Wiles, *Paul's Intercessory Prayers* (SNTSMS 24; Cambridge: Cambridge, 1974), passim; for an example, cf., e.g., *'Abot R. Nat.* 8A.

220. E.g., Manson, *Sayings,* 76; Gundry, *Matthew,* 190; Nineham, *Mark,* 170; K. Lake and H. J. Cadbury, *English Translation and Commentary,* in *The Beginnings of Christianity,* 4.160; Anderson, *Mark,* 164.

221. *M. Ber.* 9:5; *t. Ber.* 6:19; *Sipre Deut.* 258.2.2.

222. The act was purely symbolic; Roman roads were paved (Stambaugh and Balch, *Social Environment,* 37).

223. For the expression "day of judgment" meaning the final judgment here and in 11:22, cf. also Jdt 16:17; *1 Enoch* 10:6, 12; 4 Ezra 7:38; and other references cited above.

224. E.g., *Jub.* 36:10; 3 Macc 2:5; *t. Šabb.* 7:23; *Sipra Behuq.* par. 2.264.1.3; *Sipre Deut.* 43.3.5; *T. Naph.* 4:1; *T. Asher* 7:1; *T. Benj.* 9:1; cf. *CIJ* 1.417 §567.

4

• • • • • • • • • • • • • • •

THE SPIRIT AND PURIFICATION
IN THE FOURTH GOSPEL

• • • • • • • • • • • • • • •

In our first chapter we saw that in first-century Judaism, the Spirit had functioned as a purifying Spirit, as well as functioning as the Spirit of prophecy and insight into God's mysteries. The Spirit of purification lacks a prominent role in many early Jewish circles, but remained quite relevant to John, who juxtaposes the Spirit and water, the latter often symbolizing traditional rituals, in a manner meant to contrast his community's possession of the Spirit with his opponents' reliance upon, in his view, ritual forms.

This is not to say that John assumed that his opponents did not believe in fidelity to God (although they probably doubted the current experience of the Spirit in their day), nor that John completely rejects older Jewish rituals (Jesus *uses* the ritual water in ch. 9).[1] Rather, he contrasts the best of human religion, as mere "flesh," with what comes from the Spirit. Because his opponents would not have laid claim to possession of the Spirit for themselves, John's argument would have been difficult to refute without at least partly denying the validity of the continuing experience of the purifying and prophetic Spirit (a response some later rabbinic texts may suggest).

We start here from the premise, based on evidence internal to the Fourth Gospel, that John is addressing a largely Jewish-Christian community excluded from their local synagogue communities, hence probably facing pressure from Roman authorities to participate in the civic cult. We leave aside the more detailed reconstructions which appeal to the Birkath ha-Minim, conflict with Judean rabbis at Yavneh, and so forth; local synagogue conflict can sufficiently account for the data in the text, although such conflict may have been related to tensions in Palestine as well. But because the best available historical analogy anywhere close to contemporary with John is the conflict between rabbis and minim in rabbinic texts, we use some of this material to illustrate our case.[2]

Although texts in the Fourth Gospel (particularly in the Paraclete sayings) reveal the inspiratory function of the Spirit, especially with regard to revealed knowledge and insight into the Jesus tradition,[3] we focus in this chapter on the Spirit of purification in the Fourth Gospel, primarily as seen in John's water motif. While we will survey the other passages briefly, we will focus our attention on John 3:5 and 7:37–39, which provide interpretive foci for the other water motif texts by explicitly linking water and the Spirit.

1.   VIEWS CONCERNING WATER IN JOHN

Water is an indispensable substance, the appreciation for which was heightened in antiquity by the effects of drought on agrarian societies.[4] Ancient writers used water symbolically in various ways, e.g., as a symbol for life in certain philosophers,[5] or perhaps as an image for oracular speech.[6] Philo read the four rivers in Genesis as the four virtues flowing from τοῦ θείου λόγου,[7] and elsewhere also read water as divine wisdom;[8] Sirach similarly describes wisdom as water.[9] The rabbis spoke of wisdom,[10] Torah, and teaching as water[11] or a well,[12] and heresy as bad water;[13] this may be less significant,[14] of course, when we recognize that they compared Torah also with honey and other sustaining materials.[15]

The Spirit could also be symbolized by water. Although this image does occur in rabbinic texts,[16] the Spirit was a far less standard referent than the Torah, and it cannot be supposed that the average reader of the Fourth Gospel would have assumed that water there stands for the Spirit unless informed by some source other than the image circulating in rabbinic circles. This image is, however, available in OT passages referring to the Spirit of God as water poured from above.

Some have taken water to represent baptism in John, and have read it as indicating a sacramental element in Johannine theology.[17] Others, on the other hand, read the Gospel in an anti-sacramental light.[18] MacGregor feels that John is polemicizing against the sacramentalism of the mysteries, which he feels still retained a strong hold on early Christian converts.[19] Bultmann suggests a polemic against John's baptism, due to continuing rivalry with the Baptist sect.[20] Others have opted for a position between sacramentalism and anti-sacramentalism; Käsemann thinks that sacramentalism was not prominent in John (against Cullmann, Wilckens, and Barrett), but also not all redactional (against Bultmann);[21] Matsunaga thinks that the author was merely warning, in view of a substantial number of apostates (John 6), that baptism and the eucharist alone could not suffice to bring life apart from true discipleship.[22]

It will be argued below that the Fourth Gospel does indeed include polemic against the efficacy of water rituals, but that this polemic is only a part of his argument with the synagogue about the nature of true purification. By emphasizing the Spirit as the agent of purification over against ritual waters, and following an OT image of water as a symbol for the Spirit, he builds a case against his non-pneumatic opponents which is difficult to refute on their own terms.

2. THE BAPTIST'S PURIFICATIONS AND JESUS

The first apparent contrast between water and Spirit is an implicit one, in John 1:31–33. Here the description of Jesus' baptism, presumably widely known in the early church,[23] is superseded[24] by John's personal testimony regarding God's attestation of Jesus by the Spirit.[25] Because we have already surveyed John's baptism from an historical perspective, we limit our observations on this pericope to those directly bearing on its function in the context of the Johannine water motif as a whole.

Although the contrast between John's water baptism and Jesus' Spirit baptism is less striking verbally than in the Synoptic parallels, the emphasis on John's role as a forerunner in the immediate context underlines it no less strongly than it does in the Synoptics. John's purification rite is emphatically subordinated to that of Jesus. Thus, in John 1:19–28 John testifies freely to those who will be Jesus' opponents concerning the fact that Jesus is greater than he. This passage also places in perspective the early Christian comparison of John with the great prophet Elijah and with the eschatological Prophet (1:21); Jesus will be the prophetic bearer of the Spirit par excellence,[26] and the only one who washes with the purifying Spirit (1:33).

Our Evangelist does not permit John to keep any titles for himself,[27] and even where John's purification is presented as a step above that of other Jewish rituals (3:22–25), it is acknowledged to be superseded by Jesus' purification (3:26), a fact which John regards as entirely appropriate

(3:27–36). So also in 1:29–34, where he testifies to Jesus as the bearer and bestower of the Spirit, John describes his mission as revealing Jesus to Israel (1:31), and in subsequent paragraphs those affected by his testimony leave him to follow Jesus. The Fourth Gospel attests that this is as it should be.

One must ask the reason for the emphatic subordination of John's baptism and exercise of prophetic gifts. Although John's function is that of a witness, a role later taken over by believers in the Fourth Gospel,[28] this alone does not seem to explain the prominence accorded him by his place in the prologue. Consequently, many have seen here a polemic against an exalted role given to John in certain circles. Although there could be a basis for this in first-generation tradition,[29] it is even more likely by the time the Fourth Evangelist is writing. Acts 19 suggests that some followers of John still circulated in Asia later in the first century, without having become followers of Jesus.[30]

Thus, as noted in a previous chapter, Bultmann is rightly not alone in his contention that there is a polemic against the Baptist here,[31] although he naturally has his detractors.[32] Others qualify his position; Kysar suggests that while there may have been a polemic of some sort "against a Baptist messianic movement," it could also be that the Jewish opponents of the Johannine community were urging a low Christology in which Jesus was only the equivalent of a John the Baptist.[33]

What we would suggest here is that even John's role as a prophet is more clearly secured in his role as a witness to Jesus than in the other Gospels. If the Johannine Epistles reflect a stage in the development of a Johannine community not far advanced beyond that reflected in the Gospel as we have it, the nature of John's prophetic role may have naturally become an issue of contention. The false prophets of 1 John, with their questionable Christology, may have wished to compromise with "idolatry" (5:21) just like the false prophets in some of the communities in Revelation, who advocated spiritual compromise (Rev 2:14, 20). Perhaps this involved a compromise either with the demands of the Imperial cult, or with the christological demands of the synagogue (less likely), to avoid exposure to Roman harassment. At any rate, it is unlikely that these prophets who had gone beyond the Jesus tradition and seceded from the community[34] would have nicknamed their mentors "Balaam" or "Jezebel"; we undoubtedly have John the seer to thank for that. More likely, they would have chosen a prophetic figure who could have commanded respect from the Jewish community as well as the Christian community, and used him as their model for proclaiming the importance of Jesus, while coming far short of the Christology of the Johannine community.

If this were the case, the Fourth Evangelist's polemical response would be easily intelligible: only by subordinating John as a witness to the Jesus of the Johannine community could John be rescued from adoption by the secessionists with their lower Christology. This proposal is uncertain, resting on a view of the Johannine community that is not currently in vogue, namely, that the Epistles could be addressing some issues arising from the immediate milieu of the Fourth Gospel, rather than from a milieu reflecting a later, probably docetic distortion of that Gospel's teaching.

What is more clear, however, is that the polemic against John is only a part of the broader polemic against Jewish ritual. John functions as a witness for Jesus, but he functions as a witness whose purification falls short of that of Jesus just as all other purifications offered by humans will fall short in the passages that follow. Whether or not a Baptistic sect may have flourished in Asia, or false prophets may have used John's name, the Fourth Evangelist's primary polemic here is still against the synagogue. If the threat of the Baptist represents little more than that of any segment of thought in the synagogue, it is because those who claimed to be his followers at the end of the first century were viewed by the Fourth Evangelist as little beyond the views of the rest of the non-Christian Jewish community: inadequate.

3.   RITUAL PURIFICATION

One of the clearest references to Jesus superseding ceremonial purification in the Fourth Gospel is in 2:1–11.[35] Although there is no explicit mention of the Spirit in this chapter,[36] its function in the water motif that runs through John suggests that the old purification has become less important only because Jesus' purification by the Spirit is now available. A careful reader might catch that cue from the pericope about John in chapter one.[37]

i. Preliminary Questions

Some scholars read this pericope as a portrait of the obsolescence of Judaism or Jewish ritual.[38] Others, pointing to the reuse of the pots and renewal of the temple, argue that this chapter supports a renewal within Judaism, rather than its repudiation.[39] Still others see both tendencies, suggesting both Judaism's fulfillment and its destruction.[40] One's particular perspective will depend on whether one concludes, on reading the whole Gospel, that the Johannine community still considered itself part of

Judaism. Against many scholars, I have concluded that it did.[41] Thus I would tend to see this passage as arguing that Jesus has brought an eschatological renewal to Judaism, which the Jerusalem (and, by the Johannine period, Yavnian) hierarchy have rejected.

Some see the figure of wine here as an allusion to the messianic banquet;[42] rabbinic literature[43] and possibly[44] the Dead Sea Scrolls[45] speak of an eschatological banquet for the righteous. But wine does not always symbolize the future banquet; in rabbinic texts, in fact, it seems more often to symbolize the Torah.[46]

The specific milieu and thus intent of the miracle is also in question. Although similar imagery occurs in the Jesus tradition (Mark 2:18–22),[47] and especially Jesus' attitude toward ritual purification (Mark 7:1–23), wine miracles were often associated with Dionysiac fertility in the Hellenistic world,[48] and many have read John 2:1–11 against a Dionysiac background.[49] On the other hand, whatever their own source, Jewish texts also can report wine miracles,[50] though these were rare,[51] and it is possible that there are benevolent echoes of Moses' first sign in Exodus in Jesus' first sign in John.[52] For our purposes, however, the source of the tradition or subsequent influences on it are far less important than the issue it addresses in its Johannine context, namely, Jewish ritual purification (2:6).[53]

ii. Ritual Purification in Judaism

Before we can evaluate Jesus' sign in relation to the ritual of purification for which the waterpots had been set aside (2:6), we must survey how this purification would have been understood by the Johannine community and its opponents.

Old Testament models provide a background for the development of later Jewish purifications, and are rooted in the religious consciousness of ancient Near Eastern society. This is true of ancient Egyptian,[54] Mesopotamian,[55] and Hittite rituals.[56]

It is probable that Mediterranean models in the Hellenistic and Roman worlds likewise contributed to the development of Jewish purification ideas. Although some philosophers like the Cynics detested the thought behind bodily purifications,[57] other schools like the Pythagoreans[58] and Stoics[59] valued them as important. Various temples had their own rules mandating ritual purity,[60] and the Eleusinian[61] and Isis[62] cults used lustrations as preliminary purifications in their initiatory rites, although scholars have rightly pointed out that such acts were simply preliminary washings, and not initiatory of themselves.[63]

The early Jewish practice of ritual washings was widespread in Jewish Palestine long before the time of the Jesus movement.[64] *Mikvaoth*, or standard ritual immersion pools, often included steps for descending into the pool and ascending from it, as well as a conduit for water to flow into it from an adjoining pool.[65] They are in evidence in the Hasmonean[66] and Herodian[67] periods, and examples are found at Masada[68] and Jerusalem.[69] They were especially common among the well-to-do who lived in upper city Jerusalem,[70] and on the Temple Mount.[71]

Later rabbinic texts include many discussions of ritual purification.[72] The *mikveh*'s waters were thought to cleanse ritual impurity,[73] and so were important for priests[74] and menstruants,[75] and even vessels.[76] Ritual purity was required preceding a festival and was achieved mainly through immersion (John 11:55).[77]

One crucial rabbinic requirement of the ritual water was that it be "living" water, i.e., either rainwater or flowing water from another fresh source. Drawn water in excess of a very small quantity (the portion being debated by different rabbis) was not acceptable in rabbinic texts.[78] Of course, clean water could purify some of the rest,[79] and where absolute halakic purity was impossible, drawn water could be purified by contact (through a connecting conduit) with ritually pure water in an adjacent container.[80] The partial exceptions to the rule found in rabbinic texts could be due to less strictness at some distance from Jerusalem,[81] especially in dry areas like Egypt,[82] Masada, or Qumran.[83]

The purity of water also excludes other elements mixed in with it, and wine is specifically mentioned as a substance which must not be mixed with the water if it is to be valid for purifications.[84]

iii. Wine vs. Ritual Water

John underlines the purpose of the waterpots: they had been set aside for ritual purification (2:6), and John's narrative suggests that this may have been related to the nearness of Passover (2:13). The fact that the waterpots were made of stone no doubt reflects the preference for stoneware that was due to its invulnerability to levitical impurity.[85]

This point in the Johannine narrative is problematic on an historical level, although the theological point is clear enough. Since drawn water was not normally used, and the probable site of Cana received much more rainwater than Masada or other such sites, it is difficult to understand how John could have conceived of purificatory water found in pots and drawn from a well. Several solutions are possible:

(1) John is unaware of the details of Palestinian halakah, and is simply implausible in his construction of the narrative at this point.

(2) The washing of hands rather than a full *mikveh* is in view.

(3) The real site of Cana is much dryer than the sites currently regarded as most probable.

(4) John and his readers are both sufficiently familiar with ritual purification as we know it from our texts, and he wishes them to suppose the feast's host to be less than strict in his observance of the purification ritual.

(5) Most Jews, except for the Pharisees, did not insist on the use of "living water," and the host would only be seen as nonreligious by Pharisees and those who subscribed to their halakic prescriptions.

While the first explanation is plausible, it is weakened by suggestions that John does indeed know the ritual, e.g., his use of the amount of water in the six waterpots,[86] for a total of 120–150 gallons,[87] which is more than enough[88] for an immersion pool.[89]

The second explanation is not unsupportable. Excavations have uncovered hand-basins in synagogue grounds, and Tannaitic sources speak of the hands being purified by water being poured on them from a container.[90] There is support for Jesus' setting aside of this practice in the tradition (Mark 7:2–4), and some commentators have naturally seen this idea here.[91] Against such an identification of the ritual is the size of the pots, which would make pouring difficult, and the amount of water they contain, as noted above, which was far more than would be necessary for the washing of hands.

The third explanation is possible but has no evidence on which to base a case; although the site of Cana is not undisputed, the evidence does not favor any particular site in a desert area.[92]

The fourth explanation has in its favor the theological nuancing it would add to the narrative: Jesus favors a semi–religious host's social standing above ritual purification, just as he later condemns the temple and Nicodemus, but is better received by a Samaritan woman and a Galilean βασιλικός. Against it is the possibility that John's readers in Asia might not have been as familiar with the custom, especially if some of them were Gentiles; but this objection is considerably weakened by the cumulative strength of John's use of traditions more obscure than this, which he seems to expect his readers to recognize (e.g., on John 7:37–39, below).

With regard to the final explanation, Sanders has provided a strong case that most Palestinian Jews did not share the Pharisaic-rabbinic views of drawn water.[93] This could suggest that the use of these pots for purification was at least not unusual, and at most offensive especially to the strict Pharisees, whose protorabbinic successors John apparently delights to offend anyway (cf. the recurrent identification of Jesus' opponents, employed virtually interchangeably with his negative and probably ironic usage of οἱ Ἰουδαῖοι). Whether or not John's readers would have caught an antagonism to Pharisaism here is in this case a moot point.

Regardless of which explanation one chooses, however, the explicit statement of John is that these waterpots were set apart for the ceremony of ritual purification, and that Jesus replaced water that was pure at least by the host's standards, with what could not be pure for washing by anyone's standards. Preventing a social affront to his host or the dissatisfaction of the guests (cf. ch. 6) was more critical to the Johannine Jesus than the affront offered to the tradition of purification by water.

4.   PROSELYTE BAPTISM IN THE SPIRIT

The point of 2:1–11 becomes much plainer in 3:1–8. Here Jesus confronts a representative of the religious establishment, and demands the ultimate form of purification, namely, the immersion that accompanied the conversion of Gentiles to Judaism. This text also clarifies what the passage in chapter 2 left implied from chapter 1: this washing is carried out by the water of the Spirit.

i. Rebirth Language in Antiquity

Before we can determine the nuances implied by Jesus' response to Nicodemus in John 3:3–5, we must survey some of the proposed contexts for interpreting his teaching about being born from God.

Many scholars speak of a standard idea of rebirth in the mysteries,[94] although explicit references to rebirth in the mysteries are rare in the pre-Christian period. Since the mysteries exhibited differences among themselves, it is more profitable for us to examine the evidence for each cult for which these claims have been made, rather than to lump them together.

The idea of regeneration may occur at Eleusis, although the admission of Willoughby in arguing for this must be taken into account:

> It was virtually for them the experience of a new birth. True, the exact word *palingenesia* does not occur on any of the Eleusinian monuments, but Tertullian attests that the *mystae* applied this very figure of speech to their initiation experiences and to baptism especially.[95]

His dependence on Tertullian is significant; either Tertullian or his sources could have understood the mysteries through the grid of their own religious system, especially after the language of Christianity itself was becoming widespread. Perhaps more to the point is Nock's caution that the rebirth in the Eleusinian Mysteries probably took place in the initiation which followed the bathing, not in the bathing itself.[96] What the Eleusinian initiation provides is a model of intense religious experience in the Hellenistic world. What it cannot signify is the claim to a unique transformation of life distinct from all allegedly analogous experiences; it could be conjoined with a number of other initiations because, in a polytheistic society, it could make no claims to exclusivity.

For regeneration in the cult of Isis, our best evidence comes from well into the Christian period, from Apuleius.[97] The earliest significant sources are late-second-century Christian writers.[98] This need not indicate that regeneration was not an early part of popular Isis worship, but it makes the antiquity or early prominence of this detail difficult to prove. Similarly, the claim for regeneration through the taurobolium, in the cult of Cybele,[99] appears no earlier than the second century, and only in the late fourth century does it appear as a rebirth to eternity rather than for a twenty-year period.[100]

Dionysus could be called "twice-born" because of his return from death,[101] and his followers could be said to have been reborn, according to the late writer Sallustius;[102] but evidence is otherwise scant. And while Dionysiac symbolism is prominent in this period, mentions of a specific mystery cult of Dionysus are far fewer in the imperial than in the Hellenistic period. Willoughby argues at some length for regeneration in Orphism,[103] but concedes:

> Admittedly Orphic practice did not offer a new birth experience as a single catastrophic event to be realized in one's lifetime, unless initiation itself is considered that event in a proleptic way. But Orphism did furnish the possibility for a long regenerative process, beginning at initiation and ending after the death of the physical body—and a development that eventuated in happy immortality.[104]

Guthrie contrasts Orphic regeneration with the moral and ethical quality of Christian ideas of rebirth,[105] though the point in our passage is more the ability to receive revelation than moral prowess. The weakness of the Orphic parallel, besides the weakly defined nature of Orphism, is its character; gradual transformation may be an idea related to the Johannine figure of birth from above, but it is at best only *distantly* related. Rebirth images in Mithraism[106] and in Hermetic[107] sources are too late for detailed consideration here.

"Rebirth" language probably had a much less defined usage in Greco-Roman antiquity than some earlier scholars have supposed. The language could be used for reincarnation;[108] one was initially begotten by God by virtue of creation;[109] and the term could have a variety of metaphorical applications.[110] Usually scholars look for parallels with the *concept* in Greek religion, rather than with the terminology, as Bultmann illustrates:

> Although the expression γεννηθῆναι ἐκ τοῦ θεοῦ ("born of God") is not attested in the same form in the mystery religions or Gnosticism, nevertheless there can be no doubt that this manner of speaking, i.e., the notion, born of God, derives from this sphere.[111]

Or, as Nock puts it:

> Now the sentiment is Hellenistic, and belongs to the stage when the eschatological significance of the act has been replaced by one of individual rebirth. Yet it is to be noted that παλιγγενεσία is not a characteristic mystery word. Plutarch uses it, *De Is. et Os.* 35 p. 364F of the reanimation of Zagreus and Osiris—not of their worshippers; in *De carnium esu* I 7 p. 996C it refers to the destiny of the soul after death and elsewhere it is applied to transmigration. . . .[112]

Philo often speaks of God the Creator as Begetter (γεννητήν),[113] and can only much more rarely speak of death as a rebirth.[114] Of course, it was customary to call the supreme God, the creator, the father of all;[115] and Philo's predominant usage of birth language is hence readily understandable.[116] The usage in Philo and Josephus may indicate the broader semantic range of begetting language that we have already seen.[117]

Wagner argues that rebirth in the early Christian sense is rarely attested in the mysteries, and never in the first century.[118] An experience of radical transformation, of course, does occur in some of the mysteries; but it is a more standard feature of Greek philosophical "conversion,"[119] and examples from unrelated cultures[120] may call into question the significance of the parallel.

Indeed, the more general language of God as begetter may be paralleled in biblical Judaism independent of Hellenistic influence, although the pervasive influence of Hellenistic idiom certainly amplified its presence in early Judaism:

> multiple streams of Jewish tradition refer to God bearing his people or the world (Dt. 33:18a LXX—θεὸν τὸν γεννήσαντά σε; Ps. 22:9; 90:2; Nu. 11:12; 1 QH 9:35–36; Philo *Ebr.* 30; Tanhuma on Ex. 4:12; cf. also the female imagery applied to God in Is. 66:13).[121]

But more to the point is specific Jewish language concerning a new birth, even though it is not normally identified as a birth from God.[122] The idea of a new life is implied in Ps.-Philo 20:2; 27:10, whose language follows 1 Sam 10:6. Somewhat clearer is *Jos. and Asen.* 8:9, if the language has not been influenced by early Christian formulas:

> Lord, bless this virgin,
> and renew her by your spirit,
> and form her anew by your hidden hand,
> and make her alive again by your life
> (ἀνακαίνισον τῷ πνεύματί σου . . .
> ἀναζωοποίησον τῇ ζωῇ σου).[123]

But the clearest Jewish allusions to "rebirth" are found in rabbinic texts addressing Gentiles converting to Judaism (the language may have been affected by the more distant rebirth language of Hellenism illustrated in some texts surveyed above). Since we have suggested earlier, along with the current consensus of Johannine scholarship, that the Johannine community's conflict was with those elements in the synagogue allied with what was developing into rabbinic Judaism, it should not surprise us if the Fourth Gospel should use language intelligible to that segment of early Judaism, especially since the language had already become current in early Christian circles (especially 1 Pet 1:3, 23; Titus 3:5).

ii. Jewish Proselyte Baptism

We have already argued above for the antiquity and importance of Jewish proselyte baptism, as well as its relevance to early Christian baptism. At this point we must compare one aspect of descriptive language concerning Jewish proselyte baptism with the language of this passage.

The rites of conversion were considered strongly efficacious. Proselytes were to be treated well,[124] for they had good standing before God.[125] The OT גר, or stranger, was entitled to the same justice as the native,[126] and גר came to be understood as "proselyte" in many early Jewish texts.[127] Just how great a measure of status could be attributed to proselytes may be seen in the common identification of Abraham as a model proselyte,[128] or the tradition that Shemayah and Abtalion were descendants of proselytes.[129] Proselytes could become disciples of the sages.[130]

This is not to say that there were not certain restrictions on proselytes, especially regarding whom they should marry.[131] They also ranked below other members of Israel in social standing,[132] and would more quickly be accused of sin.[133] But after a thorough review of the evidence, Bamberger concludes that the halakah is overwhelmingly friendly toward converts,[134] and that rabbinic texts are by and large favorable toward them.[135] Hoenig is more convinced of this for the Tannaitic than the

Amoraic period,[136] but for our purposes it is the Tannaitic evidence which is more relevant.

Despite social disadvantages to the first-generation proselyte, a proselyte's spiritual status was in theory equal to an Israelite. Although proselytes from certain peoples could not marry directly into Israel in the first generation, according to a certain understanding of the Torah, they also could not marry pagans, because in regard to them they were of Israelite status.[137] Justin also testifies to the mid-second-century Jewish belief, apparently widespread, that the proselyte is "like one who is native born."[138]

It was, in fact, a commonplace that a proselyte's status was that of a newborn child.[139] The convert was no longer the person he or she had been as a Gentile before God, the Law, or Israel; his or her legal standing was that of an Israelite.[140] The line of demarcation, of course, was the ritual cleansing in proselyte baptism.[141]

When R. Hanania b. R. Simeon b. Gamaliel suggests that proselytes are afflicted because they disobeyed the seven Noahide laws, R. Jose responds:

> One who has become a proselyte is like a child newly born. Why then are proselytes oppressed?—Because they are not so well acquainted with the details of the commandments as the Israelites.[142]

In other words, a proselyte may still struggle to learn all the halakah for which he is responsible, but his spiritual status is secure; a Jewish nature is different than a Gentile nature, for Israel's ancestors stood before Mount Sinai, where their evil impulse was defeated.[143] Old sins no longer determined the proselyte's status; a purportedly Tannaitic tradition reports that R. Eliezer turned away a proselyte woman guilty of incest, but R. Joshua (in the spirit of Hillel) received her with the words, " 'When she set her mind on being a proselyte, she no longer lived to the world.' "[144]

In the halakah, a proselyte had lost all previous connections; the convert had begun a new life.[145] This may bear some relation to Roman law, in which one becoming a Roman citizen had to reaffirm old legal ties explicitly in order for them to remain binding.[146]

Thus, in terms of legal status, a proselyte had no relatives, and could marry paternal relatives;[147] according to legal *theory*, though not practice, a proselyte could even marry his former mother.[148] Many early Palestinian Amoraim understood Tannaitic authorities to say that a proselyte had no inheritance obligation to his former children.[149] Perhaps because one's past divorce was committed under Noahide status, a proselyte could remarry the former wife in spite of Deut 24:4.[150]

This newness is not, of course, portrayed as a supernatural birth, but as a new legal status; and it is often qualified. Although "a Noahide [Gentile] who slew his neighbour [also a Gentile] or violated his wife, and then became converted, is exempt," he is still liable to death if he did it to an Israelite, only the judicial procedure being changed to accommodate his new status as an Israelite.[151] Such qualifying of the new status can work in favor of the proselyte at times; for instance, he is still permitted to inherit:

> A proselyte and a gentile who inherited [the property of] their father, [who was] a gentile—he [the proselyte] is permitted to say to him [the gentile], "You take the idols and I [will take] the utensils; you [take] the wine and I [will take] the produce.[152]

A proselyte might deal with himself more strictly and throw out his own share;[153] but he was at least *permitted* to inherit. Yet by the Amoraic period it was agreed that this concession, allowing him to inherit, was only to dissuade him from returning to idolatry.[154]

All this appears to have functioned as more than legal theory, however. Jeremias has argued that the phrase, "[a proselyte is] like a newborn child," reflected a religious interpretation about a now complete innocence, before the legal applications gained ground.[155] To whatever extent Jeremias' interpretation might overstate the case on this specific point, early second-century examples of Roman xenophobia reflect the popular view that proselytes, perhaps by rejecting the family religion, have broken filial ties: those who are circumcised and become Jewish "have this lesson first instilled into them, to despise all gods, to disown their country, and set at nought parents, children and brethren."[156]

Language of a "new creation" was naturally used especially for eschatological newness in early Judaism;[157] in rabbinic texts, however, the emphasis falls on forensic renewing of sinners in Israel after repentance.[158] One who taught Torah to another Israelite,[159] or made converts,[160] was reckoned as if he had created them. If the evidence for such varied strands of thought could be woven together—eschatology, forensic renewal, and conversion—one might approximate some of the Pauline imagery of eschatological realignment in his new-creation language. That some such strands of thinking, besides the eschatological, could have been available in the first century is plausible, though difficult to demonstrate on the basis of our limited extant first-century evidence.

At any rate, it is clear that a conversion experience could be described by the rabbis in terms of an entirely new status, and it is very probable that this concept was sometimes expressed in terms of a proselyte being seen as "a newborn child" spiritually, and to some extent socially, in the period in which John was writing.[161] If this is the case, the synagogue represented in Nicodemus *should* have understood Jesus' point.

iii. Birth from Above, from Water and Spirit

Birth "from above" (3:3) is explained as birth "from water and Spirit" in 3:5. Nicodemus' incomprehension is used to generate the explanation.

"Above" is certainly the place of God in John's vertical dualism,[162] and "above" had become a circumlocution for God in many Jewish circles.[163] The standard meaning of ἄνωθεν is "above" in both classical and Hellenistic usage,[164] as well as in the usage elsewhere in John. But John frequently employs word-plays, which were often given hermeneutical significance in Jewish circles, and many scholars thus recognize a double entendre here: "born again" and "born from above."[165] What is clear is that Nicodemus understands Jesus only to say, "born again," and, like most of the adversarial foils of Jesus in the Fourth Gospel, misses Jesus' point (v. 4).[166]

Later in this text, Jesus functions as a witness of the realm "above" because he alone has been there and descended to report its nature to the world. This can be seen in terms of Jewish mysticism, or, given the reference to Moses, in terms of Moses' ascent to heaven.[167] One could thus read 3:3 as a christological response to Nicodemus' statement about Jesus as a teacher: Jesus has been born "from above."[168] The problem with this interpretation is that while Jesus is "from above" in the Fourth Gospel, John curiously avoids drawing attention to his "birth"; the text goes on to explain this in terms of proselyte baptism (as we shall argue below), and it is developed in general in vv. 4–8. But while the christological meaning is not solely in view, "birth from above" is certainly linked with the Son of man from above in vv. 11–14: Jesus, as the only one who has come from above, is the only one who can testify what it means to originate from above.[169] If he is a teacher "from God" (v. 2), i.e., "from above," then he is qualified to tell Nicodemus how he, a "teacher of Israel" (3:10), can also be "from above," "from God" (v. 3). Although "seeing the kingdom" could have reference to the future (cf. 8:51), in terms of the eschatological vision of God, it could also be read in terms of mystical vision, such as was experienced in Jewish mysticism. Either way, Jesus seems to be saying that unless one comes from above (either as the Son of man or from a heavenly, spiritual birth),[170] one cannot understand the nature of the things above; Nicodemus' lack of understanding only confirms this point. Like Israel of old, weighed down by corruptible bodies and barely able to understand earthly matters (τὰ ἐπὶ γῆς), Nicodemus could only understand heavenly matters (τὰ ἐν οὐρανοῖς) if divine wisdom or the Holy Spirit descended from heaven (Wis 9:15–16; cf. John 3:12).[171]

When Nicodemus misunderstands this heavenly birth, Jesus articulates it in a new way: birth from water and Spirit. A variety of solutions have been proposed to the question of the meaning of water here. One proposed solution, associating this birth with natural birth,[172] is that the water is semen, related to conception.[173] But as J. R. Michaels notes, "The problem with this view (aside from the heaping of metaphor on metaphor!) is that *water* is not among the expressions for physical birth listed in 1:13."[174]

A more popular solution is that the text refers to Christian baptism, which must include the presence of the Spirit as well as water to be properly efficacious.[175] This interpretation is common because it is thought that early Christian readers would have understood the phrase in this way; but as D. W. B. Robinson notes, this argument is somewhat circular; there is no evidence in the passage itself to suggest Christian baptism, but Christian baptism is inferred by the reconstruction of Christian tradition.[176] While this is a possible inference, Kümmel finds this passage to be the only "clear" mention of baptism in the Fourth Gospel.[177] Such a reading is less consistent with the use of the water motif in the Fourth Gospel than Jewish baptism would be, since Jewish baptism is normally in view, and a thoroughgoing polemic against Christian baptism would be unlikely (4:1), no matter how much it might be played down for its similarity with other Jewish rituals (cf. 4:2).

As Robinson points out, the water of chapter 2 referred to Jewish ritual and was transformed by Jesus; the water here may thus also apply to Jewish ritual. The opposition of flesh and Spirit in the following verses contrasts the old ritual with the new gift of life in the Spirit.[178] This fits the use of the water motif throughout the Fourth Gospel, where the water of various Jewish rites usually finds its fulfillment in the gift of Jesus, sometimes the Spirit.

But this leaves the question of the relationship between "water" and Spirit unanswered. Various scholars argue whether[179] or not[180] the construction should be read as a hendiadys with an epexegetical καί, but the issue cannot be resolved on merely grammatical grounds.[181] It is at least clear that the two terms are intended to be taken closely together.[182] But the determination as to whether the καί in this passage is epexegetical must rest on Johannine usage, and since water is explicitly used of the Spirit several chapters later (7:37–39), an identification of water and Spirit here would fit Johannine usage.

The connection of water and Spirit has considerable precedent in the Hebrew scriptures, and is applied to the renewal of Israel in the eschatological time particularly in Ezek 36:25–27, a passage which many scholars believe is at least partly in view here.[183] This passage was associated with immersion and repentance in the Qumran community,[184] used in later Jewish texts for the eschatological destruction of the evil impulse,[185] and associated with God as Israel's bath of purification:

> R. Akiba said: Blessed are ye, O Israel. Before whom are ye made clean and who makes you clean? Your Father in heaven; as it is written, And I will sprinkle clean water upon you and ye shall be clean. And again it says, O Lord the hope (mikveh) of Israel; as the Mikveh cleanses the unclean so does the Holy one, blessed be He, cleanse Israel.[186]

In this passage it is associated with the ablution of the high priest, i.e., with Israel's prescribed purifications.[187] The Spirit functions as an eschatological *mikveh* in Ezek 36, and the water of John 3:5 thus is a picture of the Spirit, rather than representing something distinct from it.

Nevertheless, given our earlier discussion of proselyte baptism and new birth, it is probable that something more specific than the *mikveh* is in view: the Johannine Jesus is calling on Nicodemus to undergo a spiritual proselyte baptism, i.e., a conversion effected by the purifying Spirit of God, a new birth. That Nicodemus should not understand such a requirement is plausible enough; why would one descended from Abraham (8:38–44), particularly a teacher of Israel, need to convert to true Judaism and thus be genuinely born of God?[188]

iv. Purification and the Spirit

If our analysis has been correct, then "water" in John 3:5 refers to a proselyte baptism by the Spirit, and thus refers to a spiritual purification. It also indicates that this kind of purification was for religious Jews as well as for Gentiles, and that it is more essential than Jewish proselyte baptism, just as it proved more essential than ceremonial washing and John's baptism in previous chapters of the Fourth Gospel.

5.   SAMARITAN HOLY WATER: JACOB'S WELL

Most of the fourth chapter of the Fourth Gospel deals with Jesus' encounter with the Samaritan woman. This encounter is set in the context of Jesus' supremacy over John and everyone else, and particularly the superiority of his baptism over other forms of purification (3:22–4:3). Part of Jesus' dialogue with the woman concerns the water of a Samaritan holy site; most of the dialogue concerns the conflict between Jewish and Samaritan religion, and involves the role of Jacob in such a way as to keep the significance of "Jacob's well" before the readers.

i. Jesus' Encounter with the Woman

Although some Samaritans apparently did live outside Palestine,[189] they would not have been widely known outside Palestine, and this can indicate one of several things: John or his tradition addressed a community with a Samaritan presence;[190] he has historical tradition which he does not wish to alter;[191] or Samaritans were theologically the closest thing to Gentiles he could find in the Jesus tradition.[192] In favor of the last possibility should be noted the parallels between the Samaritans and the Galileans in the narrative.[193] Whatever the reason Samaritans in particular appear in this narrative, their function as a dynamic contrast to the Jerusalem hierarchy,[194] including Nicodemus,[195] is not difficult to observe.

The hostility of the Samaritans toward the Jews in the first century C.E. is well-known,[196] and apparently did not decrease in later rabbinic opinion.[197] Tannaim could question whether Samaritans should be treated from the standpoint of Gentiles or Israelites in certain laws.[198] Further, in talking with a woman alone, Jesus violated standard Jewish custom,[199] an offense certainly compounded by the fact that she was a Samaritan woman, which made her perpetually unclean.[200] Samaritan bread[201] and drinking vessels[202] could also be unclean (contrast 4:7–8). The picture is intensified by the fact that she was a "sinner," in contrast to the other village women who no doubt made her come to draw water alone rather than allow her to accompany them.[203] The Samaritan woman and her people thus provide a stark contrast to Nicodemus and his community.

Although the site of the woman's town, Sychar, has been identified both with modern Askar and with Shechem,[204] the really important geographical identification in this text is with Jacob's well.[205] Sacred wells were common enough in the ancient Mediterranean,[206] and some Jewish tradition reports various miracles associated with Jacob's well in particular.[207] What is most significant about this well is its association with Jacob (4:12);[208] the woman speaks of it as the gift of Jacob "our" father, as if to link her people, but not the Jews, with Jacob.[209]

Jacob remains in the background of the whole text. There are clear echoes of Gen 24 (Rebekah and the representative of Isaac),[210] and less clear echoes of Exod 2 (Moses); but both these texts are full of parallels with Gen 29 (Jacob), whether the parallels derive from common literary patterns or the preliterary tradition. Just as Jacob met Rachel at a well and provided water for her there (Gen 29:10), Jesus, who is greater than Jacob, supplies living water for this woman.[211] Even the time that Jesus comes to the well may be significant; the sixth hour is probably noon,[212] and while that may be meant to indicate the woman's exclusion from community life,[213] or to explain Jesus' weariness and thirst,[214] it may also allude to the time Jacob met Rachel coming to water the sheep.[215] The water of Jacob's well, then, does not necessarily allude to purification, unlike the water passages of John 1–3; it is "holy" because of its association with a holy site and holy history. But the motif of purification is so important in the preceding context (3:22–4:3) that it is very likely implied in some measure in the drinking water of John 4.[216]

ii. The Water and Holy Land

As in 2:6, Jesus here ignores ritual purity questions (such as nonassociation with Samaritans) in favor of a deeper spiritual reality, and transforms water as a symbol of religious tradition to point to a deeper reality. Water in this passage has been variously associated with Torah according to standard rabbinic formulas,[217] the water flowing from the new Jerusalem,[218] etc. The use of "living water," ὕδωρ ζῶν, however, a typical Johannine double entendre[219] playing on a standard designation for fresh, flowing water,[220] and the water of life,[221] suggests the image of purification,[222] since fresh water was necessary for that purpose.[223]

The theme of Jesus' superiority to a Samaritan holy site (appropriately again associated with water) dominates the entire passage. For John, the true holy site is "in the Spirit" (4:21–24). The place of the sanctuary had become an important issue in Judaism before 70 C.E.;[224] for instance, the holy land theology of Genesis is amplified in *Jubilees*.[225] Later rabbis also emphasized the importance of the land,[226] and generally even Babylonian documents acknowledged the superior merit assigned to one living in Palestine.[227] The synagogue, which was also considered sacred space,[228] was officially supposed to be built on high ground,[229] of course on a clean site,[230] and often oriented toward Jerusalem.[231] Although rabbinic theory was not always followed in practice, it is clear that the terrestrial dimension of Jewish thought was important.[232]

When the woman points to Mount Gerizim (within sight of the well)[233] and says that the Samaritan place of worship was (aorist) on Mt. Gerizim,[234] she alludes to the fact that the Jews under John Hyrcanus had destroyed it a century and a half earlier;[235] in other words, she was reflecting the sense of hostility which Jews[236] and Samaritans felt toward one another's holy sites. This hostility is demonstrated by a number of first-century incidents,[237] and may be illustrated by an early Amoraic story about a Tanna:

> R. Jonathan was going up to worship in Jerusalem, when he passed the Palatinus [Mt. Gerizim] and was seen by a Samaritan, who asked him, 'Whither are you going?' 'To worship in Jerusalem,' replied he. 'Would it not be better to pray at this holy mountain than at that dunghill?' he jeered. 'Wherein is it blessed?' inquired he. 'Because it was not submerged by the Flood.' Now R. Jonathan momentarily forgot the teaching [on the subject], but his ass-driver said to him, 'Rabbi, with your permission I will answer him.' 'Do,' said he. 'If it is of the high mountains,' he answered, 'then it is written, AND ALL THE HIGH MOUNTAINS WERE COVERED. While if it is of the low ones, Scripture ignored it.'

Whereupon R. Jonathan dismounted and exalted his ass-driver above himself.[238] For the Samaritan woman, this geographical issue was of paramount religious significance, and any Jew who claimed to be a prophet would have to answer it.[239]

In many Jewish traditions, the Spirit tended to be localized.[240] But the point of John 4:20–24 seems to be the opposite: it is the Spirit that is the location of true worship. ("Spirit and truth" function closely together, and, like the phrase in 3:5, could be a kind of hendiadys, perhaps as the "Spirit of truth.")[241] The phrase "God is Spirit" is probably not an onto-logical philosophical statement, but a statement that God is manifested in his Spirit.[242] That God is to be worshiped "in Spirit" (4:23–24; cf. Rev 1:10) could well be taken to mean ecstatic worship.[243] Ecstatic or charismatic worship is reported among OT prophets (e.g., 1 Sam 10:5, 10) and the Chronicler says that it was transferred to the temple cult (1 Chron 25:1–6), where it probably generated many of the psalms in the Psalter. This fits our clearest NT pictures of worship, such as 1 Cor 14:14–16, 26,[244] and the heavenly worship in Revelation could be related to the Qumran idea of worshiping with the angels,[245] in which case it may indicate a more mystical form of early Jewish piety among many of the Jewish Christians of Asia. Whether or not ecstatic worship is in view, the Spirit seems to replace the temple as the location of divine activity, and the locative may function instrumentally; true worship will no longer be confined to the temple, but will be dependent on the sort of experience of the Spirit described in the Fourth Gospel.

Whereas in John 1–3 the Spirit fulfills purificatory rituals, here the Spirit's replacement of a water theme and other religious symbols (particularly geographic and Samaritan) ultimately points to a replacement of Samaritan and Jewish holy sites: not only Jacob's well (because Jesus is greater than the ancestor of the Jewish and Samaritan peoples), but also Mt. Gerizim and the temple in Jerusalem.

6. WATER OF A POPULAR HEALING SITE

The water of the pool of Bethesda, like the ritual water in most of the preceding chapters, proves ineffectual (due to its seeker's inability to appropriate its alleged power), leaving a man paralyzed for thirty-eight years until Jesus comes to heal him. While the water of such a pool would not be used in official Jewish ritual, its significance on a popular level must have been great.

Excavators have identified the site of "Bethesda"[246] with the Twin Pools beneath St. Anne's Monastery;[247] the pools were apparently as large as a football field, and about twenty feet deep.[248] The "five porticoes" (5:2) represent a porch on each of the four sides and one separating the two pools,[249] perhaps to separate the men and the women.[250] In Greco-Roman cities, porticoes, like temples, theaters, baths, and gymnasia, were public places,[251] so it would not be unusual to find beggars and other people in such locations.[252]

Water was often associated with healing shrines in Greek religion,[253] and the masses of sick people who crowded Palestinian Jewish hot springs and healing baths[254] may suggest some degree of transference of the Greek expectation of supernatural intervention at such sites. Despite the fact that the late texts that add 5:3b–4 may no longer have had any tradition concerning the original reason the man expected the waters to heal him (v. 7),[255] there is some evidence that healing properties had been attributed to this pool in folklorish tradition:

> In 1866 a broken marble foot was found in the debris in the vaults of the Church of St. Anne. On the top was this inscription in Greek: ... "Pompeia Lucilia dedicated (this as a votive gift)" ... The donor, a Roman lady to judge by her name, had certainly visited the place and left a sign of her visit; it could be that the foot commemorates a healing. Paleographically the inscription may be from the second century. At that time the Pool of Bethesda may have been a pagan healing sanctuary.[256]

If the second-century date is correct, it is unlikely that the pagan tradition derived from a Christian interpretation of the Fourth Gospel; it is far more likely that it reflects an earlier popular Jewish tradition. No doubt this use of Bethesda as a healing bath would have been regarded as unorthodox by the establishment,[257] but Theissen is surely right when he notes, "In Jn 5.1ff. Jesus is in competition with ancient healing sanctuaries."[258]

The water in this case serves more as a stage prop for the miracle that leads to a proclamation of Jesus' supremacy over the Sabbath and Moses, than to focus on the issue of purification itself.

The unnamed feast of 5:1 has been identified with Purim,[259] Pentecost,[260] or perhaps Rosh Hashanah,[261] since many early manuscripts omit the article. If "the feast" is read, Sukkoth is surely in view;[262] but since no special associations with Sukkoth appear (unlike in John 7–9), it is probable that the "feast" is simply an explanation for why Jesus has returned to Jerusalem. The real calendrical issue in this chapter is not an annual feast, but the Sabbath,[263] and Jesus' claim to divine authority as God's *shaliach* to modify Sabbath rules. The chapter ultimately leads into a comparison of Jesus with God's earlier messenger, Moses, arguing that Jesus is much greater than Moses.[264]

While some see the passage as a baptismal reference,[265] others find the basis for baptismal interpretation "fragile,"[266] or see an anti-baptismal motif reflected in the fact that the water was not efficacious.[267] The last point is the most likely, given earlier references to water in the Gospel, but it depends almost entirely on the cumulative support of the other references. There is no mention of purification, and while replacement by the Spirit could have been implied by replacement of a popular healing shrine, there is no definite evidence that this is the case in this text, apart from implication by its function in the Johannine water motif.

What demonstrates that this water text fits into the others is the clear antithetical parallel it provides with chapter 9,[268] where the evidence of ritual water and the Spirit (in the context of Sukkoth) is much clearer. Culpepper lays out the parallel structure of the passages as follows:[269]

Lame man
(1) History described (5:5)
(2) Jesus takes initiative (5:6)
(3) Pool's healing powers (5:7)
(4) Jesus heals on Sabbath (5:9)
(5) Jews accuse him of violating Sabbath (5:10)
(6) Jews ask who healed him (5:12)
(7) Doesn't know where or who Jesus is (5:13)
(8) Jesus finds him and invites belief (5:14)
(9) Jesus implies relation between his sin and suffering (5:14)
(10) Man goes to Jews (5:15)
(11) Jesus works as his Father is working (5:17)

Blind man
(1) History described (9:1)
(2) Jesus takes initiative (9:6)
(3) Pool of Siloam, healing (9:7)
(4) Jesus heals on Sabbath (9:14)
(5) Pharisees accuse Jesus of violating Sabbath (9:16)
(6) Pharisees ask who healed him (9:15)
(7) Doesn't know where or who Jesus is (9:12)
(8) Jesus finds him and invites belief (9:35)
(9) Jesus rejects sin as explanation for his suffering (9:3)
(10) Jews cast man out (9:34–35)
(11) Jesus must do the works of one who sent him (9:4)

The close relationship between them suggests that the function of water in the two passages is analogous or antithetically parallel. That in the first case the water is not effective, and in the second case, the water heals (a promise tradition had not made for the pool of Siloam as it had for the pool of Bethesda) only because Jesus "sent" the man there, suggests that Jewish piety is still in the background, and that Jesus' touch in person symbolizes for the Johannine community how the other Paraclete, Jesus' presence in the Spirit, functions in their time. This suggestion is further strengthened by the fact that the waters of the pool of Siloam come to point to the work of the Spirit in the one water passage intervening between chapters 5 and 9, John 7:37–39.

7.   WATERS OF THE ESCHATOLOGICAL TEMPLE
. . . .

John 7:2, 37, explicitly invite us to examine John 7–9[270] in light of the theology and customs of the Feast of Tabernacles. This was a feast particularly characterized by joyous celebration[271] and by the ceremony of the water libation, in which water drawn from the pool of Siloam was carried in procession to the temple, where it was poured out at the altar.[272] The water-pouring ceremony on the feast of Sukkoth was a ritual related to a prayer for rain, appropriate to that time of year,[273] but it had taken on far greater dimensions.

Although some later rabbis traced the ceremony back to Moses[274] or Ruth,[275] it was probably a Pharisaic innovation in Maccabean times.[276] But the customs known to us were certainly practiced in the first century C.E., and were known, by means of Diaspora pilgrims, to the Jewish community throughout the Roman world. This can be demonstrated, for example, by the image of the golden flagon for the water-drawing ceremony on a souvenir amphorisk found on Cyprus.[277] This ceremony would still be known to Jewish readers of the Fourth Gospel two or three decades after the destruction of the temple, as shown both by rabbinic documents[278] and archaeological data.[279]

Perhaps more significant for our text is the theology that was associated with the water-drawing ceremony. By the third century, some rabbis had begun to associate the water-drawing at Sukkoth with the drawing out of the Holy Spirit,[280] and since it is not inherently likely that the rabbis derived this tradition from the Jewish Christians who might have preserved it on the basis of John 7:37–39, this tradition with early Amoraic attestation may have far older roots. On the other hand, John could have made the link midrashically from OT texts without a prior

Jewish tradition on which to build; it certainly suits his *Tendenz,* as we have already observed in the Fourth Gospel, just as much as it might have been suppressed in some Tannaitic circles.

What may be more significant is the Scripture to which the Johannine Jesus makes reference in 7:38. Although the lectionary thesis for the Fourth Gospel is at best unproved and at worst disproved, due in part to the very late date that must be assigned to the extant system of readings, it is perhaps possible to ascertain what texts might have been commonly read on the Feast of Tabernacles.[281] The only readings in the prophets which discuss the feast are Hos 12:9, which does not use σκηνοπηγία and is not conducive to joyful celebration in the context, and Zech 14:16–21,[282] a text of pilgrimage and Israel's triumphant exaltation over the nations. It is therefore intrinsically likely, on a priori grounds, that the Scripture readings for Sukkoth should have included Zech 14. Tannaitic sources appear to confirm this expectation:

> It required bringing the water-offering on the Festival [of Tabernacles] so that the rain would be blessed on its account, and it says, *And if any of the families of the earth do not go up to Jerusalem to worship the King, the Lord of hosts, there will be no rain upon them. And if the family of Egypt do not go up and present themselves, then upon them [shall come the plague with which the Lord afflicts the nations that do not go up to keep the festival of Tabernacles]* (Zech. 14:17–18).[283]

Significantly, the preceding context in Zechariah describes the event that would initiate this eschatological era of peace and blessing for Israel:

> On that day living waters shall flow out from Jerusalem, half of them to the eastern sea and half of them to the western sea; it shall continue in summer as in winter. And the LORD will become king over all the earth; on that day the LORD will be one and his name one.[284]

This text could naturally be connected midrashically with a number of other texts about the Spirit of God being poured out as water, such as Isa 44:3 and Joel 3:1 (2:28, English), but its closest affinities could be with Ezek 47, which also turns up in Tannaitic discussions of Sukkoth:

> Then he brought me back to the door of the temple; and behold, water was issuing from below the threshold of the temple toward the east (for the temple faced east); and the water was flowing down from below the south end of the threshold of the temple, south of the altar . . .[285]

The passage goes on to describe the water becoming a deep river bringing life to all the world (Ezek 47:3–12). The Tosephta expounds Ezek 47 and applies it to the future, prefigured by the flask of water at the Sukkoth festival.[286]

Why is it called "the Water Gate" [*M. Sukka* 4:9]? Because through it they bring a flask of water for the water libation on the Festival. R. Eliezer b. Jacob says, *Through it the water comes out [on the south side]* (Ez. 47:2). This teaches that they will flow outward like the water of a flask. And they are destined to *flow down from below the south end of the threshold of the Temple.*[287]

On Ezek 47:10, the Tosephta declares, "This teaches that all the waters created at the Creation are destined to go forth from the mouth of this little flask."[288] The waters of Ezek 47, associated with Sukkoth, would purify: "There will be a single source [of purification-water] for sin and for menstrual uncleanness."[289]

The use of Ezekiel's new-temple image is probably more significant for the Fourth Gospel than has been hitherto realized. John speaks three times of the Father's house, in 2:16, 8:35, and 14:2. The first text refers to the temple and then goes on to define it in terms of Christ's resurrection body; the second text employs the image of a father's household, noting that only a descendant, not slaves, holds a permanent inheritance therein; the third text is pointedly obscure until explained by its following context and the preceding references to the house, as the place where believers may dwell forever in Jesus' presence through the Spirit. In Ezek 46:16–17, it is stated that the prince's inheritance of land is permanent only for his descendants, not for his servants; further, only the undefiled ministers would have a place in God's house, the temple (44:9–16; cf. 48:11), where God would dwell with his people forever (43:7, 9; 48:35).[290]

The square configurations of a holy allotment in the eschatological city (Ezek 48:16, 20) may reflect the old holy of holies, the place of God's presence, which is probably also implied by the shape of the new Jerusalem in Rev 21:16. Jesus is the new temple, where believers and God experience one another's presence, in John's realized eschatology (John chs. 14–15; cf. Rev 21:3, 22); some of John's conception of that new temple is apparently derived from Ezekiel. This is why the waters flow, not from the Jerusalem temple, but from the glorified Jesus (19:34; cf. Rev 22:1). It is possible that John's reference to the last day of the feast[291] as "the last day, the great one," is another of his double entendres, this one with an implied eschatological significance.[292]

John's allusion to "Scripture" in v. 38 has sent scholars looking for the exact source of his reference. Some have looked to the well in Numbers,[293] which also was associated with the Sukkoth flask;[294] others feel that Zech 14[295] or Ezek 47 are more likely backgrounds.[296] Although I believe that John makes most use of the new-temple material in Ezekiel, I concur with those scholars who argue that John regularly blends various texts midrashically and that he is following that practice here.[297]

The case inevitably turns to the question of the meaning of the text. Who is the source of the living waters, Christ or the believer? Most Hellenistic contexts (such as Epicurean philosophy's location of the rational part of man in the chest)[298] could support a reading of the waters flowing from the believer, but this has little precedent in Jewish or Christian sources, except possibly John 4:14 (below). Discussions of the Semitic original behind "belly"[299] attempt to identify the OT text in view and thus its probable Johannine referent, but presume too much knowledge of Hebrew or Aramaic for the readers of the Johannine community; reading an eclectic text arranged by someone with a knowledge of Hebrew is not the same as reading Hebrew, so this method will not help us identify either the OT passages or their Johannine referent.

Those who argue that the waters of John 7:37–38 flow from the believer[300] argue on the basis of the antecedent of αὐτοῦ,[301] the parallel with 4:14,[302] the emphasis on receiving in 7:39,[303] the weakness of the opposing view's parallelism,[304] and, perhaps the strongest point, the traditional punctuation in the oldest punctuated manuscripts, which reflects such an interpretation.[305]

Others favor a punctuation which more easily permits the waters to flow from Jesus instead of from the believer.[306] They challenge the patristic support for the opposing view[307] and argue from parallelism,[308] grammar,[309] and formal considerations.[310] But the strongest arguments are: (1) it is much more likely that John would cite Scripture with a christological interpretation than that he would apply it to the believer;[311] and (2) context—John interprets the believers as the *recipients* of the Spirit, thereby implying that the glorified Christ is the Spirit's source (v. 39).[312] This would also better explain why the Spirit is not available[313] before Jesus is glorified, particularly if the specific event of 19:34 is in view here.[314]

It was commonly believed that Jerusalem,[315] and (especially in rabbinic texts) specifically the temple[316] and the foundation stone beneath the altar[317] were at the center of the world. From this center would flow the rivers of life to inundate the whole world;[318] and in John, where Jesus' body becomes the new temple (2:19–21), he becomes the shattered cornerstone from which flows the water of the river of life.[319]

8.   RITUAL WATER EMPOWERED

This passage finally makes clear that John does not oppose ritual waters per se; rather, he contends that the rituals of contemporary Judaism are not efficacious apart from an encounter with Jesus. This is presumably one reason why "knowledge" about Jesus is stressed in this passage so thoroughly: in the dispute between the former blind man and his accusers, verbs of knowing are used eleven times (9:13–34), and then, defending the blind man, Jesus proceeds to use a different (but in John interchangeable) word for knowing which indicates that those who truly know Jesus are his covenant people (10:1–18). The water motif here runs into one of the main themes in the Fourth Gospel, that of knowing God, which in turn is related in the Farewell Discourses to the revelation of the Spirit, all of which are contrasted with what the writer regarded as mere religious forms.[320]

John tells of a man whose blindness[321] was not due to sin[322] (9:2), in contrast to a blindness of sin among his opponents (9:41). This narrative probably reflects the dilemma of his community in a particularly strong way:[323] faithfulness to Jesus and thus to the covenant, or acceptability within the broader Jewish community. Jesus heals the man in part with spittle, a substance occasionally used for healings in antiquity.[324] But what is more significant for our treatment here is the other part of the healing: Jesus sends the man to the Pool of Siloam to wash off the spittle-mud from his eyes, and it is only after the man obeys this command that he returns seeing.[325]

The Pool of Siloam was an ancient site associated with much of Jerusalem's history,[326] and was used for some purifications,[327] probably including proselyte baptism.[328] But perhaps most significant is the fact that the water of this pool was used for the water libation at the Feast of Tabernacles (above), and that the lack of a definitive break between chapter 7 and 8:12–10:18, once 7:53–8:11 is seen as an interpolation, indicates that this was still the last day of the feast. Jesus had left the temple and found this man near the temple on the last day of the feast,[329] and commanded him to wash his eyes with water that had been used in the water-drawing ceremony on the first seven days of the feast. As E. E. Ellis notes,

> Siloam was the pool from which the water for the Temple ceremony was taken: at Jesus' word the impotent water of religious Judaism became the instrument of God's redemptive power.[330]

The man is healed not by the waters themselves, but precisely because he is "sent" there by Jesus, a point which is underscored by the false etymology[331] given the pool of Siloam.

9. WASHING AND DEATH

It is commonly agreed that Jesus' act of washing his disciples' feet represents a prefiguration of the cross.[332] This is probably indicated by the double entendre involved in loving his disciples "to the end" and its temporal context in 13:1,[333] and by the "laying aside" and "taking" in v. 4 (cf. 10:18).[334] But it is more explicit in Jesus' explanation of the act, which merges into an announcement of the betrayal (13:11–30)[335] and of his going away to glorification (13:31–38). To call his disciples to follow his example of service (13:14–16) and love (13:34–35) was to summon them to lay down their lives for one another; the commandment was "new" (v. 34) not because love was a new commandment (cf. Lev 19:18), but because the model to be followed ("as I have loved you," i.e., in the cross) was new.[336] Such unity would be necessary to stand in the face of the "world's" hostility which the community was facing (15:18–16:4), which made the apostasy of secessionists (cf. 15:6) all the more grievous.[337]

Those who were truly part of the community were already clean (13:10; 15:3; cf. Rev 7:14; 1:5 [v.l.]), but needed to continue to be cleansed (pruned, 15:2, is καθαίρει; cf. 13:10; 1 John 1:7, 9). To continue to be cleansed meant to continue to abide in Jesus the vine, and thus in the community with the true Christology (15:4),[338] the community united by the fruit of love for one another (15:5–14; cf. 15:8 with 13:35).

10. CONCLUSION

In the final analysis, it was Christ's death that would bring the true, spiritual cleansing (19:34),[339] and this would be administered by the Spirit who would reveal the glorified Christ (7:37–39; 16:12–15). While this would not always rule out the usefulness of other Jewish purification ceremonies (9:7; cf. the second paragraph of our ch. 4), they could henceforth derive their meaning only from an encounter and continuing relationship of fellowship with him through the Spirit. Nothing associated with purity among the opponents of the Johannine community was adequate to sustain its own holiness; for this, the Spirit of purification was necessary, and the Spirit of purification was available only to those who were followers of Jesus, who alone was qualified to bestow the Spirit (1:32–34; 3:31–35).

This theme is developed in the Farewell Discourses, where the emphasis shifts, however, to another, more prominent characterization of the Spirit of God in early Judaism, namely, the Spirit of prophecy. At this point we will turn, however, to a sample in a writer who emphasizes the Spirit of inspiration almost to the exclusion of other aspects of the Spirit's work: Luke.

NOTES

· ·

1. Jewish Christians may have continued the practice of ritual baths; cf. Meyers and Strange, *Archaeology,* 130; perhaps Heb 6:2. Christian baptism almost certainly reflects standard Jewish models, as we argued in ch. 2, above.

2. The proposed context of the Fourth Gospel assumed here, along with a response to various other proposals, is treated more thoroughly in C. S. Keener, "The Function of Johannine Pneumatology in the Context of Late First Century Judaism" (Ph.D. diss., Duke University; Ann Arbor: University Microfilms, 1991) 1–57; for the sake of space, I have summarized here only the conclusions of that study. In the dissertation I argued that Johannine pneumatology (prophetic as well as purificatory, the former with an emphasis on illumination as at Qumran, represented in the Paraclete passages) played a central role in the Fourth Gospel's polemic against the synagogue leadership.

3. The particular emphasis of inspiration resembles again Qumran's emphasis on the Spirit of inspiration. For a more detailed approach to the Spirit in the Paraclete sayings, and background for the Paraclete image itself, see Keener, "Pneumatology," 217–323.

4. It was naturally coupled with bread to represent the basic staples of life, e.g., Sir 29:21.

5. Thales, in the sixth century B.C.E., in *Greek Philosophy: Thales to Aristotle* (ed. R. E. Allen; New York: Free Press, 1966) 2. In Socratics, *Ep.* 25 (*Cynic Epistles,* 278–79), one may thirst (ἐδίψων) after philosophy, and in Plutarch a proper education is a source, a fountain (πηγή), of goodness (as well as its root, ῥίζα: *Educ.* 7, *Moralia* 4C). Marc. Aur., *Med.* 7.59, wrote that "within [ἔνδον] is the fountain of Good [ἡ πηγὴ τοῦ ἀγαθοῦ], ready always to well forth . . . " (LCL; cf. John 4:14, although the latter may be modeled on Jewish interpretation of the well springing up in the wilderness). Nile water may have been linked with immortality; see R. A. Wild, *Water in the Cultic Worship of Isis and Sarapis* (ÉPROER 87; Leiden: Brill, 1981) 97–99.

6. Plut., *Obsolescence of Oracles* 5, *Moralia* 411F, which refers to prophecy as flowing like water; this may be an image chosen for the moment, rather than a standard one, but the possibility of broader usage derives some support from Sir 24:30, *Odes Sol.* 40:2, and perhaps the wise speech which "flowed" (ῥείουσι) from Adam and Eve in *Sib. Or.* 1:33–34.

7. *Post.* 127–29; *Somn.* 2.242–43.

8. *Somn.* 2.242–43; *Det.* 117 (the "fountain of divine wisdom"); *Fug.* 166 (on this drink, however, one may become intoxicated in a good way); see Knox, *Gentiles,* 87–88; A. W. Argyle, "Philo and the Fourth Gospel," *ExpT* 63 (1952) 386. Cf. 1QS 10.12, in a hymn, apparently of the משכיל, which speaks of God as the מקור דעת ומעין קודש, the "fountain of knowledge and the spring of holiness"; rabbinic Hebrew uses "fountain" and "spring" also with reference to issuing from the womb, but the image here is more likely for the source of water; cf. further 3.19, 11.3, 5, 6–7; probably CD 3.16–17. Arabic and Syriac A Ahiqar 1:15 (Charles, 2.726–27) compares a father's wisdom instruction to bread and water.

9. 15:3; 24:25 (understanding, compared to rivers); 24:30–33 (where Wisdom also ἐκχεῶ her teaching like prophecy). Cf. similarly Wis 7:25.

10. E.g., *Exod. Rab.* 31:3.

11. *M. ʾAbot* 1:4 (attributed to a pre-Tannaitic sage); 2:8 (attributed to ben Zakkai, though the form is heavily redacted); *Mek. Vayassa* 1:74ff. (Lauterbach, 2.89–90), *Bahodesh* 5.99 (237, allegorizing the Hebrew Bible on water); *Sipre Deut.* 48.2.7, 306.19.1, 306.22, 23, 24, 25, etc.; *ʾAbot R. Nat.* 18A; cf. *b. Taʿan.* 7a; *B.Qam.* 17a, 82a; *Gen. Rab.* 41:9, 54:1, 69:5, 70:8–9, 84:16, 97:3; *Exod. Rab.* 47:5 (and bread); *Song Sol. Rab.* 1:2 §3.

12. R. Akiba in *Sipre Deut.* 48.2.7; *Pesiq. Rab Kah.* 24:9; cf. L. L. Belleville, " 'Born of Water and Spirit,' " *TJ* 1 (1980) 130, arguing that the rabbis used a well as a symbol of Torah more than they used water in general, to bolster her argument that the water of John 3:5 is not Torah.

13. *M. ʾAbot* 1:11 (attributed to Abtalion, first century B.C.E.); *Sipre Deut.* 48.2.5.

14. Of course, Jesus the Word never appears as "water" in the Fourth Gospel, but only as its source, as R. A. Culpepper, *Anatomy of the Fourth Gospel* (Philadelphia: Fortress, 1983) 196, has pointed out.

15. E.g., *Gen. Rab.* 71:8; Montefiore and Loewe, *Anthology*, 163ff.

16. Abrahams, *Studies* (1), 43; E. D. Freed, *Old Testament Quotations in the Gospel of John* (NovTSup 11; Leiden: Brill, 1965) 29; McNamara, *Targum*, 110.

17. E.g., S. S. Smalley, "The Christ-Christian Relationship in Paul and John," in *Pauline Studies* (ed. D. A. Hagner and M. J. Harris; Exeter: Paternoster, 1980) 97, although he sees it as less developed than Paul's. R. E. Brown, *The Gospel according to John* (AB 29; Garden City, N.Y.: Doubleday, 1966–70) 1.cxi, cites Cullmann, Vawter, Hoskyns, Lightfoot, and Barrett as tending toward the sacramental view. R. Kysar, *The Fourth Evangelist and his Gospel* (Minneapolis: Augsburg, 1975) 256, thinks that sacramental interpreters presuppose a more widespread emphasis on sacraments in the early church than has been substantiated.

18. Brown, *John*, 1.cxi, cites Bornkamm, Bultmann, Lohse, and Schweizer as holding a non-sacramental or anti-sacramental understanding of John. For a summary of the major views before 1945, see especially W. F. Howard, *The Fourth Gospel in Recent Criticism and Interpretation* (3d ed.; London: Epworth, 1945) 206–14.

19. G. H. C. MacGregor, "The Eucharist in the Fourth Gospel," *NTS* 9 (1963) 118. It should be noted, however, that "the 'sacramental' cults" could involve ecstasy (Lake, "Spirit," 104), and thus that an opposition of sacrament and πνεῦμα (if the Johannine Christians could associate the latter with ecstatic inspiration) would not be as useful in opposing such sacramentalism as MacGregor hopes.

20. Besides the references in his commentary, see Bultmann, *History*, 165–66. L. Mowry, "The Dead Sea Scrolls and the Gospel of John," *BA* 17 (1954) 92, suggests an anti-Essene polemic; this is answered by Belleville, "Water and Spirit," 126.

21. *The Testament of Jesus* (Philadelphia: Fortress, 1978) 32.

22. K. Matsunaga, "Is John's Gospel Anti-Sacramental?," *NTS* 27 (1981) 516–24. Cf. Paul's similar argument in his midrash in 1 Cor 10:1–13.

23. Its presence in both Mark and Q may suggest double attestation, although it is equally possible that Mark compressed Q for the sake of the succinctness of his literary introduction.

24. Of course, the baptism proper tends to be passed over rapidly in all the Gospels, especially after Mark; it was an established rhetorical principle that the

narrator "should narrate most concisely whatever is likely to distress the audience" (Theon, *Progymn.* 5.52–56).

25. Michaels, *Servant and Son*, 36, thinks that none of the Gospels contradict the impression one gets in Mark, that only Jesus saw the dove and heard the heavenly voice; but John 1:32 certainly suggests that John saw it. Other scholars have also suggested that Jesus had a vision at his baptism: Hill, *Prophecy*, 59; Borg, *Vision*, 41. Bultmann, *History*, 251, takes the Synoptic account as Hellenistic and inauthentic; but the event at least should be regarded as historical: see Sanders, *Jesus and Judaism*, 11.

26. Cf. 4:19, 44; 6:14; 7:40; 9:17. For the portrayal of Jesus and the Spirit as prophets in John, see M. E. Boring, "The Influence of Christian Prophecy on the Johannine Portrayal of the Paraclete and Jesus," *NTS* (1978) 113–23; M. E. Isaacs, "The Prophetic Spirit in the Fourth Gospel," *HeyJ* 24 (1983) 392–99 (the Spirit), 399–402 (Jesus); O. Betz, *Der Paraklet Fürsprecher im häretischen Spätjudentum* (AGSU 2; Leiden: Brill, 1963) 128–30 (as teacher, 130–33; witness, 133–34; protector of righteousness, 134–36); G. Bornkamm, "Der Paraklet im Johannesevangelium," in *Festschrift Rudolf Bultmann zum 65. Geburtstag überreicht* (Stuttgart: Kohlhammer, 1949) 18–20; Hill, *Prophecy*, 150; B. Vawter, "Ezekiel and John," *CBQ* 26 (1964) 450–58 (the model supplied from Ezekiel). Compare the portrayal of Jesus being accused of "having a demon" with Joshua ben Ananiah in Jos. *J.W.* 6.303, 305 (δαιμονιώτερον).

27. Acknowledgment of the Fourth Gospel's polemical motivation does not, of course, deny possible historical tradition behind such a denial; cf. Luke 3:15–17.

28. Rissi, "Jn 1:1–18," 398; Hooker, "John the Baptist," 354–58; E. F. Harrison, "A Study of John 1:14," in *Unity and Diversity in NT Theology* (ed. R. A. Guelich; Grand Rapids, Mich.: Eerdmans, 1978) 25; R. A. Culpepper, *The Johannine School* (SBLDS 26; Missoula, Mont.: Scholars, 1975) 278; J. M. Boice, *Witness and Revelation in the Gospel of John* (Grand Rapids, Mich.: Zondervan, 1970) 26. F. C. Burkitt, *Church and Gnosis* (Cambridge: Cambridge, 1932) 97, suggests that the original readers of the Fourth Gospel knew of John, but not of Jesus, but this is unlikely, especially if it can be shown that the writer assumes some knowledge of the Jesus tradition (e.g., 6:17).

29. Sanders, *Jesus and Judaism*, 91–92, thinks Jesus was a disciple of John the Baptist; cf. Marxsen, *Mark the Evangelist*, 39, on the question of the chronological succession of John and Jesus in the Markan and Johannine narratives.

30. Bultmann, *History*, 165; Fritsch, *Community*, 117. The third-century *Pseudo-Clementine Homilies* also seem to reflect a polemic; cf. Daniélou, *Theology*, 62; J. R. Michaels, *John* (NIBC 4: Peabody, Mass.: Hendrickson Publishers, 1989) 25–26.

31. Cf. R. H. Strachan, *The Fourth Gospel* (London: SCM, 1917) 70; Hengel, *Charismatic Leader*, 36; Morris, *John*, 88; Painter, "Christology," 51.

32. E.g., Smalley, *John*, 127. G. N. Stanton, *The Gospels and Jesus* (Oxford: Oxford, 1989) 167, refuses to rule out a polemical intention, but does not believe it is John's primary concern.

33. "Contributions of Prologue," 359; his concessions to Bultmann, but with the warning that he certainly exaggerated, are in n. 32.

34. There may be indications of this in the Fourth Gospel as well, where Christology is often a cause for apostasy from initial faith: 6:41–71 (climaxing in Judas, the ultimate paradigm of betrayal and secession); 8:31–59; cf. 2:23–25; etc.

35. Keener, "Pneumatology," provides a more extensive exegesis of this passage, and most of the passages discussed in this chapter. The present chapter focuses merely on the water and Spirit contrasts.

36. G. Schulze-Kadelbach, "Zur Pneumatologie des Johannes Evangeliums," *ZNW* 46 (1955) 279–80, sees the gift of the Spirit in the transformation sign.

37. A. Geyser, "The Semeion at Cana of the Galilee," in *Studies in John* (NovTSup 24; ed. W. C. van Unnik; Leiden: Brill, 1970) 20–21, suggests that 2:1–11 is anti-Baptistic, especially in light of 3:25–26, but if so, one wonders why our author would specifically address other Jewish purification rites, especially given the polemic with the synagogue the Fourth Gospel presupposes.

38. P. F. Ellis, *The Genius of John* (Collegeville, Minn.: Liturgical, 1984) 43; E. J. Epp, "Wisdom, Torah, Word," in *Current Issues in Biblical and Patristic Interpretation* (ed. G. F. Hawthorne; Grand Rapids, Mich.: Eerdmans, 1975) 145; S. D. Toussaint, "The Significance of the First Sign in John's Gospel," *BSac* 134 (1977) 50; R. F. Collins, "Cana—the First of His Signs or the Key to His Signs?" *ITQ* 47 (1980) 79–95.

39. C. Bryan, "Shall We Sing Hallel in the Days of the Messiah?" *StLukeJ* 29 (1985) 25–36. Cf. B. E. Thiering, *The Gospels and Qumran* (ANZSTR; Sydney: Theological Explorations, 1981) 57, despite her eccentric view of a polemic against the Teacher at Qumran here.

40. E. L. Allen, "The Jewish Christian Church in the Fourth Gospel," *JBL* 94 (1955) 89.

41. See Keener, " 'The Jews' and Johannine Irony," Appendix A in "Pneumatology," 330–49.

42. T. Worden, "The Marriage Feast at Cana," *Scripture* 20 (1968) 101; K. Hanhart, "The Structure of John i 35–iv 54," in *Studies in John,* 39; cf. Culpepper, *Anatomy,* 193; B. Olsson, *Structure and Meaning in the Fourth Gospel* (Lund: Gleerup, 1974) 19.

43. *ʾAbot* 3:16 (לסעודה), 4:16; *b. Ber.* 34b; *Gen. Rab.* 51:8, 62:2; *Exod. Rab.* 45:6, 50:5; *Lev. Rab.* 13:3; *Num. Rab.* 13:2; *Pesiq. Rab.* 41:5, 48:3; cf. A. Marmorstein, *The Doctrine of Merits in Old Rabbinical Literature* (New York: KTAV, 1968) 46, 59, 120, 135; Bonsirven, *Judaism,* 244. In *Sib. Or.* 3:622 (probably second century B.C.E.) good wine is one of the blessings of the new age, but along with honey, milk, and (623) wheat; see Jeremias, *Theology,* 106, for other eschatological references. Aside from OT passages about eschatological abundance, Greek beliefs about an everlasting banquet in the Elysian fields may have influenced this idea; cf. in Koester, *Introduction,* 1.161.

44. The matter is disputed; cf. M. Smith, " 'God's Begetting the Messiah' in 1QSa," *NTS* 5 (1958–59) 224. It is understandable that the eschatological triumph would include meals patterned after the meals of the community; this does not need to imply, however, that the regular meals of the community were patterned after the far more rarely mentioned eschatological banquet.

45. E.g., J. F. Priest, "The Messiah and the Meal in 1QSa," *JBL* 82 (1963) 95–100.

46. *Sipre Deut.* as cited in Patte, *Hermeneutic,* 26; *Qoh. Rab.* 2:3 §1; *Song Sol. Rab.* 6:10 §1; *Pesiq. Rab. Kah.* 12:5; *Pesiq. Rab.* 51:1. None of these references are Tannaitic except those in *Sipre Deut.* For wine symbolism in antiquity, see Goodenough, *Symbols,* 12.107–22.

47. C. L. Blomberg, "The Miracles as Parables," in *Gospel Perspectives*, 6.334, suggests that this was an acted parable with roots in historical tradition; more scholars think the parable generated the miracle story (Dodd, Lindars) or the reverse (Smalley; citations from ibid.).

48. Otto, *Dionysus*, 97–98; Grant, *Gods*, 65; O. Broneer, "Corinth: Center of Paul's Missionary Work in Greece," *BA* 14 (1951) 86.

49. Smith, *Magician*, 25, 120; Theissen, *Miracle Stories*, 277; Bousset, *Kyrios Christos*, 102–3; Grant, *Gods*, 96; Bultmann, *History*, 238; id., *John*, 118; Martin, *Religions*, 95 (following Bultmann); Jeremias, *Theology*, 88; cf. I. Broer, "Noch einmal: Zur religionsgeschichtlichen 'Ableitung' von Jo 2,1–11," *SNTU* 8 (1983) 103–12; contrast Blackburn, " 'ΘΕΙΟΙ ΑΝΔΡΕΣ,' " 192, Blomberg, "Miracles," 335; R. A. Batey, *New Testament Nuptial Imagery* (Leiden: Brill, 1971) 51–52; E. C. Hoskyns, *The Fourth Gospel* (2d rev. ed.; London: Faber, 1947) 191–92; J. D. M. Derrett, *Law in the New Testament* (London: Darton, Longman, & Todd, 1970) 243–44; cf. E. K. Lee, *The Religious Thought of St. John* (London: SPCK, 1962) 17.

50. *B. Ber.* 5b; cf. E. Haenchen, *A Commentary on the Gospel of John* (Philadelphia: Fortress, 1984) 1.174, who rejects Billerbeck's use of *Num. Rab.* 16. J. Bowman, *The Fourth Gospel and the Jews* (PTMS 8; Pittsburgh: Pickwick, 1975) 208, connects this miracle with the Jewish prayers for fertility leading up to the feast.

51. Cf. *b. Šabb.* 53b, where an amora argues that while miracles often happen, the miracle of creation of food is rare.

52. See Glasson, *Moses*, 26; R. H. Smith, "Exodus Typology in the Fourth Gospel," *JBL* 81 (1962) 334–35; cf. Exod 7:19; *Jub.* 48:5; Rev 8:8; a Stoic mentions a similar portent in Cic., *De Divin.* 1.43.98.

53. If the relatively isolated Philonic connection between ecstatic inspiration and intoxication may be read in here (cf. Acts 2:13; Eph 5:18; Keener, *Paul, Women, & Wives*, 262, 272), the Spirit of prophecy may also lie in the background; but there is no explicit indication that such is in view in our text.

54. E.g., *Book of Dead* Spell 20; James Moyer, "The Concept of Ritual Purity among the Hittites" (Ph.D. diss., Brandeis, 1969) 130; A. M. Blackman, "Purification: Egyptian," in *The Encyclopedia of Religion and Ethics* (ed. J. Hastings; Edinburgh: T. & T. Clark, 1908–26) 10.476; Philo, *Mos.* 1.14.

55. Moyer, "Purity," 130.

56. Ibid., 132; cf. importance of ritual purity in "Instructions for Palace Personnel to Insure the King's Purity," *ANET* 207; "Instructions for Temple Officials," 14, *ANET* 209. The principle is frequent in a wide variety of apparently unrelated cultures; cf., e.g., Mbiti, *Religions*, 169, 172; postpartum purificatory water rituals among Eskimos, in Fiji, and Uganda (E. N. Fallaize, "Purification: Introductory and Primitive," in *Encyclopedia of Religion and Ethics*, 10.455–66; cf. Hindu water purifications before approaching a deity in C. G. Fry, J. R. King, E. R. Swanger, and H. C. Wolf, *Great Asian Religions* [Grand Rapids, Mich.: Baker, 1984] 61, and, to a lesser extent, in Shinto tradition in Japan [ibid., 154]), as well as possibly related cultures (cf. Islamic purifications in A. Guillaume, *Islam* [New York: Penguin, 1956] 88; Mandaeans in E. S. Drower, *The Mandaeans of Iraq and Iran* [Leiden: Brill, 1962] 100–23); it suggests that the ancient Near Eastern parallels provide a reasonable context for the Israelite washings.

57. Diogenes, in Diog. Laert., *Lives* 6.2.42. Plutarch condemns the βάπτισ-μους of superstitious religion and magic (*Superst.* 2, *Moralia* 166A), though this need not imply that he felt so toward all immersion.

58. Cf. Diog. Laert., *Lives* 8.1.33; Culpepper, *School,* 49 (following Iamblichus, *V.P.* 71–74).

59. Diog. Laert., *Lives* 7.1.119.

60. E.g., the inscription (Dittenberger, *Sylloge* [2], 566, 2–9) from Athena's temple at Pergamum, in Grant, *Religions,* 6. Aune, *Prophecy,* 30, cites the Pythia's ritual bath preceding sacrifice. Ach. Tat., *Clit.* 8.3.2, speaks of a fountain of τὸ ἱερὸν ὕδωρ used for ablutions in the temple of Artemis in Ephesus. Cf. *IG* 2.2.1366; *PGM* 1.54.

61. Epict., *Disc.* 3.21.14; Mylonas, *Eleusis,* 248; S. Angus, *The Mystery-Religions and Christianity* (New York: Scribner's, 1928) 81–82.

62. Plut., *Isis* 75, *Moralia* 381D; Apul., *Metam.* 11.1. For such ablutions deriving from older Egyptian traditions, see Wild, *Water,* 129–48.

63. Burkert, *Cults,* 101; Nock, *Gentile Christianity,* 60–62, 133; G. Wagner, *Pauline Baptism and the Pagan Mysteries* (Edinburgh: Oliver & Boyd, 1967) 71–72, 102–3; Meeks, *Urban Christians,* 152–53. Some initiatory baths were, however, used to secure pardon from the gods: Apul., *Metam.* 11.23.

64. It is assumed, e.g., by Jos., *Ant.* 6.235, who reads it into the David narrative; cf. his comments on the form of purification used by Essenes at the temple in *Ant.* 18.19. W. Wirgin, *The Book of Jubilees and the Maccabaean Era of Shmittah Cycles* (LUOSM 7; n.p.: Leeds, 1965) 27–38, adduces numismatic evidence that may argue for priestly use of holy water for their hands and feet in the Maccabean period. The Pharisees probably did more to extend ritual washing beyond the priesthood than anyone else (e.g., Stambaugh and Balch, *Social Environment,* 87).

65. E.g., Yadin, *Masada,* 164; Avigad, *Discovering Jerusalem,* 142; F. F. Bruce, *Second Thoughts on the Dead Sea Scrolls* (Grand Rapids, Mich.: Eerdmans, 1956) 50–51; David Kotlar, "Mikveh," in *EJ,* 11.1134–44, esp. 1535.

66. Avigad, *Discovering Jerusalem,* 85–86; notes in *Josephus: The Jewish War* (ed. Gaalya Cornfeld; Grand Rapids, Mich.: Zondervan, 1982) 50; probably at Gezer, in R. Reich, "Mqww'wt-thrh yhwdyym btl gzr," *Qadmoniot* 15 (1982): 74–76; E. Netzer, "Mqww'wt-hthrh mymy byt sny byryhw," *Qadmoniot* 11 (1978) 54–59.

67. E.g., Reich, "Miqweh," 220–23.

68. Pearlman, *Zealots,* 179, who identified this *mikveh* as the earliest known at the time of his writing.

69. See Avigad, *Discovering Jerusalem,* 139–43. *M. Para* 3:7 also mentions a place of immersion at the Mount of Olives.

70. Avigad, *Discovering Jerusalem,* 139, 142. Neusner, *Beginning,* 24–25, argues that Jerusalemites were more concerned with ritual purity than were the provincials "who purified themselves mainly for the festal pilgrimages."

71. Cf. the "chamber of immersion" (*m. Mid.* 1:9) and, for the immersion of lepers, the chamber of lepers (*m. Neg.* 14:8). See Meyers and Strange, *Archaeology,* 55; B. Mazar, "Excavations near Temple Mount Reveal Splendors of Herodian Jerusalem," *BARev* 6 (1980) 52; Cornfeld, *Josephus,* 272. The list of "officers" in the temple (*m. Šeqal.* 5:1–2) includes one Nehemiah as "over the water," literally,

a "trench-digger," and he was "in charge of the aqueduct and the Temple cisterns, and to look after the baths" used for ablutions (Jeremias, *Jerusalem,* 174).

72. See especially the Mishnah, Tosephta, and talmudic tractates *Miqva'oth.* The most extensive discussion of this material to date is in Jacob Neusner, *A History of the Mishnaic Law of Purities* (Leiden: E. J. Brill, 1974–77), vols. 1–22. Mikveh was considered a commandment of God (cf. the Amoraic blessing in *b. Ber.* 51a).

73. *M. Para* 11:6; *b. Šabb.* 64b; *p. Šeb.* 2:1 §6. Proselyte baptism, by extension, cleanses away Gentile impurity when accompanied by circumcision; cf. *t. Pisha* 7:14 (the same type of *mikveh* is used for both; see Bamberger, *Proselytism,* 43–44). For its cleansing power, cf. the play on words with "fountain" and "hope" in the discussion of God's cleansing of Israel on Yom Kippur in *b. Yoma* 85b (cf. *Bek.* 22a).

74. *B. Ber.* 2b (purportedly Tannaitic).

75. *B. Pesaḥ.* 90b; *Šabb.* 84a; *Yoma* 6b; the importance of this may be underlined by the haggadic illustration on an OT narrative in *Lev. Rab.* 19:6, and the illustration of R. Gamaliel's maidservant in *Pesiq. Rab Kah.* 12:15.

76. *M. Makš.* 4:6; *Miqw.* 9:5–7, 10; *Sipra Šemini* pq. 9.115.1.6–8; *b. Šabb.* 15b, 34a, 84a; *Zebaḥ.* 22a; *Menaḥ.* 101a; *Bek.* 22a; *Ḥul.* 123a; *p. Ḥag.* 3:8 §§1–3; cf. *m. Ṭohar.* 8:9; CD 10.12; 11.3–4. The sacred washings of sacred objects in the Phrygian cult of Cybele (Mart., *Epig.* 3.47) may or may not be analogous.

77. *B. Pesaḥ.* 59a ("our rabbis"); references in Urbach, *Sages,* 1.582–83 (including *Sipra Šemini* 4.49a). Cf. Jdt 16:18 (the people ἐκαθαρίσθη before offering sacrifices); cf. John 2:6 with 2:13.

78. *M. Ter.* 5:6; Ed. 1:3, 7:3–4; *Miqw.* 2:3ff., 3:1–4, 4:1–5, 5:1–6; *t. Miqw.* 2; *Sipra Šemini* par. 9.118.1.1; *b. Šabb.* 16b, 65a, 144b; *Pesaḥ.* 17b, 34b; *Beṣa* 18; *Giṭ.* 16a; *B.A.* 66a; *Mak.* 4a; *Bek.* 55b; *p. Ter.* 4:12, 5:7; cf. CD 10.12 (11.1–2, for Sabbath, as in *Jub.* 2:29); Kotlar, "Mikveh," 1536–37. Hillel argued for one hin of drawn water, Shammai for nine kabs, and the Sages for three logs (*m. Ed.* 1:3, *t. Ed.* 1:3, etc.). R. Eleazar b. R. Yose suggests that even Samaritans follow this practice (*p. ʿAbod. Zar.* 5:4 §3). Water should also not be stagnant from disuse, in *p. Ter.* 1:8 (purportedly Tannaitic).

79. Cf. *m. Ber.* 3:5; for degrees of impurity by the percentage of pure water, as noted in the previous note, see especially *p. Ter.* 5:6; cf. *Qoh. Rab.* 4:17 §1.

80. Besides the note on the design of mikvaoth above, see especially Avigad, *Discovering Jerusalem,* 139; Pearlman, *Zealots,* 180–81; Yadin, *Masada,* 166; R. Hachlili and A. Killebrew, "The Saga of the Goliath Family," *BARev* 9 (1983) 44, 46.

81. Neusner, *Beginning,* 24–25. Variations within Upper City Jerusalem *mikvaoth* were between those that met the minimal requirements, and those that exceeded them (Avigad, *Discovering Jerusalem,* 142).

82. The use of the water in the synagogues of Arsinoe, 113 C.E., may not be for *mikvaoth,* but since they each pay about twice as much as the local baths for their water pumped in, their great consumption is probably more than a reflection of mere hospitality or boarding houses and one wonders if handwashing alone would account for the difference; see in *CPJ* 2.220–24 §432.

83. Masada is in an area which currently receives less than 5 inches (100 mm) of rainfall annually (H. G. May, ed., *The Oxford Bible Atlas* [London: Oxford, 1962]

51), but, interestingly enough for our treatment of Cana, below, the probable site of Cana receives 20–25 inches (500–600 mm).

84. *T. Miqw.* 5:10 (allowing up to three logs, as with drawn water); *Sipra VDDen.* pq. 6.9.7.2; *b. Ḥul.* 25b; *p. Maʾaś.* 5:5; cf. *Sipra Šemini* par. 9.118.1.4; *p. ʿAbod. Zar.* 5:11 §1; *Ter.* 8:5; Safrai, "Home," in *JPFC,* 740.

85. S. Safrai, "Home," 741; N. Avigad, "Jerusalem Flourishing," *BARev* 9 (1983) 59; id., *Discovering Jerusalem,* 183; cf. Y. Magen, "Yrwslym kmrkz sl t'syyt kly-'bn btqwpt hwrdws (Jerusalem as the Center for Stone-Ware Production in Herodian Times)," *Qadmoniot* 17 (4, 1984) 124–27 (NTA 30.198). This reason for the use of stoneware has been pointed out by many commentators, e.g., R. Schnackenburg, *The Gospel according to St. John* (New York: Herder & Herder, Seabury, Crossroad, 1968–82) 1.332; R. E. Brown, *John,* 1.100; cf. B. F. Westcott, *The Gospel according to St. John* (Grand Rapids, Mich.: Eerdmans, 1950) 37. Olsson, *Structure,* 48, objects that "stone ware" was usually made of hard clay, *pace* Schnackenburg.

86. Lee, *Thought,* 17, allegorizes the six waterpots in Philonic style; J. Gamble, "The Philosophy of the Fourth Gospel," *The Expositor,* 9th ser., 4 (1925) 51–52, regards the amount as an historical reminiscence.

87. J. Villescas, "John 2.6: The Capacity of the Six Jars," *BibTrans* 28 (1977) 447; Toussaint, "Significance," 49; Schnackenburg, *John,* 1.332 n. 25; Bultmann, *John,* 117 n. 3; Brown, *John,* 1.100; A. M. Hunter, *The Gospel according to John* (Cambridge: Cambridge, 1965) 31.

88. Some *mikvaoth* would have more than the prescribed amount, which was only a minimum; see Avigad, *Discovering Jerusalem,* 139.

89. Forty se'ahs was the required minimum: *m. Miqw.* 2:1–2, 7:6–7; *t. Ber.* 2:12; *Sipra VDDen.* pq. 6.9.7.1; *Sipra Šemini* par. 9.118.1.1; *Sipra Zabim* pq. 6.158.2.1–2; *b. Ber.* 22ab; *Qidd.* 66b, 79a; *ʿErub.* 35b (purportedly Tannaitic); *Pesaḥ.* 109; *Yoma* 31; *Zebaḥ.* 22a; *Ḥul.* 31a; *p. Ḥag.* 2:5 §3; Yadin, *Masada,* 166. The important halakic point was that the water covered the entire body; *m. Miqw.* 9:1–4; *Sipra Zabim* pq. 6.158.2.1–2, 3.5; *b. Ḥul.* 10a, 106b; *Qidd.* 25a; cf. *M. Ṭohar.* 8:9 (the whole immersion of objects); CD 10.10–11; Kotlar, "Mikveh," 588. The tradition from one amora that Torah weighed 40 se'ahs (*p. Taʿan.* 4:5 §1) could be a play on the idea of purification, but given the fact that this is also the weight of pigeons for sacrifice in *p. Taʿan.* 4:5 §13, this surmise is unlikely.

90. S. Safrai, "Religion in Everyday Life," in *JPFC* 830, citing *Sipra Šemini* 8; *Sipra Mezora Zabim* 6; *m. Miqw.*

91. M. McNamara, *Palestinian Judaism and the New Testament* (GNS 4; Wilmington: Glazier, 1983) 196, assumes it; J. H. Bernard, *A Critical and Exegetical Commentary on the Gospel according to St. John* (ICC; Edinburgh: T. & T. Clark, 1928) 1.77, applies this to the washing of hands before and after meals. *P.Ḥag.* 2:5 §3 demonstrates that the pool of 40 se'ahs could also be used for the washing of hands.

92. Kefar-Kenna has not turned up materials from the first Roman period (cf. S. Loffreda, "Scavi a Kafr Kanna," *SBFLA* 19 [1969] 328–48); most scholars now favor the site of Khirbet-Qanah: R. Mackowski, "Scholars' Qanah," *BZ* 23 (1979) 278–84; Brown, *John,* 1.98; Derrett, *Law,* 235 n. 2. The village "Cana" in Jos., *J.W.* 1.102, lacks necessities for survival, but it seems unlikely that John could have expected his readers to have known of this; "Cana" does not appear in the LXX.

93. E. P. Sanders, *Jewish Law from Jesus to the Mishnah* (Philadelphia: Trinity, 1990) 31–32, 214–27.

94. Reitzenstein, *Mystery-Religions,* 333–37; Angus, *Mystery-Religions,* 95ff.; Bultmann, *Primitive Christianity,* 159; E. Lohse, *The New Testament Environment* (Nashville: Abingdon, 1976) 234; cf. Kümmel, *Theology,* 309; White, *Initiation,* 252; Schoeps, *Paul,* 112; among commentators, e.g., R. G. Bury, *The Fourth Gospel and the Logos-Doctrine* (Cambridge: Heffer, 1940) 34; J. N. Sanders, *A Commentary on the Gospel according to St. John* (HNTC; New York: Harper & Row, 1968) 123; M. Dibelius and H. Conzelmann, *The Pastoral Epistles* (Hermeneia; Philadelphia: Fortress, 1972) 148–50 (on Titus 3:5). R. H. Lightfoot, *St. John's Gospel* (London: Oxford, 1960) 131, argues that John 3:3, 5 must depend on non-Jewish Greek thought, because "the thought of spiritual rebirth, although Ezekiel comes very near to it in Ezek 36.25–27, was indeed unfamiliar in Jewish thought at this time," an inaccurate statement, as will be observed below.

95. H. R. Willoughby, *Pagan Initiation* (Chicago: University of Chicago, 1929) 65.

96. *Gentile Christianity,* 61.

97. Apul., *Metam.* 11.23–24, etc.; cf. Reitzenstein, *Mystery-Religions,* 39. Nock, *Conversion,* 138–55, argues that this is largely autobiographical. Cf. Tram Tam Tinh, "Sarapis and Isis," in *Self-Definition* 3.113.

98. Cited in Willoughby, *Initiation,* 187.

99. E.g., CIL 6.510 from Rome, 376 C.E., in Grant, *Religions,* 147; Stambaugh and Balch, *Social Environment,* 136–37; G. S. Gasparro, *Soteriology and Mystic Aspects in the Cult of Cybele and Attis* (ÉPROER 103; Leiden: Brill, 1985) 118.

100. Wagner, *Baptism,* 250.

101. Otto, *Dionysus,* 154.

102. Guthrie, *Orpheus,* 209.

103. *Initiation,* 90–113.

104. Ibid., 108.

105. Guthrie, *Orpheus,* 269.

106. G. Bornkamm, "The Heresy of Colossians," in *Conflict at Colossae* (SBS 4; ed. F. O. Francis and W. Meeks; Missoula, Mont.: SBL, 1973) 127, on the Mithras liturgy.

107. Willoughby, *Initiation,* 196–24; Dodd, *Interpretation,* 45–46; Barrett, *John,* 2.206–7; Lee, *Thought,* 45; Reitzenstein, *Mystery-Religions,* 47–48, 55, 62, 453–54.

108. Plato, *Meno* 81BC (πάλιν γίγνεσθαι); Plut., *Divine Vengeance* 32, *Moralia* 567EF (ἐπὶ δευτέραν γένεσιν).

109. Cleanthes, *Hymn to Zeus* (in Stobaeus, *Eclogae* 1.1.12; in Grant, *Religions,* 152); Epict., *Disc.* 4.10.16; Marc. Aur., *Med.* 10.1; Plut., *Table-Talk* 8.1.3 (on Plato, e.g., *Timaeus* 28C). For rebirth of the world, cf. Plato, *The Statesman* 270DE.

110. E.g., Artem., *Oneir.* 1.12, where a father whose wife bears a son that looks like him "would seem to be born again" in a dream.

111. R. Bultmann, *The Johannine Epistles* (Hermeneia; Philadelphia: Fortress, 1973) 45–46, on 1 John 2:29.

112. Nock, "Vocabulary," 132. His comments on the Hermetica are also appropriate.

113. E.g., *Decal.* 53, 107; *Spec.* 1.96, 209; cf. *Spec.* 3.189; *Virt.* 62.

114. *Cher.* 114 (παλιγγενεσίαν); see Wolfson, *Philo,* 1.405, and especially F. W. Burnett, "Philo on Immortality," *CBQ* 46 (1984) 447–70.

115. E.g., Cleanthes, *Hymn to Zeus,* passim; Diog. Laert., *Lives* 7.147; Plut., *Sayings of Kings, Alex.* 15, *Moralia* 180D; *R.Q.* 40, *Moralia* 274B; *Plat. Questions* 2.1, *Moralia* 1000E; 2.2, 1000E–1001C; Epict., *Disc.* 1.3.1, 6.40, 9.4–7, 13.3–4, 9, 12; 3.22.82; Sen., *Dial.* 50.1.5; Mart., *Epig.* 10.28 (Janus); *Orph. H.* 4.1 (Ouranos), 12.6 (Herakles), 15.7 and 19.1 (Zeus); cf. Cornutus in Grant, *Gods,* 78. Jos., *Ag. Ap.* 2.241, protests at the use of this title for Zeus.

116. Philo, *Conf.* 170; *Mos.* 2.238; *Decal.* 32, 51, 105; *Spec.* 1.14, 22, 32, 41, 96; 2.6, 165; 3.178, 189; *Virt.* 64, 77, 218; *Praem.* 24; *Contempl.* 90; *Aet.* 13; *Legat.* 115, 293; *QG* 60. So also *Sib. Or.* 3:604, ἀθάνατον γενέτην (probably second century B.C.E., maybe of Egyptian Jewish provenance); 5:284, 328, 360, 406, 498, 500, 726 (probably second century B.C.E.); Theophilus 1.4; Athenagoras, *Plea* 13, 27.

117. So also E. G. Selwyn, *The First Epistle of St. Peter* (2d ed.; New York: Macmillan, 1947) 122.

118. Wagner, *Baptism,* 270. M. Vellanickal, *The Divine Sonship of Christians in the Johannine Writings* (AnBib 72; Rome: Biblical Institute, 1977) 49, 360, also concurs that Hellenistic sonship language is not at work in John.

119. E.g., Polemo in Diog. Laert., *Lives* 4.16; Diogenes the Cynic in Diog. Laert., *Lives* 6.2.56. See especially Nock, *Conversion,* 164–86; cf. Meeks, *Moral World,* 44, 54; Stambaugh and Balch, *Social Environment,* 45–46, 142, 144; S. K. Stowers, *Letter Writing in Greco-Roman Antiquity* (LEC 5 [Philadelphia: Westminster, 1986]) 37, 112–13; Malherbe, *Exhortation,* 56–57. For similarities and differences, see especially R. MacMullen, "Conversion: A Historian's View," *Sec-Cent* 5 (1985–86) 67–81.

120. E.g., the shaman's change of behavior in Eliade, *Rites and Symbols,* 88.

121. P. Davids, *The Epistle of James* (NIGTC; Grand Rapids, Mich.: Eerdmans, 1982) 89; cf. Vellanickal, *Sonship,* 27; for community birth, besides passages in seventh-century B.C.E. prophets, see ibid., 38–39, on 1QH 3.7–12.

122. The standard Jewish notion of Israel as God's children could have encouraged thought in this direction, however.

123. *OTP* 2.213; the Greek enumeration, p. 158 of the Greek text, is 8:10–11 here. The prayer for the regeneration of catechumens in *Apost. Const.* 8.6.6 might be from an earlier Jewish prayer, as some have thought, but there is no clear evidence for this suggestion.

124. *Mek.* 22:20 (in Smith, *Parallels,* 104–5); *Sipra Qed.* pq. 8.205.1.4, 6; *Sipre Num.* 78.3.1, 5.1; *b. B.Meṣiʿa* 59b; *Pesiq. Rab.* 42:1. These passages especially stress not reminding the proselyte of his or her former life; see below.

125. Jos., *Ant.* 20.89–91; *p. Sanh.* 6:7 §2; *Exod. Rab.* 27:5; *Lev. Rab.* 1:2, 2:9, 3:2; *Num. Rab.* 8:1, 2, 9; 13:15–16; *Ruth Rab.* 3:5; *Qoh. Rab.* 7:8 §1; the thirteenth benediction of the ʾAmida (in Oesterley, *Liturgy,* 65). Cf. *t. Peʾa* 4:18, which extols the piety of Monobases, king of Adiabene. Like Israelites, proselytes have accepted the covenant (*Sipra VDDen.* par. 2.3.3.1) and must keep the Law (*Sipra Qed.* pq. 8.205.1.5; *Sipre Num.* 71.2.1); because he could not depend on ancestral merits, his part in the world to come would have been acquired through his own merit entirely (*Num. Rab.* 8:9; cf. *2 Bar.* 42:4–6; *Exod. Rab.* 19:4). Proselytes would testify against the nations on the day of judgment (*Lev. Rab.* 2:9; *Pesiq. Rab.* 35:3).

126. For a summary of the OT data, see Moore, *Judaism,* 1.330–31; R. R. De Ridder, *Discipling the Nations* (Grand Rapids: Baker, 1971) 46.

127. Cf. *Sipra Qed.* par. 4.206.1.2; *Sipra Emor* par. 7.223.1.1; pq. 19.243.1.12; *Sipra A.M.* par. 7.190.1.1; pq. 11.191.1.1; *Pesiq. Rab Kah.* 3:16; *Pesiq. Rab.* 12:9; also Montefiore and Loewe, *Anthology,* 566. It probably still means "foreigner" in CD 6.21, where it is conjoined with the poor as those needing aid; M. Ohana, "Prosélytisme et Targum palestinien," *Bib* 55 (1974) 317–32, argues from targumic usage that the identification is later. But the identification had already begun in the LXX; see J. Blauw, *The Missionary Nature of the Church* (Grand Rapids, Mich.: Eerdmans, 1962) 56; Lake, "Proselytes," 84.

128. *Mek. Nez.* 18.36ff. (Lauterbach, 3.140); *b. Sukka* 49b; *Gen. Rab.* 39:8; *Num. Rab.* 8:9; cf. Bamberger, *Proselytism,* 175–76; T. F. Torrance, "The Origins of Baptism," *SJT* 11 (1958) 170; Abraham and Sarah also made proselytes of others (*Song Sol. Rab.* 1:3 §3; Bamberger, *Proselytism,* 176–79).

129. *B. Yoma* 71b; *Giṭ.* 57b; cf. also Bamberger, *Proselytism,* 222–23. Cf. the eminent descendants of Rahab the proselyte in *b. Meg.* 14b; similarly, on Ruth in *Gen. Rab.* 88:7 (implied in Matt 1:5).

130. *Sipre Deut.* 253.2.2; *Pesiq. Rab.* 14:2 (purportedly Tannaitic); *Qoh. Rab.* 7:8 §1 (purportedly Tannaitic). Aquila, who made the extremely literal Greek translation, was said to be a disciple of the sages, though he was a proselyte; *Gen. Rab.* 70:5; *Exod. Rab.* 19:4.

131. See *Sipre Deut.* 253.2.2; *p. Yeb.* 8:2 §7; *Pesiq. Rab Kah.* 16:1, for specific kinds of proselytes. In general, they were restricted only from marrying into priestly families (M. Stern, "Aspects of Jewish Society: The Priesthood and Other Classes," in *JPFC* 623; cf. C. Keener, *And Marries Another* [Peabody, Mass.: Hendrickson, 1991] 56–61), although the second generation was only restricted, if ever, if both parents were proselytes (*m. Qidd.* 4:7; *b. Yeb.* 77a; cf. *b. Qidd.* 73a–74b), and marrying proselytes could be discouraged (*b. Pesah.* 112b); but an amora, citing tradition purportedly from Hillel, advocates the ability of all classes to intermarry in Israel, including proselytes (*b. Yeb.* 37a). The prohibition against proselytes marrying priests was perhaps solely due to the rabbinic distrust of Gentiles' virginity after the age of three years and one day, taken together with the Torah's requirement that priests marry virgins or the widows of priests (*b. Yeb.* 60b; *Qidd.* 78a, both purportedly Tannaitic). Some kinds of discrimination could work in one's favor, however: strangulation, the more lenient form of punishment, could be applied to a proselyte not native-born, as opposed to one born into Israel of a proselyte mother (*m. Ketub.* 4:3).

132. *M. Hor.* 3:8; *Num. Rab.* 6:1; perhaps CD 14.4 (depending on the meaning of הגר); cf. J. D. M. Derrett, *Jesus's Audience* (New York: Seabury, 1973) 47; Jeremias, *Jerusalem,* 272, 323. They would be excluded from the eschatological sanctuary in Qumran, and this reflected some broader Jewish conceptions of their social inferiority; see J. M. Baumgarten, "The Exclusion of 'Netinim' and Proselytes in 4QFlorilegium," *RevQ* 8 (1972) 87–96; G. Blidstein, "4Q Florilegium and Rabbinic Sources on Bastard and Proselyte," *RevQ* 8 (1974) 431–35.

133. *B. Šabb.* 33b–34a; *Lev. Rab.* 27:8; *Pesiq. Rab.* 23:4. In *b. Pesah.* 91b, however, because proselytes do not know the Law well enough they may err by being *too* strict.

134. *Proselytism,* 145.

135. Ibid., 149–61; for the few unfavorable ones, see 161–65; for mixed opinions, see 165–69. Converts are as dear to God as born Jews (149–54), or dearer (154–56); Israel's dispersion was God's way to increase proselytes (156–58); converts were protected by (mainly Tannaitic) laws against harm from Jews (158–61). Bamberger argues that this favorable attitude carries through the whole talmudic period, although at times the popular prejudices did affect the rabbis (277–78). Proselytes had no place in the land, but neither did priests (66–67); there is also some evidence that some people were proud to trace their ancestry from converts (230).

136. Hoenig, "Conversion," 43.

137. *P. Yeb.* 8:2 §7 (purportedly Tannaitic), attributed to Akiba and his circle. R. Joshua, cited in the majority opinion against R. Gamaliel II, argued the case that Ammonite proselytes should be accepted (*b. Ber.* 28a), which has implications for how Deut 23:3 came to be read by the rabbis.

138. *Dialogue with Trypho* 123:1; see Barnard, "Old Testament in Justin," 403; A. L. Williams, *Justin Martyr: The Dialogue with Trypho* (New York: Macmillan, 1930) xxxii.

139. Often noted in current literature: Hoenig, "Conversion," 54; Moore, *Judaism,* 1.335; R. Schnackenburg, *Baptism in the Thought of St. Paul* (Oxford: Blackwell, 1964) 15; Bultmann, *John,* 137.

140. *Mek. Nez.* 1.47ff. (Lauterbach, 3.5), R. Ishmael; *b. Yeb.* 47b; Moore, *Judaism,* 1.328, 333–34; Hoenig, "Conversion," 48, 54; Bamberger, *Proselytism,* 60. Legal standing, of course, does not mean that he was received as a social equal.

141. *B. Pesah.* 92a, a Babylonian amora interpreting a mishnah of Beth Hillel. *B. Yeb.* 47b: "When he comes up after his ablution he is deemed to be an Israelite in all respects." This is after circumcision, which is assumed.

142. *B. Yeb.* 48b.

143. *P. Qidd.* 4:1 §2. See further G. W. Buchanan, *The Consequences of the Covenant* (NovTSup 20; Leiden: Brill, 1970) 201. This is not to suggest that the rabbinic imagery is more ontological than forensic; but it may have an ontological component; see below.

144. *Qoh. Rab.* 1:8 §4.

145. Bamberger, *Proselytism,* 63–64.

146. *CIL* 2.1963, 82–84 C.E., in *Empire* (ed. Sherk) 138 §97.

147. *B. Yeb.* 98a; *Gen. Rab.* 18:5 (the sages against R. Meir; this could reflect the idea that Gentiles could not know who their father was); cf. *b. Sanh.* 58a (continuing relations depended on the time of conversion: one was converted with one's mother if in the womb, but with both parents if in the loins); *Yeb.* 22a.

148. Bamberger, *Proselytism,* 86.

149. *B. Bek.* 47a; *Yeb.* 62a.

150. *Gen. Rab.* 18:5, probably third-century Palestinian amora.

151. *B. Sanh.* 71b.

152. *M. Demai* 6:10, in Neusner, *Tosefta* 1.114; Danby, 26–27.

153. *T. Demai* 6:13.

154. *B. Qidd.* 17b.

155. Jeremias, *Jerusalem,* 324.

156. Tac., *Hist.* 5:5 (Church and Brodribb, 660).

157. *1 Enoch* 72:1; *Jub.* 1:29, 4:26; 1QS 4.25 (עשות הדשה, but Ringgren, *Faith,* 165, also thinks new creation is in view).

158. *Lev. Rab.* 29:12; references in Moore, *Judaism,* 1.533, and Bonsirven, *Judaism,* 117 (on *Sipre Deut.*); cf. *Jub.* 1:20–21. For renewing of individuals who obey God to perform their calls, see the late materials in *Exod. Rab.* 3:15; *Midr. Ps.* 2 §9; Buchanan, *Covenant,* 210.

159. *B. Sanh.* 99b; I have not yet found this in Tannaitic material.

160. *Sipre Deut.* 32.2.1; *Song Sol. Rab.* 1:3 §3; and texts in Davies, *Paul,* 119.

161. The fact that this language is spread through many early Christian writers, e.g., James (1:18, 21), 1 Peter (1:23; 2:2), Paul (as new creation/life imagery; cf. Titus 3:5), and probably the Jesus tradition (Matt 18:3; cf. Mark 9:37; Luke 9:48) also strongly suggests the antiquity of this concept (though Justin, *First Apology* 61, is probably dependent on Johannine tradition, given the similarity of language).

162. Cf. also Epict., *Disc.* 1.30.1 (God watches ἄνωθεν); Philo, *Her.* 64; *Fug.* 137–38; *Mut.* 259–60. The contrast between upper and lower realities is standard: Diogenes, *Ep.* 7 (*Cynic Epistles,* 98–99); Heraclitus, *Ep.* 5 (ibid., 194–95); Plut., *Isis* 78, *Moralia* 382F; *T. Sol.* 6:10 (though the τῶν ἐπουρανίων turn out to consist mainly of a lecture on folk magic); *Sipre Deut.* 306.28.2; Theophilus 1.13; *Ladder of Jacob* 7:2, 16.

163. *Sib. Or.* 3:307 (probably second century B.C.E.); Rom 1:18; Luke 15:18; Jas 1:17, 3:17; *3 Enoch* 28:9; *b. Pesaḥ.* 54a; *Gen. Rab.* 51:3; *Qoh. Rab.* 10:11 §1; cf. also the references in Jeremias, *Theology,* 10; Marmorstein, *Names and Attributes,* 91.

164. Vellanickal, *Sonship,* 172; Hoskyns, *Gospel,* 211–12.

165. F.-M. Braun, "La vie d'en haut," *RSPT* 40 (1956) 3–24 (also on ὑψοθῆναι in v. 14); Brown, *John,* 1.cxxxv; Hunter, *John,* 38; Ellis, *John,* 53; R. Shedd, "Multiple Meanings in the Gospel of John," in *Issues in Biblical and Patristic Interpretation* (ed. Hawthorne) 255; W. H. Cadman, *The Open Heaven* (New York: Herder & Herder, 1969) 64. Double entendres often fulfill an ironic function related to Jesus' interlocutors' misunderstanding (Culpepper, *Anatomy,* 155).

166. Culpepper, *Anatomy,* 135; J. C. Fenton, *The Gospel according to John* (London: Oxford, 1970) 53; for John in general, cf., e.g., Ellis, *John,* 7; J. Painter, *John: Witness and Theologian* (London: SPCK, 1975) 9. The misunderstanding motif was familiar from both the Greek sources (Aune, *Environment,* 34, 55–56) and Jewish traditions (4 Ezra 5:34–35; E. E. Lemcio, "External Evidence for the Structure and Function of Mark iv.1–20, vii.14–23 and viii.14–21," *JTS* 29 [1978] 323–38; cf. *Herm. Vis.* 3.6, 10; *Herm. Man.* 12.4; *Herm. Sim.* 9.12). For other examples in the Jesus tradition, see Lemcio, "Evidence"; Wrede, *Messianic Secret,* 143–45. G. Johnston, *The Spirit-Paraclete in the Gospel of John* (SNTSMS 12; Cambridge: Cambridge, 1970) 149, says that "our sympathy goes to the perplexed interlocutors." But he bases his position on a modern reading of the text that ignores the likelihood that the Johannine community would have been encouraged by the denseness of Jesus' opponents who prefigured their own. Nicodemus's idea of return to the womb may be paralleled in initiatory symbolism in many cultures; see Eliade, *Initiation,* 51–64.

167. See P. Borgen, "God's Agent in the Fourth Gospel," in *Religions in Antiquity,* 146; Aune, *Cultic Setting,* 91; and references under Moses' ascent in our first chapter, on the Spirit in early Judaism. For Israel's "birth" at Sinai in some Jewish traditions, see *Song Sol. Rab.* 8:2 §1; cf. *b. Šabb.* 145b–146a; P. Borgen, "Some Jewish Exegetical Traditions as Background for Son of Man Sayings

in John's Gospel," in *L'Évangile de Jean*, 254–58. For the ascending-descending redeemer in pre-Gnostic tradition, see Wis 18:15 (God's Word descending from heaven at the death of the firstborn in Exodus); Longenecker, *Christology*, 58–62; C. H. Talbert, "The Myth of a Descending-Ascending Redeemer in Mediterranean Antiquity," *NTS* 22 (1976) 418–40; id., *What Is a Gospel?* (Philadelphia: Fortress Press, 1977) 54–57, especially on wisdom tradition; for Torah itself as the object of comparison, see *ʾAbot R. Nat.* 47 §130B; Smith, *Parallels*, 158–59.

168. Nicholson, *Departure*, 81–82; he suggests on 83 that in vv. 4–8 the focus changes to others who need to be born from above.

169. See especially Meeks, *Prophet-King*, 298; id., "The Man from Heaven in Johannine Sectarianism," *JBL* 91 (1972) 53. The argument has its closest parallels in Sen., *Apocol.* 1; Diogenes, *Ep.* 38 (*Cynic Epistles*, 160–61); *T. Job* 38:5; 4 Ezra 4:5–9, 21; cf. perhaps Diog. Laert., *Lives* 8.1.21, on Pythagoras' knowledge from his descent to Hades.

170. Meeks, *Prophet-King*, 298–99.

171. Cf. Wis 10:10, where wisdom, which has come from the heavens (9:10), ἔδειξεν Jacob the *kingdom of God* (cf. John 3:3). Cf. similarly Bar 3:29–30, which appears to be modeled on Deut 30:12–13; cf. the comparable midrash in Rom 10:6–7.

172. Less commonly proposed than semen, but also associated with natural birth, is the breaking of the amniotic sac at birth; so D. G. Spriggs, "Meaning of 'Water' in John 3:5," *ExpT* 85 (1974) 149–50; M. Pamment, "John 3:5," *NovT* 25 (1983) 189–90. Against this, Michaels, *John*, 39, observes that the point of v. 6 is precisely that the spiritual birth is not fleshly birth.

173. For semen, *m. ʾAbot* 3:1 (מטפה סרוחה); *ʾAbot. R. Nat.* 16, 19A; *b. ʿAbod. Zar.* 20a (about R. Akiba); *Gen. Rab.* 63:8 (possibly; purportedly Tannaitic); *Lev. Rab.* 14:2, 18:1 (repeating *m. ʾAbot* 3:1); cf. also references in Urbach, *Sages*, 1.232. The solution is especially associated with Odeberg, *Fourth Gospel*, 49–52; he also finds allusions to the celestial waters, given the heavenly mysticism theme, on pp. 51–66 (though most sources cited after p. 55 are late, influenced by Christianity).

174. Michaels, *John*, 39; so also Burge, *Community*, 161 (following Lindars). Saliva could also be called "water" (e.g., *Lev. Rab.* 16:4); prayer for rain was connected with the resurrection of the dead (*p. Taʿan.* 1:1 §2); so a connection between water and semen is far from self-evident.

175. Culpepper, *Anatomy*, 193; White, *Initiation*, 254, 262 (the addition of the Spirit counters the sacramentalism of the mysteries).

176. D. W. B. Robinson, "Born of Water and Spirit," *RTR* 25 (1966) 15. That Christian tradition could indeed be taken this way may be inferred, e.g., from Rom 6:3–4; 1 Pet 3:21; *Herm. Vis.* 3.3; Justin, *First Apology* 61.

177. *Theology*, 310.

178. Robinson, "Baptism?" 20–21. Proselyte baptism is listed as one of the possibilities by Howard, *Gospel*, 202. Belleville, "Water and Spirit," 126–27, challenges Robinson's assertion by arguing that water and Spirit are not opposed (1:26, 33), but coordinated; but this is probably because in this passage the true water (as in ch. 4) is the Spirit, rather than merely ritual water (chs. 2, 9, perhaps 5); the motif is clarified when the reader reaches 7:37–39, particularly if she or he understands the associations with Sukkoth. Burge, *Community*, 165–70, suspects that this text may address sacramental abuse in the church, but thinks it is not

anti-sacramental; his association specifically with John the Baptist here (ibid., 165) is too narrow, given the waterpots of 2:6.

179. Dunn, *Baptism*, 192; W. H. Bates, "Born of Water," *BSac* 85 (1928) 235; Burge, *Community*, 166. This was the view of Origen, the English Reformers, the Lollards, Calvin, and others (Robinson, "Baptism?" 19–20).

180. Westcott, *John*, 49; F. Porsch, *Pneuma und Wort* (FTS 16; Frankfurt: Knecht, 1974) 128–29. Robinson, "Baptism?" 19–20, who does not hold it to be a hendiadys, admits that there is considerable evidence in its favor.

181. So also Michaels, *John*, 43.

182. E.g., Morris, *John*, 218. Belleville, "Water and Spirit," 134–35, 140, and D. A. Carson, *Exegetical Fallacies* (Grand Rapids, Mich.: Baker, 1984) 42, following her, believe that the passage refers to the dual work of the Spirit: purifying (water) and imparting a new nature (God's nature as spirit).

183. Cf. Ladd, *Theology*, 285; Smalley, *John*, 227; Hoskyns, *Gospel*, 214; J. N. Suggit, "Nicodemus—the True Jew," *Neot* 14 (1981) 96; Bruce, *History*, 156–57; Belleville, "Water and Spirit," 140. Z. C. Hodges, "Part 3 of Problem Passages in the Gospel of John," *BSac* 135 (1978) 206–20, relates the water (v. 5, as an OT symbol for the Spirit) and wind (v. 8, as an OT symbol for the Spirit) to heaven, the "above" of v. 3.

184. 1QS 3.8–9, 4.21.

185. *B. Sukka* 52a; *Pesiq. Rab Kah.* 24:17; *Exod. Rab.* 41:7; *Lev. Rab.* 35:5; *Song Sol. Rab.* 6:11 §1; cf. *Pesiq. Rab.* 14:15; *Num. Rab.* 7:10. *Gen. Rab.* 26:6 (purportedly Tannaitic) applies the passage to the eschatological bestowal of the Spirit on all the righteous; in *Gen. Rab.* 96:5, *Exod. Rab.* 48:4, the related Ezek 37:12–14 is naturally applied to the association of the Spirit with the resurrection of the body (cf. *ʿAbod. Zar.* 20b, associating the Holy Spirit directly with eternal life).

186. *M. Yoma* 8:9.

187. Torrance, "Proselyte Baptism," 153; idem, "Origins," 166.

188. One may compare the probable offense of John's baptism, as portrayed in Q (Matt 3:9; Luke 3:8).

189. See A. T. Kraabel, "New Evidence of the Samaritan Diaspora has been Found on Delos," *BA* 47 (1984) 44–46; P. W. van der Horst, "De Samaritaanse diaspora in de oudheid," *NedTT* 42 (1988) 134–44; much later, in *CPJ* 3.102–4 §513 (103, line 7), 3.105 §514.

190. J. D. Purvis, "The Fourth Gospel and the Samaritans," *NovT* 17 (1975) 161–98 (Samaria or Samaria-Galilee); cf. J. Bowman, "Samaritan Studies," *BJRL* 40 (1958) 298–329. There is possible evidence of a later Samaritan Christianity; cf. P. E. Dion and R. Pummer, "A Note on the 'Samaritan-Christian Synagogue' in Ramat-Aviv," *JSJ* 11 (1980) 217–22, though in extant (medieval) Samaritan literature about Jesus, he appears as a prophet like those of the Hebrew Bible—a false prophet (S. Isser, "Jesus in the Samaritan Chronicles," *JSJ* 32 [1981] 166–94).

191. The statement of 4:4 that Jesus had (ἔδει) to pass through Samaria is strictly true only if he was under temporal constraint (Jos., *Life* 269: ἔδει, for a three-day trip from Galilee to Jerusalem), and this route was often used (*J.W.* 2.232); but Samaritan land came to be considered unclean by the early third century (*b. Ḥag.* 25a; probably *p. Ḥag.* 3:4 §1). But if Jesus had been in the Jordan valley (3:22), he could have easily circumvented Samaria (Brown, *John*, 1.169;

Michaels, *John*, 59), and the "necessity" may function as the divine will of God, as elsewhere in John (Morris, *John*, 255).

192. R. E. Brown, *The Community of the Beloved Disciple* (New York: Paulist, 1979) 37, sees the reconciliation of disciples and Samaritans as a statement about the history of the Johannine community, which, though it began with a lower Christology of its own, joined those with a higher Christology; but this is speculative, and presupposes that John's readers would have had much knowledge about Samaritan messianology, which was probably quite limited in this period anyway.

193. See R. T. Fortna, "Theological Use of Locale in the Fourth Gospel," *ATRSup* 3 (1974) 83; cf. Olsson, *Structure*, 143.

194. See the intricate theory of J. S. King, "Sychar and Calvary," *Th* 77 (1974) 417–22.

195. E.g., Sanders, *John*, 137; B. Witherington, *Women in the Ministry of Jesus* (SNTSMS 51; Cambridge: Cambridge, 1984) 57; Fortna, "Locale," 83.

196. *Ant.* 20.125; *J.W.* 2.232–45. Josephus starts the conflict immediately after the return from exile; *Ant.* 11.84; 12.156. R. Marcus, "Josephus on the Samaritan Schism," in Josephus, *Works* (LCL; Cambridge, Mass.: Harvard, 1926–65) 6.498–511, suggests that Josephus had an "anti-Samaritan source." Cf. *4 Bar* 8; Samaria was founded by those who rejected Jeremiah's call to repentance, contradicting the OT account. But Josephus allows that they were friendly to Herod the Great; e.g., *J.W.* 1.229.

197. E.g., *p. Ta'an.* 4:5 §10 (on Betar); *Qoh. Rab.* 10:8 §1 (purportedly Tannaitic); cf. *Lam. Rab.* 1.1 §§14–15. In some rabbinic texts, Samaria had its own local Shedim demons (Alexander, *Possession*, 29), and Samaritans often defined their laws polemically by the differences with Jewish laws (*Samaritan Documents Relating to Their History, Religion, and Life* [POTTS 2; tr. and ed. John Bowman; Pittsburgh: Pickwick, 1977] 299). For other examples of Jewish antipathy toward Samaritans, see, e.g., F. Dexinger, "Limits of Tolerance in Judaism," in *Self-Definition*, 2.88–114; *b. B.Qam.* 38b; *p. Ḥag.* 3:4 §1; Sir 50's remarks on "Sichem" (see also Manson, *Sayings*, 179–90).

198. *T. Ter.* 4:14; *'Abod. Zar.* 2:8 (contrast 3:1, 3, 5); *p. Ketub.* 3:1 §3 (purportedly Tannaitic); cf. *m. Giṭ.* 1:5; *Ter.* 3:9; *b. Bek.* 11b; *Sanh.* 57a; *Meg.* 25b. They were often viewed as "lion-proselytes," not true converts, given the record in 2 Kgs 17:24–41: *b. Qidd.* 75b (R. Ishmael vs. R. Akiba); *Num. Rab.* 8:9; Hoenig, "Conversion," 58; they are lax Jews in *Deut. Rab.* 2:33. I. Sonne, "The Use of Rabbinic Literature as Historical Sources," *JQR* 36 (1945–46) 154–62, accentuates the more positive elements in the tradition, and R. J. Coggins, *Samaritans and Jews* (Atlanta: Knox, 1975) 163–64, thinks the formative period in the schism was gradual, from the third century B.C.E. to the beginning of the Christian period. Whatever one thinks of this theory, Elephantine Jews in the fifth century B.C.E. still regarded both Jerusalem and Samaria as Jewish centers (Bright, *History of Israel*, 407); yet Justin Martyr (*First Apology* 53) identifies Samaritans with Jews as Israel (though he also regards himself both as a geographical Samaritan and a Gentile; cf. Osborn, *Justin Martyr*, 6).

199. *M. 'Abot* 1:5; *b. Ber.* 43b; *'Erub.* 53b; *p. Soṭa* 1:1 §7; *'Abod. Zar.* 2:3 §1; in some later traditions even God avoids talking with women (*Gen. Rab.* 48:20; 63:7). Asking for water would not be considered promiscuous (cf. *b. Qidd.* 9a), but could have conjugal connotations (e.g., the girl who acts like Rebekah and wishes

R. Joshua to act like Eliezer, in *Lam. Rab.* 1.1.19), especially since Jacob, the presupposed foil for Jesus in the narrative, met Rachel at a well (Gen 29:8–12). The woman's denial of marriedness (4:17a) could have been construed (and intended) as an invitation (cf. *b. Soṭa* 10a).

200. *M. Ṭohar.* 5:8; *Nid.* 4:1; *t. Nid.* 5:1; *b. Šabb.* 17a; cf. *Yeb.* 86a. It may be homiletical hyperbole, but its effect would at the very least be the avoidance of social intercourse with Samaritan women; Daube, *New Testament and Judaism,* 373, thinks the rule had been observed in strict Jewish circles before it had acquired legal force. *Mikveh* was crucial in cleansing Jewish menstruants (*m. Miqw.* 8:5; *b. Šabb.* 84a; *Nid.,* passim).

201. *M. Šeb.* 8:10; *p. ʿAbod. Zar.* 5:11 §2 (in R. Eliezer's name); selectively, *t. Demai* 1:11, 5:24; *p. ʿAbod. Zar.* 5:4 §3. The rabbis regarded eating untithed food as a terrible offense (cf., e.g., *Gen. Rab.* 60:8; *Lam. Rab.* 1.3.28).

202. *M. Kelim,* passim. But while this was always true of Gentile vessels (*b. ʿAbod. Zar.* 67b, 75b; *Pesaḥ.* 44b, all purportedly Tannaitic), it had not always been true of Samaritan wine (*b. ʿErub.* 36b–37a; cf. *p. ʿAbod. Zar.* 5:4 §3).

203. For Samaritan religious strictness, see S. Dar, "Three *Menorot* from Western Samaria," *IEJ* 34 (1984) 177–79 and plate 20BC.

204. Cf. Westcott, *John,* xii; Haenchen, *John,* 1.218–19; Brown, *John,* 1.169.

205. See Finegan, *Archeology of New Testament,* 36–42; E. M. Yamauchi, *The Stones and the Scriptures* (Grand Rapids, Mich.: Baker, 1972) 102–3. S. Pancaro, *The Law in the Fourth Gospel* (Leiden: Brill, 1975) 482–85, sees Jacob's well as a symbol of Torah, but this does not fit 4:10, where Jesus interprets the well image's function for this text.

206. Besides OT examples, cf., e.g., Philostr., *V.A.* 1 §6.

207. For the Targums, see McNamara, *Targum,* 145–46. For motifs of the wandering well in the wilderness (1 Cor 10:4), see, e.g., Olsson, *Structure,* 165ff.

208. The tradition linking Jacob to this land is ancient (Schnackenburg, *John,* 1.423), and even R. Meir's challenge to the Samaritan heritage is difficult to sustain (*Gen. Rab.* 94:7).

209. "Our father Jacob" was a fairly standard phrase in Judaism as well (e.g., *Pesiq. Rab Kah.* 23:2). Jews complained that Samaritans identified themselves with Jewry only when it was convenient (Jos., *Ant.* 11.340–41); but they always identified themselves with Israel.

210. N. R. Bonneau, "The Woman at the Well—John 4 and Genesis 24," *BT* 67 (1973) 1252–59; Glasson, *Moses,* 57.

211. For a more detailed analysis of Jacob traditions in this passage, see J. H. Neyrey, "Jacob Traditions and the Interpretation of John 4:10–26," *CBQ* 41 (1979) 419–37.

212. Against Westcott, *John,* 68.

213. R. A. Whitacre, *Johannine Polemic* (SBLDS 67; Chico: Scholars, 1982) 111. Of course, this is derived from the fact that she came alone, not from the time of day; in some cultures, midday heat is the best time to draw water (e.g., the Ankore of Uganda in Mbiti, *Religions,* 25).

214. I. H. Marshall, "Historical Criticism," in *Interpretation* (ed. Marshall) 126; G. H. C. MacGregor, *The Gospel of John* (MNTC; London: Hodder & Stoughton, 1928) 96. Weariness could be used as a sign of human mortality, as Plutarch uses it for Alexander of Macedon (*Table-Talk* 8.1.3, *Moralia* 717F); but sitting on a well was not an unusual posture (cf. Diog. Laert., *Lives* 6.2.52, ἐπὶ φρέατι

καθήμενον). Submitting to thirst could be viewed as ignoble (Lysimachus #1 in Plut., *Sayings of Kings, Moralia* 183E; Theron in Char., *Chaer.* 3.3.17 [ποτόν]; 4 Macc 3:6–18), but Abraham's servant Isaac initiated the conversation with Rebekah by asking for water (Gen 24:14, 17–20).

215. Gen 29:7, "high day": היום גדול; ἡμέρα πολλή.

216. Oscar Cullmann, *Early Christian Worship* (Philadelphia: Westminster, 1953) 83, may well be correct in moving from drinking water to baptismal water by addressing the nature of the conversation; his appeal to later Gnostic baptismal sects' drinking their baptismal water is, however, anachronistic. We further see a replacement of ritual holy water here rather than its affirmation, and again doubt that it is *Christian* baptism that is in view.

217. Whitacre, *Polemic,* 86–87; Brown, *John,* 1.176; Odeberg, *Fourth Gospel,* 150–51, noting the use of "God's gift" for Torah (cf., perhaps analogously in a Greek setting, τοῦ δώρου τοῦ Διονύσου, [Ps.-] Plut., *Frg.* 54, of wine).

218. D. C. Allison, "The Living Water," *SVTQ* 30 (1986) 143–57; cf. C. H. H. Scobie, "North and South," in *Biblical Studies* (ed. J. R. McKay and J. F. Miller; Philadelphia: Westminster, 1976) 97–98; this derives support from John 7:37–39 and the discussion in 4:20–21, but does not appear to be in the foreground in this passage. The water "springing up" probably alludes to Num 21, which appears frequently in contemporary Jewish tradition; see Glasson, *Moses,* 55–56.

219. Cullmann, *Worship,* 82; Olsson, *Structure,* 213. J. MacDonald, *The Theology of the Samaritans* (Philadelphia: Westminster, 1964) 425, observes that "living water" was a favorite expression of some later Samaritan writers; but they are late enough to have been influenced by Christianity.

220. Even well water could be valid for immersion, if it were somehow flowing; cf. *m. Miqw.* 5:5, if I have understood it properly.

221. "Living waters" are associated with a "fountain of life" also in CD 19.34; 1QH 8.7, 12.14, from the Law (J. C. Coetzee, "Life in St. John's Writings and the Qumran Scrolls," *Neot* 6 [1972] 64). CD 6.3–4 uses "the well" of Num 21:18 for the well dug by the wise of Israel, the Law (התורה), dug also by the Covenanters (6.5). The Messiah is a πηγὴ ζωήν in some manuscripts of *T. Jud.* 24:4, but this may be Christian interpolation. Likewise, in some Amoraic haggadah, the water sprang up for Rebekah whenever she came to the well (*Gen. Rab.* 60:5), but this may be too late to parallel John 4:14; cf. the water flowing up for Jacob in targumic traditions in McNamara, *Judaism,* 228–29.

222. E.g., *Jos. and Asen.* 14:12 (ὕδατι ζῶντι); cf. Bernard, *John,* 1.138.

223. See the discussion of John 2:6 above.

224. In postbiblical times, e.g., *Jub.* 4:26; 32:23; *Sipra A.M.* par. 6.187.1.1; *Gen. Rab.* 56:2.

225. E.g., *Jub.* 9:1–15, 27–34. It may be played *down* in Josephus to avoid revolutionist implications; cf. B. H. Amaru, "Land Theology in Josephus' *Jewish Antiquities,*" *JQR* 71 (1981) 201–29.

226. R. Simeon b. Yohai claimed that it was one of three precious gifts God gave to Israel (*b. Ber.* 5a, purportedly Tannaitic; *Exod. Rab.* 1:1; *Lev. Rab.* 13:2, also purportedly Tannaitic; cf. *Gen. Rab.* 39:8; 68:12; *Num. Rab.* 23:7; and the *Sipre Deut.* reference in Urbach, *Sages,* 1.349). Sages associate the land with distinct eschatological hopes, as one would expect from the Hebrew Bible; *b. Meg.* 29a; *Pesah.* 113a; *Pesiq. Rab.* 1:3; for resurrection in the land, *b. Ketub.* 111a; *p. Ketub.* 12:4 §8; *Gen. Rab.* 74:1, 96:5; 96 (MV); *Deut. Rab.* 2:9; *Pesiq. Rab.* 1:4–6;

cf. *Gen. Rab.* 36:6, and archaeological data in S. Safrai, "Relations between the Diaspora and the Land of Israel," in *JPFC* 213; Bonsirven, *Judaism,* 230–33.

227. E.g., *b. Qidd.* 31b; *Ketub.* 110b; *Mo²ed Qat.* 25a; but contrast *b. Ber.* 24b.

228. *M. Meg.* 3:1–3; *b. Ber.* 6a.

229. *T. Meg.* 3(4):23; cf. J. F. Strange and H. Shanks, "Has the House Where Jesus Stayed in Capernaum Been Found?" *BARev* 8 (1982) 29. Israel was higher and thus more praiseworthy than other lands (*Sipre Deut.* 37.3.6; *b. Qidd.* 69a), and the sanctuary was the highest place of all (*Sipre Deut.* 317.2.1; *b. Qidd.* 69a; *Song Sol. Rab.* 7:5 §3; also *b. Zer.* 54b in J. D. Hester, *Paul's Concept of Inheritance* [SJTOP 14; Edinburgh: Oliver & Boyd, 1968] 76). Certain places made prayers more likely to be heard, in early Jewish texts; see Johnson, *Prayer,* 44–46; but R. Jose b. Hanina suggested that one should pray in a low spot rather than a high one (*b. Ber.* 10b).

230. E.g., *b. Ber.* 25a; cf. *Ber.* 60b, 62a (purportedly Tannaitic), on excretory practices; for the cleanness of Jerusalem, *m. Šeqal.* 8:1. The legend of R. Simeon b. Yohai having removed the bones from Tiberias had to have been circulating before the site could be declared clean of the graves on which it had been built, allowing the rabbinic academy to move there.

231. It is mandated in *t. Ber.* 3:15–16; *Sipre Deut.* 29.3.2; cf. *t. Meg.* 3:21–22 (doors open toward the east); *²Abot R. Nat.* 40A (do not stand naked facing the holy of holies); Stambaugh and Balch, *Social Environment,* 48; S. Safrai, "The Synagogue," in *JPFC* 938; Meyers and Strange, *Archaeology,* 143–44. But this is not the only tradition that was followed in practice; see Z. U. Ma'oz, "Ancient Synagogues of the Golan," *BA* 51 (1988) 119; J. Wilkinson, "Orientation, Jewish and Christian," *PEQ* 116 (1984) 16–30; cf. Greek temples, which normally, though not always, faced east (S. C. Herbert, "The Orientation of Greek Temples," *PEQ* 116 [1984] 31–34). Even in a later period, rabbinic views may not have been enforced (R. A. Stewart, "The Synagogue," *EvQ* 43 [1971] 36–46).

232. This has been developed at length by Davies, *Land,* passim, but terrestrial theology may not be played down in early Christianity as much as Davies argues; see E. M. Meyers, "Early Judaism and Christianity in the Light of Archaeology," *BA* 51 (1988) 75.

233. Schnackenburg, *John,* 1.434.

234. Cf. Jos., *Ant.* 13.74–79; 18.85–89; *J.W.* 3.307–8. They were said to circumcise in the name of Mt. Gerizim (*t. ᶜAbod. Zar.* 3:13; *b. ᶜAbod. Zar.* 27a; *p. Yeb.* 8:1 §10, both purportedly Tannaitic), and Gerizim was seen as the Samaritan counterpart of the Jewish temple (*b. Yoma* 69a). In support of this it may be noted that the Ten Commandments in the Samaritan text include as the tenth (having combined the "ninth" and "tenth" of the Judean text) the command to build an altar on Gerizim (Deut 27:3–5) (Bowman, *Samaritan Documents,* 14), and a probable Samaritan synagogue points toward Gerizim (Goodenough, *Symbols,* 1.262–63).

235. Jos., *J.W.* 1.64–66; R. J. Bull, "Field Report XII," *BASOR* 180 (1965) 41; id., "An Archaeological Context for Understanding John 4:20," *BA* 38 (1975) 54–59; Finegan, *Archeology of New Testament,* 35. The Samaritans expected their temple's restoration (Olsson, *Structure,* 190). For more data on the Samaritan temple, from archaeological sources, see R. J. Bull and G. E. Wright, "Newly Discovered Temples on Mt. Gerizim in Jordan," *HTR* 58 (1965) 234–37; H. C. Kee,

"Tell-Er-Ras and the Samaritan Temple," *NTS* 13 (1967) 401–2; G. G. Garner, "The Temples of Mt. Gerizim," *BH* 11 (1975) 33–42.

236. Some Jews felt that idols were buried at the Samaritan site; *p. ʿAbod. Zar.* 5:4 §3 (purportedly Tannaitic).

237. Jos., *Ant.* 18.30; see the material in Jeremias, *Jerusalem*, 352–58; and *Gen. Rab.* 64:10, a fiction about Samaritan antipathy toward the temple in Hadrianic times.

238. *Gen. Rab.* 32:10; also *Deut. Rab.* 3:6; *Song Sol. Rab.* 4:4 §5; a similar story is told of R. Ishmael b. Jose, early second century, in *Gen. Rab.* 81:3. R. Levi, an early Palestinian amora, says that Eretz Israel was not submerged by the Flood (*Gen. Rab.* 33:6); perhaps the editor(s) of *Gen. Rab.* were particularly interested in such stories because of Genesis' diluvian tradition. We may be sure that pilgrims to Jerusalem faced hostility in Samaria in the first century; Luke 9:53; Jos., *J.W.* 2.323–45.

239. Pointed out by other commentators, e.g., Westcott, *John*, 71; Strachan, *Fourth Gospel*, 105; cf. Fenton, *John*, 61.

240. See especially Davies, "Reflections in Mekilta"; Reif, "Review," 158, summarizing Schäfer.

241. Brown, *John*, 1.180.

242. H. Schlier, "Zum Begriff des Geistes nach dem Johannesevangelium," in *Besinnung auf das Neue Testament* (Freiburg: Herder, 1964) 264; Burge, *Community*, 192; Brown, *John*, 1.172. This is quite different from the more Stoic language of similar phrases in Philo (e.g., *Sacr.* 95; cf. A. Marmorstein, *The Old Rabbinic Doctrine of God: Essays in Anthropomorphism* [New York: KTAV, 1968] 4–6) or Tatian, *Address to the Greeks* 4.

243. Scott, *Spirit*, 196; cf. Aune, *Cultic Setting*, 104; against Johnston, *Spirit-Paraclete*, 44 (who acknowledges it in Acts, Paul, and Rev 1:10, but not here). Strabo, *Geog.* 16.2.36 notes admiringly that Moses introduced a simpler kind of worship than his predecessors, and to have simplified ritual still beyond that point, or to reduce it to ecstatic experience of the divine, might have appealed to more hellenized readers.

244. 1 Cor 14 speaks of an ecstatic worship "in spirit," but there it refers to a nonrational human dimension, not to God's Spirit (*pace* Fee, *Presence*, 125, 229; cf. pp. 484–86; 645–46, who translates "S/spirit"). That God's Spirit undoubtedly inspires Paul's spirit when he prays in tongues in 1 Cor 14:14–15 (cf. Acts 2:4) does not mean that *"my* spirit" here includes God's Spirit; praying with the understanding in this context refers to interpreting tongues, which also occurs by God's Spirit, yet we do not render this Spirit/mind (that "Spirit" and "spirit" are the same term reflects the word's semantic range in Jewish Greek, not a theological peculiarity of Pauline usage).

245. On worship with angels at Qumran, see 4Q Shir Shab (in G. Vermes, *The Religion of Jesus the Jew* [Minneapolis: Fortress, 1993] 128); cf. 1QS 11.8; 1QM 12.1–2; *Jub.* 30:18; 31:14; *Prayer of Manasseh* 15; *Sipre Deut.* 306.31.1; S. E. Robinson, "The Testament of Adam and the Angelic Liturgy," *RevQum* 12 (1985) 105–10. In Revelation, cf., e.g., Rev 4:7–11; 5:8–14; 8:4; 7:10–12; 11:15–18; 15:1–4; 19:1–9. Some scholars think that Col 2:18 disavows worship *with* angels (e.g., Francis, "Humility and Angelic Worship," 178–80; W. Carr, *Angels and Principalities* [Cambridge: Cambridge University, 1981] 70–72); more likely it attacks worship or veneration of angels (E. Schweizer, *The Letter to the Colossians*

[Minneapolis: Augsburg, 1982] 159–60; cf. R. P. Martin *Colossians and Philemon* [NCBC; Grand Rapids: Eerdmans, 1978] 14–15). For invocation of angels, see, e.g., *PGM* 3.145–50; 7.1012–13; 35.1–42; 36.170–75; 43.15–20; A. T. Kraabel, "Judaism in Western Asia Minor under the Roman Empire" (Th.D. diss., Harvard, 1968) 143–45; Cohen, *Maccabees to Mishnah*, 84.

246. On the probability of this reading, see D. J. Wieand, "John V2 and the Pool of Bethesda," *NTS* 12 (1966) 394–95; E. J. Vardaman, "The Pool of Bethesda," *BT* 14 (1963) 29; Cullmann, *Worship*, 84–85 n. 2; Finegan, *Archeology of New Testament*, 143.

247. Wieand, "Bethesda," 396–97; Cornfeld, *Josephus*, 338, 364; Finegan, *Archeology of New Testament*, 145; on sheep pool, ibid., 142–43. Although widely held, this identification does not command universal consensus and may face more rigorous challenges.

248. Yamauchi, *Stones*, 104.

249. Vardaman, "Bethesda," 28. The view of J. E. Bruns, *The Art and Thought of John* (New York: Herder & Herder, 1969) 65; and Ellis, *John*, 88, that they symbolize the five books of the Law, is needless allegorization, despite references to the Law later in the chapter.

250. J. Jeremias, *Unknown Sayings of Jesus* (2d ed.; London: SPCK, 1964) 55.

251. Cary and Haarhoff, *Life and Thought*, 105.

252. E.g., Acts 3:2.

253. For Aesculapia, Ps.-Luc., *Hippias/The Bath* (LCL 1.40–41); Koester, *Introduction*, 1.174; E. M. Yamauchi, *The Archaeology of New Testament Cities in Western Asia Minor* (Grand Rapids, Mich.: Baker, 1980) 45–49. On the Asclepius cult, see, e.g., H. C. Kee, "Self-Definition in the Asclepius Cult," in *Self-Definition*, 3.118–36; for healings, 3.129–33.

254. Cf., e.g., Hammat Gader, in Y. Hirschfeld and G. Solar, "Sumptuous Roman Baths Uncovered near Sea of Galilee," *BARev* 10 (1974) 22–40.

255. G. D. Fee, "On the Inauthenticity of John 5:3b–4," *EvQ* 54 (1982) 207–18; against Z. C. Hodges, "Problem Passages in the Gospel of John. Part 5," *BSac* 136 (1979) 25–39.

256. Finegan, *Archeology of New Testament*, 147. J. Klinger, "Bethesda and the Universality of the Logos," *SVTQ* 27 (1983) 169–85, wrongly assumes that this means Jesus visited a pagan sanctuary, since John's readers would rightly assume that pre-70 Jerusalem, in which Jesus lived, was a Jewish city.

257. J. Wilkinson, *Jerusalem as Jesus Knew It* (London: Thames & Hudson, 1978) 95–104, especially 102.

258. Theissen, *Miracle-Stories*, 51; also 277.

259. Bowman, *Gospel*, 36–38, 99–159. Bowman does a better job of establishing the possibility (99–109) than attempting to draw parallels between Purim and John 5 (111–59).

260. Bruns, *Art*, 26; cf. Brown, *John*, 1.206, who sees this as possible due to discussion of Torah in John 5.

261. Bruce, *Documents*, 49; cf. Fenton, *John*, 67.

262. *Jub.* 16:27; *m. Giṭ.* 3:8; *b. B. Meṣiʿa* 28a (purportedly Tannaitic); *Sukka* 33b; *Pesaḥ.* 34b (in 36a it is Pesach, but this is clear from the context); *p. Giṭ.* 3:8 §4; *Gen. Rab.* 6:5, 35:3; S. Safrai, "The Temple," in *JPFC* 894.

263. Brown, *John*, 1.206.

264. This theme is further developed in ch. 6, where Jesus becomes a manna-giver far greater than Moses. The continuity between the chapters is considerably greater than advocates of transposition (such as Bultmann, *John*, 209) recognize (for continuity, see P. Borgen, *Bread from Heaven* [Leiden: Brill, 1965]; D. M. Smith, *The Composition and Order of the Fourth Gospel* [New Haven, Conn.: Yale, 1965]).

265. Richardson, *Theology*, 360.

266. Brown, *John*, 1.211.

267. Dunn, *Baptism*, 187.

268. Meeks, *Prophet-King*, 59; Hoskyns, *Gospel*, 360–61; cf. Pancaro, *Law*, 9. The "lame" and the "blind" often function as the most dramatic cures in summaries of miraculous healings; cf., e.g., Epidauros inscriptions in Grant, *Religions*, 57–58.

269. *Anatomy*, 139.

270. If John 7:53–8:11 is an interpolation, as is extremely probable given the textual evidence, as well as style, etc. (see B. M. Metzger, *A Textual Commentary on the Greek New Testament* [New York: United Bible Societies, 1975] 219–221), then 8:12–10:21 apparently occur on the last day of Sukkoth.

271. *Jub.* 16:27, 29, 18:19; *m. Sukka* 5:1; *Sipre Deut.* 142.3.1; *b. Sukka* 51a, 53a; *Pesiq. Rab Kah.* 27:2, *Pesiq. Rab Kah. Sup.* 2:8; Safrai, "Temple," 894; compare the celebration at the Lesser Mysteries of Eleusis, in Mylonas, *Eleusis*, 241.

272. *M. Sukka* 4:9; *m. Mid.* 2:7; *t. Sukka* 3:3 (4), 14, 16; *b. Ta'an.* 2b–3a; Safrai, "Diaspora and Israel," 198; id., "Temple," 866–67, 894; Westcott, *John*, 123; see especially B. H. Grigsby, " 'If Any Man Thirsts . . . ,' " *Bib* 67 (1986) 100–108. For other kinds of festival libations, cf., e.g., *p. Ter.* 9:8; libations and sacred processions were standard in Greek religion as well. In time haggadic traditions arose about the place of water-pouring, e.g., that it was from the time of creation (*t. Sukka* 3:15; *b. Sukka* 49a) or that the pits beneath the altar descended to the abyss (*t. Sukka* 3:15); the Amoraic tradition about the centrality of the temple in the world actually has pre-Tannaitic Jewish antecedents (see below).

273. *M. Ta'an.* 1:1; *t. Sukka* 3:18; *Sipre Deut.* 40.4.2; *b. Ta'an.* 25b; *B. Meşi'a* 28a (purportedly Tannaitic); *p. Ta'an.* 1:1 §§1–10; *Roş Hoş.* 1:3 §§43–46; *Pesiq. Rab Kah. Sup.* 7:2; *Qoh. Rab.* 7:14 §3; *Song Sol. Rab.* 7:2 §2; cf. Moore, *Judaism*, 2.44–45; Harrelson, *Fertility Cult*, 69. In contexts unrelated to Sukkoth, cf. *Pesiq. Rab Kah.* 1:4; *'Abot R. Nat.* 4A; Johnson, *Prayer*, 13–14.

274. *B. Mo'ed Qaṭ.* 3b; *Zebaḥ.* 110b (purportedly Tannaitic).

275. *Ruth Rab.* 4:8.

276. Bowman, *Gospel*, 35, noting that Alexander Jannaeus opposed it. Charles, *Jubilees*, lxv, suggests that *Jubilees* omits it probably because it was unknown to the author; but the omission could also imply Essene disapproval of a Pharisaic innovation. S. Belkin, *Philo and the Oral Law* (HSS 11; Cambridge, Mass.: Harvard, 1940) 192–218, finds more Philonic parallels for Tannaitic teachings on the Sabbath, Rosh Hashanah, and Yom Kippur than on Sukkoth. J. Daniélou, "Le symbolisme eschatologique de la Fête de Tabernacles," *Irénikon* 31 (1958) 19–40, traces the development of Sukkoth themes from the prophets up through the fourth century C.E.

277. See A. Engle, "An Amphorisk of the Second Temple Period," *PEQ* 109 (1977) 117–22. The frequency of the lulab and ethrog in Diaspora inscriptions may

also indicate a familiarity with some aspects of the Sukkoth ritual; see Goodenough, *Symbols*, 4.145–66, 12.86–88; H. J. Leon, *The Jews of Ancient Rome* (Peabody: Hendrickson Publishers, 1995) 198.

278. E.g., the early second-century debate on the proper context of the water-drawing in the temple, reported by R. Johanan in *p. Sukka* 4:6 §1. This is not as significant as the epigraphic data because one would expect the rabbis to maintain their interest in details of the Law even if current applications were necessarily restricted.

279. If A. St. Clair, "The Torah Shrine at Dura-Europos," *JAC* 29 (1986) 109–17, is correct, the Torah shrine mural reflects Sukkoth. The surviving Jews in second-century Egypt also apparently kept the feast, although its temple associations are not clear; see *CPJ* 3.5–6 §452a (τῆς σκηνοπηγίας, in the context of Jewish names).

280. *P. Sukka* 55a (from Moore, *Judaism*, 2.45–46); *Gen. Rab.* 70:8; *Ruth Rab.* 4:8; *Pesiq. Rab.* 1:2 (R. Joshua b. Levi); cf. Bowman, *Gospel*, 323; Barrett, *John*, 329; Schnackenburg, *John*, 2.155; Lee, *Thought*, 217; R. H. Lightfoot, *Gospel*, 184; Hunter, *John*, 84. Freed, *Quotations*, 30, rightly notes that the attestation for this is late. Dodd, *Interpretation*, 350–51, thinks there may be a vague association of the Messiah's coming with this feast as well.

281. The public reading of Torah at the feast is at least as old as Neh 8:1–18; note also the association with the Water Gate (8:1), which becomes more prominent in rabbinic tradition.

282. Schnackenburg, *John*, 2.155 (citing *b. Meg.* 31a); Dodd, *Interpretation*, 350; Bruce, *Time Is Fulfilled*, 46; and Hunter, *John*, 84–85, note Zech 14's use in the later lection for Sukkoth. While we may not be able to depend on the late tradition, we should also not use it to rule out the possibility of an earlier tradition, which is inherently likely on its own terms. Haenchen, *John*, 2.17, curiously takes the tradition for Zech, Ezek, and Isa 12 back to 90 C.E. (R. Eliezer b. Jacob), but then denies its relevance to the Fourth Gospel.

283. *T. Sukka* 3:18 (Neusner, 2.222–23).

284. Zech 14:8–9, RSV.

285. Ezek 47:1–2, RSV.

286. *T. Sukka* 3:3–10.

287. *T. Sukka* 3:3 (4) (Neusner, 2.218–19).

288. *T. Sukka* 3:10 (Neusner, 2.220).

289. *T. Sukka* 3:9 (Neusner, 2.220).

290. The gate of John 10 could allude to the prince and his people going in and out through the gate of Ezek 46:9–10, but the phraseology may be much broader than that: Num 27:17; 2 Sam 5:2; 1 Kgs 3:7; 1 Chron 11:2.

291. The eighth day was different from the first seven; see *t. Mo᾽ed Qaṭ.* 2:13; *Sukka* 4:17; *Sipra Emor* par. 12.236.1.1; *b. Sukka* 47ab; *p. Ned.* 6:1 §1; *Pesiq. Rab Kah.* 28:8; *Pesiq. Rab.* 52:6; cf. *Jub.* 32:27–29; *m. Sukka* 4:6; *p. Roṣ Haṣ.* 1:3 §43; *Lev. Rab.* 37:2. But this does not support the contention of some (Glasson, *Moses*, 72; Sanders, *John*, 212) that the seventh day is in view here.

292. Z. C. Hodges, "Rivers of Living Water," *BSac* 136 (1979) 247; the other uses of "last day" in the Fourth Gospel are eschatological. We base this opinion on John's propensity for double entendres and his customary use of "last day"; the construction itself is acceptable in the form in which it appears (cf., e.g., 1QM 18.1).

293. Westcott, *John*, 123; Longenecker, *Exegesis*, 153. Glasson, *Moses*, 48, finds evidence in the early linking of the water from the rock with manna, as in 1 Cor 10:3–4, *b. Šabb.* 35a, etc.

294. *T. Sukka* 3:11. The artistic attestation of this motif is considerably less than that of the Sukkoth motifs above, especially if Leon, *Jews*, 214, is correct about the Christian nature of the fragment in Rome; but the OT text is commonly cited in antiquity.

295. See note 282 on lections, above.

296. E.g., Hodges, "Rivers," 244.

297. Freed, *Quotations*, 23; C. K. Barrett, "The Old Testament in the Fourth Gospel," *JTS* 48 (July 1947) 156; P. Grelot, "Jean. vii,38," *RB* 70 (1963) 43–51.

298. Long, *Philosophy*, 52. Cf. *Sib. Or.* 3:762, where minds (φρένας) are located in the breasts (στήθεσιν).

299. C. F. Burney, "The Aramaic Equivalent of ἐκ τῆς κοιλίας in Jn. VII 38," *JTS*, 1st ser., 24 (1923) 79–80; cf. Freed, *Quotations*, 24.

300. G. D. Fee, "John 7:37–39," *ExpT* 89 (1978) 116–18; J. Blenkinsopp, "John VII.37-9," *NTS* 6 (1959) 95–98; Hodges, "Rivers"; Bernard, *John*, 1.282; J. B. Cortés, "Yet Another Look at Jn 7,37–38," *CBQ* 29 (1967) 75–86.

301. Fee, "John 7:37–39," 117; Morris, *John*, 423–24; Hodges, "Rivers," 242–43. But if John is citing Scripture this is weakened; "my" would not have been a preferred substitute.

302. Hodges, "Rivers," 242; Cortés, "Look," 78–79; but cf. 6:35 as a parallel if the source is Christ.

303. Fee, "John 7:37–39," 116–17. But 7:38 speaks of giving, not receiving, waters, and Jesus seems to be the source of believers receiving in v. 39.

304. Cortés, "Look," 79; Hodges, "Rivers," 240.

305. Barrett, *John*, 326; Cortés, "Look," 77; K. H. Kuhn, "St. John vii.37-8," *NTS* 4 (1957) 65.

306. Dodd, *Interpretation*, 349; Brown, *John*, 1.321–23; Dunn, *Baptism*, 179–80; cf. J. R. Michaels, "The Temple Discourse in John," 200–213 in *New Dimensions in New Testament Study* (ed. R. N. Longenecker and M. C. Tenney; Grand Rapids, Mich.: Zondervan, 1974), esp. 208–9.

307. Brown, *John*, 1.321; C. H. Turner, "On the Punctuation of St. John VII 37,38," *JTS* 24 (1923) 66–70; cf. some of the early textual evidence in Bruce, *Time Is Fulfilled*, 46. Cf. *Odes Sol.* 30:1–7.

308. Hoskyns, *Gospel*, 321; Jeremias, *Theology*, 159.

309. Cf. G. D. Kilpatrick, "The Punctuation of John VII.37-38," *JTS* 11 (1960) 340–42; Brown, *John*, 1.321; Strachan, *Gospel*, 132.

310. Note J. Blenkinsopp, "The Quenching of Thirst," *Scripture* 12 (1950) 40, for the structure; it is an invitation formula (41). Cf. Glasson, *Moses*, 50–51.

311. Cf. W. C. Allen, "St. John vii.37, 38," *ExpT* 34 (1922–23) 329–30; Sanders, *John*, 213–14; D. W. B. Robinson, "Baptism?" 164.

312. Schnackenburg, *John*, 2.154.

313. I.e., the era of the Spirit's outpouring had not yet come; cf. Lightfoot, *Gospel*, 184; D. E. Holwerda, *The Holy Spirit and Eschatology in the Gospel of John* (Kampen: Kok, 1959) 1. S. H. Hooke, " 'The Spirit Was Not Yet,' " *NTS* 9 (1963) 379, argues for the significance of the newness of this event. For the connection of the Spirit, Jesus, and glory in the Fourth Gospel, see L. Floor, "The Lord and the Holy Spirit in the Fourth Gospel," *Neot* 2 (1968) 122–30.

314. Most scholars agree that the hour of Jesus' glorification includes his death (12:23–28); e.g., Taylor, *Atonement*, 139; Lindars, *Apologetic*, 58.

315. *Jub.* 8:12, 19; *Sib. Or.* 4:249–50 (probably late first to early-second-century C.E. Egypt); *b. Yoma* 54b; cf. Ezek 38:12; P. S. Alexander, "Notes on the 'Imago Mundi' of the Book of Jubilees," *JJS* 33 (1982) 197–213; Davies, *Land*, 7. *Ep. Arist.* 83 (cf. 115, μέση for seaports, also) places it in the midst of Judea, as does Jos., *J.W.* 3.52. Curiously, *1 Enoch* 18:2 ignores the opportunity to identify *where* the cornerstone of the earth is located, but this does not mean the tradition was unknown in that period, against *Jubilees*; *1 Enoch* 26:1 may place the middle of the earth in Jerusalem (26:2–6).

316. Some of the references in the preceding note, in addition to *b. Sanh.* 37a; *Num. Rab.* 1:4; *Lam. Rab.* 3:64 §9; *Pesiq. Rab.* 10:2; cf. P. Hayman, "Some Observations on Sefer Yesira: (2)," *JJS* 37 (1986) 176–82; P. Schäfer, "Tempel und Schöpfung," *Kairos* 16 (1974) 122–33. For the site of the temple as the "pupil of God's eye," cf. *b. Ber.* 62b. Cf. the pagan tradition in which the earth's center was at Delphi (Varro, *Lat. Lang.* 7.2.17), although Harrelson, *Fertility Cult*, 36, may be correct in citing Mesopotamian parallels.

317. *T. Kip.* 2:14; *Lev. Rab.* 20:4 (purportedly Tannaitic); *Num. Rab.* 12:4 (purportedly Tannaitic); *Pesiq. Rab Kah.* 26:4; cf. F. Böhl, "Über das Verhältnis von Shetija-Stein und Nabel der Welt in der Kosmogonie der Rabbinen," *ZDMG* 124 (1974) 253–70.

318. Besides clearer data above, cf. *3 Enoch* 22B:7 (from the throne); *Odes Sol.* 6:7–13 (to the temple). *Ep. Arist.* 88–91 speaks of an underground water system beneath the temple, no doubt part of its utopian idealization of the temple.

319. Gaston, *Stone*, 211; Hooke, "Spirit," 377–78. Some naturally see baptismal associations here (Blenkinsopp, "Quenching," 48; Cullmann, *Worship*, 82).

320. I argued this at some length in my unpublished master's thesis (including a chapter concerning Johannine vocabulary of knowledge), and hope to develop the connection in a forthcoming commentary on the Fourth Gospel with Hendrickson Publishers.

321. This was seen as a miserable state analogous to death; cf. *b. Beṣa* 32b; *p. Ketub.* 11:3 §2 (both purportedly Tannaitic); *Gen. Rab.* 71:6.

322. Blindness was often attributed to sin (*t. Ber.* 6:3; *b. Ber.* 58b; *Taʿan.* 21a; cf. Plut. *Profit by Enemies* 5, *Moralia* 88F; perhaps Qumran rules excluding those with a physical blemish, including blindness). Other maladies were also often attributed to personal sin (e.g., *Jub.* 35:10–11 with 37:5, 11; *1 Enoch* 98:5; Ps.-Philo 45:3; *m. ʾAbot* 2:7 [Hillel]; *Mek. Nezikin* 18.55ff. [Lauterbach, 3.141–42]; *Sipre Deut.* 238.3.1; *b. Ber.* 5a; *ʿAbod. Zar.* 17b (purportedly Tannaitic); *Sanh.* 107b [in Montefiore and Loewe, *Anthology*, 332]; *p. Ḥag.* 2:1 §3; *Gen. Rab.* 79:8, 80:4; *Exod. Rab.* 1:9; cf. Abrahams, *Studies* (1), 108ff.; Sanders, *Paul*, 125; Jeremias, *Theology*, 183; Bonsirven, *Judaism*, 110–11; Brown, *John*, 1.371), though this need not cover all cases (*m. ʾAbot* 4:15; references in Urbach, *Sages*, 1.443, 446). Prenatal sin on the part of the parents (Exod 20:5; *b. Ned.* 20ab; *p. Ḥag.* 2:1 §9; *Lev. Rab.* 15:5) or perhaps the fetus (Barrett, *John*, 356; cf. Greek story of Osiris and Isis consorting together in the womb before birth, Plut., *Isis* 12, *Moralia* 356A) could also lead to judgment. Among some peoples today mental inadequacies "are attributed to the action of a witch upon the fetus" (Gelfand, "Shona," 165; cf. B. Kaplan and D. Johnson, "The Social Meaning of Navaho Psychopathology and Psychotherapy," in *Magic, Faith, and Healing*, 209).

323. Noted first and foremost by J. L. Martyn, *History and Theology in the Fourth Gospel* (Nashville: Abingdon, 1968) 40; cf. also Pancaro, *Law*, 247ff.; P. J. Riga, "The Man Born Blind," *BT* 22 (1984) 168–73. J. Painter, "John 9 and the Interpretation of the Fourth Gospel," *JSNT* 28 (1986) 31–61, expands on the part of Martyn's thesis most difficult to prove methodologically, separating tradition from redaction, but with equally dubious results.

324. *B. Šebu.* 15b (condemned); Barrett, *John*, 358 (citing *t. Sanh.* 12:10); Vermes, *Jesus the Jew*, 65 (citing *b. Šabb.* 108b; *p. Šabb.* 14d; *Deut. Rab.* 5:15); Urbach, *Sages*, 1.102 (citing *b. B.Bat.* 126b); cf. *T. Sol.* 7:3. In paganism, see Bultmann, *Tradition*, 233; Aune, "Magic," 1537; Yamauchi, "Magic," 137–40. Perhaps this was considered effective because spittle was a despised substance (cf. Ps.-Philo 7:3, 12:4; 4 Ezra 6:56; *2 Bar.* 82:5; *Sipre Num.* 106.1.1; *b. Nid.* 33b, 55b [if from one unclean]; *Pesiq. Rab Kah.* 10:8), but a Tannaitic tradition suggests that Jerusalem spittle was clean (*b. Pesaḥ.* 19b), and various other substances can fulfill the same magical/healing function (Tob. 11:11–13; the blood of a white cock, 138 C.E., *CIG* 5980 in Deissmann, *Light*, 135–36; Theissen, *Miracle-Stories*, 63, 93).

325. Obedience to an "absurd" command was used as a technique in healings, both in the OT tradition (e.g., 2 Kgs 5:10–14; T. L. Brodie, "Jesus as the New Elisha," *ExpT* 93 [1981] 39–42, makes perhaps *too* much of this parallel) and the dream revelations at the temples of Asclepius (inscription of M. Julius Apellas in Grant, *Religions*, 58–59).

326. See 2 Kgs 20; A. Issar, "The Evolution of the Ancient Water Supply in the Region of Jerusalem," *IEJ* 26 (1976) 131–33; F. J. Bliss and A. C. Dickie, *Excavations at Jerusalem, 1894–1897* (London: Palestine Exploration Fund, 1898) 154–57, 191–92, 224ff. N. Shaheen, "The Siloam End of Hezekiah's Tunnel," *PEQ* 109 (1977) 107–12, argues that the pool may have originally been outside the city; but by the first century C.E., although Josephus is unclear, Siloam was certainly within the walls (D. Adan, "The 'Fountain of Siloam' and 'Solomon's Pool' in First-Century C.E. Jerusalem," *IEJ* 29 (1979) 92–100; *pace* Finegan, *Archeology of New Testament*, 114).

327. *T. Taʿan.* 1:8; cited in *p. Taʿan.* 2:1 §8, stresses its power for purification. It was also used for the ritual of the red heifer (*m. Para.* 3:2, in Davies, *Land*, 315). Kotlar, "Mikveh," 1543, observes that the pool of Siloam has been "popularly called to this day 'the *mikveh* of the high priest Ishmael.'" Bliss and Dickie, *Excavations*, 225ff., mention baths near the pool of Siloam, but provide little data of use to us here.

328. If Jeremias, *Jerusalem*, 320, is correct. B. Grigsby, "Washing in the Pool of Siloam," *NovT* 27 (1985) 227–35, sees an anticipation of 19:34 here.

329. Also Hoskyns, *Gospel*, 352, on "passed by," although not emphasizing a connection with Siloam and the feast here.

330. *World*, 69; cf. Davies, *Land*, 314–15; Bruns, *Art*, 27.

331. A common enough practice in antiquity, e.g., Plato, *Cratylus*, passim; Hierocles, *Duties* 3.39.34 (in Malherbe, *Exhortation*, 89); Marc. Aur., *Med.* 8.57; Plut., *Isis* 2, 351F and throughout Plutarch; throughout Philo (cf. A. Hanson, "Philo's Etymologies," *JTS* 18 [1967] 128–39); perhaps Exod 2:10 (cf. N. M. Sarna, *Exploring Exodus* [New York: Schocken, 1986] 32–33). Although some writers probably thought their derivations historically accurate, others (such as the rabbis and Philo) probably exercised more liberty.

332. Cf. G. G. Nicol, "Jesus' Washing the Feet of the Disciples" *ExpT* 91 (1979) 20–21. The "servant" motif here may be linked to that of Isa 53.

333. Brown, *John*, 2.550; Michaels, *John*, 231. Glasson, *Moses*, 74, cites the Jerusalem Targum for an interesting parallel, but Johannine style is sufficient to explain the double entendre here.

334. Brown, *John*, 2.551; Sanders, *John*, 306; Hoskyns, *Gospel*, 376; Fenton, *John*, 141–42. Schnackenburg, *Gospel*, 2.510, thinks this suggestion reads too much into the narrative.

335. Cf. K. Grayston, *The Johannine Epistles* (NCBC; Grand Rapids, Mich.: Eerdmans, 1984) 81.

336. Cf. Lee, *Thought*, 246–47.

337. F. F. Segovia, *Love Relationships in the Johannine Tradition* (SBLDS 58; Chico: Scholars, 1982) 124–25, 133–79, assigns the love passages of the Farewell Discourse to the *Sitz im Leben* of 1 John, differentiating them (perhaps too much) from earlier parts of the Gospel (contrast his helpful later work reading narratives as a whole). A. Lacomara, "Deuteronomy and the Farewell Discourse," *CBQ* 36 (1974) 75–77, finds the background for the love passages, as for much of the rest of the discourse, in Deuteronomy.

338. In early Judaism, the vine usually functioned as a communal symbol; Israel was both vineyard (Isa 4:2; 5:7; 27:6; Matt 21:33; *3 Bar.* 1:2; *Mek. Pisha* 1.162 [Lauterbach, 15]; *Pesiq. Rab Kah* 16:9; *Exod. Rab.* 30:17; 34:3; *Song Sol. Rab.* 7:13 §1) and vine (Ps 80:8; Hos 10:1, 4, 11–13; 14:5–8; 4 Ezra 5:23–24; Ps.-Philo 12:8–9; 23:12; 28:4; *b. Ḥul.* 92a; *Gen. Rab.* 88:5; 98:9; *Exod. Rab.* 44:1; *Num. Rab.* 8:9; *Esth. Rab.* 9:2; cf. 1QS 8.5; *2 Bar.* 39:7). Thus one thinks of the golden vine in the temple, significant enough that the pilgrims should remember it (Jos., *J.W.* 5.211; Tac., *Hist.* 5.5). Many commentators recognize the community symbol as important to John 15: e.g., D. A. Carson, *The Farewell Discourse and Final Prayer of Jesus* (Grand Rapids, Mich.: Baker, 1980) 91; Barrett, "Old Testament," 164; id., *John*, 472; Morris, *John*, 668; Fenton, *John*, 158; Strachan, *Gospel*, 176; J. A. T. Robinson, "The Destination and Purpose of St. John's Gospel," *NTS* 6 (1960) 121–22; C. van der Waal, "The Gospel according to John and the Old Testament," *Neot* 6 (1972) 36; C. J. A. Hickling, "Attitudes to Judaism in the Fourth Gospel," in *L'Évangile de Jean*, 353; Hunter, *John*, 148; id., *Message*, 78; Sanders, *John*, 337; Painter, *John*, 48. John probably does not intend the vine to evoke Sukkoth imagery (*b. Sukka* 11a; cf. 22b).

339. Only John records this, and C. H. Dodd, *Historical Tradition in the Fourth Gospel* (Cambridge: Cambridge, 1965) 133, is almost certainly wrong to view this report as unrelated to Johannine theology. I here concur with most scholars, who see symbolic significance in John's reporting the water as well as blood flowing from Jesus (although his theological use need not make the tradition ahistorical; cf. points at which Synoptic tradition corroborates the basic Johannine tradition, e.g., in 1:27, 32–33); cf. E. C. Hoskyns, "Genesis I–III and St. John's Gospel," *JTS* 21 (1919) 213 (despite the Eve allegory he finds here); M. Vellanickal, "Blood and Water," *Jeevadhara* 8 (1978) 218–30; Glasson, *Moses*, 52.

5

● ● ● ● ● ● ● ● ● ● ● ● ● ●

PENTECOST, PROPHECY, AND PROCLAMATION TO ALL PEOPLES

● ● ● ● ● ● ● ● ● ● ● ● ● ●

Luke–Acts refers to the Spirit frequently, but in most cases focuses solely on the Spirit of prophecy or inspired speech (e.g., Luke 1:15–17, 41–42, 67; 2:26; 12:12; Acts 1:2,[1] 8; 2:4, 17; 4:31; 5:32; 6:10; 7:51; 11:28; 13:2, 4, 9; 20:23; 21:4, 11), and in other cases usually on ideas more related to this activity than to moral transformation (e.g., visions and instructions like biblical prophets experienced, Acts 7:55; 8:29; 10:19, 45–46; 16:6–9; cf. 10:38; 15:28).[2] Luke 3:16 may represent the one clear exception, because following Q it reports John's contrast between Spirit and fire; but in the whole context of Luke–Acts, even this announcement becomes an announcement of the eschatological Spirit of prophecy. Because Luke's emphasis on this aspect of the Spirit is so self-evident and pervasive, a brief sample should suffice to establish the point.

As Jesus' announcement of his Spirit-anointing in Luke 4:18–19 (interpreting Isa 61:1–2; cf. Acts 10:38) is programmatic for Luke, Acts 1:8 and 2:16–21 (interpreting Joel) are programmatic for Acts.[3] An examination of Acts 1–2 demonstrates Luke's emphasis that the Spirit was sent to empower NT believers, like the prior biblical prophets, to speak God's utterances. Luke regards tongues (2:4) and prophecy (2:17) as important manifestations of this prophetic empowerment whose ultimate purpose is to bear witness of Jesus to all peoples (1:8).[4]

1. THE PROMISE OF PENTECOST
· ·

While paraphrasing differently for the sake of variation,[5] Acts 1:4–11 recapitulates Luke 24:44–53, following a practice sometimes applied in two-volume works.[6] Jesus' primary instructions to the disciples before he ascended to heaven were to wait for the empowerment of the Spirit so they could carry out Jesus' mission of proclaiming him to all peoples (Luke 24:46–49; Acts 1:4–8). The eschatological character of both the Spirit and the kingdom in the relevant circles of Judaism explains their relationship in this context (Acts 1:3–4) and why the disciples would assume that a promise concerning the Spirit implied the imminent restoration of Israel (1:6).

Yet because the biblical prophets had associated the coming of the Spirit with the restoration of Israel (e.g., Isa 44:3–4; 59:20–21; Ezek 36:27–28; 37:14; 39:28–29; Joel 2:28–3:1) and subsequent Jewish interpreters had associated this event with the time of the kingdom,[7] the disciples' question ("Are you restoring the kingdom to Israel at this time?") represents a natural one. The message of John the Baptist provided the same association; Jesus reminds them of John's message (Acts 1:4–5; cf. Luke 3:16) after teaching them about the kingdom (Acts 1:3).

Proclaiming the imminent kingdom of God and fiery judgment (Luke 3:7–9, 16–17), John the Baptist did not distinguish different aspects of the Spirit's ministry; coupled with the fire of eschatological judgment (Luke 3:9, 16–17), Spirit baptism was simply the blessing promised the righteous in the time of the kingdom. In the Baptist's ministry, "Spirit baptism" must include eschatological salvation because of its contrast with fiery judgment. But in early Judaism the title, "Holy Spirit," generally indicated also prophetic empowerment,[8] and that is the only clear sense in which it appears in all other passages in Luke–Acts.

Theologically, all of the Spirit's ministry is one package (2:38–39); but in the *experience* of the early church depicted in Luke–Acts, the prophetic empowerment dimension of the Spirit sometimes occurs subsequent to conversion (Acts 8:14–17; 19:5–6).[9] Thus the Fourth Gospel invests the experience of John 20:19–23 with the theological significance of Pentecost before closing his Gospel, but Luke, whose narrative extends into his second volume, feels free to include his Pentecost at a subsequent time.[10] For John the Baptist, his first Jewish hearers, and presumably Luke's implied audience, the main point is that the baptism in the Spirit signals the time of the kingdom.

Thus the disciples inquire when the kingdom would be restored to Israel (1:6), not grasping Luke's understanding of Isaiah's eschatological mission (cf. Acts 13:47), which involved witness to the nations as well as Spirit empowerment (Isa 43:10–11; 44:11): the kingdom must first be preached to all nations (cf. Matt 24:14; Rom 11:25–26; 2 Pet 3:9, 15; Rev 5:9) and Israel must first repent (Acts 3:19–21; Matt 23:39; Rom 11:26).[11] For Luke as for many other early Christian writers, disciples cannot know the time of God's kingdom,[12] but can in a sense hasten it by proclaiming it (1:7–8; 2 Pet 3:9, 12, 15). Jesus here declares that his followers are Isaiah's Spirit-anointed witnesses, the remnant of Israel, who would testify to the nations in the end time (1:8).[13]

The geographical expansion of 1:8 provides an outline for the progress of the Gospel in Acts,[14] and in light of the emphasis on the Gentile mission in Luke–Acts,[15] it is clear that Luke intends us to understand this in its Isaian sense: the purpose of Spirit anointing is missions. The "ends of the earth" is a general phrase[16] which could easily apply to "Ethiopia"[17] (Africa south of Egypt),[18] to Spain,[19] or to any other region viewed as standing on the perimeter of the encircling river Oceanus,[20] but which in Acts itself climaxes proleptically in Rome.[21] Luke undoubtedly intends the implications of the mission for his audience to continue beyond the close of Acts itself, however.[22]

That Jesus ascends immediately after these words, and that Luke records it, parallels the emphasis of other traditions about Jesus' final words in Matt 28:18–20; John 14–16; 20:21–23: although Jesus is going and will come again, believers will have his presence and power to enable them to proclaim his message in the meantime.[23]

Some writers cite Hellenistic parallels of heroes divinized at death;[24] but Aune has correctly pointed out the weaknesses of the parallel.[25] Others cite Jewish ascension narratives applied to figures such as Enoch, Elijah, and angels like Raphael in Tobit.[26] Most human ascents were postmortem, but some bodily ascents appear, too.[27] Many writers argue that the point in this case is less spatial than emphatic with regard to Christ's exaltation and reign;[28] this is probable, although it communicates the point particularly well in the context of both Hellenistic and apocalyptic vertical dualisms.

Because in the prophets the Spirit constituted a sign of the future kingdom, and because Jesus here links the two, it is clear that the text portrays the Spirit as a present sign of the world to come, the downpayment of his coming kingdom (cf. Eph 1:13–14; Heb 6:5).

2.   THE PROOFS OF PENTECOST

Luke sets the stage carefully for what he presents as one of the most unique moments in salvation history.[29] The location is ideal: Jerusalem (cf., e.g., Joel 2:32–3:1; MT 3:5–4:1); the state of the believers is likewise ideal: unity;[30] perhaps most significantly, the occasion is the day of Pentecost (2:1).

Some writers may overemphasize Luke's mention of Pentecost.[31] After all, he does not explicitly develop his mention of the festival in his narrative, and Diaspora readers may have been unfamiliar with its Palestinian associations. Scholars point to specific associations between the day of Pentecost and Acts 2. According to later rabbis, Pentecost was the day on which Moses received the Law from Mount Sinai, and gave it as a gift to Israel on earth.[32] Those inclined to make much of this connection point out that just as Moses had ascended to receive the gift of God's word for his people below, Jesus had ascended to receive the gift of the Spirit for his people; 2:33, 38.[33] In earlier times, Pentecost was at least celebrated as a feast of covenant renewal.[34] Yet regardless of the themes stressed by his sources, Luke's own primary point may simply be that Pentecost was one of Judaism's three great pilgrimage festivals; Jerusalem would thus be flooded with Diaspora Jews visiting from throughout the world at this time.[35]

The external signs more clearly function as divinely bestowed symbols of the impending kingdom of God. Wind (2:2) would have convinced the gathered believers that the coming age had arrived, for it symbolizes the breath of resurrection life in Ezek 37, a passage which some later rabbis naturally linked to Gen 2:7 and which may have been in the minds of some early Christian preachers (cf. John 20:22).[36]

Fire, of course, could symbolize the imminent time of the eschatological judgment (Acts 2:3). God had marked the dedications of physical temples with fire in Exod 40:34–35 and 1 Kgs 8:10–11. But both Israelite prophets and John the Baptist had repeatedly spoken of God's judgment in terms of fire (e.g., Isa 66:15; Zeph 1:18; Luke 3:9, 16–17). Jesus himself, drinking the cup of wrath, endured this baptism of fire on behalf of believers (Luke 12:49–50), and in the Gospel tradition, partakers of Christ's sufferings might still experience the purging of his fiery trials in the form of suffering for his name; cf. Mark 10:39; 1 Pet 4:12.[37] The fire, therefore, serves as a small reminder of the fire to be unleashed in God's vengeance at the end of the age.[38]

The clearest sign in Acts 2:1–12 that the power of the eschatological kingdom is erupting into history is the phenomenon of glossolalia in 2:4.[39] As noted above, the Spirit of prophecy was an eschatological phenomenon,[40] and as will be shown below, Luke recognizes speaking in unknown tongues as a form of prophetic (i.e., inspired) speech,[41] and uses this phenomenon to mark the fact that in the new era all God's people would be prophets in some sense (Joel 2:28–29).[42] The point seems to run: if Jesus' followers could be inspired to speak for God in a language that they did not know (2:4),[43] how much more would they be prepared to speak for God in a language that they did know (1:8)?

3.   THE PEOPLES OF PENTECOST

But Luke reports another eschatological sign more extensively: the remnant of the nations have gathered at Jerusalem (albeit in a proleptic sense) for the outpouring of God's Spirit. Luke allows representative spokespersons of the hearers to enumerate their places of origin.[44] Probably they were present only for the feast,[45] but what is certain is that they were Diaspora Jews from all over the Roman and Parthian worlds. Although there are different views on why precisely this listing is given, it is interesting that the places seem to correspond with the table of nations in Gen 10, using updated terms.[46] In other words, these Jewish hearers had gathered from all the nations of the known earth.

This represents another sign of the kingdom era. According to the Jesus tradition (most explicit in Matt 24:14), Christ's message had to be preached to all the nations before the end could come (cf. Mark 13:10; Acts 1:6–8; Rom 11:25–27; 2 Pet 3:9–15). In a sense, the gospel was offered to all these nations proleptically at Pentecost.[47] As in the other signs of the new age in Acts 2, this sign merely foreshadows greater events to come; but the signs leave no doubt as to the eschatological significance of Spirit-empowerment.

Unfortunately, one gets the impression from reading Acts 3–8 that perhaps the Twelve thought this proleptic sense was all that was needed: it was left to the Hellenist Christians to evangelize beyond Jerusalem (cf. 8:2)[48] and the apostles remained in Jerusalem as late as Acts 15:2! Perhaps they felt that evangelizing the nations merely meant evangelizing visiting or immigrant Diaspora Jews, of whom there were plenty in Jerusalem.

Luke develops contemporary Jewish expectations. In the end-time, representatives from all peoples would gather before the Lord (Isa 60:3–16; Zech 14:16–19; cf. Rev 7:9); in Acts 2, the Spirit had come in advance of that time to initiate the church into the eschatological unity of an ethnically reconciled, cross-cultural people of God in the midst of the present age. The church in Acts, initially divided between Jewish and Gentile believers, had some problems with this reality; but those truly obedient to the Spirit were ultimately forced to cross ethnic boundaries (8:29; 10:19–20; 11:12–18). Thus Luke intimately connects the Spirit with his theme of the Gentile mission, a theme which in Acts almost consumes the more diverse representatives of marginalized classes in the Gospel. Thus, Luke implies, those who are truly led by God's Spirit will labor on behalf of the Gentile mission.

4.   THE PROPHECY OF PENTECOST

Peter's sermon in Acts 2:14–40 clearly connects baptism in the Holy Spirit with prophetic witness and the present experience of God's future reign.[49] Luke accomplishes this purpose by having Peter respond to the first remark of the crowd, arguing that the manifestation of inspired speech (in this instance, tongues) proves that God's people have been anointed as prophets (2:17–18), and this anointing is evidence that the time of Israel's salvation has come (2:19–20), and that they can therefore be saved by calling on the Lord's name (2:21). The rest of his sermon argues that the name of the Lord (Yahweh in Joel 2:32; MT 3:5) is "Jesus of Nazareth" (Acts 2:22–38).

The crowd's two objections provide the foil for Peter's message. Peter answers the second, the accusation of drunkenness (2:13),[50] first (2:15).[51] The first question (2:12), however, becomes the occasion for his sermon. When the Diaspora Jews heard "*this* sound" (2:6), they asked, "What does *this* mean?" (2:12), in reference to the miracle of speaking in tongues.[52] Peter answers that *this* (tongues) is the fulfilment of Joel's prophecy about all Israel being anointed as prophets.[53] Lest Joel's emphasis on prophetic empowerment (prophecy, visions, and dreams) be missed, Peter adds to Joel's words the line "and they shall prophesy" in 2:18.[54] He also changes Joel's "afterward" to "in the last days" to make explicit what the context in Joel already implies: this prophecy refers to the end time; cf. Joel 3:1 (MT 4:1).[55] In Joel, the pouring forth of the Spirit, or baptism in the Spirit, is evidenced by prophetic activity; inspired speech (in this case tongues) likewise fulfills that function in Acts 2.[56] Prayer and praise in tongues, sometimes coupled with prophecy, continue to function as evidence for initial Spirit baptism at strategic points in the narrative of Acts (cf. Acts 10:45–47; 19:6).[57]

It is doubtful that Luke understands the wonders in heaven and earth, prerequisites for the end-time (2:19–20), as fulfilled in the wind and fire; nevertheless Peter makes it clear that a proleptic fulfilment of the eschatological signs has already taken place. Peter adds the word "signs" to Joel's "wonders" and explains that "signs and wonders" have occurred in Jesus' ministry, in the first verse after he finishes his quotation from

Joel (2:22).[58] "Signs and wonders," an OT motif (notable, e.g., in the exodus account, e.g., Deut 4:34; 7:19), function as a sign of God's eschatological Spirit throughout Acts.[59]

Thus, while Luke allows that the day of judgment remains future (cf. Acts 17:31), he also announces that it has broken into history in the person of Jesus of Nazareth, whose first coming has called people to give account and respond to his summoning presence by his Spirit. If that day has begun to dawn in some sense (cf. 1 Thess 5:5–6), then the rest of Joel's prophecy is true: the time has come to call on God for his eschatological deliverance (Acts 2:21). But "the Name" of God was not to be pronounced; "Adonai" or "kyrios" were substituted for the tetragrammaton, except in magical usage.[60]

On which name of the Lord were they then to call? The fact that Peter breaks off his quote of Joel here and returns to it only in 2:39[61] suggests that the rest of this sermon answers that question, expounding (in Jewish midrashic style) the last line read ("whoever calls on the LORD's name will be saved"). The name of Yahweh they must invoke is none other than "Jesus" (2:36, 38).[62]

5.   THE PROCLAMATION OF PENTECOST

After Peter recites Joel's prophecy and indicates that the outpouring of the Spirit fulfills the first lines, he must demonstrate that the final line applies to Jesus: his is the name on which people must call for salvation (cf. also 4:12). Peter begins by explaining that Jesus' death was no accident, but a divine plan executed by disobedient Israel and godless Gentiles; he suffered the pangs of death (a phrase perhaps reminiscent of "the birth pangs of the Messiah" in Jewish eschatology).[63] But the real issue that establishes Jesus' identity as Lord is not merely his death but his resurrection. Peter argues persuasively that since Ps 16 was obviously not fulfilled literally for David—he has undergone decay—it must apply instead to David's ultimate seed of promise (cf. also Acts 13:35–37).

This argument sounds close to the *pesher* statement of 2:17, but is equally legitimate in principle: Jesus' unique fulfilment of the hope of all Israel (4:2; 23:6–8; 24:15; 26:6–8) had validated that hope for David's people.[64] Peter points to the solid connection between Ps 16[65] and the Son of David tradition so central to Israel's worship (Ps 89:3 in 2:30).[66] Peter does not think here in terms of *sensus plenior*; in his view, David knew exactly what he was saying (2:30–31). Just as David was a prophet before the event, the apostles were witnesses after it.[67]

Peter then argues the second point which their anointing with the Spirit proves: what they "see and hear"[68] proves that Jesus is indeed at the right hand of God (2:33); as remarked above, most Jews believed that the Spirit would only be made available once the messianic era had arrived. David did not fulfill this prophecy of Ps 110 either (2:34), but knew his descendant would do so (2:34–35; cf. Luke 20:41–44). Linking texts by common key words (as in the rabbinic hermeneutical principle of *gezerah shavah*),[69] Peter points out that just as the Lord would be at the Messiah's right hand (Ps 16:8 in Acts 2:25), the Messiah would also figuratively be at God's (Ps 110:1 in Acts 2:34). The one who would later return to subdue his enemies (Acts 2:35) would first be enthroned with God, and called David's "Lord." In Aramaic and Greek, this is the same title as Yahweh's, which would strengthen Peter's case with his hearers. If the day of Israel's salvation has come, Israel must call on the name of God the deliverer, the forerunner who has conquered death and will soon subdue all enemies: Jesus of Nazareth.

The resurrection thus proves that Jesus is not only David's Son, the Christ, as implied in Ps 16, but also his "Lord" as in Ps 110 (2:36). Cut to the heart (2:37; cf. 5:33, 7:54) over their corporate guilt, Peter's hearers asked how to be saved (2:37; cf. 16:30; Luke 3:10, 12, 14). Peter's response demanded a clear demarcation. In his interpretation, to "call on the name of the Lord" (2:21) was to repent and be baptized in his name (2:38), the same requirements placed on Gentiles wishing to convert to Judaism.[70] This act constituted a radical statement of commitment to Christ and faith in his claims.[71]

Peter concludes by announcing that his hearers could all receive the gift of the Spirit through repentance (2:38); by this he means both conversion and, in keeping with the literary function of the Spirit in this narrative and elsewhere in Luke–Acts, the promise of prophetic empowerment.[72] But Peter also made a statement the full implications of which may have eluded him (unless he had to relearn its point in Acts 10–11); like the "all flesh" of 2:17, the "afar off"[73] of 2:39, in the larger context of Luke–Acts, includes the Gentiles who are grafted into the spiritual remnant of Israel.[74]

The phrases "and your children" and "as many as God shall call" likewise make clear that Luke does not envision the outpouring of the Spirit as a past, temporary gift; if Luke does not regard it as still available, then by his argument God's calling, the new era, and the availability of salvation must have also been retracted. In this case Luke expects his Christian audience to reject the whole point of Peter's sermon, as he reports that Peter's unrepentant Jewish hearers did. The implications of such an interpretation run totally counter to Luke's theology; clearly he assumes that Pentecost's endowment of the Spirit and dynamic manifestations of the Spirit such as glossolalia are to continue until Jesus' return. If "the last days" did in fact begin on Pentecost (2:17), and if, in the words of many scholars today, Luke's view of the kingdom is "already" as well as "not yet," Luke believes that Spirit baptism remains normative for God's community, both to Israel and to "far off" Gentiles.

Interestingly, Peter's sermon is structurally a chiasmus, and the motif of "witness" is twice connected with prophecy. Even in the subtlest way, Luke again connects Spirit anointing with evangelization of the nations.[75]

6.   THE POWER OF PENTECOST

While Luke gives attention to initial aspects of the Pentecost experience, i.e., various forms of inspired speech and evangelism, he focuses on the Spirit's evidence in transformed lives, what Paul would call the "fruit" of the Spirit. The people who responded to Peter's message persevered;[76] it may be significant that Peter in his call for baptism had refused to compromise the radical demands of the gospel (cf. Luke 9:22–26, 57–62; 12:33; 14:25–35; 18:22–30). The converts devoted themselves to the apostolic teaching and to fellowship,[77] with communal meals[78] and prayer (2:42).

The eschatological enthusiasm and awe of the first Pentecost experience did not wear off quickly. According to Acts, signs and wonders continued in the apostolic church (2:43);[79] as noted above (ch. 3), non-Christians continued to note Christian miracle-working at least into the second century. Acts assumes that such attestation should continue; many missiologists note the continuance of signs in Christian evangelism today.

Yet Pentecost issued in another kind of sign as well: believers were committed enough to one another to share with those in need (2:44). Although some theologians have tried to depict the church's primitive communalism as a failure, Luke depicts in glowing terms what was regarded as an ideal in many cultures.[80] In light of Jesus' teachings recorded in Luke (e.g., 12:13–34; 14:33) and glimpses of the social life of Christians in the rest of Acts (4:32–35),[81] there is every indication that the sharing of possessions continued.[82]

Ancient views on possessions were hardly monolithic, but in a world which typically viewed traveling sages as greedy (cf. 1 Thess 2:5; 3 John 7), those who might complain that these Christians were naive at least would not charge that they were insincere. Views on wealth varied among thinkers in the Greco-Roman world, though most people then like most people today pursued whatever material advancement was available. For the wealthy, that meant greater wealth; for most of the empire, it meant continued subsistence. Modern scholars who associate Jesus' views strictly with those of Cynic philosophers miss the diversity in both Greek and Jewish thought on wealth.

Many ancient writers expressed the worthlessness of wealth, although some such critics (like Seneca and Philo) did not object to their own possession of it.[83] Greek sages often claimed that wealth could be used positively,[84] but many praised the moral blessing of poverty[85] and condemned the danger of wealth;[86] to them, wealth appeared worthless compared to knowledge.[87] Most philosophers and moralists thus stressed the virtue of contentment.[88] Some other countercultural sages in antiquity also advocated lack of attachment to material possessions. Epictetus remarked that you can only lose what you have, so if you had had more, you would have lost more; had you had less to lose, you would have complained about not having much.[89] Unlike some philosophers, however, Jesus did not oppose possessions because he supposed them evil;[90] he merely insisted that a higher priority demanded the entire resources of one who shared the kingdom's values.

Jewish views on wealth varied similarly, usually depending on how people used wealth: some could regard wealth positively, as a sign of blessing;[91] yet many also acknowledged the spiritual dangers of wealth[92] and "love of gain,"[93] a vice also in Greek tradition.[94] Sometimes Jewish writers even contrast the uselessness of worldly wealth with the true treasure of the world to come.[95] Jewish contemporaries of the apostolic church often stressed that obedience on earth led to treasure in heaven.[96] Jesus' views, hence those of his followers, make sense against such a context, although they sometimes differ.[97] Although one first-century Jewish teacher insisted that one should value one's neighbor's property as highly as one's own,[98] nearly all Jesus' extant statements on wealth go beyond the rabbinic model; some scholars thus suggest that "closer to Qumran, Jesus disdains all earthly wealth."[99] Qumran, however, practiced a rigid communalism,[100] whereas the early Christians shared possessions voluntarily as needs arose (Acts 2:45; 4:32–35).[101] Jesus did not establish a council to enforce his teachings on possessions as at Qumran, but his views were no less countercultural and radical than Qumran's.

Of course, Acts 2:44 and 4:34 do not imply that anyone sold his or her sole place to live, but only that they sold what was in excess of their own needs when others were in need and continued to share what they kept (cf. also Luke 3:11; 12:15, 33).[102] Those who kept their homes used them for public prayer (Acts 12:12) and offered their hospitality to missionaries (16:15; 17:5; 18:2–3, 7; 21:16), the latter a practice they had learned especially from Jewish hospitality to Jewish travelers.[103] The key is that believers cared for one another and made sure no one was in need; there was enough provision in the whole community that, when distributed, everyone would have enough. (Paul later applies the same principle in dealing with the churches of Achaia helping the famine-pressed churches of Judea—2 Cor 8:14–15.) Such a radical view on possessions could not be legislated (5:4); it was the result of the eschatological enthusiasm of the Spirit in a community whose reference points were no longer possessions for status but the presence and hope of the kingdom of God. People mattered more to them than possessions did.

Acts 2:46–47 show that a further feature of the Spirit-filled community was continuing worship. In light of OT passages about the inspired worship of the prophets (e.g., 1 Sam 10:5–6; cf. 2 Kgs 3:15; Hab 3:19), especially in the temple (e.g., 1 Chron 25:1–8), we may suspect that their worship was as vibrant and inspired as that of David's temple ministers who composed the Psalms (cf. 2 Chron 29:30). It was in the context of such worship (Acts 3:1) and feeling of social concern (3:3–4) that another crucial miracle would occur (3:5–10).

Just as Jesus' baptism and commission (Luke 4:18–19) are programmatic for Jesus in Luke, Acts 2 is programmatic for the church in Acts. The church is a missionary church in the rest of Acts because they waited first to receive divine enablement. Luke's narrative examples in Acts 2 of prophetic inspiration in speech and longer-range witness of lifestyle presents his readers with the ideal model for Spirit-empowered Christianity, a lifestyle intended to display the character of the coming kingdom. The fruits of this initiation (2:42–47) provided a corporate witness to the rest of Israel and the spiritual foundation for the Gentile mission.

7.   THE PURPOSE OF PENTECOST

Throughout Acts, Luke calls the message about Jesus "the word," "the word of God," or "the word of the Lord," OT language for the Law or, more often, for the prophetic message. Visions, the Spirit's direct words to believers, and other forms of divine direction remain the normal experience of the missionary church in Acts.[104] Pentecost thus marks Luke's church as a prophetic people, a people empowered to witness by God's Spirit.

For Luke, whatever the ways in which the Spirit's empowerment is manifested, the purpose of Spirit baptism is witness (1:8). The signs of 2:1–12 are signs of the kingdom. The message of Peter stresses that God's people have been anointed as witnesses like the prophets, and the enthronement of Jesus as king at God's right hand has ushered in the time of salvation. While God's unchallenged rule over the world will be complete only at Jesus' return, Jesus' present rule in his church by the Spirit is the dynamic manifestation of the kingdom of God in this age, and this is divine empowerment for mission.

NOTES

1. On the sense here, see most convincingly Dunn, *Baptism*, 46.

2. Stronstad, *Charismatic Theology*, 35, notes that Luke retains most Markan and Q references to the Spirit and adds others; for the Spirit in Luke, with each point recurring in Acts (and the special emphasis on prophetic inspiration), see ibid., 34–48. See especially the thorough analysis of Menzies, *Pneumatology*, especially 205–77 (on Acts); his case in Luke–Acts is largely secure, even if he has been too one-sided in his evaluation of the Spirit as the Spirit of prophecy in early Judaism (ibid., 53–112). I regret that I discovered Menzies, whose research is quite thorough, only after completing the bulk of this manuscript in 1994.

3. On the connection between Luke's Jesus and the Spirit-baptized community of Acts, cf., e.g., R. L. Brawley, *Luke–Acts and the Jews* (SBLMS 33; Atlanta: Scholars, 1987) 24–25; R. F. Zehnle, *Peter's Pentecost Discourse* (SBLMS 15; Nashville: Abingdon, 1971) 128; R. F. O'Toole, "Parallels between Jesus and His Disciples in Luke–Acts," *BZ* 27 (1983) 195–212; W. Russell, "The Anointing with the Holy Spirit in Luke–Acts," *TJ* 7 (1986) 47–63; Stronstad, *Charismatic Theology*, 34–48. Luke–Acts is as much theology as Paul's letters are (see, e.g., J. R. Michaels, "Evidences of the Spirit, or the Spirit as Evidence?" in *Initial Evidence* [Peabody, Mass.: Hendrickson, 1991] 203); for a recent survey of literary approaches on Luke–Acts, see F. S. Spencer, "Acts and Modern Literary Approaches," in *The Book of Acts in Its First Century Setting* (Grand Rapids, Mich.: Eerdmans, 1993) 1.381–414.

4. I have adapted this article from an earlier treatment which has also been adapted for publication in the *A.M.E. Zion Quarterly Review* ("Pentecost, Prophecy, and Proclamation to All Peoples," *The A.M.E. Zion Quarterly Review* 108 [1, Jan. 1996] 43–66); some homiletical features (such as alliteration of points) stem from its previous use.

5. For this Lukan stylistic characteristic see H. J. Cadbury, "Four Features of Lucan Style," in *Studies in Luke–Acts*, 90–97. For paraphrase as a standard ancient writing technique, see Theon, *Progymn.* 1.93–171; cf., e.g., Epict., *Disc.* 1.9.23–25, with the Loeb note referring to Plato, *Apol.* 29C, 28E (LCL 1.70–71).

6. See Aune, *Environment*, 90 (citing Diodorus 1.42; 2.1.1–3; 3.1.1–3; 18.1.1–6). For details in the recapitulation, see Goulder, *Type and History*, 16–17. Menzies, *Pneumatology*, 198, is undoubtedly correct to suggest this "promise" of

the Spirit provides a thematic link between the volumes, but that Luke depends on pre-Lukan tradition (cf. John 20:21–23).

7. See ch. 1, above.

8. Ibid.

9. Dunn's objections in Acts 8 (e.g., Dunn, *Baptism,* 65, which declares the Samaritans' initial faith inadequate and could imply that the apostles imparted the experience of salvation through laying on of hands) are probably too ingenious to have occurred to the implied readers without clearer prompting and thus probably miss Luke's point. Cf. E. A. Russell, " 'They Believed Philip Preaching' (Acts 8.12)," *IBS* 1 (1979) 169–76; F. F. Bruce, "The Holy Spirit in the Acts of the Apostles," *Int* 27 (1973) 166–83; M. Hodges, *A Theology of the Church and Its Mission* (Springfield, Mo.: Gospel Publishing, 1977) 41; Ladd, *Theology,* 346; Menzies, *Pneumatology,* 248–60. See the exegetical cautions (to both sides) in Carson, *Exegetical Fallacies,* 46–47.

10. For several views on the relationship of the Johannine and Lukan Pentecosts, see J. A. T. Robinson, "The One Baptism," in *Twelve Studies,* 166; P.-H. Menoud, "La Pentecôte lucanienne et l'histoire," *RHPR* 42 (1962) 141–47; M. de Jonge, *Jesus: Stranger from Heaven and Son of God* (Missoula, Mont.: Scholars, 1977) 174; Dunn, "Spirit," 704; H. M. Ervin, *Conversion-Initiation and the Baptism in the Holy Spirit* (Peabody, Mass.: Hendrickson, 1984) 133–40; cf. Chrysostom, *Hom.* 86. The two-stage argument fits only Acts, probably falters in John (unless he assumes his audience's knowledge of Pentecost), and surely fails in Paul (cf. Fee, *Presence,* on the relevant Pauline texts, especially 406–7, 670, 863–64). For one discussion of the historicity of the first Pentecost experience (and the continuing experience of early Christians at minimum presupposes that some such experience was "first"), see Dunn, *Jesus and Spirit,* 135–56.

11. Cf. O. Cullmann, "Eschatology and Missions in the New Testament," in *Background and Eschatology,* 416–17; G. Baum, *The Jews and the Gospel* (London: Bloomsbury, 1961) 167. On Acts 3:19, cf. T. F. Glasson, *The Second Advent* (3d rev. ed.; London: Epworth, 1963) 155; cf. *Mekilta Pisha* 5.38ff. (Lauterbach, 1.36); *b. Sanh.* 97a–98b; ʿ*Abod. Zar.* 9b–10a (bar.); *B.Bat.* 10a; *Nid.* 13b; *Exod. Rab.* 25:12; *Lev. Rab.* 15:1; *Deut. Rab.* 3:2; *Lam. Rab.* Proem 21; *Lam. Rab.* 1:13 §41; *Song Sol. Rab.* 2:5 §3; 4:8 §3; 5:2 §2; 8:14 §1; T. W. Manson, *On Paul and John* (SBT 38; London: SCM, 1963) 23–24; Zehnle, *Pentecost Discourse,* 72.

12. Cf. Sir 4:20; *b. Sanh.* 97b; Bowman, *Samaritan Documents,* 43, 46–47; comments in Bonsirven, *Judaism,* 178; Moore, *Judaism,* 2.231; Daube, *Judaism,* 289–90; D. Ford, *The Abomination of Desolation in Biblical Eschatology* (Washington, D.C.: University Press, 1979) 28. Rabbinic Judaism held two conflicting traditions, namely, that God had appointed the time and that Israel's righteousness could hasten it (cf. Bonsirven, *Judaism,* 53); early Christians likewise accepted both these views: the time of God's coming kingdom is unknown, but the church through proclaiming and suffering can hasten the time (2 Pet 3:11–12; Rev 6:10–11). In the OT prophets the time of the Lord's day was in God's hands, but would come when Israel truly repented in the final eschatological distress.

13. On Isaiah here, see also F. F. Bruce, *Commentary on the Book of Acts* (NICNT; Grand Rapids, Mich.: Eerdmans, 1977) 39; on the Spirit for witness, cf. I. H. Marshall, "The Significance of Pentecost," *SJT* 30 (1977) 347–69; for community witness in Acts, see G. E. Ladd, *The Young Church* (New York: Abingdon, 1964) 93–94. The most thorough analysis of the witness concept in the Bible and

its context is A. A. Trites, *The New Testament Concept of Witness* (SNTSMS 31; Cambridge: Cambridge, 1977).

14. As commonly noted, e.g., H. N. Ridderbos, "The Speeches of Peter in the Acts of the Apostles" (TNTL 1961; Rushden: Hunts, 1962) 6; J. Dupont, *The Salvation of the Gentiles* (New York: Paulist, 1979) 12–13; Goulder, *Type and History*, 68.

15. Cf., e.g., J. Jervell, "Das gespaltene Israel und die Heidenvölker," *ST* 19 (1965) 68–96; S. G. Wilson, *The Gentiles and the Gentile Mission in Luke–Acts* (SNTSM 23; Cambridge: Cambridge, 1973); Dupont, *Salvation*, 11–33; F. Stagg, "The Unhindered Gospel," *RevExp* 71 (1974) 451–62; cf. S. J. Case, *The Social Origins of Christianity* (New York: Cooper Square, 1975) 179–80; J. C. O'Neill, *The Theology of Acts in Its Historical Setting* (2d ed.; London: SPCK, 1970) 75, 133.

16. E.g., Ps 67:7; 98:3; Isa 45:22; 49:6; 52:10; Crates, *Ep.* 31, to Hipparchia. For the most complete analysis of "the ends of the earth" in Lukan theology and context, see J. M. Scott, "Luke's Geographical Horizon," in *The Book of Acts in Its First Century Setting* (Grand Rapids, Mich.: Eerdmans, 1994) 2.483–544.

17. E.g., Strabo, *Geog.* 1.1.6, following Homer. Some see this idea in Acts itself; see T. C. G. Thornton, "To the End of the Earth: Acts 1:8," *ExpT* 89 (1978) 374–75. Luke may wish us to see the conversion of the African court official as the proleptic fulfillment of the southward part of the "ends of the earth" mission; see more fully Scott, "Horizon," 533–38.

18. For this meaning of "Ethiopia" in Greco-Roman literature, see especially Snowden, *Blacks in Antiquity*, passim. For Ethiopians' blackness, cf., e.g., Petr., *Sat.* 102; Sen., *Dialogues* 5.27.3; Sextus Empiricus, *Against the Ethicists* 3.43; Philo, *Leg.* 2.67; *Apoc. Mos.* 35:4–36:3; *Gen. Rab.* 73:10; 86:3.

19. E.g., *Greek Anth.* 4.3.84–85; Davies, *Land*, 279, thinks Acts 1:8 points to Spain. *1 Clem.* 5:5–7 sees Paul's mission as extending to Spain in the extremity of the "west"; see Grant, "Introduction," 16 (Lake and Cadbury, *Commentary*, 9, finds Rome there, but regards it as irrelevant to this verse).

20. Cf., e.g., Homer, *Iliad* 14; *1 Enoch* 33:2–3; 24:1–2; 25:1 36:2. Hellenistic geography (or its broader ancient Near Eastern source) was known in Palestine; cf. *Jub.* 8:12 (especially *OTP* 2.72 n. *i*); 1QM 10.13 ("circle of the waters"). If a Semitic original stood behind an original logion in Acts 1:8, it could refer to the "end of this world" (*ʿolam*), indicating a mission until the end (cf. Matt 24:14); but an *ʾeretz* or equivalent better fits this context as well as Lukan theology as a whole—not to mention the Isaian source from which Luke's language probably ultimately derives (cf. Acts 13:47; the geographical phrase is not uncommon in the Bible, e.g., Ps 67:7; Isa 49:6; cf. also 1QM 1.8).

21. Rome is the "end of the earth" in *Pss. Sol.* 8.16; Italy is the "west" in *Sib. Or.* 4.102–3. But *Psalms of Solomon* may provide merely an example of the much broader sense of "ends of the earth" as found in the Septuagint (cf. Bruce, *Acts: Greek Text*, 71; id., *Commentary*, 39 n. 30); "In contrast to Jerusalem, the . . . center of the worship of the true God, the ends of the earth represent the pagan nations" (Dupont, *Salvation*, 18–19; cf. Luke 24:47).

22. Cf. Brawley, *Jews*, 39.

23. On the principle of the Spirit as Jesus' "successor" in view of Jewish parallels, see Keener, "Pneumatology," 261–64, especially comments on the genre of "parallel lives" (developed most notably in Plutarch; see C. B. R. Pelling,

"Plutarch's Method of Work in the Roman Lives," *JHS* 99 [1979] 74–96; for comparison with Lukan historiography, cf. Kee, *Miracle*, 190); cf. also U. B. Müller, "Die Parakletenvorstellung im Johannesevangelium," *ZTK* 71 (1974) 57–60; D. B. Woll, *Johannine Christianity in Conflict: Authority, Rank, and Succession in the First Farewell Discourse* (SBLDS 60; Chico, Calif.: Scholars Press, 1981) 48, 79–80; H. Windisch, *The Spirit-Paraclete in the Fourth Gospel* (Philadelphia: Fortress, 1968) 5; F. Gryglewicz, "Die Aussagen über den Heiligen Geist im vierten Evangelium," *SNTU* 4 (1979) 45–53; Stronstad, *Charismatic Theology*, 20–21.

24. Diog. Laert., *Lives* 8.2.68; C. H. Talbert, "The Concept of Immortals in Mediterranean Antiquity," *JBL* 94 (1975) 419–36; Talbert, *Gospel*, 39.

25. D. E. Aune, "The Problem of the Genre of the Gospels," in *Gospel Perspectives* 2.47–48. The contrast of E. Haenchen, *The Acts of Apostles* (Philadelphia: Westminster, 1971) 149, is far less significant.

26. Cf. 1 Macc 2:58; Tob 12:20–22; *1 Enoch* 14:8; 39:3; *2 Enoch* 3:1–2 J; 67:1–3; *Jos. and Asen.* 17:8/6 v.1.; *T. Ab.* 4, 8–10, 15A; 4, 7–8, 10, 12B; *Gr. Ezra* 5:7; *Pesiq. Rab.* 1:3; e.g., P. Palatty, "The Ascension of Christ in Luke-Acts," *Biblebhashyam* 12 (2, 1986) 100–117. For a full survey of a variety of ascent traditions, see A. F. Segal, "Heavenly Ascent in Hellenistic Judaism, Early Christianity, and Their Environment," in *ANRW* 2.23.2.1333–94 (although he depends too heavily on structuralist models, e.g., pp. 1337–40). On comparisons with Elijah in view of the whole of Luke–Acts, cf., e.g., Stronstad, *Charismatic Theology*, 44; earlier in Gospel tradition, cf. V. K. Robbins, *Jesus the Teacher* (Minneapolis: Fortress, 1992) 54.

27. See, e.g., the examples in Segal, "Ascent," passim; this was especially common in Hellenistic ascents, but also *T. Ab.* 20A; 14B.

28. J. A. T. Robinson, "Ascendancy," *ANQ* 5 (1964) 5–9, stresses ascendancy rather than change of location; P. Benoit, *Jesus and the Gospels* (New York: Seabury, 1974) 2.209–53, refers to a spiritual world. Luke undoubtedly understands the ascension as a prefiguring of the parousia (1:11), the language of which appears here by way of allusion to Dan 7:13; see H. Flender, *St Luke: Theologian of Redemptive History* (London: SPCK, 1967) 93; H. J. Cadbury, "Acts and Eschatology," in *Background and Eschatology*, 309; cf. discussion of various biblical sources in P. A. Van Stempvoort, "The Interpretation of the Ascension in Luke and Acts," *NTS* 5 (1958) 38; Lake and Cadbury, *Commentary*, 9; P. S. Minear, *Christian Hope and the Second Coming* (Philadelphia: Westminster, 1954) 119ff.. Nevertheless, there is no reason to think Luke interpreted the narrative event only symbolically, *pace* L. Goppelt, *Apostolic and Post-Apostolic Times* (Grand Rapids, Mich.: Baker, 1980) 18. Too much in Luke's narrative (from Luke 9:51 forward; cf. 24:37–43; Acts 1:3) hinges on its corporeality; cf. C. H. Talbert, *Literary Pattern, Theological Themes, and the Genre of Luke–Acts* (SBLMS 20; Missoula, Mont.: SBL, 1974) 112, though without an anti-docetic tone. Nor is it likely that it is a purely Lukan construction, *pace* Goulder, *Type and History*, 182–83; cf. John 20:17; the possibly non-Lukan tradition in Mark 16:19.

29. All was ripe for the dawn of the new era, as many scholars observe, e.g., G. Herrthorst, "The Apologetic Aspect of Acts 2:1–13," *Scripture* 9 (1957) 33–43; Ladd, *Church*, 34–52; A. M. Hunter, *The Gospel according to Paul* (Philadelphia: Westminster, 1966) 36; O. Cullmann, *Early Christian Worship* (Philadelphia: Westminster, 1953) 21; W. Barclay, "Acts ii.14–40," *ExpT* 70 (1958–59) 198–99;

C. F. Sleeper, "Pentecost and Resurrection," *JBL* 84 (Dec. 1965) 390; Ridderbos, "Speeches," 12; Cadbury, "Eschatology," 300; cf. Bruce, *History,* 206.

30. Cf. *Mekilta Bahodesh* 1.108ff. (Lauterbach, 2.200); on the Sinai motif here, see Dupont, *Salvation,* 38–39. The crowds could indicate the temple courts (Bruce, *Commentary,* 56; Lake and Cadbury, *Commentary,* 17, think it is difficult to know), but this is an unusual use of "house" for Luke (Haenchen, *Acts,* 168 n. 1; cf. E. F. F. Bishop, *Apostles of Palestine* (London: Lutterworth, 1958) 32–33. But a house with an "upper room" (1:13) would no doubt be in the upper city, hence near the temple. A normal upper room could not fit 120 people at one time (on which cf. Lake and Cadbury, *Commentary,* 10; F. J. Foakes-Jackson, *The Acts of the Apostles* [MNTC; London: Hodder & Stoughton, 1931] 6; which could limit the number present to the apostles and women—Dupont, *Salvation,* 37; cf. Lake and Cadbury, *Commentary,* 17); but cf. *m. Šabb.* 1:4; *t. Soṭa* 13:3; *b. Soṭa* 48b; *Qidd.* 40b; *Sanh.* 11a.

31. E. g., R. R. Williams, *Acts of the Apostles* (London: SCM, 1965) 40; cf. the greater cautions in Sleeper, "Pentecost," 390; S. G. Wilson, *Gentiles,* 126–27; Dupont, *Salvation,* 35. Crowds always gathered for the feast (Jos., *Ant.* 17.254, *J.W.* 1.253; *b. Yoma* 21a; *Song Sol. Rab.* 7:2 §2) when, as in Acts 2:1, the days were "fulfilled" (cf. Dupont, *Salvation,* 36; Haenchen, *Acts,* 167 n. 2; Bruce, *Greek Text,* 81; R. J. Knowling, "The Acts of the Apostles," in *The Expositor's Greek Testament* [Grand Rapids, Mich.: Eerdmans, 1979] 2.71; though cf. Luke 24:49).

32. *B. Pesaḥ.* 68b (cited in Bruce, *History,* 208; Goulder, *Type and History,* 150); *Exod. Rab.* 31:16; cf. various scholars (some also citing Qumran evidence on covenant renewal), e.g., Foakes Jackson, *Acts,* 10; M. Weinfeld, "Pentecost as a Festival of the Giving of the Law," *Immanuel* 8 (1978) 7–18; M. Delcor, "Das Bundesfest in Qumran und das Pfingstfest," *Bibel und Leben* 4 (1963) 188–204; cf. B. H. Charnov, "Shavuot, 'Matan Torah,' and the Triennial Cycle," *Judaism* 23 (1974) 332–36; J. Potin, "Approches de la fête juive de la Pentecôte," *Foi et Vie* 80 (1981) 91–95; Dunn, *Baptism,* 48.

33. In some late traditions, Moses ascended as far as heaven to receive Torah (e.g., *Exod. Rab.* 28:1; 47:5; *Pesiq. Rab.* 20:4; cf., e.g., Lincoln, *Paradise,* 157, for other texts).

34. See *Jub.* 6:17; B. Noack, "The Day of Pentecost in Jubilees, Qumran, and Acts," *ASTI* 1 (1962) 89; R. Le Déaut, "Savu'ot och den kristna pingsten i NT," *SEÅ* 44 (1979) 148–70; Flusser, *Judaism,* 48; Black, *Scrolls and Origins,* 92; cf. Zehnle, *Pentecost Discourse,* 62; James Parker III, "The Concept of Apokatastasis in Acts: A Study in Primitive Christian Theology" (Th.D. diss., University of Basel, 1978) 58–61; cf. Harrelson, *Fertility Cult,* 25. On Pentecost and Jubilee (cf. Luke 4:18–19) in this connection, see Patte, *Hermeneutic,* 149.

35. Jos., *Ant.* 17.254; *J.W.* 1.253; *Song Sol. Rab.* 7:2 §2; cf. the hyperbole in *b. Yoma* 21a. Some other scholars are also skeptical of a Sinai connection in Acts 2, e.g., R. F. O'Toole, "Acts 2:30 and the Davidic Covenant of Pentecost," *JBL* 102 (1983) 245–58; Sleeper, "Pentecost," 390; Menzies, *Pneumatology,* 229–44; cf. F. Cocchini, "L'evoluzione storico-religiosa della festa di Pentecoste," *RivB* 25 (1977) 297–326; Ps.-Philo, *Bib. Ant.* 11:1.

36. Cf. Keener, "Pneumatology," 317–18; J. Grassi, "Ezekiel xxxvii.1–14 and the New Testament," *NTS* (1965) 164; Bruce, *Commentary,* 54. Others connect wind with Sinai imagery (Dupont, *Salvation,* 39–41; Stronstad, *Charismatic Theology,* 58) or see in it merely a symbol of the divine presence (Knowling, "Acts,"

72). The phenomena of 2:2–3, taken together, may be reminiscent of Sinai (A. P. O'Hagan, "The First Christian Pentecost," *SBFLA* 23 [1973] 50–66; Goulder, *Type and History*, 151), but an eschatological connection is most obvious (cf. J. Abri, "The Theological Meaning of Pentecost," *Kator Shin* [1965] 133–51). Strong winds were common in Jerusalem (Bishop, *Apostles*, 31–32), but Luke's language demands a special significance.

37. For a discussion of the baptism of fire in Lukan theology, see Dunn, *Baptism*, 9–12; Mattill, *Luke and Last Things*, 6–7, 217, 222–24. Some others see Sinai imagery in the language of Acts 2:3 (Dupont, *Salvation*, 41–42; Zehnle, *Pentecost Discourse*, 116–18; Stronstad, *Charismatic Theology*, 58), which might play a subsidiary role.

38. Luke's explicit future eschatology in Acts is rare by comparison with Matthew or Mark, especially in Acts (Acts 1:11; 3:20–21; 10:42; 17:31; 24:15; 26:6–8); Pentecost functions for Luke as proleptic or partially realized eschatology, inaugurating the interim mission of witness.

39. Scholars generally concur that this event or one like it occurred (cf. C. H. Dodd, *The Apostolic Preaching and Its Developments* [London: Hodder & Stoughton, 1936] 58; Conzelmann, *Theology*, 37–38). This fits the character of OT prophetic speech but is a unique kind (Bruce, *Commentary*, 56; contrast W. Neil, *The Epistle of Paul to the Thessalonians* [MNTC; London: Hodder & Stoughton, 1950] 129). The experience marked a new stage in salvation history but was not wholly new in character (cf. D. P. Fuller, *Gospel and Law* [Grand Rapids, Mich.: Eerdmans, 1980] 173–74.

40. Tongues has eschatological significance in other passages also (cf. Hamilton, *Spirit and Eschatology*, 36). Its eschatological character for Luke precludes its disappearance in this era in his thinking (for Paul, cf. 1 Cor 13:8–13; P. Elbert, "Face to Face: Then or Now?" [paper presented to the annual meeting of the Society for Pentecostal Studies, Springfield, Mo., 1977]; H. E. Dollar, "A Cross-Cultural Theology of Healing" (D.Miss. diss., Fuller Theological Seminary School of World Mission, 1981) 48; G. D. Fee, *The First Epistle to the Corinthians* (NICNT; Grand Rapids, Mich.: Eerdmans, 1987) 600; Carson, *Exegetical Fallacies*, 77–78; R. Banks and G. Moon, "Speaking in Tongues: A Survey of the New Testament Evidence," *Churchman* 80 [4, 1966] 278–94). Goulder's view that glossolalia had ceased by Luke's time (*Type and History*, 77) thus misses Luke's point; Luke, regarding glossolalia as evidence of the Spirit's coming, uses it to demonstrate disciples' reception of the Spirit.

41. For tongues as inspired speech here, see Dupont, *Salvation*, 51; Knowling, "Acts," 72–73; A. D. Palma, "*Apophthengomai*: Declare under Inspiration," *Advance* (1978) 31 (the term often connotes this, e.g., Diog., *Ep.* 21 in Cynic Epistles; but not always, e.g., Diog. Laert., *Lives* 1.88).

42. Some other Jewish thinkers also held this view; see especially the discussion of the eschatological Spirit in Davies, *Paul*, 208–17.

43. Although some have proposed pagan parallels to the phenomenon (e.g., C. G. Williams, "Glossolalia as a Religious Phenemenon: 'Tongues' at Corinth and Pentecost," *Religion* 5 [1975] 16–32; cf. Scholem, *Jewish Gnosticism*, 33; J. G. Griffiths, "Some Claims of Xenoglossy in the Ancient Languages," *Numen* 33 [1986] 141–69; J. H. Van Halsema, "De historische betrouwbaarheid van het Pinksterverhaal," *NTTid* 20 [1966] 218), the parallels are scanty and not particularly relevant (see the thorough analysis of Aune, "Magic," 1549–51; cf. id.,

Prophecy, 31, 199, 230). Further, the biblical accounts suggest contrasts more than similarities (R. H. Gundry, " 'Ecstatic Utterance'?" *JTS* 17 [1966] 299–307); Luke understands tongues as genuine languages (cf. also 1 Cor 13:1). Meeks, *Urban Christians,* 119, 232 n. 27 (following Felicitas Goodman's cross-cultural studies) thinks the biblical accounts represent the same phenomenon as modern glossolalia (contrast, e.g., K. Preus, "Tongues: An Evaluation from a Scientific Perspective," *CTQ* 46 [1982] 277–93).

44. By transcending language barriers glossolalia can symbolize unity; see Ladd, *Church,* 56; cf. Dupont, *Salvation,* 52, who also thinks that it alludes to the dividing of tongues at Sinai in rabbinic legend (59).

45. Although the wording suggests those who had settled in Jerusalem (cf. Acts 6:1; Dupont, *Salvation,* 55; Knowling, "Acts," 73), temporary dwellers would fit Luke's point better. They were certainly Jewish (whether by birth or conversion; Bruce, *Greek Text,* 83; *Commentary,* 60–61), and while different theories for the source of this information have been proposed (cf. K. Stendahl, *Paul among Jews and Gentiles and Other Essays* [Philadelphia: Fortress, 1976] 118–19; M. Dibelius, "Style Criticism of the Book of Acts," in *Studies in the Acts of the Apostles* [London: SCM, 1956] 15; Knox, *Church of Jerusalem,* 32–33), there is nothing intrinsically improbable about the account.

46. On the places, see, e.g., De Ridder, *Discipling,* 10 n. 33; R. A. Kraft, "Judaism on the World Scene," in *Catacombs,* 82–83; J. Neusner, *There We Sat Down* (Nashville: Abingdon, 1972) 32, 48; Bruce, *Commentary,* 61 n. 21; id., *Greek Text,* 84; F. J. Foakes Jackson and K. Lake, "The Dispersion," in *Beginnings,* 1.151; for Cyrene and Libya, Jos., *Ant.* 16.160, 162; *J.W.* 7.437; for Mesopotamia, Jos., *Ant.* 18.310; for Egypt, cf. Sandmel, *Beginnings,* 257; Foakes Jackson and Lake, "Dispersion," 151; for Rome, E. A. Judge, *The Social Pattern of the Christian Groups in the First Century* (London: Tyndale, 1960) 55; among Arabs, cf. Guillaume, *Islam,* 12. Some attribute this specific listing to ancient zodiacal geography (Grant, "Introduction," 15; Zehnle, *Pentecost Discourse,* 121); while this could account for "every nation under heaven" and would fit Jewish synagogue zodiacs and angelology, the OT background is better, particularly given Luke's *heilsgeschichtliche* orientation (see Goulder, *Type and History,* 151–55, 158; C. F. D. Moule, *Christ's Messengers* [New York: Association, 1957] 24).

47. See Dupont, *Salvation,* 58; Martin Dibelius, "The Acts of the Apostles as an Historical Source," in *Studies,* 106; Robinson, "Baptism," 167; Foakes Jackson, *Acts,* 11; cf. Bruce, *Commentary,* 64. If the Sinai motif is present, one may compare the universalistic theme that motif bore in Judaism: cf. Knox, *Gentiles,* 95; Bruce, *Commentary,* 59f; Moule, *Messengers,* 24. Others have suggested, sometimes in addition, a reversal of the Tower of Babel events of Gen 11: Bruce, *Commentary,* 64; Stendahl, *Paul,* 117; J. C. Kirby, *Ephesians: Baptism and Pentecost* (Montreal: McGill, 1968) 117; Moule, *Messengers,* 23. On Babel, cf. Jos., *Ant.* 1.116–18.

48. This is particularly likely if the Hellenist-Jewish Christians (Diaspora immigrants) were scattered; cf. M. Simon, *St. Stephen and the Hellenists in the Primitive Church* (New York: Longmans, Green, 1958) 28; Dunn, *Baptism,* 67 n. 47; Koester, *Introduction,* 2.91.

49. It is not possible here to explain in detail the oft-debated issue of historicity of ancient speeches; suffice it to say that Luke probably adapts the language of the original speech, as was customary when information was available. Acts

demonstrates consistent use of devices such as interruption (G. H. R. Horsley, "Speeches and Dialogues in Acts," *NTS* 32 [1986] 609–614) and common structural patterns (cf., e.g., Goulder, *Type and History*, 83; Zehnle, *Pentecost Discourse*, 19–23). Scholars who have noted such patterns have sometimes assumed them to indicate wholesale secondary composition; see J. T. Townsend, "The Speeches in Acts," *ATR* 42 (2, April 1960) 150–59; Eduard Schweizer, "Concerning the Speeches in Acts," in *Studies in Luke–Acts* (Nashville: Abingdon, 1966) 208–16; Dibelius, *Studies in Acts*, 138–85; id., *Paul* (Philadelphia: Westminster, 1953) 11; id., *Tradition*, 16–18). But this assumption need not be the case (Ridderbos, "Speeches," 9, compares Jesus' Matthean discourses). Robinson, *Twelve Studies*, 139–53, pointed to theological divergences in some speeches (Acts 3 reflecting very primitive features), suggesting prior tradition. In favor of some tradition behind the speeches may be Luke's historiographic style elsewhere (M. B. Dudley, "The Speeches in Acts," *EvQ* 50 [1978] 147–55), awkward expressions uncharacteristic of Lukan style (W. W. Gasque, "The Speeches of Acts: Dibelius Reconsidered," in *Dimensions in New Testament Study*, 248–49), possible Semitisms (cf. Dodd, *Developments*, 17–19; R. A. Martin, "Syntactical Evidence of Aramaic Sources in Acts i–xv," *NTS* 11 [1964] 59; D. F. Payne, "Semitisms in the Book of Acts," in *Apostolic History and the Gospel* [Grand Rapids, Mich.: Eerdmans, 1970] 134–50; A. Ehrhardt, *The Acts of the Apostles* [Manchester: Manchester, 1969] 1), and possible reminiscences of the speakers' own style at points (Selwyn, *First Peter*, 33–36; J. Munck, *The Acts of the Apostles* [AB 31; Garden City, N.Y.: Doubleday, 1967] xliii–xliv; Doeve, *Jewish Hermeneutics*, 176; though cf. the practice of *prosopopoia* noted in Theon, *Progymn.* 8).

50. I have explored the relationship among ancient concepts of drunkenness, inspiration, loss of control, and the religious experience of the mysteries in Keener, *Paul, Women & Wives*, 259–65.

51. That wine would have some alcohol content by Pentecost was inevitable, the grape vintage having come around the end of summer or early autumn (cf. N. Lewis, *Life in Egypt under Roman Rule* [Oxford: Clarendon, 1983] 125, for the time in Egypt).

52. The responses of the crowds ("wonder," cf. *T. Ab.* 3, 6 A) in early Christian narratives usually follow miracles (cf., e.g., Theissen, *Miracle Stories*, 161), and in Luke is often a prelude to faith (Dupont, *Salvation*, 53).

53. For the programmatic significance of Joel 2 here, see L. T. Johnson, *The Literary Function of Possessions in Luke–Acts* (SBLDS 39; Missoula, Mont.: SBL, 1977) 41; for views on sermon structure cf. Lindars, *Apologetic*, 361; Zehnle, *Pentecost Discourse*, 27–28. On the rabbinic use of Joel 2 (MT 3), see *Deut. Rab.* 6:14; Zehnle, *Pentecost Discourse*, 29–30; Lake and Cadbury, *Commentary*, 22; Davies, *Paul*, 216.

54. Not uncommonly noted; see Menzies, *Pneumatology*, 221, 224.

55. On "the last days" here, cf. Johnson, *Function of Possessions*, 44; Patte, *Hermeneutic*, 138; Oscar Cullmann, *Christ and Time* (tr. F. V. Filson; Philadelphia: Westminster, 1950) 156; Ridderbos, "Speeches," 13; cf. 1 Tim 4:1; 2 Tim 3:1; Heb 1:2; 1 Pet 1:20; 2 Pet 3:3; Ignatius *Ep. to Eph.* 11; but note that in the Hebrew Bible it usually represents the day of YHWH (cf. Isa 2:2; Mic 4:1; for a broader usage, see Daniel 2:28; 10:14). For the *pesher*, cf. D. L. Tiede, *Prophecy and History in Luke–Acts* (Philadelphia: Fortress, 1980) 89; Longenecker, *Exegesis*, 100; cf. Dodd, *Preaching*, 21.

56. Haenchen, *Acts,* 179, also notes the identification of prophecy and tongues here. On the case as a whole, see particularly Ladd, *Theology,* 345, which is worth quoting: "Peter explained that this marvelous power to speak in other tongues *(glossolalia)* was the outward sign of the fulfilment of Joel's prophecy that God would pour out his Holy Spirit on all his people. In Joel this promise was associated with the Day of the Lord; Peter asserts that this event has now occurred in history . . . "

57. See also Dunn, *Jesus and Spirit,* 189–90, noting that tongues seems to accompany every instance of initial reception of the Spirit in Acts, probably even (by implication) in Acts 8. Dunn does argue, however, that Luke, who is not explicit about tongues in Acts 8 and elsewhere emphasizes other dramatic expressions of the Spirit's empowerment—such as praise (10:45), prophecy (19:6), and boldness (4:8, 31)—does not present tongues as a *necessary* evidence of baptism in the Holy Spirit.

58. Barclay, "Acts ii," 198, sees the signs as fulfilled at the cross, but it is more likely they were fulfilled in Jesus' ministry, given the context; cf. also G. N. Stanton, *Jesus of Nazareth in New Testament Preaching* (Cambridge: Cambridge, 1974) 16, 72; Johnson, *Function of Possessions,* 44–45; Lake and Cadbury, *Commentary,* 23; Zehnle, *Pentecost Discourse,* 34.

59. For the importance and structural employment of signs and wonders in Acts, cf., e.g., G. B. Caird, *The Apostolic Age* (London: Duckworth, 1955) 64; Goulder, *Type and History,* 106–7; J. Fenton, "The Order of the Miracles Performed by Peter and Paul in Acts," *ExpT* 77 (1966) 381–83; Dollar, "Cross-Cultural Theology of Healing," 10, 47. Throughout Acts miracles are one of the main means of drawing crowds to hear the gospel (2:5–41, 43; 3:11–4:4; 5:10–11, 12–16; 6:3, 5, 8–10; 8:6–7, 13, 39–40; 9:34–35, 40–42; 13:9–12; 14:3, 9; 15:12; 16:25–34; 19:11–20; 28:5–6, 8–10; cf. 8:18; 9:1–9; 10:3, 44–48; 12:23–24; 16:18; 20:10–12); the writer explicitly views these signs as continuing God's work in ancient Israel (7:36) and Jesus (2:19, 22; 10:38). For visions and similar supernatural guidance in evangelism, etc., see 2:17; 9:1–10; 10:10; 16:9; 22:17; 23:11; they seem to have been a normal part of early Christian experience (cf. 2 Cor 12:1); on literary forms for vision reports, see John S. Hanson, "Dreams and Visions in the Graeco-Roman World and Early Christianity," *ANRW* 2 (Principat), 23.2.1395–1427. The motif "seen and heard" (2:33) often relates to signs, sometimes to the ultimate sign of the resurrection (Luke 7:22; Acts 2:33; 4:20; 8:6; 22:15; 28:26–28).

60. On the use of "the Name," cf., e.g., R. N. Longenecker, "Some Distinctive Early Christological Motifs," *NTS* 14 (1968) 533–36; Bietenhard, " Ὄνομα," 268–69.

61. As noted, e.g., by Dupont, *Salvation,* 22; Haenchen, *Acts,* 184 n. 5; Zehnle, *Pentecost Discourse,* 34.

62. In general, see W. C. Van Unnik, "Jesus: Anathema or Kyrios (1 Cor. 12:3)," in *Christ and Spirit in the New Testament* (Cambridge: Cambridge, 1973) 123; D. Juel, "Social Dimensions of Exegesis: The Use of Psalm 16 in Acts 2," *CBQ* 43 (1981) 544–45; Lake and Cadbury, *Commentary,* 22; Knowling, "Acts," 81; cf. Ladd, *Theology,* 338–41; id., *Church,* 50–51; Hunter, *Paul,* 65; id., *Message,* 41; Hengel, *Son,* 77, 80; contrast Bultmann, *Theology,* 1.124.

63. Haenchen, *Acts,* 183, calling Luke "inept," misses the Hebraic concept of corporate responsibility; for "lawless," cf. Lake and Cadbury, *Commentary,* 23; Bruce, *Commentary,* 70; on the divine purpose, cf. Taylor, *Atonement,* 18. On the

pangs, cf. Doeve, *Jewish Hermeneutics*, 170–71; Bruce, *Greek Text*, 92; id., *Commentary*, 71 n. 56; Lindars, *Apologetic*, 39; Haenchen, *Acts*, 180; Lake and Cadbury, *Commentary*, 23; Mattill, *Luke and Last Things*, 32; cf. Poly., *Phil.* 1.

64. The Sadducees, who differed from most other Jews in rejecting this future hope (23:8; cf. Jos., *Ant.* 18.16; polemic in *b. Sanh.* 90a, bar.; *Šabb.* 152b, v.1.; for a different view, cf. S. T. Lachs, "The Pharisees and Sadducees on Angels," *GCAJS* 6 [1977] 35–42), were especially perturbed by the Christian proclamation of the resurrection, since for the Christians this represented not merely a theoretical hope for the future, but an attested fact of recent history (4:2; Ladd, *Theology*, 324; id., *The Last Things* [Grand Rapids, Mich.: Eerdmans, 1978] 79; cf. Caird, *Age*, 83; Haenchen, *Acts*, 214–15).

65. See Juel, "Dimensions"; Lake and Cadbury, *Commentary*, 23–24; cf. Ladd, *Theology*, 336–37; A. Schmitt, "Ps 16, 8–11 als Zeugnis der Auferstehung in der Apg," *BZ* 17 (1973) 229–48 (reading LXX against MT; Doeve, *Jewish Hermeneutics*, 1045, shows dependence on LXX, but LXX may read MT correctly here). Cf. *Midr. Ps.* 57:3.

66. On the Son of David as Messiah (or messianic line) tradition, see, e.g. (some more explicit than others), Ps 18:50; 132:10–12; Isa 9:6–7; 11:1; 16:5; 55:3–4; Jer 17:25; 22:4; 23:5; 30:9; 33:15–26; Ezek 34:23–24; 37:24–25; Hos 3:5; Amos 9:11; Zech 12:7–8; *Pss. Sol.* 17:21; 4QFlor.; *p. Sukka* 5:1 §7; *Gen. Rab.* 88:7; *Song Sol. Rab.* 2:13 §4; *Pesiq. Rab.* 15:14/15; see Fitzmyer, *Essays*, 113–26.

67. Witness is a frequent motif in Acts; cf. 1:8; 3:15; 4:33; 5:32; 10:39; 13:31; 22:15, 18, 20; 23:11; 26:16.

68. A characteristic Lukan phrase; cf. Luke 7:22; Acts 4:20; 8:6; 22:15. In this case, "this" refers again to tongues.

69. *Gezerah shavah* is a frequent interpretive technique, e.g., in *Mek. Pisha* 5:103 (Lauterbach, 1.41); *Mek. Nezikin* 10:15f, 26, 38, 17:17 (3.75–77, 130); *b. Ber.* 9a, 35a; *Šabb.* 64a; *Naz.* 48a; *Qidd.* 15a, 35b; *Ter.* 16a; *Ker.* 5a; *Nid.* 22b–23a; *Roš Haš.* 3b, 34a; *Sanh.* 40b, 51b; *Zebaḥ.* 18a, 49b–50b; *Menaḥ.* 76a; *Giṭ.* 49a; *B.Qam.* 25b; *Exod. Rab.* 1:20; Paul uses it, e.g., in Rom 4. Others note its use here; e.g., Longenecker, *Exegesis*, 97. The more specifically Hellenistic background proposed by W. R. G. Loader, "Christ at the Right Hand," *NTS* 24 (1978) 199–217, is thus improbable. Christians continued to apply Ps 110 to Jesus (e.g., Eph 1:20–21; Heb 1:13; Justin Martyr, *Dialogue with Trypho* 32; *First Apology* 45), but later rabbis applied it to Abraham (*Midr. Ps.* 110; for Hezekiah, cf. Williams, *Justin Martyr*, 175).

70. See, e.g., De Ridder, *Discipling*, 107; Abrahams, *Studies* (1), 45; R. P. Martin, *The Worship of God* (Grand Rapids, Mich.: Eerdmans, 1982) 127; in more detail, see ch. 2, above. Given the baths (strictly for ritual purposes) on the Temple Mount (and perhaps those of hospitably disposed homeowners in the nearby Upper City), there would be no shortage of water for the mass baptisms implied in Acts 2:38, 41 (cf. Avigad, *Discovering Jerusalem*, 139–43; Meyers and Strange, *Archaeology*, 25–26, 55; *Josephus*, ed. Cornfeld, 272; Mazar, "Excavations," 52; *m. Mid.* 1:9; *Neg.* 14:8; *Para.* 3:7).

71. It should be mentioned that baptism "in Jesus' name" appears only with the passive, not with the active, uses of the verb in Acts. In other words, this refers to Christian baptism as distinct from Jewish baptism (cf. Jewish repentance in God's "name"; *Jos. and Asen.* 15:7; cf. *1 Enoch* 48:7), and to one's own confession

of faith (2:21; 22:16), not to a formula the baptizer utters over the person being baptized.

72. As noted above, this is theologically one package, even if believers in Acts did not always *experience* the full reality of their empowerment at the moment of their conversion; cf. 8:12–17, discussed briefly above.

73. The phrase comes from Isa 57:19, and is used in Eph 2:17 for the Gentile remnant. See Kirby, *Ephesians*, 157 (noting that rabbis in the late text *Num. Rab.* 8:4 apply the text to proselytes); cf. Tob 13:11.

74. E.g., Dupont, *Salvation*, 23. It is Luke and his audience, rather than Peter and his, that can catch the allusion to Gentiles here (Haenchen, *Acts*, 184, citing Acts 22:21); even later rabbis could apply an explicit quotation of Isa 57:19 to Jews (*b. Ber.* 34b).

75. See the appendix for this structure, borrowed from K. E. Bailey, *Poet and Peasant* (Grand Rapids, Mich.: Eerdmans, 1976) 65–67.

76. For a study of the theme in Lukan theology in general, see S. Brown, *Apostasy and Perseverance in the Theology of Luke* (Rome: Pontifical Biblical Institute, 1969); cf. Luke 22:21–23, 31–32.

77. The Greek term undoubtedly implies "sharing" possessions, like its cognate in 2:44. See G. Panikulam, *Koinonia in the New Testament* (AnBib 85; Rome: Biblical Institute, 1979) 123–24, 129.

78. I.e., the love feast, probably inseparable at this time from the Lord's Supper. Cf. Justin Martyr, *First Apology* 67; J. Jeremias, *The Sermon on the Mount* (Philadelphia: Fortress, 1963) 20; F. J. A. Hort, *Judaistic Christianity* (Grand Rapids, Mich.: Baker, 1980) 43; Derrett, *Jesus's Audience*, 39.

79. Cf. Dollar, *Theology of Healing*; e.g., Acts 3:6–4:12; 4:30; 5:12; 6:8; 8:6–7; 9:32–42; 12:7–10; 13:10; 14:3, 8–9; 16:18, 26; 19:11–12; 20:10–12; 28:8–9, besides other leadings by the Spirit (e.g., Acts 8:29; 10:3–6, 10–16, 19; 11:12). Luke clearly envisions signs and wonders as normative in the missionary endeavor. Paul's undisputed letters also mention them, in three cases appealing to his audience's eyewitness testimony of what he describes (Rom 15:19; 1 Cor 12:10; 2 Cor 12:12; Gal 3:5).

80. Cf. Malherbe, *Social Aspects*, 90; Dupont, *Salvation*, 88–90; M. Hengel, *Property and Riches in the Early Church* (Philadelphia: Fortress, 1974) 8–9, 31. The meaning of "fellowship" *(koinonia)* here is financial as well as spiritual; see Panikulam, *Koinonia*, 123–24, 129; Dupont, *Salvation*, 86–87, 99; cf. Lampe, *Seal*, 51, for the fellowship of the Spirit. Among the Essenes, see 1QS 1; Philo, *Prob.* 76, 85–86; *Hypoth.* 11:4–5; Jos., *J.W.* 2.122; Fitzmyer, *Essays*, 284–88; id., "Jewish Christianity," 243; Haenchen, *Acts*, 234; D. R. A. Hare, *The Theme of Jewish Persecution of Christians in the Gospel according to St. Matthew* (Cambridge: Cambridge, 1967) 15–16; cf. Jeremias, *Theology*, 222–23; Vermes, *Jesus and Judaism*, 128. The entire section (2:41–47) probably serves an apologetic function, emphasizing the virtue of the earliest Christian community (see G. E. Sterling, " 'Athletes of Virtue': An Analysis of the Summaries in Acts (2:41–47; 4:32–35; 5:12–16)," *JBL* 113 [4, Winter 1994] 679–96).

81. Some of the phenomena in Acts 2 may be best explained by the practice Jesus' disciples learned while following him; see Betz, *Jesus*, 73; Munck, *Acts*, 22; Hengel, *Property*, 32–33; Goppelt, *Apostolic Times*, 50. On the rest of Judaism, however, cf. L. T. Johnson, *Sharing Possessions* (Philadelphia: Fortress, 1981) 133; on Jos., *Ant.* 18.12, see the note in the Loeb edition.

82. The practice of community continued well into the next century; Justin Martyr, *First Apology* 14; Tert., *Apol.* 39:11–12; Luc., *Peregrinus* 13; see also Hengel, *Property,* 42–43; R. J. Sider, *Rich Christians in an Age of Hunger* (Dallas: Word, 1990) 81–82; cf. E. Troeltsch, *The Social Teaching of the Christian Churches* (tr. O. Wyon; London: Allen & Unwin, 1931) 1.59. Among later Christian revival movements, Wesley favored the model of economic distribution found in Acts 2 (T. W. Jennings, Jr., *Good News to the Poor* [Nashville: Abingdon, 1990] 25, 97–117, and esp. 111–16). Dunn, *Jesus and Spirit,* 161, argues that the communal charity program presupposed in Acts 2 is historically probable; "the discontent and division implied in Acts 6.1 was hardly an invention of Luke."

83. On Philo, cf. T. E. Schmidt, "Hostility to Wealth in Philo of Alexandria," *JSNT* 19 (1983) 85–97; F. G. Downing, "Philo on Wealth and the Rights of the Poor," *JSNT* 24 (1985) 116–18; D. L. Mealand, "The Paradox of Philo's Views on Wealth," *JSNT* 24 (1985) 111–15; id., "Philo of Alexandria's Attitude to Riches," *ZNW* 69 (1978) 258–64.

84. Plato, *Laws* 9.870AB; Diog. Laert., *Lives* 6.6.95; Sen., *De Benef.* 6.3.1–2.

85. Sen., *Ep. Lucil.* 4; 17:4; *Dialogues* 2.13.3; 5.2.1; 12.10.10–11.2; Diog. Laert., *Lives* 6.9.104; *Pythagorean Sentences* 17 in Malherbe, *Moral Exhortation,* 110.

86. Lucret., *Nat.* 5.1105–42; Sen., *Dialogues* 5.33.1; Luc., *Wisdom of Nigrinus*; Heraclitus, *Ep.* 8, to Hermodorus; Plut., *Educ.* 8, *Moralia* 5D.

87. Dio Chrys., *79th Disc.* §6; Diog. Laert., *Lives* 2.115.

88. Horace, *Ode* 2.18; 3.16; Mart., *Epig.* 4.77.2; Juv., *Sat.* 14.303–4; Cic., *Tusc. Disp.* 5.31–32; Diogenes, *Ep.* 46, to Plato; Sen., *Ep. Lucil.* 61.4; Plut., *Love of Wealth, Moralia* 523C–28B; Diog. Laert., *Lives* 6.1.11; 10.1.11; Dio Chrys., *6th Disc.*; Marc. Aur., *Med.* 5.1, 14; 8.45.1.

89. Epict., *Disc.* 1.18.15–16.

90. Cf. Lucret., *Nat.* 5.1105–42; Sen., *Dialogues* 5.33.1.

91. *Sib. Or.* 3.783; *Ep. Arist.* 204–5; *m.* *'Abot.* 4:9; *Qidd.* 4:14; cf. *Sipre Deut.* 352.1.1.

92. *1 Enoch* 63:10; 94:8; 96:4; 97:8; 1QS 10.18–19; 11.2; CD 4.17; 8.7; Sir 31:8–11; *Ep. Arist.* 211; Jos. *J.W.* 2.250; *m.* *'Abot.* 2:7; *Sipre Deut.* 43.3.1–2, 5; 318.1.1–4.

93. *Sib. Or.* 3.189, 234–36, 640–42; Ps.-Phoc. 42–47; *1 Enoch* 108:8; *T. Levi* 17.11; *T. Judah* 17.1; 18.2; 19.1; Sir 31:5–8; Philo, *Spec.* 1.281.

94. Isoc., *Demon.* 9, 27–28, *Or.* 1; Plato, *Hipparchus,* 225A–32C; Plut., *Bravery of Women,* Chiomara, *Moralia* 258E; Diog. Laert., *Lives* 4.48; 6.2.50; Theon, *Progymn.* 3.91–92.

95. *1 Enoch* 100:6; *m.* *'Abot.* 4:1; 6:9; *b.* *B.Meşi'a.* 114b; *Gen. Rab.* 67:5; cf. *Herm. Vis.* 1.1. True wealth could thus include contentment; cf. *m.* *'Abot.* 4:1; L. Finkelstein, *Akiba: Scholar, Saint, and Martyr* (New York: Atheneum, 1970) 187.

96. 4 Ezra 7:77; *2 Bar.* 14:12; 24:1; 44:14; cf. Tob 4:8–10; 12:8; *T. Levi* 13:5; *Qoh. Rab.* 1:3 §1; *Song Sol. Rab.* 7:14 §1; Marmorstein, *Merits,* 20; Sandmel, *Beginnings,* 190–91; Guelich, *Sermon,* 327. Second-century tradition declared that a first-century king who gave to the poor dispensed with earthly treasures to gain heavenly ones (*t.* *Pe'a* 4:18); a later teacher insisted that if his disciples sought wealth in this world they would lose their reward in the world to come, where alone their labor in the law would be rewarded (Montefiore and Loewe, *Anthology,* 205–6).

97. For Jesus, the treasure is not merely *in* heaven (Matt 19:21); it represents the kingdom of heaven (13:44). Idolaters who value Mammon too highly to abandon it for what Jesus values will have no place in his kingdom (19:21–30; cf. Luke 14:33).

98. *M. ʾAbot.* 2:12; cf. Exod 22:6; 23:4–5; Deut 22:1–4.

99. Meier, *Matthew,* 65; cf. Flusser, *Judaism and Origins of Christianity,* 194–95.

100. 1QS 6.22–23; Jos., *Ant.* 18.20; *J.W.* 2.122; Philo, *Prob.* 85–86; *Hypoth.* 11.4–5; Mealand, "Community."

101. See Fitzmyer, "Jewish Christianity," 243. Scholars propose various reasons for why Jesus' rhetoric in Luke is stronger than the church's behavior in Acts (S. Arai, "Individual und Gemeindeethik bei Lukas," *AJBI* 9 [1983] 88–127; D. B. Kraybill and D. M. Sweetland, "Possessions in Luke–Acts," *PRS* 10 [1983] 215–39), but given Jesus' own home base in Capernaum and earlier in Nazareth, Jesus' rhetoric may be radical not so that all believers immediately sell all possessions on conversion, but that they relinquish all valuing and ownership of them and hence stop acquiring possessions of merely personal value.

102. Cf. Dunn, *Jesus and Spirit,* 161, emphasizing the imperfect tense.

103. On hospitality in the NT and in Judaism, see Koenig, *Hospitality.*

104. E.g., Acts 8:29; 9:10–16; 10:3–16, 19–20; 11:5–10, 12. Joel's prophecy serves programmatically in this regard (Acts 2:17), although Luke does not emphasize dreams; of the four Gospels only Matthew does so.

6

• • • • • • • • • • • • • •

CONCLUSION:

CLOSING WORDS

• • • • • • • • • • • • • •

In our opening chapter we noted that early Jewish pneumatology involved primarily two streams of thought: an emphasis on purification (particularly found in Essene circles) and a more pervasive emphasis on inspiration (whether in prophecy or in specially revealed insights). Both emphases recur frequently in early Christian texts, although they do not exhaust the categories of early Christian pneumatology.

In seeking to compare the understanding of the Spirit in early Christian narrative texts, we focused on several sample texts that provided windows into the larger narrative worlds they depicted. First, we examined John's proclamation of the Spirit-baptizer in Mark's introduction, in a pericope that functions programmatically for the Second Gospel. This passage can approximate the prophetic dimension of Jewish pneumatology, although extending the prophetic mission beyond inspired speech to a more pervasive conflict with demonic forces. The special Markan emphasis is that the Spirit also empowers disciples to suffer, to participate in Jesus' cross.

Second, we examined sample passages in Matthew, which included a purificatory function in Spirit baptism but continued to emphasize the prophetic dimension. Probably due to the polemical situation which then engaged Matthew's audience (and early Jewish Christians in general), Matthew's pneumatology includes a sustained apologetic that distinguishes the Spirit-empowered ministry of Jesus and his followers from sorcery. Jesus is a *true* prophet rather than a "deceiver," and genuine signs of the Spirit identify him as Messiah and Kingdom-bringer.

Third, we examined samples of the Fourth Gospel's "water motif," in which John contrasted Christian experience with traditional Jewish rituals involving water. The most explicit passages supporting this motif emphasize the Spirit's activity in Christian experience, underlining the purificatory aspect of the Spirit's work. (John emphasizes the prophetic element particularly in the Farewell Discourses.) In John the Spirit marks the true spokespersons of God and again serves a polemical function within the narrative.

Finally, we examined the Pentecost experience of Acts 1–2, which functions programmatically for the book of Acts. Here the pneumatological emphasis is explicitly prophetic, and points to eschatological fulfillment and consequently functions as evidence that Jesus is Lord and Christ. The transformed community also testifies to the reality of their pneumatic experience, hence functions apologetically to vindicate their faith.

Each of the above writers addressed a milieu which shared some particular expectations about the Spirit's activity. Early Christianity was no less distinctive than other groups of its day, but was not so distinctive as to remain unintelligible to the broader Jewish community. Although the Christians were less "sectarian" than a wilderness community like Qumran, they did share many elements of its conception of the Spirit (purification as well as prophecy). Like the Qumran community which believed that the presence of the Spirit indicated the nearness of the eschatological time and thus vindicated their agendas, the early Christians often appealed to the Spirit's activity among them for apologetic or polemical purposes, an appeal that defined rather than abrogated the boundaries for its own community.

At the same time, the Christian movement was readily distinguishable from other groups of its day, sharing among themselves some understandings of the Spirit that separated them from others. While early Christian experience of the Spirit did fulfill basic contemporary expectations of the Spirit's work, it spilled beyond those categories into other categories identifiable within and beyond the Hebrew Bible. Because it is not this book's purpose to trace these other dimensions of the Spirit's activity in early Christianity, we mention three of them only briefly. Especially Matthew, Mark, and Luke–Acts indicate that many of those empowered by the Spirit would not only prophesy but, like some Israelite prophets, perform signs and wonders. John and Paul especially emphasize moral transformation that causes believers to share Christ's divine character. John in particular emphasizes the nature of intimate communion with Christ not usually specified in Jewish texts roughly contemporary with his Gospel (except in terms of ecstasy).

Despite the differing (not necessarily incompatible) emphases of different early Christian authors, however, two common features permeate much of the Spirit material in those texts surveyed in this book. First, many of the writers employ their portrayals of the Spirit's activity in a polemical or apologetic manner. To some degree, this usage reflects the hostile situation in which Jesus' followers found themselves in the second half of the first century. They also, however, point back to the matrix in which the Jesus movement began: like Mark, the early Christians learned to connect their sufferings with those of Jesus, and had to understand pneumatic experience in the shadow of the cross. Second, these polemical texts point to an understanding of the Spirit that appears also in texts directed only toward problems within the Christian community (e.g., 1 Cor 12:3; 1 John 4:2–3): the true Spirit points to Jesus. Many features of early Christian pneumatology may be distinctive, but the most basic is its inseparability from the characteristic which specifically demarcated Christians from others—early Christian Christology.

APPENDIX:
THE LITERARY STRUCTURE
OF PETER'S SERMON

A Jesus whom you crucified
  B Is Lord and Christ
    C David says, "The Lord . . . is at my right hand"
    MEN . . . IT IS NECESSARY TO SPEAK BOLDLY . . .
      D David died and was buried . . .
        E Being therefore a prophet, and knowing
          F That God had sworn an oath to him . . .
            G one of his descendants on his throne
              H he foresaw and spoke
                I of Christ's resurrection
                  J not abandoned to Hades
                  J' did not see corruption
                I' This Jesus God raised up
              H' Of that we are all witnesses
            G' Being exalted at God's right hand
          F' Having received . . . the promise of the Spirit
        E' He has poured out this which you see and hear
      D' For David did not ascend into the heavens
    C' But he himself says, "The Lord said to my Lord, Sit at my right hand"
    ASSUREDLY THEREFORE LET ALL THE HOUSE OF ISRAEL KNOW
  B' That God has made Him Lord and Christ
A' This Jesus whom you crucified[1]

Most significant for the present study are the subtle parallels in E/E′ and H/H′, which connect OT prophecy first with the baptism in the Holy Spirit and second with the NT apostolic witness. Both these connections support the thesis emphasized in this essay.

NOTE

1. This chiasmus has been adapted from Bailey, *Poet and Peasant*, 65–66; he also provides other structural clues for the exegesis of Peter's sermon.

SELECT BIBLIOGRAPHY
OF SOURCES CITED

The original, complete bibliography of sources cited included 1100 entries, but has been shortened here to save space.

Abelson, Joshua. *The Immanence of God in Rabbinical Literature.* 2d ed. New York: Hermon Press, 1969. 1st ed., with different pagination, London, 1912.

Abrahams, I. *Studies in Pharisaism and the Gospels.* 1st series. Prolegomenon by Morton S. Enslin. Library of Biblical Studies. New York: KTAV Publishing House, 1967; reprint of Cambridge: Cambridge University Press, 1917.

_____. *Studies in Pharisaism and the Gospels.* 2d series. Cambridge: Cambridge University Press, 1924.

Abri, J. "The Theological Meaning of Pentecost." *Kator Shin* (1, 1965) 133–51.

Adan, David. "The 'Fountain of Siloam' and 'Solomon's Pool' in First-Century C.E. Jerusalem." *Israel Exploration Journal* 29 (2, 1979) 92–100.

Allen, Willoughby C. "St. John vii.37, 38." *Expository Times* 34 (1922–23) 329–30.

Allison, Dale C. "The Living Water (John 4:10–14; 6:35c; 7:37–39)." *St. Vladimir's Theological Quarterly* 30 (2, 1986) 143–57.

Amaru, Betsy Halpern. "Land Theology in Josephus' *Jewish Antiquities.*" *Jewish Quarterly Review* 71 (4, April 1981) 201–29.

Applebaum, Shim'on. *Jews and Greeks in Ancient Cyrene.* Studies in Judaism in Late Antiquity 28. Leiden: E. J. Brill, 1979.

Arnold, Clinton E. *Ephesians: Power and Magic: The Concept of Power in Ephesians in Light of Its Historical Setting.* Society for New Testament Studies Monograph 63. Cambridge: Cambridge University Press, 1989.

Artemidori Daldiani. *Onirocriticon Libri V.* Bibliotheca Scriptorum Graecorum et Romanorum Teubneriana. Leipzig: B. G. Teubneri, 1963.

"Assyrian Oracles and Prophecies." Trans. Robert H. Pfeiffer. In *Ancient Near Eastern Texts Relating to the Old Testament.* 2d ed. Ed. J. B. Pritchard. Pages 449–450. Princeton, N.J.: Princeton University Press, 1955.

Aune, David Edward. *The Cultic Setting of Realized Eschatology in Early Christianity.* Supplements to Novum Testamentum 28. Leiden: E. J. Brill, 1972.

_____. "Magic in Early Christianity." In *Aufstieg und Niedergang der römischen Welt* Pages 1507–1557. II.(Principat) 23.2.

_____. *The New Testament in Its Literary Environment.* Library of Early Christianity 8. Philadelphia: Westminster Press, 1987.

_____. "The Problem of the Genre of the Gospels: A Critique of C. H. Talbert's *What Is a Gospel?*" In *Gospel Perspectives.* Vol. 2: *Studies of History and Tradition in the Four Gospels.* Ed. R. T. France and David Wenham. Pages 9–60. Sheffield: JSOT Press, 1981.

_____. *Prophecy in Early Christianity and the Ancient Mediterranean World.* Grand Rapids, Mich.: Eerdmans, 1983.

_____. "The Use of προφήτης in Josephus." *Journal of Biblical Literature* 101 (3, September 1982) 419–21.

Avigad, Nahman. *Discovering Jerusalem.* Nashville: Thomas Nelson Publishers, 1980.

Avi–Yonah, Michael. *Hellenism and the East: Contacts and Interrelations from Alexander to the Roman Conquest.* Jerusalem: Institute of Languages, Literature and the Arts, Hebrew University; University Microfilms International, 1978.

Baer, Richard A., Jr. *Philo's Use of the Categories Male and Female.* Arbeiten zur Literatur und Geschichte des Hellenistischen Judentums 3. Leiden: E. J. Brill, 1970.

Bagatti, Bellarmino. *The Church from the Circumcision.* Jerusalem: Franciscan Printing Press, 1971.

Bailey, Kenneth Ewing. *Poet and Peasant: A Literary Cultural Approach to the Parables in Luke.* Grand Rapids, Mich.: Eerdmans, 1976.

Bamberger, Bernard J. "The Changing Image of the Prophet in Jewish Thought." In *Interpreting the Prophetic Tradition: The Goldman Lectures 1955–1966.* Ed. Harry M. Orlinski. Pages 301–23. Cincinnatti: Hebrew Union College Press, 1969; New York: KTAV Publishing House, 1969.

————. *Proselytism in the Talmudic Period.* 2d ed. Foreword by Julian Morgenstern. New York: KTAV Publishing House, 1968.

Barclay, William. "Acts ii.14–40." *Expository Times* 70 (1958–59) 196–99.

Barnard, L. W. "Matt. III.ll//Luke III.16." *Journal of Theological Studies* 8 (1, 1957) 107.

Barrett, C. K. *The Holy Spirit and the Gospel Tradition.* London: SPCK, 1966.

Basser, Herbert W. "The Rabbinic Attempt to Democratize Salvation and Revelation." *Studies in Religion/Sciences Religieuses* 12 (1, 1983) 27–33.

Bates, William H. "Born of Water." *Bibliotheca Sacra* 85 (338, April 1928) 230–36.

Baumgarten, Joseph M. "The Exclusion of 'Netinim' and Proselytes in 4QFlorilegium." *Revue de Qumran* 8 (1, June 1972) 87–96.

Baumgarten, Joseph, and Menahem Mansoor. "Studies in the New *Hodayot* (Thanksgiving Hymns)—II." *Journal of Biblical Literature* 74 (3, September 1955) 188–95.

Beasley-Murray, G. R. *Baptism in the New Testament.* Grand Rapids, Mich.: Eerdmans, 1962.

————. "The Holy Spirit, Baptism, and the Body of Christ." *Review and Expositor* 63 (Spring 1966) 177–85.

Belkin, Samuel. *Philo and the Oral Law: The Philonic Interpretation of Biblical Law in Relation to the Palestinian Halakah.* Harvard Semitic Series 11. Cambridge: Harvard University Press, 1940.

Belleville, Linda L. " 'Born of Water and Spirit': John 3:5." *Trinity Journal* 1 (2, Fall 1980) 125–41.

Best, Ernest. *The Temptation and the Passion: The Markan Soteriology.* Society for New Testament Studies Monograph 2. Cambridge: Cambridge University Press, 1965.

————. "The Use and Non-Use of Pneuma by Josephus." *Novum Testamentum* 3 (3, October 1959) 218–25.

Betz, Otto. *Der Paraklet Fürsprecher im häretischen Spätjudentum, im Johannes-Evangelium, und in neu gefundenen gnosticischen Schriften.* Arbeiten zur Geschichte des Spätjudentums und Urchristentums 2. Leiden/Köln: E. J. Brill, 1963.

Black, Matthew. *An Aramaic Approach to the Gospels and Acts.* 3d ed. Oxford: Clarendon Press, 1967.

————. *The Scrolls and Christian Origins.* London: Thomas Nelson & Sons, 1961.

Black, Matthew, ed. *The Scrolls and Christianity: Historical and Theological Significance.* London: SPCK, 1969.

Blackburn, Barry L. " 'Miracle Working ΘΕΙΟΙ ΑΝΔΡΕΣ' in Hellenism (and Hellenistic Judaism)." In *Gospel Perspectives.* Vol. 6: *The Miracles of Jesus.* Ed. David Wenham and Craig Blomberg. Pages 185–218. Sheffield: JSOT Press, 1986.

Blackman, Aylward M. "Purification (Egyptian)." In *The Encyclopedia of Religion and Ethics.* Ed. James Hastings. 10.476–82. Edinburgh: T. & T. Clark, 1908–26.

Blenkinsopp, Joseph. "John VII.37–9: Another Note on a Notorious Crux." *New Testament Studies* 6 (1, October 1959) 95–98.

————. "The Quenching of Thirst: Reflections on the Utterance in the Temple, John 7:37–9." *Scripture* 12 (18, 1950) 39–48.

Blidstein, Gerald. "4Q Florilegium and Rabbinic Sources on Bastard and Proselyte." *Revue de Qumran* 8 (3, March 1974) 431–35.

Bliss, Frederick Jones, and Archibald Campbell Dickie. *Excavations at Jerusalem, 1894–1897.* London: Committee of the Palestine Exploration Fund, 1898.

Böhl, Felix. "Über das Verhältnis von Shetija-Stein und Nabel der Welt in der Kosmogonie der Rabbinen." *Zeitschrift der Deutschen Morgenländischen Gesellschaft* 124 (2, 1974) 253–70.

Bonneau, Norman R. "The Woman at the Well—John 4 and Genesis 24." *Bible Today* 67 (October 1973) 1252–59.

Bonsirven, Joseph. *Palestinian Judaism in the Time of Jesus Christ.* New York: Holt, Rinehart & Winston, 1964.

Borg, Marcus J. *Jesus: A New Vision (Spirit, Culture, and the Life of Discipleship).* San Francisco: Harper & Row, Publishers, 1987.

Borgen, Peder. *Bread from Heaven: An Exegetical Study of the Concept of Manna in the Gospel of John and the Writings of Philo.* Leiden: E. J. Brill, 1965.

————. "God's Agent in the Fourth Gospel." In *Religions in Antiquity: Essays in Memory of Erwin Ramsdell Goodenough.* Studies in the History of Religions. Supplements to Numen 14. Ed. Jacob Neusner. Pages 137–48. Leiden: E. J. Brill, 1968.

Boring, M. Eugene. "How May We Identify Oracles of Christian Prophets in the Synoptic Tradition? Mark 3:28–29 as a Test Case." *Journal of Biblical Literature* 91 (December 1972) 501–21.

————. "The Influence of Christian Prophecy on the Johannine Portrayal of the Paraclete and Jesus." *New Testament Studies* 24 (1, October 1978) 113–23.

————. *Sayings of the Risen Jesus: Christian Prophecy in the Synoptic Tradition.* Society for New Testament Studies Monograph 46. Cambridge: Cambridge University Press, 1982.

Bornkamm, Günther. "Der Paraklet im Johannesevangelium." In *Festschrift Rudolf Bultmann zum 65. Geburstag überreicht.* Pages 12–35. Stuttgart: W. Kohlhammer Verlag, 1949.

Botha, F. J. "*Ebaptisa* in Mark i. 8." *Expository Times* 64 (9, June 1952) 268.

Bowman, John. "Prophets and Prophecy in Talmud and Midrash." *Evangelical Quarterly* 22 (2, April 1950) 107–14; (3, July 1950) 205–20; (4, October 1950) 255–75.

Braun, François-M. "La vie d'en haut." *Revue des Sciences Philosophiques et Théologiques* 40 (1956) 3–24.

Brawley, Robert L. *Luke–Acts and the Jews: Conflict, Apology, and Conciliation.* Society of Biblical Literature Monograph 33. Atlanta: Scholars Press, 1987.

Brodie, Thomas L. "Jesus as the New Elisha: Cracking the Code." *Expository Times* 93 (2, November 1981) 39–42.

Broer, Ingo. "Noch einmal: Zur religionsgeschichtlichen 'Ableitung' von Jo 2,1–11." *Studien zum Neuen Testament und seiner Umwelt* 8 (1983) 103–12.

Brown, Raymond E. "The Dead Sea Scrolls and the New Testament." In *John and Qumran.* Ed. James H. Charlesworth. Pages 1–8. London: Geoffrey Chapman Publishers, 1972.

Brownlee, William H. "A Comparison of the Covenanters of the Dead Sea Scrolls with Pre-Christian Jewish Sects." *Biblical Archaeologist* 13 (3, September 1950) 50–72.

Bruce, F. F. "The Holy Spirit in the Acts of the Apostles." *Interpretation* 27 (2, 1973) 166–83.

_____. "Holy Spirit in the Qumran Texts." *Annual of Leeds University Oriental Society* 6 (1966) 49–55.

_____. "The Spirit in the Apocalypse." In *Christ and Spirit in the NT: Studies in Honour of C. F. D. Moule.* Ed. Barnabas Lindars and Stephen S. Smalley. Pages 333–44. Cambridge: Cambridge University Press, 1973.

Bryan, Christopher. "Shall We Sing Hallel in the Days of the Messiah? A Glance at John 2:1–3:21." *Saint Luke's Journal of Theology* 29 (1, December 1985) 25–36.

Büchsel, D. Friedrich. *Der Geist Gottes im Neuen Testament.* Gütersloh: Bertelsmann, 1926.

Bull, Robert J. "An Archaeological Context for Understanding John 4:20." *Biblical Archaeologist* 38 (1, March 1975) 54–59.

Bull, Robert J., and G. Ernest Wright. "Newly Discovered Temples on Mt. Gerizim in Jordan." *Harvard Theological Review* 58 (2, 1965) 234–37.

Bultmann, Rudolf. *Theology of the New Testament.* 2 vols. Trans. Kendrick Grobel. New York: Charles Scribner's Sons, 1951.

Burge, Gary M. *The Anointed Community: The Holy Spirit in the Johannine Tradition.* Grand Rapids, Mich.: Eerdmans, 1987.

Burkert, Walter. *Ancient Mystery Cults.* Cambridge: Harvard University Press, 1987.

_____. *Greek Religion.* Trans. John Raffan. Cambridge: Harvard University Press, 1985.

Burkert, Walter, et al. "Orphism and Bacchic Mysteries: New Evidence and Old Problems of Interpretation." In *The Center for Hermeneutical Studies in Hellenistic and Modern Culture, 28th Colloquy.* Ed.

W. Wuellner. Berkeley, Calif.: Center for Hermeneutical Studies in Hellenistic and Modern Culture, 1977.

Burnett, Fred W. "Philo on Immortality: A Thematic Study of Philo's Concept of *palingenesia.*" *Catholic Biblical Quarterly* 46 (3, July 1984) 447–70.

Burney, C. F. "The Aramaic Equivalent of ἐκ τῆς κοιλίας in Jn. VII 38." *Journal of Theological Studies,* 1st ser., 24 (93, October 1923) 79–80.

Carcopino, Jérôme. *Daily Life in Ancient Rome: The People and the City at the Height of the Empire.* Ed. Henry T. Rowell. Trans. E. O. Lorimer. New Haven: Yale University Press, 1940.

Chariton. *Charitonis Aphrodisiensis: De Chaerea et Callirhoe Amatoriarvm Narrationvm Libri Octo.* Oxford: Clarendon Press; London: Humphrey Milford, 1938.

Charlesworth, James H. "Christian and Jewish Self-Definition in Light of the Christian Additions to the Apocryphal Writings." In *Jewish and Christian Self-Definition.* 3 vols. Ed. E. P Sanders. 2.27–55. Philadelphia: Fortress Press, 1980–82.

_____, ed. *The Old Testament Pseudepigrapha.* 2 vols. Garden City, N.Y.: Doubleday: 1983–85.

Charnov, Bruce H. "Shavuot, 'Matan Torah,' and the Triennial Cycle." *Judaism* 23 (3, Summer 1974) 332–36.

Chernus, Ira. "Individual and Community in the Redaction of the Hekhalot Literature." *Hebrew Union College Annual* 52 (1981) 253–74.

Chevallier, Max–Alain. *Esprit de Dieu, paroles d'hommes: Le rôle de l'esprit dans les ministères de la parole selon l'apôtre Paul.* Bibliothèque Théologique. Neuchatel, Switz.: Éditions Delachaux et Niestlé, 1966.

_____. *L'Esprit et le Messie dans le bas-judaïsme et le Nouveau Testament.* Études d'Histoire et de Philosophie Religieuses 49. Paris: Presses Universitaires de France, 1958.

_____. "Le souffle de Dieu dans le judaïsme, aux abords de l'ère chrétienne." *Foi et Vie* 80 (1, January 1981) 33–46.

_____. *Souffle de Dieu: le Saint-Esprit dans le Nouveau Testament.* Vol. 1: *Ancien Testament, hellénisme et judaïsme, la tradition synoptique, l'oeuvre de Luc.* Le Point Théologique 26. Paris: Éditions Beauchesne, 1978.

Cocchini, F. "L'evoluzione storico-religiosa della festa di Pentecoste." *Rivista Biblica* 25 (3, 1977) 297–326. (*NTA* 23.297.)

Coetzee, J. C. "Life (Eternal Life) in St. John's Writings and the Qumran Scrolls." *Neotestamentica* 6 (1972) 48–66.

Cohen, Boaz. *Jewish and Roman Law: A Comparative Study.* 2 vols. New York: Jewish Theological Seminary of America, 1966.

Cohen, Shaye J. D. "Conversion to Judaism in Historical Perspective: From Biblical Israel to Postbiblical Judaism." *Conservative Judaism* 36 (4, Summer 1983) 31–45.

————. *From the Maccabees to the Mishnah.* Library of Early Christianity 7. Philadelphia: Westminster Press, 1987.

Collins, John J. *The Sibylline Oracles of Egyptian Judaism.* Society of Biblical Literature Dissertation 13. Missoula, Mont.: Society of Biblical Literature, 1972.

Coppens, J. "Le don de l'Esprit d'après les textes de Qumrân et le quatrième Évangile." In *L'Évangile de Jean: Études et Problèmes.* Recherches Bibliques 3. Pages 209–23. Louvain: Desclée de Brouwer, 1958.

Corpus Inscriptionum Iudaicarum: Recueil des inscriptions juives qui vont du IIIe siècle avant Jésus-Christ au VIIe siècle du notre ère. 3 vols. Ed. P. Jean-Baptiste Frey. Rome: Pontifical Institute of Christian Archaeology, 1936–52.

Corpus Papyrorum Judaicarum. 3 vols. Vols. 1–2, ed. Victor A. Tcherikover, with Alexander Fuks. Vol. 3, ed. Victor A. Tcherikover, Alexander Fuks, and Menahem Stern, with David M. Lewis. Cambridge: Harvard University Press, for Magnes Press, Hebrew University, 1957–64.

Cortés, Juan B. "Yet Another Look at Jn 7,37–38." *Catholic Biblical Quarterly* 29 (1, January 1967) 75–86.

Couturier, Guy. "La vision du conseil divin: Étude d'une forme commune au prophétisme et à l'apocalyptique." *Science et Esprit* 36 (1, January 1984) 5–43.

Craghan, John F. "Mari and Its Prophets: The Contributions of Mari to the Understanding of Biblical Prophecy." *Biblical Theology Bulletin* 5 (February 1975) 32–55.

Cranfield, C. E. B. "The Baptism of Our Lord—a Study of St. Mark 1.9–11." *Scottish Journal of Theology* 8 (1, March 1955) 53–63.

Cullmann, Oscar. *Early Christian Worship.* Philadelphia: Westminster Press, 1953.

The Cynic Epistles: A Study Edition. Ed. Abraham J. Malherbe. Society of Biblical Literature Sources for Biblical Study 12. Missoula, Mont.: Scholars Press, 1977.

Dalman, Gustaf. *Jesus Christ in the Talmud, Midrash, Zohar, and the Liturgy of the Synagogue.* New York: Arno Press, 1973; Cambridge: Deighton, Bell, 1893.

————. *Jesus-Jeshua: Studies in the Gospels.* New York: Macmillan Press, 1929.

Daniel, Constantin. " 'Faux prophètes': Surnom des Esséniens dans le Sermon sur la Montagne." *Revue de Qumran* 7 (1, December 1969) 45–79.

Daniélou, Jean. "Le symbolisme eschatologique de la fête de Tabernacles." *Irénikon* 31 (1, 1958) 19–40.

Dar, S. "Three *Menorot* from Western Samaria." *Israel Exploration Journal* 34 (2–3, 1984) 177–79 and plate 20BC.

Daube, David. *The New Testament and Rabbinic Judaism.* New York: Arno Press, 1973; London: University of London, 1956.

Davies, Stevan L. "John the Baptist and Essene Kashruth." *NTS* 29 (1983) 569–71.

Davies, W. D. "Reflections on the Spirit in the Mekilta: A Suggestion." *Journal of the Ancient Near Eastern Society of Columbia University* 5 (1973) 95–105.

_____. "Reflexions on Tradition: The Aboth Revisited." In *Christian History and Interpretation: Studies Presented to John Knox.* Ed. W. R. Farmer, C. F. D. Moule, and R. R. Niebuhr. Pages 129–37. Cambridge: Cambridge University Press, 1967.

Davies, W. D., and David Daube, eds. *The Background of the New Testament and Its Eschatology: Essays in Honour of Charles Harold Dodd.* Cambridge: Cambridge University Press, 1964.

Deissmann, G. Adolf. *Bible Studies: Contributions Chiefly from Papyri and Inscriptions to the History of the Language, the Literature, and the Religion of Hellenistic Judaism and Primitive Christianity.* Trans. Alexander Grieve. Winona Lake, Ind.: Alpha Publications, 1979; Edinburgh: T. & T. Clark, 1923.

_____. *Light from the Ancient East.* Grand Rapids, Mich.: Baker, 1978.

De Jonge, Marinus, ed. *L'Évangile de Jean: Sources, rédaction, théologie.* Bibliotheca Ephemeridum Theologicarum Lovaniensium 45. Gembloux: J. Duculat; Leuven: University Press, 1977.

Delcor, Mathias. "Das Bundesfest in Qumran und das Pfingstfest." *Bibel und Leben* 4 (3, 1963) 188–204.

Delmore, J. "La pratique du baptême dans le judaïsme contemporain des origines chrétiennes." *Lumière et Vie* 26 (1956) 165–204.

Dibelius, Martin. "The Isis Initiation in Apuleius and Related Initiatory Rites." In *Conflict at Colossae: A Problem in the Interpretation of Early Christianity Illustrated by Selected Modern Studies.* Biblical Study 4. Ed. and trans. Fred O. Francis and Wayne A. Meeks. Pages 61–121. Missoula, Mont.: Society of Biblical Literature, 1973.

_____. *Studies in the Acts of the Apostles: Essays by Martin Dibelius.* Ed. Heinrich Greeven. London: SCM Press, 1956.

Dix, Gregory. "The Ministry in the Early Church." In *The Apostolic Ministry: Essays on the History and the Doctrine of the Episcopacy.* Ed. Kenneth E. Kirk. Pages 183–303. New York: Morehouse-Gorham Co., 1946; London: Hodder & Stoughton, 1947.

Doeve, J. W. *Jewish Hermeneutics in the Synoptic Gospels and Acts.* Assen: Van Gorcum & Company, 1954.

Dollar, Harold Ellis. "A Cross-Cultural Theology of Healing." D.Miss. diss., Fuller Theological Seminary School of World Mission, 1981.

Dowd, Sharyn Echols. *Prayer, Power, and the Problem of Suffering: Mark 11:22–25 in the Context of Markan Theology.* Society of Biblical Literature Dissertation Series 105. Atlanta: Scholars Press, 1988.

Downing, F. Gerald. "Philo on Wealth and the Rights of the Poor." *Journal for the Study of the New Testament* 24 (1985) 116–19.

Dunn, James D. G. *Baptism in the Holy Spirit: A Re-examination of the New Testament Teaching on the Gift of the Spirit in Relation to Pentecostalism Today.* Studies in Biblical Theology, 2d ser., 15. London: SCM Press, 1970.

_____. *Jesus and the Spirit: A Study of the Religious and Charismatic Experience of Jesus and the First Christians as Reflected in the New Testament.* London: SCM Press, 1975.

_____. "Spirit." *NIDNTT.* 3.688–707.

_____. "Spirit and Kingdom." *Expository Times* 82 (November 1970) 36–40.

Dupont, Jacques. *The Salvation of the Gentiles: Essays on the Acts of the Apostles.* Trans. John R. Keating. New York: Paulist Press, 1979.

Ehrhardt, Arnold. *The Apostolic Ministry.* Scottish Journal of Theology Occasional Papers 7. Edinburgh: Oliver & Boyd, 1958.

Eickelman, Dale F. *The Middle East: An Anthropological Approach.* 2d ed. Englewood Cliffs, N.J.: Prentice Hall, 1989.

Elbert, Paul. "Face to Face: Then or Now?" Paper presented to meeting of the Society for Pentecostal Studies, Springfield, Missouri, 1977.

Eliade, Mircea. *Rites and Symbols of Initiation: The Mysteries of Birth and Rebirth.* Trans. Willard R. Trask. New York: Harper & Row, Publishers, 1958.

Engle, Anita. "An Amphorisk of the Second Temple Period." *Palestine Exploration Quarterly* 109 (1977) 117–22.

The Ethiopic Book of Enoch: A New Edition in the Light of the Aramaic Dead Sea Fragments. 2 vols. Ed. Michael A. Knibb, in consultation with Edward Ullendorff. Oxford: Clarendon Press, 1978.

Farmer, W. R., C. F. D. Moule, and R. R. Niebuhr, eds. *Christian History and Interpretation: Studies Presented to John Knox.* Cambridge: Cambridge University Press, 1967.

Fee, Gordon D. *God's Empowering Presence: The Holy Spirit in the Letters of Paul.* Peabody, Mass.: Hendrickson Publishers, 1994.

_____. "Once More—John 7:37–39." *Expository Times* 89 (4, January 1978) 116–18.

_____. "On the Inauthenticity of John 5:3b–4." *Evangelical Quarterly* 54 (4, October 1982) 207–18.

Felder, Cain Hope. *Troubling Biblical Waters: Race, Class, and Family.* The Bishop Henry McNeal Turner Studies in North American Black Religion 3. Maryknoll, N.Y.: Orbis Books, 1989.

Fenton, J. C. "The Order of the Miracles Performed by Peter and Paul in Acts." *Expository Times* 77 (12, September 1966) 381–83.

Finegan, Jack. *The Archeology of the New Testament.* Princeton: Princeton University Press, 1969.

_____. *The Archeology of World Religions.* Princeton: Princeton University Press, 1952.

Finkelstein, Louis. *Pharisaism in the Making: Selected Essays.* New York: KTAV,1972.

Fiorenza, Elizabeth Schüssler, ed. *Aspects of Religious Propaganda in Judaism and Early Christianity.* University of Notre Dame Center for the Study of Judaism and Christianity in Antiquity 2. South Bend, Ind.: University of Notre Dame Press, 1976.

Fishbane, Michael A., and Paul R. Flohr, eds. *Texts and Responses: Studies Presented to Nahum N. Glatzner on the Occasion of His Seventieth Birthday by His Students.* Leiden: E. J. Brill, 1975.

Fitzmyer, Joseph A. "Jewish Christianity in Acts in Light of the Qumran Scrolls." In *Studies in Luke–Acts: Essays in Honor of Paul Schubert.* Ed. Leander E. Keck and J. Louis Martyn. Pages 233–57. Nashville: Abingdon Press, 1966.

Floor, L. "The Lord and the Holy Spirit in the Fourth Gospel." *Neotestamentica* 2 (1968) 122–30.

Flowers, H. J. "En pneumati hagiō kai puri." *Expository Times* 64 (5, February 1953) 155–56.

Flusser, David. *Judaism and the Origins of Christianity.* Jerusalem: Magnes Press, Hebrew University, 1988.

Foakes Jackson, F. J., and Kirsopp Lake, eds. *The Beginnings of Christianity.* 5 vols. Reprint ed.: Grand Rapids, Mich.: Baker, 1979.

Foerster, Werner. "Der heilige Geist im Spätjudentum." *New Testament Studies* 8 (2, Jan. 1962) 117–34.

Forbes, Christopher. "Early Christian Inspired Speech and Hellenistic Popular Religion." *Novum Testamentum* 28 (3, July 1986) 257–70.

France, R. T., David Wenham, and Craig Blomberg, eds. *Gospel Perspectives.* 6 vols. Sheffield: JSOT Press, 1980–86.

Francis, Fred O., and Wayne A. Meeks, eds. *Conflict at Colossae: A Problem in the Interpretation of Early Christianity Illustrated by Selected Modern Studies.* Sources for Biblical Study 4. Missoula, Mont.: Society of Biblical Literature, 1973.

Freedman, David Noel. "Pottery, Poetry, and Prophecy: An Essay on Biblical Poetry." *Journal of Biblical Literature* 96 (March 1977) 5–26.

Garner, G. G. "The Temples of Mt. Gerizim: Tell er Ras—Probable Site of the Samaritan Temple." *Buried History* 11 (1, 1975) 33–42.

Gärtner, Bertril. *The Temple and the Community in Qumran and the New Testament.* Cambridge: Cambridge University Press, 1965.

Gager, John G. *The Origins of Anti-Semitism: Attitudes toward Judaism in Pagan and Christian Antiquity.* New York: Oxford University Press, 1983.

Gasparro, Giulia Sfameni. *Soteriology and Mystic Aspects in the Cult of Cybele and Attis.* Études Préliminaires aux Religions Orientales dans l'Empire Romain 103. Published for M. J. Vermaseren. Leiden: E. J. Brill, 1985.

Geyser, A. "The Semeion at Cana of the Galilee." In *Studies in John Presented to Professor Dr. J. N. Sevenster on the Occasion of His Seventieth Birthday.* Novum Testamentum Supplements 24. Ed. W. C. van Unnik. Pages 12–21. Leiden: E. J. Brill, 1970.

Gill, David W. J., and Conrad Gempf, eds. *Greco-Roman Setting.* Vol. 2 of *The Book of Acts in Its First Century Setting.* 6 vols. Grand Rapids, Mich.: Eerdmans; Carlisle, Penn.: Paternoster Press, 1994.

Glasson, T. Francis. *Moses in the Fourth Gospel.* Studies in Biblical Theology. Naperville, Ill.: Alec R. Allenson, 1963.

Glatzer, Nahum Norbert. "A Study of the Talmudic Interpretation of Prophecy." *Review of Religion* 10 (2, January 1946) 115–37.

Goldin, Judah. "The Magic of Magic and Superstition." In *Aspects of Religious Propaganda in Judaism and Early Christianity.* Ed. Elisabeth Schüssler Fiorenza. University of Notre Dame Center for the Study of Judaism and Christianity in Antiquity 2. Pages 115–47. South Bend, Ind.: University of Notre Dame Press, 1976.

Goodenough, Erwin R. *Jewish Symbols in the Greco-Roman Period.* 13 vols. Bollingen Series 37. Vols. 1–12: New York: Pantheon Books for the Bollingen Foundation, 1953–65. Vol. 13: Princeton: Princeton University Press for the Bollingen Foundation, 1968.

Goulder, Michael Douglas. *Type and History in Acts.* London: SPCK, 1964.

Grant, Frederick C., ed. *Hellenistic Religions: The Age of Syncretism.* The Library of Liberal Arts. Indianapolis: Bobbs-Merrill Company, Liberal Arts Press, 1953.

Grant, Robert M. *Gods and the One God.* Library of Early Christianity 1. Philadelphia: Westminster Press, 1986.

Grassi, Joseph A. "Ezekiel xxxvii.1–14 and the New Testament." *New Testament Studies* 11 (2, January 1965) 162–64.

———. "The Last Testament-Succession Literary Background of Matthew 9:35–11:1 and Its Significance." *Biblical Theology Bulletin* 7 (1977) 172–76.

The Greek Magical Papyri in Translation (Including the Demotic Spells). 2d ed. Ed. Hans Dieter Betz. Chicago: University of Chicago Press, 1992.

Grelot, Pierre. "Jean. vii,38: Eau du rocher ou source du temple?" *Revue Biblique* 70 (1, January 1963) 43–51.

Griffiths, J. G. "Some Claims of Xenoglossy in the Ancient Languages." *Numen* 33 (1, 1986) 141–69.

Grigsby, Bruce H. " 'If Any Man Thirsts . . .': Observations on the Rabbinic Background of John 7,37–39." *Biblica* 67 (1, 1986) 100–108.

———. "Washing in the Pool of Siloam—a Thematic Anticipation of the Johannine Cross." *Novum Testamentum* 27 (3, July 1985) 227–35.

Grudem, Wayne A. *The Gift of Prophecy in 1 Corinthians.* Lanham, Md.: University Press of America, 1982.

Gryglewicz, Feliks. "Die Aussagen über den Heiligen Geist im vierten Evangelium: Überlieferung und Redaktion." *Studien zum Neuen Testament und seiner Umwelt* 4 (1979) 45–53.

Guelich, Robert A., ed. *Unity and Diversity in New Testament Theology: Essays in Honor of G. E. Ladd.* Grand Rapids, Mich.: Eerdmans, 1978.

Gundry, Robert H. " 'Ecstatic Utterance' (N.E.B.)?" *Journal of Theological Studies* 17 (2, 1966) 299–307.

Guthrie, W. K. C. *Orpheus and Greek Religion: A Study of the Orphic Movement.* 2d ed. New York: W. W. Norton & Company, 1966.

Hadas, Moses, ed. and trans. *Aristeas to Philocrates (Letter of Aristeas).* New York: Harper & Brothers for the Dropsie College for Hebrew and Cognate Learning, 1951.

Hagner, Donald A., and Murray J. Harris, eds. *Pauline Studies: Essays Presented to Professor F. F. Bruce on His 70th Birthday.* Exeter: Paternoster Press, 1980.

Halperin, David J. "Ascension or Invasion: Implications of the Heavenly Journey in Ancient Judaism." *Religion* 18 (1, January 1988) 47–67.

_____. "Merkabah Midrash in the Septuagint." *Journal of Biblical Literature* 101 (3, September 1982) 351–63.

Hamilton, Neill Q. *The Holy Spirit and Eschatology in Paul.* Scottish Journal of Theology Occasional Papers 6. Edinburgh: Oliver & Boyd, 1957.

Hanson, John S. "Dreams and Visions in the Graeco-Roman World and Early Christianity." *Aufstieg und Niedergang der römischen Welt* 2 (Principat). 23.2. 1395–1427.

Haran, Menahem. "From Early to Classical Prophecy: Continuity and Change." *Vetus Testamentum* 27 (October 1977) 385–97.

Hare, Douglas R. A. *The Theme of Jewish Persecution of Christians in the Gospel according to St. Matthew.* Cambridge: Cambridge University Press, 1967.

Hawthorne, Gerald F., ed. *Current Issues in Biblical and Patristic Interpretation: Studies in Honor of Merrill C. Tenney Presented by His Former Students.* Grand Rapids, Mich.: Eerdmans, 1975.

Hayman, Peter. "Some Observations on Sefer Yesira: (2) The Temple at the Centre of the Universe." *Journal of Jewish Studies* 37 (2, Autumn 1986) 176–82.

Heitmann, Claus, and Heribert Mühlen, eds. *Erfahrung und Theologie des Heiligen Geistes.* Hamburg: Agentur des Rauhen Hauses, 1974.

Hengel, Martin. *The Charismatic Leader and His Followers.* Ed. John Riches. Trans. James Greig. New York: Crossroad, 1981.

_____. *Judaism and Hellenism: Studies in Their Encounter in Palestine during the Early Hellenistic Period.* 2 vols. Trans. John Bowden. Philadelphia: Fortress Press, 1974.

Herbert, Sharon C. "The Orientation of Greek Temples." *Palestine Exploration Quarterly* 116 (1, January 1984) 31–34.

Herford, R. Travers. *Christianity in Talmud and Midrash*. Library of Philosophical and Religious Thought. Clifton, N.J.: Reference Book Publishers, 1966.

Hill, David. *New Testament Prophecy*. New Foundations Theological Library. Atlanta: John Knox Press, 1979.

Hodges, Zane C. "Problem Passages in the Gospel of John. Part 5: The Angel at Bethesda—John 5:4." *Bibliotheca Sacra* 136 (541, January 1979) 25–39.

————. "Rivers of Living Water: John 7:37–39: Part 7 of Problem Passages in the Gospel of John." *Bibliotheca Sacra* 136 (543, July 1979) 239–48.

————. "Water and Spirit—John 3:5: Part 3 of Problem Passages in the Gospel of John." *Bibliotheca Sacra* 135 (539, July 1978) 206–20.

Hoenig, Sidney B. "Conversion during the Talmudic Period." In *Conversion to Judaism: A History and Analysis*. Ed. David Max Eichhorn. Pages 33–66. New York: KTAV Publishing House, 1965.

Holwerda, David Earl. *The Holy Spirit and Eschatology in the Gospel of John: A Critique of Rudolf Bultmann's Present Eschatology*. Kampen: J. H. Kok, 1959.

Hooke, S. H. " 'The Spirit Was Not Yet.' " *New Testament Studies* 9 (4, July 1963) 372–80.

Horwitz, Riska G. "Ru'ah ha-Kodesh." In *Encyclopaedia Judaica*. 14.364–68. Jerusalem: Keter Publishing Company, 1972.

Huffmon, Herbert B. "Prophecy in the Mari Letters." *Biblical Archaeologist* 31 (December 1968) 101–24.

Isaacs, Marie E. *The Concept of Spirit: A Study of Pneuma in Hellenistic Judaism and Its Bearing on the New Testament*. Heythrop Monographs 1. London: Heythrop College, 1976.

————. "The Prophetic Spirit in the Fourth Gospel." *Heythrop Journal* 24 (4, October 1983) 391–407.

Issar, Arie. "The Evolution of the Ancient Water Supply in the Region of Jerusalem." *Israel Exploration Journal* 26 (2, 1976) 130–36.

Jeremias, Joachim. *Jesus' Promise to the Nations*. Studies in Biblical Theology 24. Trans. S. H. Hooke. London: SCM, 1958.

————. *New Testament Theology*. New York: Charles Scribner's Sons, 1971.

————. "The Qumran Texts and the New Testament." *Expository Times* 70 (December 1958) 68–69.

Jervell, Jacob. "Das gespaltene Israel und die Heidenvölker: Zur Motivierung der Heidenmission in der Apostelgeschichte." *Studia Theologica* 19 (1–2, 1965) 68–96.

Johnson, Luke Timothy. *The Literary Function of Possessions in Luke–Acts*. Society of Biblical Literature Dissertation Series 39. Missoula, Mont.: Society of Biblical Literature, 1977.

Johnston, George. " 'Spirit' and 'Holy Spirit' in the Qumran Literature." In *New Testament Sidelights: Essays in honor of Alexander Converse Purdy.* Ed. Harvey K. McArthur. Pages 27–42. Hartford: Hartford Seminary Foundation Press, 1960.

_____. *The Spirit-Paraclete in the Gospel of John.* Society for New Testament Studies Monograph 12. Cambridge: Cambridge University Press, 1970.

Joseph et Aséneth: Introduction, texte critique, traduction, et notes. Ed. Marc Philonenko. Studia Post-Biblica 13. Leiden: E. J. Brill, 1968.

Judge, E. A. *The Social Pattern of the Christian Groups in the First Century: Some Prolegomena to the Study of New Testament Ideas of Social Obligation.* London: Tyndale Press, 1960.

Juel, Donald. "Social Dimensions of Exegesis: The Use of Psalm 16 in Acts 2." *Catholic Biblical Quarterly* 42 (October 1981) 543–56.

Keck, Leander E. "The Introduction to Mark's Gospel." *New Testament Studies* 12 (4, July 1966) 352–70.

Keck, Leander E., and J. Louis Martin, eds. *Studies in Luke-Acts.* Philadelphia: Fortress Press, 1980.

Kee, Howard Clark. *Miracle in the Early Christian World: A Study in Sociohistorical Method.* New Haven: Yale University Press, 1983.

Keener, Craig S. . . . *And Marries Another: Divorce and Remarriage in the Teaching of the New Testament.* Peabody, Mass.: Hendrickson Publishers, 1991.

_____. *The Function of Johannine Pneumatology in the Context of Late First Century Judaism.* Ph.D. diss., Duke University. Ann Arbor, Mich.: University Microfilms International, 1991.

_____. "Matthew 5:22 and the Heavenly Court." *Expository Times* 99 (2, 1987) 46.

_____. *Paul, Women, & Wives: Marriage and Women's Ministry in the Letters of Paul.* Peabody, Mass.: Hendrickson Publishers, 1992.

_____. "Pentecost, Prophecy, and Proclamation to All Peoples." *The A. M. E. Zion Quarterly Review* 108 (1, January 1996) 43–66.

_____. *Three Crucial Questions about the Holy Spirit.* Grand Rapids, Mich.: Baker, 1996.

Kiev, Ari, ed. *Magic, Faith, and Healing: Studies in Primitive Psychiatry Today.* New York: Free Press, 1964.

Kilpatrick, G. D. "The Punctuation of John VII.37–38." *Journal of Theological Studies* 11 (2, October 1960) 340–42.

Kirk, J. Andrew. "Apostleship since Rengstorf: Towards a Synthesis." *New Testament Studies* 21 (2, January 1975) 249–64.

Kittel, G., and G. Friedrich, eds. *Theological Dictionary of the New Testament.* 10 vols. Trans. G. Bromiley. Grand Rapids, Mich.: Eerdmans, 1964–76.

Knox, Wilfred L. *St. Paul and the Church of the Gentiles.* Cambridge: Cambridge University Press, 1939.

Kobelski, Paul Joseph. *Melchizedek and Melchiresa: The Heavenly Prince of Light and the Prince of Darkness in the Qumran Literature.* Ph.D. diss., Department of Theology at Fordham University, 1978. Ann Arbor, Mich.: University Microfilms International, 1979.

Koester, Helmut. *Introduction to the New Testament.* Vol. 1: *History, Culture, and Religion of the Hellenistic Age.* Vol. 2: *History and Literature of Early Christianity.* Hermeneia Foundations and Facets Series. Philadelphia: Fortress Press, 1982.

Kotlar, David. "Mikveh." In *Encyclopaedia Judaica.* 11.1534–44. Jerusalem: Keter Publishing House, 1972.

Kraabel, A. Thomas. "Judaism in Western Asia Minor under the Roman Empire, with a Preliminary Study of the Jewish Community at Sardis, Lydia." Th.D. dissertation, Harvard Divinity School, 1968.

Kraeling, Carl H. *John the Baptist.* New York: Charles Scribner's Sons, 1951.

Kraybill, Donald B., and Dennis M. Sweetland. "Possessions in Luke–Acts: A Sociological Perspective." *Perspectives in Religious Studies* 10 (1983) 215–39. (*NTA* 28.250.)

Kuhn, K. H. "St. John vii.37–8." *New Testament Studies* 4 (1, October 1957) 63–65.

Ladd, George Eldon. *A Theology of the New Testament.* Grand Rapids, Mich.: Eerdmans, 1974.

————. *The Young Church.* New York: Abingdon Press, 1964.

Lake, Kirsopp. "The Holy Spirit." In *The Beginnings of Christianity.* Ed. F. J. Foakes Jackson and Kirsopp Lake. 5.96–111. Reprint ed.: Grand Rapids, Mich.: Baker Book House, 1979.

————. "Proselytes and God-Fearers." In *The Beginnings of Christianity.* Ed. F. J. Foakes Jackson and Kirsopp Lake. 5.74–96. Reprint ed.: Grand Rapids, Mich.: Baker Book House, 1979.

Lampe, G. W. H. *The Seal of the Spirit.* New York: Longmans, Green & Company, 1951.

Le Déaut, R. "Shavu'ot och den kristna pingsten i NT." *Svensk Exegetisk Årsbok* 44 (1979) 148–70. (*NTA* 24.250.)

Légasse, S. "Baptême juif des prosélytes et baptême chrétien." *Bulletin de Littérature Ecclésiastique* 77 (1, January 1976) 3–40.

Leisegang, Hans. *Pneuma Hagion: Der Ursprung des Geistbegriffs der synoptischen Evangelien aus der griechischen Mystik.* Veröffentlichungen des Forschungsinstituts für Vergleichende Religionsgeschichte an der Universität Leipzig 4. Leipzig: J. C. Hinrichs'sche Buchhandlung, 1922; Hildesheim: George Olms Verlag, 1970.

Leivestad, Ragnar. "Das Dogma von der prophetenlosen Zeit." *New Testament Studies* 19 (3, April 1973) 288–99.

Levison, John R. "The Debut of the Divine Spirit in Josephus's *Antiquities.*" *Harvard Theological Review* 87 (2, 1994) 123–38.

✓ _____. "Inspiration and the Divine Spirit in the Writings of Philo Judaeus." *Journal for the Study of Judaism* 26 (3, 1995) 271–323.

_____. "The Prophetic Spirit as an Angel according to Philo." *Harvard Theological Review* 88 (2, 1995) 189–207.

Liefeld, Walter Lewis. *The Wandering Preacher as a Social Figure in the Roman Empire.* Ph.D. diss., Columbia University, 1967. Ann Arbor: University Microfilms International, 1976.

"Life of Adam and Eve." "Greek Text of the Vita of Adam and Eve, and the Apocalypse of Moses." In *Apocalypses Apocryphae.* Ed. Konstantin von Tischendorf. Pages 1–23. Hildesheim: Georg Olms, 1966.

✓ Lindars, Barnabas, and Stephen S. Smalley, eds. *Christ and Spirit in the New Testament: Studies in Honor of C. F. D. Moule.* Cambridge: Cambridge University Press, 1973.

"Lives of the Prophets." In *The Old Testament Pseudepigrapha.* Introduction and trans. D. R. A. Hare. Ed. James H. Charlesworth. 2.379–99. Garden City, N.Y.: Doubleday & Company, 1983–85. Greek text in Theodor Schermann, ed., *Propheten und Apostellegenden nebst Jüngerkatalogen.* Leipzig, 1907.

Lohse, Eduard. *Die Texte aus Qumran.* Munich: Kösel-Verlag, 1971.

Long, A. A. *Hellenistic Philosophy: Stoics, Epicureans, Sceptics.* New York: Charles Scribner's Sons, 1974.

Longenecker, Richard N., and Merrill C. Tenney, eds. *New Dimensions in New Testament Study.* Grand Rapids, Mich.: Zondervan, 1974.

Lys, Daniel. *"Rûach." Le souffle dans l'Ancien Testament: Enquête anthropologique a travers l'histoire théologique d'Israël.* Études d'Histoire et de Philosophie Religieuses 56. Paris: Presses Universitaires de France, 1962.

MacMullen, Ramsay. "Conversion: A Historian's View." *Second Century* 5 (2, 1985–86) 67–81.

McEleney, Neil J. "Conversion, Circumcision, and the Law." *New Testament Studies* 20 (April 1974) 319–41.

Malherbe, Abraham J. *Social Aspects of Early Christianity.* 2d ed. Philadelphia: Fortress Press, 1983.

Malina, Bruce J. *The New Testament World: Insights from Cultural Anthropology.* Atlanta: John Knox Press, 1981.

Mansfield, M. Robert. *"Spirit & Gospel" in Mark.* Peabody, Mass.: Hendrickson Publishers, 1987.

Manson, T. W. *The Sayings of Jesus.* Grand Rapids, Mich.: Eerdmans, 1979; London: SCM Press, 1957.

Marshall, I. Howard. "The Significance of Pentecost." *Scottish Journal of Theology* 30 (4, 1977) 347–69.

_____. "Son of God or Servant of Yahweh? A Reconsideration of Mark i.11." *New Testament Studies* 15 (3, April 1969) 326–36.

Marshall, I. Howard, ed. *New Testament Interpretation: Essays on Principles and Methods.* Grand Rapids, Mich.: Eerdmans, 1977.

Martin, Luther H. *Hellenistic Religions: An Introduction.* New York: Oxford University Press, 1987.

Matsunaga, Kikuo. "Is John's Gospel Anti-Sacramental?—A New Solution in the Light of the Evangelist's Milieu." *New Testament Studies* 27 (4, July 1981) 516–24.

Mattill, A. J., Jr. *Luke and the Last Things: A Perspective for the Understanding of Lukan Thought.* Dillsboro, N.C.: Western North Carolina Press, 1979.

Mauser, Ulrich. *Christ in the Wilderness.* Studies in Biblical Theology 39. London: SCM Press, 1963.

Mealand, David L. "Community of Goods at Qumran." *Theologische Zeitschrift* 31 (May 1975) 129–39.

————. "The Paradox of Philo's Views on Wealth." *Journal for the Study of the New Testament* 24 (1985) 111–15.

————. "Philo of Alexandria's Attitude to Riches." *Zeitschrift für die Neutestamentliche Wissenschaft* 69 (1978) 258–64.

Meeks, Wayne A. *The First Urban Christians: The Social World of the Apostle Paul.* New Haven: Yale University Press, 1983.

Meier, John P. "John the Baptist in Josephus: Philology and Exegesis." *Journal of Biblical Literature* 111 (2, Summer 1992) 225–37.

Menoud, Philippe H. "La Pentecôte lucanienne et l'histoire." *Revue d'Histoire et de Philosophie Religieuses* 42 (2–3, 1962) 141–47.

Menzies, Robert P. *The Development of Early Christian Pneumatology with Special Reference to Luke-Acts.* Journal for the Study of the New Testament Supplement Series 54. Sheffield: Sheffield Academic Press, 1991.

Meyers, Eric M. "Early Judaism and Christianity in the Light of Archaeology." *Biblical Archaeologist* 51 (2, June 1988) 69–96.

Meyers, Eric M., and James F. Strange. *Archaeology, the Rabbis, & Early Christianity.* Nashville: Abingdon Press, 1981.

Michaels, J. Ramsey. "Christian Prophecy and Matthew 23:8–12: A Test Exegesis." In *SBL Seminar Papers 1976.* Pages 305–10.

————. "Evidences of the Spirit, or the Spirit as Evidence? Some Non-Pentecostal Reflections." In *Initial Evidence: Historical and Biblical Perspectives on the Pentecostal Doctrine of Spirit Baptism.* Ed. Gary B. McGee. Pages 202–18. Peabody, Mass.: Hendrickson Publishers, 1991.

————. "The Temple Discourse in John." In *New Dimensions in New Testament Study.* Ed. Richard N. Longenecker and Merrill C. Tenney. Pages 200–213. Grand Rapids, Mich.: Zondervan, 1974.

The Mishnah. 7 vols. 2d ed. Pointed Hebrew text, introductions, translations, notes, and supplements by Philip Blackman. New York: Judaica Press, 1963.

Moore, George Foot. *Judaism in the First Centuries of the Christian Era.* 2 vols. New York: Schocken Books, 1971.

Moran, William L. "New Evidence from Mari on the History of Prophecy." *Biblica* 50 (1969) 15–56.

Müller, Ulrich B. "Die Parakletenvorstellung im Johannesevangelium." *Zeitschrift für Theologie und Kirche* 71 (1, March 1974) 31–78.

Mussner, Franz. "1QHodajoth und das Gleichnis von Senfkorn (Mk 4.30–32 Par.)." *Biblische Zeitschrift* 4 (1960) 128–30.

Neusner, Jacob. "The Conversion of Adiabene to Judaism." *Journal of Biblical Literature* 83 (March 1964) 60–66.

_____. "The Development of the *Merkavah* Tradition." *Journal for the Study of Judaism* 2 (2, December 1971) 149–60.

_____. *A History of the Mishnaic Law of Purities.* 22 vols. Leiden: E. J. Brill, 1974–77.

Neyrey, Jerome H. "Jacob Traditions and the Interpretation of John 4:10–26." *Catholic Biblical Quarterly* 41 (3, July 1979) 419–37.

Neyrey, Jerome H., ed. *The Social World of Luke–Acts: Models for Interpretation.* Peabody, Mass.: Hendrickson Publishers, 1991.

Nicol, George G. "Jesus' Washing the Feet of the Disciples: A Model for Johannine Christology?" *Expository Times* 91 (1, October 1979) 20–21.

Nilsson, Martin Persson. *Cults, Myths, Oracles, and Politics in Ancient Greece.* Skrifter Utgivna av Svenska Institutet i Athen, 8°, I. Lund: C. W. K. Gleerup, 1951.

_____. *Greek Piety.* Trans. Herbert Jennings Rose. Oxford: Clarendon Press, 1948.

Noack, Bent. "The Day of Pentecost in Jubilees, Qumran, and Acts." *Annual of the Swedish Theological Institute* 1 (1962) 73–95.

_____. "Qumran and the Book of Jubilees." *Svensk Exegetisk Årsbok* 22–23 (1957–58) 119–207.

Nock, Arthur Darby. *Conversion: The Old and the New in Religion from Alexander the Great to Augustine of Hippo.* Oxford: Clarendon Press, 1933.

_____. *Early Gentile Christianity and Its Hellenistic Background.* New York: Harper & Row, Publishers, 1964.

_____. "The Vocabulary of the New Testament." *Journal of Biblical Literature* 52 (1933) 131–39.

Nolland, J. "Uncircumcised Proselytes?" *Journal for the Study of Judaism* 12 (2, December 1981) 173–94.

Nussbaum, Kurt. "Abnormal Mental Phenomena in the Prophets." *Journal of Religion and Health* 13 (3, July 1974) 194–200.

O'Hagan, A. P. "The First Christian Pentecost (Acts 2:1–13)." *Studii Biblici Franciscani Liber Annuus* 23 (1973) 50–66. (*NTA* 18.319.)

Ohana, Moise. "Prosélytisme et Targum palestinien: Données nouvelles pour la datation de Néofiti 1." *Biblica* 55 (3, 1974) 317–32.

Die Oracula Sibyllina. Ed. Johannes Geffcken. GCS 8. Leipzig, 1902.

The Orphic Hymns: Text, Translation, and Notes. Trans. Apostolos N. Athanassakis. Society of Biblical Literature Texts and Translations

12. Graeco-Roman Religion Series 4. Missoula, Mont.: Scholars Press, 1977.

O'Toole, Robert F. "Acts 2:30 and the Davidic Covenant of Pentecost." *Journal of Biblical Literature* 102 (2, June 1983) 245–58.

_____. "Parallels between Jesus and His Disciples in Luke–Acts: a further study." *Biblische Zeitschrift* (n.s.) 27 (2, 1983) 195–212.

Otto, Walter F. *Dionysus: Myth and Cult.* Trans. Robert B. Palmer. Bloomington, Ind.: Indiana University Press, 1965.

Pamment, Margaret. "John 3:5: 'Unless one is born of water and the Spirit, he cannot enter the kingdom of God.'" *Novum Testamentum* 25 (2, April 1983) 189–90.

Parke, H. W. *A History of the Delphic Oracle.* Oxford: Basil Blackwell, 1939.

_____. *The Oracles of Zeus: Dodona, Olympia, Ammon.* Oxford: Basil Blackwell, 1967.

_____. *Sibyls and Sibylline Prophecy in Classical Antiquity.* Ed. B. C. McGing. New York: Routledge, 1988.

Parker, Simon B. "Possession, Trance, and Prophecy in Pre-Exilic Israel." *Vetus Testamentum* 28 (July 1978) 271–85.

Parratt, J. K. "The Holy Spirit and Baptism." *Expository Times* 82 (8, May 1971) 231–35.

Paul, Shalom M. "Prophets and Prophecy (in the Bible)." In *Encyclopaedia Judaica.* Ed. Horwitz and Kotlar. 13.1160–64. Jerusalem: Keter Publishing House, 1972.

Pelling, C. B. R. "Plutarch's Method of Work in the Roman Lives." *Journal of Hellenic Studies* 99 (1979) 74–96.

Porsch, Felix. *Pneuma und Wort: Ein exegetischer Beitrag zur Pneumatologie des Johannesevangeliums.* Frankfurter Theologische Studien 16. Frankfurt: Josef Knecht, 1974.

Potin, Jean. "Approches de la fête juive de la Pentecôte." *Foi et Vie* 80 (1, January 1981) 91–95.

Pritchard, J. B., ed. *Ancient Near Eastern Texts Relating to the Old Testament.* 2d ed. Princeton, N.J.: Princeton University Press, 1955.

Pryke, John. "John the Baptist and the Qumran Community." *Revue de Qumran* 4 (4, April 1964) 483–96.

_____. "'Spirit' and 'Flesh' in the Qumran Documents and Some New Testament Texts." *Revue de Qumran* 5 (3, November 1965) 345–60.

Pseudo-Philo's Liber Antiquitatum Biblicarum. Ed. Guido Kisch. Publications in Mediaeval Studies, University of Notre Dame. South Bend, Ind.: University of Notre Dame, 1949.

Pusey, Karen. "Jewish Proselyte Baptism." *Expository Times* 95 (4, February 1984) 141–45.

Reich, Ronny. "A Miqweh at 'Isawiya near Jerusalem." *Israel Exploration Journal* 34 (4, 1984) 220–23.

Reif, S. C. "Review of P. Schäfer, *Die Vorstellung vom Heiligen Geist.*" *Journal of Semitic Studies* 18 (1, Spring 1973) 156–62.

Ringgren, Helmer. *Word and Wisdom: Studies in the Hypostatization of Divine Qualities and Functions in the Ancient Near East.* Lund: Häkan Ohlssons Boktryckeri, 1947.

Robinson, D. W. B. "Born of Water and Spirit: Does John 3:5 Refer to Baptism?" *Reformed Theological Review* 25 (1, January 1966) 15–23.

Robinson, James M. *The Problem of History in Mark and Other Marcan Studies.* Philadelphia: Fortress Press, 1982.

Robinson, John A. T. *Twelve New Testament Studies.* Studies in Biblical Theology 34. London: SCM Press, 1962.

Rodd, C. S. "Spirit or Finger." *Expository Times* 72 (5, February 1961) 157–58.

Russell, E. A. " 'They Believed Philip Preaching' (Acts 8.12)." *Irish Biblical Studies* 1 (3, 1979) 169–76.

Russell, Walt. "The Anointing with the Holy Spirit in Luke–Acts." *Trinity Journal* 7 (1, Spring 1986) 47–63.

Safrai, S., and M. Stern, with D. Flusser and W. C. van Unnik, eds. *The Jewish People in the First Century: Historical Geography, Political History, Social, Cultural, and Religious Life and Institutions.* Section 1 of Compendia Rerum Iudaicarum ad Novum Testamentum. 2 vols. Vol. 1: Assen: Van Gorcum & Comp. B.V, 1974; Vol. 2: Philadelphia: Fortress Press, 1976.

St. Clair, A. "The Torah Shrine at Dura-Europos: A Re-evaluation." *Jahrbuch für Antike und Christentum* 29 (1986) 109–17.

Sanders, E. P. *Jesus and Judaism.* Philadelphia: Fortress Press, 1985.

_____. *Jewish Law from Jesus to the Mishnah: Five Studies.* London: SCM Press; Philadelphia: Trinity Press International, 1990.

Sanders, E. P., ed. *Jewish and Christian Self-Definition.* 3 vols. Philadelphia: Fortress Press, 1980–82.

Sandmel, Samuel. *Judaism and Christian Beginnings.* New York: Oxford University Press, 1978.

Schäfer, Peter. "Tempel und Schöpfung: Zur Interpretation einiger Heiligtums-Traditionen in der rabbinischen Literatur." *Kairos* 16 (2, 1974) 122–33.

_____. "Die Termini „heiliger Geist" und „Geist der Prophetie" im den Targumim und das Verhältnis der Targumim zueinander." *Vetus Testamentum* 20 (3, July 1970) 304–14.

_____. *Die Vorstellung vom Heiligen Geist in der rabbinischen Literatur.* Studien zum Alten und Neuen Testament 28. Munich: Kösel-Verlag, 1972.

Schiffman, Lawrence H. "At the Crossroads: Tannaitic Perspectives on the Jewish Christian Schism." In *Jewish and Christian Self-Definition.* Ed. E. P. Sanders. 2.115–56. Philadelphia: Fortress Press, 1980–82.

Schlier, Heinrich. "Zum Begriff des Geistes nach dem Johannesevangelium." In *Besinnung auf das Neue Testament: Exegetische Aufsätze und Vorträge II*. Pages 264–71. Freiburg: Herder, 1964.

Schmid, H. H. "Ekstatische und charismatische Geistwirkungen im Alten Testament." In *Erfahrung und Theologie des Heiligen Geistes*. Ed. Claus Heitmann and Heribert Mühlen. Pages 83–99. Hamburg: Agentur des Rauhen Hauses, 1974.

Schmidt, T. Ewald. "Hostility to Wealth in Philo of Alexandria." *Journal for the Study of the New Testament* 19 (1983) 85–97.

Schnackenburg, Rudolf. *Baptism in the Thought of St. Paul*. Oxford: Basil Blackwell, 1964.

Scholem, Gershom G. *Jewish Gnosticism, Merkabah Mysticism, and Talmudic Tradition*. New York: Jewish Theological Seminary of America, 1965.

_____. *Major Trends in Jewish Mysticism*. 3d rev. ed. New York: Schocken Books, 1971.

Schultz, Joseph P. "Two Views of the Patriarchs: Noahides and Pre-Sinai Israelites." In *Texts and Responses: Studies Presented to Nahum N. Glatzner on the Occasion of His Seventieth Birthday by His Students*. Ed. Michael A. Fishbane and Paul R. Flohr. Pages 43–59. Leiden: E. J. Brill, 1975.

Schulze-Kadelbach, Gerhard. "Zur Pneumatologie des Johannes Evangeliums." *Zeitschrift für die Neutestamentliche Wissenschaft* 46 (3/4, 1955) 279–80.

Schweizer, Eduard. *The Holy Spirit*. Trans. Reginald H. and Ilse Fuller. Philadelphia: Fortress Press, 1980.

Scott, E. F. *The Spirit in the New Testament*. London: Hodder & Stoughton; New York: George H. Doran Company, 1923.

Scott, James M. "Luke's Geographical Horizon." In *Graeco-Roman Setting*. Ed. David W. J. Gill and Conrad Gempf. Vol. 2 of *The Book of Acts in Its First Century Setting*. 6 vols. 1993–. Pages 483–544. Grand Rapids, Mich.: Eerdmans; Carlisle: Paternoster Press, 1994.

Segal, Alan F. "Heavenly Ascent in Hellenistic Judaism, Early Christianity, and Their Environment." *Aufstieg und Niedergang der römischen Welt*. 2.23.2.1333–94.

Sevenster, J. N. *The Roots of Pagan Anti-Semitism in the Ancient World*. Supplements to Novum Testamentum 41. Leiden: E. J. Brill, 1975.

Shaheen, Naseeb. "The Siloam End of Hezekiah's Tunnel." *Palestine Exploration Quarterly* 109 (July 1977) 107–12.

Sherk, Robert K., ed. and trans. *The Roman Empire: Augustus to Hadrian*. Translated Documents of Greece and Rome 6. New York: Cambridge University Press, 1988.

Sifra: An Analytical Translation. 3 vols. Trans. Jacob Neusner. Brown Judaic Studies 138–140. Atlanta, Ga.: Scholars Press, 1988.

Sifre to Deuteronomy: An Analytical Translation. 2 vols. Trans. Jacob Neusner. Brown Judaic studies 98 and 101. Atlanta, Ga.: Scholars Press, 1987.

Sifre to Numbers: An American Translation and Explanation. 2 vols. Trans. Jacob Neusner. Brown Judaic Studies 118–119. Atlanta, Ga.: Scholars Press, 1986.

Sleeper, C. F. "Pentecost and Resurrection." *Journal of Biblical Literature* 84 (December 1965) 389–99.

Smith, Derwood C. "Jewish Proselyte Baptism and the Baptism of John." *Restoration Quarterly* 25 (1, 1982) 13–32.

Smith, Morton. *Jesus the Magician.* San Francisco: Harper & Row, Publishers, 1978.

Sommer, Benjamin D. "Did Prophecy Cease? Evaluating a Reevaluation." *Journal of Biblical Literature* 115 (1, Spring 1996) 31–47.

Spriggs, D. G. "Meaning of 'Water' in John 3:5." *Expository Times* 85 (5, February 1974) 149–50.

Stambaugh, John E., and David L. Balch. *The New Testament in Its Social Environment.* Library of Early Christianity 2. Philadelphia: Westminster Press, 1986.

Stanton, Graham N. *The Gospels and Jesus.* Oxford Bible Series. Oxford: Oxford University Press, 1989.

Sterling, Gregory E. " 'Athletes of Virtue': An Analysis of the Summaries in Acts (2:41–47; 4:32–35; 5:12–16)." *Journal of Biblical Literature* 113 (4, Winter 1994) 679–96.

Stronstad, Roger. *The Charismatic Theology of St. Luke.* Peabody, Mass.: Hendrickson Publishers, 1984.

Suggit, J. N. "Nicodemus—the True Jew." *Neotestamentica* 14 (1981) 90–110.

Sutcliffe, Edmund Felix. "Baptism and Baptismal Rites at Qumran?" *Heythrop Journal* 1 (3, 1960) 179–88.

Talbert, Charles H. *Literary Patterns, Theological Themes, and the Genre of Luke–Acts.* Society of Biblical Literature Monograph Series 20. Missoula, Mont.: Scholars Press, 1974.

Taylor, T. M. "The Beginnings of Jewish Proselyte Baptism." *New Testament Studies* 2 (February 1956) 193–98.

Teeple, Howard M. *The Mosaic Eschatological Prophet.* Journal of Biblical Literature Monograph Series 10. Philadelphia: Society of Biblical Literature, 1957.

The Temple Scroll: An Introduction, Translation, and Commentary. Trans. and ed. Johann Maier. Journal for the Study of the Old Testament Supplement 34. Sheffield: Journal for the Study of the Old Testament Press, 1985.

The Testament of Abraham: The Greek Recensions. Trans. Michael E. Stone. Society of Biblical Literature Texts and Translations 2. Pseudepigrapha Series 2. Missoula, Mont.: Society of Biblical Literature, 1972.

The Testament of Job according to the SV Text. Ed. Robert A. Kraft with Harold Attridge, Russell Spittler, and Janet Timbie. Society of Biblical Literature Texts and Translations 5. Pseudepigrapha Series 4. Missoula, Mont.: Scholars Press, Society of Biblical Literature, 1974.

The Testament of Solomon. (Greek text.) Ed. Chester Charlton McCown. Leipzig: J. C. Hinrichs'sche Buchhandlung, 1922.

The Greek Version of the Testaments of the Twelve Patriarchs, edited from nine mss. Together with the variants of the Armenian and Slavonic versions and some Hebrew fragments. Edited by R. H. Charles. Oxford: Clarendon Press, 1908.

Theissen, Gerd. *The Gospels in Context: Social and Political History in the Synoptic Tradition.* Trans. Linda M. Maloney. Minneapolis: Fortress Press, 1991.

————. *The Miracle Stories of the Early Christian Tradition.* Trans. Francis McDonagh. Ed. John Riches. Philadelphia: Fortress Press, 1983.

Theon. *The Progymnasmata of Theon: A New Text with Translation and Commentary.* By James R. Butts. Ann Arbor, Mich.: University Microfilms International, 1989.

Thiering, Barbara E. "Inner and Outer Cleansing at Qumran as a Background to New Testament Baptism." *New Testament Studies* 26 (January 1980) 266–77.

————. "Qumran Initiation and New Testament Baptism." *New Testament Studies* 27 (October 1981) 615–31.

Thornton, T. C. G. "To the End of the Earth: Acts 1:8." *Expository Times* 89 (12, 1978) 374–75.

Thurston, Bonnie. *Spiritual Life in the Early Church: The Witness of Acts and Ephesians.* Minneapolis: Augsburg Fortress Press, 1993.

Tiede, David Lenz. *The Charismatic Figure as Miracle Worker.* Society of Biblical Literature Dissertation 1. Missoula, Mont.: Society of Biblical Literature, 1972.

————. *Prophecy and History in Luke–Acts.* Philadelphia: Fortress Press, 1980.

Tigerstedt, E. N. "Plato's Idea of Poetical Inspiration." *Commentationes Humanarum Litterarum (Societas Scientiarum Fennica)* 44 (2, 1969) 5–76.

Torrance, T. F. "The Origins of Baptism." *Scottish Journal of Theology* 11 (June 1958) 158–71.

————. "Proselyte Baptism." *New Testament Studies* 1 (November 1954) 150–54.

The Tosefta. Trans. Jacob Neusner. (Vol. 1 trans. Alan J. Avery-Peck et al.) New York: KTAV Publishing House, 1977–86.

Toussaint, Stanley D. "The Significance of the First Sign in John's Gospel." *Bibliotheca Sacra* 134 (533, January 1977) 45–51.

Trites, Allison A. *The New Testament Concept of Witness.* Society for New Testament Studies Monograph 31. Cambridge: Cambridge University Press, 1977.

Turner, C. H. "On the Punctuation of St. John VII 37,38." *Journal of Theological Studies* 24 (93, October 1923) 66–70.

Twelftree, Graham H. " 'ΕΙ ΔΕ . . . ΕΓΩ ΕΚΒΑΛΛΩ ΤΑ ΔΑΙΜΟΝΙΑ . . .' " In *Gospel Perspectives.* Ed. R. T. France, David Wenham, and Craig Blomberg. 6.361–400. Sheffield: JSOT Press, 1980–86.

Uprichard, R. E. Henry. "The Baptism of Jesus." *Irish Biblical Studies* 3 (1981) 187–202.

Urbach, Ephraim E. *The Sages: Their Concepts and Beliefs.* 2d ed. 2 vols. Trans. Israel Abrahams. Jerusalem: Magnes Press, Hebrew University, 1979.

Vardaman, E. Jerry. "The Pool of Bethesda." *Bible Translator* 14 (1, January 1963) 27–29.

Vawter, Bruce. "Ezekiel and John." *Catholic Biblical Quarterly* 26 (4, October 1964) 450–58.

Vermes, Geza. *The Religion of Jesus the Jew.* Minneapolis: Augsburg Fortress, 1993.

Villescas, J. "John 2.6: The Capacity of the Six Jars." *Bible Translator* 28 (4, October 1977) 447.

Wagner, Günter. *Pauline Baptism and the Pagan Mysteries: The Problem of the Pauline Doctrine of Baptism in Romans VI.1–11, in Light of Its Religio-Historical "Parallels."* Trans. J. P. Smith. Edinburgh: Oliver & Boyd, 1967.

Weinfeld, Moshe. "Pentecost as a Festival of the Giving of the Law." *Immanuel* 8 (1978) 7–18.

Whitacre, Rodney A. *Johannine Polemic: The Role of Tradition and Theology.* Society of Biblical Literature Dissertation 67. Chico, Calif.: Scholars Press. 1982.

White, R. E. O. *The Biblical Doctrine of Initiation.* Grand Rapids, Mich.: Eerdmans, 1960.

Wieand, D. J. "John V.2 and the Pool of Bethesda." *New Testament Studies* 12 (July 1966) 392–404.

Wild, Robert A. *Water in the Cultic Worship of Isis and Sarapis.* Études Préliminaires aux Religions Orientales dans l'Empire Romain, 87. Published for M. J. Vermaseren. Leiden: E. J. Brill, 1981.

Wilkinson, John. "Orientation, Jewish and Christian." *Palestine Exploration Quarterly* 116 (1, January 1984) 16–30.

Willoughby, Harold R. *Pagan Initiation: A Study of Mystery Initiations in the Graeco-Roman World.* Chicago: University of Chicago Press, 1929.

Wilson, R. McL. "The Spirit in gnostic literature." In *Christ and Spirit in the New Testament: Studies in honour of C. F. D. Moule.* Ed. Barnabas Lindars and Stephen S. Smalley. Pages 345–55. Cambridge: Cambridge University Press, 1973.

Wilson, R. R. "Prophecy and Ecstacy: A Reexamination." *Journal of Biblical Literature* 98 (September 1979) 321–37.

Wilson, Stephen G. *The Gentiles and the Gentile Mission in Luke–Acts.* Society for New Testament Studies Monograph 23. Cambridge: Cambridge University Press, 1973.

Windisch, Hans. *The Spirit-Paraclete in the Fourth Gospel.* Trans. James W. Cox. Facet Books Biblical Series 20. Philadelphia: Fortress Press, 1968.

Winter, Bruce D., and Andrew D. Clarke, eds. *Ancient Literary Setting.* Vol. 1 of *The Book of Acts in Its First Century Setting.* Grand Rapids, Mich.: Eerdmans; Carlisle: Paternoster Press, 1993.

Wirgin, Wolf. *The Book of Jubilees and the Maccabaean Era of Shmittah Cycles.* Leeds University Oriental Society Monograph 7. N.p.: Leeds University, 1965.

Wood, Bryant G. "To Dip or Sprinkle? The Qumran Cisterns in Perspective." *Bulletin of the American Schools of Oriental Research* 256 (Fall 1984) 45–60.

Worden, T. "The Marriage Feast at Cana (John 2.1–11)." *Scripture* 20 (52, October 1968) 97–106.

Yamauchi, Edwin M. "Magic or Miracle? Diseases, Demons, and Exorcisms." In *Gospel Perspectives.* Ed. R. T. France, David Wenham, and Craig Blomberg. 6.89–183. Sheffield: JSOT Press, 1980–86.

Zehnle, Richard F. *Peter's Pentecost Discourse: Tradition and Lukan Reinterpretation in Peter's Speeches of Acts 2 and 3.* Society of Biblical Literature Monograph 15. Nashville: Abingdon Press, for Society of Biblical Literature, 1971.

INDEX OF MODERN AUTHORS

Cothenet, E., 36
Couturier, G., 40
Craghan, J. F., 43
Cranfield, C. E. B., 77, 78, 79, 87, 122
Cross, F. M., 39, 75, 83
Cullmann, O., 76, 88, 125, 137, 164,
    180, 183, 187, 202, 204, 208
Culpepper, A. F., 85, 164, 165, 166,
    168, 175, 176, 184

Dahl, N. A., 78
Dalman, G., 28, 126, 127, 128, 129, 133
Danby, H., 174
Daniel, C., 32
Daniélou, J., 71, 75, 165, 184
Danker, F. W., 124
Dar, S., 179
Daube, D., 72, 73, 121, 179, 202
Davey, F. N., 80
Davids, P., 172
Davies, S. L., 74
Davies, W. D., 33, 35, 38, 39, 40, 72, 79,
    121, 122, 175, 181, 182, 187, 188,
    203, 206, 208
Deissmann, A., 29, 45, 87, 88, 128, 133,
    188
De Jonge, M., 202
De Kruijf, Th. C., 80
Delcor, M., 205
Delmore, J., 86
Delorme, J., 132
De Ridder, R. R., 73, 173, 207, 210
Derrett, J. D. M., 167, 170, 173, 211
Detienne, M., 46
De Vaux, R., 79
Dewey, J., 71
Dexinger, F., 178
Dibelius, M., 43, 72, 122, 123, 171, 207,
    208
Dickie, A. C., 188
Dion, P. E., 177
Dittenberger, W., 168
Dix, G., 131
Dixon, S., 122
Dodd, C. H., 28, 80, 119, 120, 127, 166,
    171, 185, 186, 189, 206, 208
Doeve, J. W., 79, 208, 210
Dollar, H. E., 206, 209, 211
Donahue, J. R., 76

Dowd, S. E., 90
Downing, F. G., 212
Driver, G. R., 84
Drower, E. S., 167
Drury, J., 74
Dudley, M. B., 208
Dunn, J. D. G., 4, 35, 79, 82, 87, 119,
    120, 124, 127, 177, 184, 186, 201,
    202, 205, 206, 207, 209, 212, 213
Du Plessis, I. J., 80
Dupont, J., 203, 205, 206, 207, 208,
    209, 211
Dupont-Sommer, A., 31, 42, 75, 79

Edersheim, A., 124, 131
Edgar, S. L., 126
Ehrhardt, A., 131, 208
Eichhorn, D. M., 85
Eickelman, D. F., 134
Elbert, P., 206
Eliade, M., 44, 172, 175
Ellis, E. E., 33, 161, 188
Ellis, P. F., 125, 132, 166, 175, 183
Engle, A., 184
Epp, E. J., 166
Ervin, H. M., 202

Fabry, H.-J., 133
Faierstein, M. M., 74
Falk, H., 86
Fallaize, E. N., 167
Fant, M. B., 128
Fee, G. D., 3, 5, 27, 182, 183, 186, 202,
    206
Felder, C. H., 130
Fenton, J. C., 119, 128, 175, 182, 183,
    189, 209
Filson, F. V., 87, 208
Finegan, J., 27, 87, 179, 181, 183, 188
Finkelstein, L., 85, 212
Fishbane, M. A., 85
Fitzmyer, J. A., 74, 89, 133, 210, 211,
    213
Flender, H., 204
Floor, L., 186
Flowers, H. J., 82, 119
Flusser, D., 39, 85, 126, 128, 205, 213
Foakes Jackson, F. J., 28, 205, 207

INDEX OF ANCIENT SOURCES

OTHER RABBINIC LITERATURE

OTHER EARLY JEWISH AND CHRISTIAN TEXTS